STUDIES ON

SCARAB SEALS

Volume Three

Scarab Typology and Archaeological Context

An Essay on Middle Bronze Age Chronology

William A. Ward
and
William G. Dever

Van Siclen Books
San Antonio, Texas

ISBN 0-933175-33-7
Printed in U.S.A.

Contents

Text Figures and Tables

Preface

The *Studies on Scarab Seals* project was conceived some four decades ago when Olga Tufnell prepared her volumes on the Lachish excavations. As she studied the hundreds of scarabs found there, it was evident that the then current criteria for dating scarabs were insufficient. Tufnell set out to remedy this deficiency, her main goal being the possible use of a stylistic history of scarabs as a help in establishing absolute dates for the Canaanite Middle Bronze Age. To that end, she laid out a new typology and began the long search for the relevant material. In 1962, I joined the project and we began a happy collaboration between archaeologist and Egyptologist that lasted more than two decades. The first two volumes of the project (Ward 1978; Tufnell 1984) established the new criteria for a history of scarab style, and incorporated the wealth of archaeological data discovered since the older theories on dating scarabs had become fixed in the literature.

The argument presented in these volumes, however, needs refinement and it is that refinement which is offered here, again from the dual standpoint of Canaanite archaeology and Egyptology. A few years ago, during a three-month seminar at the University of Arizona that concentrated on scarabs, Prof. William G. Dever and I agreed that a great deal remained to be done on both scarabs and Middle Bronze Age chronology. More scarab groups could be incorporated and the erroneous ideas in the first two volumes corrected. On the Canaanite side, much new material is now available and the archaeological phases of the Middle Bronze Age can be better defined. Since we had been looking independently at this problem for many years, it was inevitable that we should combine forces, take a new look at what has already been done, and present an up-to-date review of Tufnell's original project.

W. A. W.

CHAPTER 1

INTRODUCTION

A. THE PRESENT CONTROVERSY

For the past century, many scholars have examined the problem of utilizing scarabs as a chronological guide for both Egyptian archaeological deposits and those in Canaan where scarabs appear in abundance in the Middle and Late Bronze Periods. No satisfactory solution has been forthcoming. While scarabs remain a potentially valuable dating criterion, that potential has yet to be realized. The general methodological approach has been to create a typological history of scarab style based on excavated groups from Egypt, or one derived from scarabs bearing royal names, or a combination of both, the royal name scarabs producing the absolute chronology.

In recent years, the application of scarabs as a chronological tool has reached a crossroads. There is now a clear-cut disagreement in both methodology and conclusions between specialists on Canaan and some Egyptologists concerning the absolute dates for the several archaeological phases of the Canaanite Middle Bronze Age. While there is general agreement that the Canaanite MB III phase falls within the time of the 15th Dynasty, the so-called "Hyksos Period," there are major differences of opinion on the earlier MB phases.

Specialists on Canaan are more and more inclined to place the beginning of MB I in the 20th century B.C., the beginning of MB II around 1800 B.C.; cf. the dates proposed by various writers listed by Dever (1973: 38) and Gerstenblith (1983: 104.) On the other hand, Bietak (1984: 478-79, 483-85), O'Connor (1983: 168-69; 1987: 37), and Kemp and Merrillees (1980: 44-45) prefer an absolute date of ca. 1700 B.C. or later for the beginning of MB II and Weinstein (1975:11; 1992: 38) suggests a date in the late 18th century B.C. There is an even greater gap in opinion on the date of the Montet Jar deposit from Byblos. This deposit, clearly of the MB I period, is dated to the early 2d millennium B.C. by Canaanite specialists (Gerstenblith 1983: 74; Tubb 1983: 49-50; Saghieh 1983: 50; etc.). The scarabs from this deposit are currently placed from the late 12th to the early 15th Dynasties by several Egyptologists (O'Connor 1987: 36-37; Kemp and Merrillees 1980: 45; Giveon 1973: 88), though Hornung and Stahelin (1976: 49) and Lilyquist 1979: 28-29) accept an earlier date as proposed by Tufnell (1984, passim) and Ward (1987: 531). The latter date the Montet Jar deposit to the 20th century B.C. and the beginning of MB II in the second half of the 19th century B.C. The present work lowers the beginning of MB II to 1750 B.C. with a transitional MB I/II *ca.* 1775-1750 B.C. largely because of current adjustments in Egyptian absolute chronology (cf. Kitchen 1987; 1989).

Now the lower date assigned by some to the beginning of MB II, largely on the basis of scarab evidence, automatically reduces the time-span for MB II-III in Canaan to no more than a century and a half, ca. 1700-1550 B.C. This, as the present study will show, is highly unlikely. Whether these scholars saw beyond the immediate problem or not, their dating affects the whole of Canaanite Middle Bronze chronology. The pottery, weapons and other objects at Ruweisé, Byblos and Jericho -- the key sites in the discussion -- are not isolated, but stand in relation to the same material from all over Canaan. As the argument stands, all sites must be dated similarly so that, for example, the MB II at Megiddo, Hazor, Shechem and a host of other ancient cities would begin *ca.* 1700 B.C. There are even wider implications, The Canaanite Middle Bronze Age is related to the Syrian Middle Bronze, the Aegean Middle Minoan and Middle Cypriote, and all are connected not only to Egyptian chronology but to that of Mesopotamia as well. The application of the lower absolute dating now being proposed thus has the effect of a somewhat radical reduction in the chronology of much of the ancient world.

The basic problem is that the proponents of the lower chronology do not sufficiently consider the archaeological deposits in which the scarabs they date to the late 13th and 15th Dynasties are found . These scarabs have an abundant archaeological context and this fits into the broader context of the MB Age throughout Canaan. This, in turn, is part of an even wider context stretching from the Aegean to Mesopotamia. In treating the scarabs from Canaan, some write as if these scarabs exist in a kind of limbo, that they belong to no archaeological assemblage or, if they do, that assemblage is of little importance. This is methodologically unsound. If one wishes to defend what is essentially a new chronology for Canaan, Syria, the Aegean World and Mesopotamia, the whole archaeological context -- building strata, pottery, weapons, and the like -- is important. It cannot be ignored as if it never existed.

The error is that many scholars assume that the antiquated dating criteria for scarabs set out decades ago are still valid and that they are sufficient to date deposits both in Egypt and elsewhere. In point of fact, many of the old criteria do not apply -- they never did apply (Ward 1987: 523-26) -- and we are still at the stage where there is a wide disagreement as to whether scarabs date archaeological contexts or the contexts date the scarabs. Those who favor the low chronology have assumed the former, hence feel free to propose a new chronology for the Canaanite Middle Bronze Age with little or no consideration of the total archaeological evidence of that period.

There has thus come about a significant difference of opinion between some Egyptologists and Canaanite specialists with regard to the absolute dating of the Canaanite MB archaeological phases. The former concentrate on the scarab evidence and propose a low chronology; the latter emphasize the Canaanite archaeological material and have increasingly come to prefer a high chronology. There has been little communication or dialogue between the two groups, hence the two bodies of evidence have sometimes been treated separately. The result is a disturbing debate in the literature in which the two assemblages of material -- scarabs and Canaanite archaeological material -- are examined separately. In reality, they ought to be seen as parts of a single spectrum of evidence bearing on the same problem and integrated into a single line of argument. That this has not been the case is amply shown by the widely divergent views noted above.

The present study is concerned with *all* the evidence bearing on the approximate absolute dates for the Canaanite Middle Bronze Age. It is perhaps understandable that Egyptological studies should emphasize Egyptological material, but scarabs found at Canaanite sites have an archaeological context that must be taken into account. Antiquated ideas on dating scarab style established decades ago no longer apply in the face of major discoveries in Syria-Palestine. It is thus necessary to begin over again and establish new criteria for the history of scarab style based on the wealth of new archaeological material discovered after the older theories had become fixed in the literature. The first two volumes of *Studies on Scarab Seals* (Ward 1978; Tufnell 1984) attempt to do precisely that, though the argument presented there needs further refinement. It is that refinement which is offered here.

B. Terminology

In the present study we use the MB Age terminology proposed by Dever (1973) and Gerstenblith (1980) since that established by Albright and Wright no longer reflects the actual archaeological situtation. Hence: Dever EB IVA (= Albright EB IV); EB IVB-C (= MB I); MB I (= MB IIA); MB II (= MB IIB); MB III (= MB IIC).

On the Egyptian side, the phrase "Second Intermediate Period" has been variously used to include either (1) part or all of the 13th Dynasty plus the 15th Dynasty period, including the 17th Dynasty, or (2) the 15th/17th Dynasties alone. This is due to differing views as to the political strength and geographical extent of the 13th Dynasty. For the sake of clarity, the chronological dynastic sequence used here is as follows:[1] 12th Dynasty: *ca.* 1963-1786 B.C.; 13th Dynasty: *ca.* 1786-1660 B.C.; 15th Dynasty; *ca.* 1660-1552 B.C.

The 17th Dynasty was roughly contemporary to the 15th. The 14th and 16th Dynasties of the Manethoan tradition were not historical dynasties, but groups of local rulers who were probably vassals of the 13th and 15th Dynasties, respectively (Von Beckerath 1964: 86-93, 137-38; Ward 1984: 155). Except where quoting other scholars, the phrase "Second Intermediate Period" is avoided in the present discussion.

The term "Hyksos" causes several problems in that it is often used to imply a distinct cultural or geographical entity. In reality, the older idea of a "Hyksos culture" stretching over a "Hyksos empire" embracing part of Canaan as well as Egypt has no basis in fact. This term properly applies only to the six kings of the 15th Dynasty who ruled from Avaris (Helck 1971: 90). The terms "Hyksos" or "Hyksos period" as used in the present work are thus synonymous with the 15th Dynasty.

This, of course, reflects our own choice of alternatives in the continuing debate on the nature and extent of 15th Dynasty rule as well as the mechanism by which this dynasty came to power. Opinion remains divided between (1) an actual invasion of Asiatics who took advantage of the weak later decades of the 13th Dynasty to establish a foreign kingdom in the eastern Delta, and (2) a peaceful build-up of Asiatics in that region over many years to the point where a local family of Asiatic origin assumed the kingship at Avaris ca, 1660 B.C., much as a local native family assumed the kingship at Thebes around the same time.

In our opinion, the latter alternative best suits the evidence at hand (Dever 1985; Ward 1994), though this is not conclusive as witness the number of authorities who still support the invasion theory (e.g. Redford 1992:103-11). While this is not the context in which this problem can be fully discussed, a few remarks are pertinent.

Too much has been made of the Egyptian tradition recounted by Manetho and his copyists, mainly Josephus, who describe a destructive, barbarian invasion. It is generally assumed that such an event is reflected in the Speos Artemidos inscription of Hatshepsut. This summarizes that Queen's political policies and includes her boast:

> I raised up what had formerly been in ruins since the Asiatics were in Avaris in the midst of the Delta, with Nomads among them, destroying what had (previously) been built. They ruled without Re, nor did he (Re) act by divine command down to the time of my majesty (after Gardiner 1946: 47-48).

The text that precedes this statement speaks of a decline in religious observance, the falling into ruin of temples, and government neglect of the army and priesthoods, The text makes it clear that Hatshepsut claims she has corrected evils which had existed during the Hyksos period and which had continued to prevail throughout the first 60 years or so of the 18th Dynasty, a claim which is patently untrue.

Hatshepsut's statements must be seen in the context of a usurper justifying an illegal reign made legitimate by such things as public oracles and the fiction of divine birth described in other texts of her reign.[2] Indeed, later Egyptian tradition considered her a usurper since, like the Amarna pharaohs, she was habitually omitted from official lists of kings compiled during the Empire.

On the other hand, the fact that the Turin Canon (Col. X, 16-21) in its original state listed six Hyksos kings, noting that they reigned 106 years, indicates that Egyptian historical tradition considered this dynasty to be legitimate. This lends credence to the charge that the Speos Artemidos text is little more than another propagandistic document intended to give divine authority to an otherwise sacrilegious act. To bolster this act, Hatshepsut claims that the god Re was inactive from the Hyksos period to her own lifetime, at which moment he began again to function on behalf of the land. In such an obviously biased context, Hatshepsut's statements about the destructive Asiatics cannot be taken at face value.[3]

Josephus (*Contra Apionem* 1, §§ 227-87), of course, had his own reasons for positing an Asiatic invasion since he could tie this to the movements of the biblical patriarchs to and from Egypt. Manetho, whom Josephus purports to quote, based his own account of the ravaging foreign hordes on "an Egyptian (Demotic) piece composed sometime in the 5th century B.C., or during the 28th through 30th Dynasties, and redolent of the patriotism of the times" (Redford 1986: 242). This source obviously confused earlier events so that the account recorded by Josephus cannot be taken seriously.

The so-called "Hyksos culture" extending from the Egyptian Delta into Canaan is still postulated by some though this, in fact, did not exist. This theory was effectively challenged over 40 years ago by Säve-Söderbergh (1951) who showed that there is nothing in the material culture of the period which can be identified as specifically "Hyksos" (cf. Dever 1985). The MB III culture of Canaan is quite distinct from that of contemporary Egypt, the only feature identifying the Hyksos as such and tying them to Canaan being their personal names (Ward 1976). One can therefore speak of a "Hyksos period," meaning the Canaanite MB III and contemporary Egyptian 15th Dynasty, but not a "Hyksos culture" common to both areas.

C. Changes in the Present Volume

During the years following the publication of the first two volumes (Ward 1978; Tufnell 1984), several important changes have been made in both the typological system and the scarab groups used in these two volumes as elements in the dated archaeological series. Most of these are noted in the appropriate context in the following chapters, though it is best to list them at this point since those who consult the present volume should be aware of such alterations in methodology from the start.

1. The final stage of scarab history prior to the introduction of the classical Middle Kingdom scarab style, defined as "FIP Period 4" in Ward 1978, has been discarded altogether; see below, n. 4.

2. The typology of scarab backs used in the first two volumes -- based on whether the back is plain or has one or more lines dividing the elytra -- has been abandoned in favor of a modified version of that proposed by O'Connor. See Chap. 9B.

3. The date for the burial of the Montet Jar deposit proposed in the first two volumes has been slightly lowered. The 68 scarabs in this collection constitute Scarab Period II in the present work and date to around the mid-20th century B.C.

4. The ten scarabs from Hazor Cistern 9024, Strata 5-4, included among the early scarab groups in Tufnell 1984: 56-57 and passim, have been omitted in the present volume as part of the excavated series. This is a mixed deposit and the scarabs are better placed in Periods III-IV; see Chap. 8C.

5. The earliest (MB I) groups from Jericho, Megiddo, and the Tel Aviv Harbor Cemetery have been redefined in accordance with Dever's observations in Chap. 3.

6. The division of the design scarab material into chronological Periods instituted in Ward 1987 has been continued here, with the addition of Period IIA; see following Sect. D.

7. The present volume has considerable additional material which is noted as it appears in the discussion.

D. The Periods in Scarab History

The main design scarab sample used in the present work is divided into seven chronological periods defined by archaeological context. As will be shown in the discussion of this sequence in Chap. 7, scarab typology evidences a regular historical development which more or less conforms to these archaeological periods. The scarabs used in this study are as follows.

Period I consists of the earliest scarab groups from Egypt as studied in Ward 1978.[4] While this material does show three distinct stages in the early history of scarabs, for the present purpose it is sufficient to consider them together. This stage dates to the FIP and 11th Dynasty and may run into the early years of the 12th.

Period II is the scarab collection from the Montet Jar summarized in Chap. 4. While there has been wide disagreement as to the date of these scarabs, their typological profile shows that they belong at this point in scarab history and no other. This group follows closely on Period I and dates *ca.* 1950 B.C.

Period IIA is defined and discussed in Chap. 5. It consists of 79 scarabs from various Canaanite deposits dating to the later MB I and transitional MB I/II phases. This is a new grouping in the project and labelled IIA so the new numbering of Periods (Ward 1987) can be retained . 12th Dynasty.

Period III is made up of the scarabs from the earlier MB II tomb deposits at Jericho (Groups I-II) and Megiddo (Phases A-D), minus a few belonging to the Period

IIA group. These two collections are closely related archaeologically and the scarabs show an almost identical typological profile. Note that the Jericho material in this and the following periods is divided according to Tufnell's restudy (1984) of the MB tomb material, not according to the dating originally proposed by Kenyon who agreed to all points of Tufnell's reassessment. Periods IIA-III plus Early and Late 12 of the royal name series make up the classical Middle Kingdom scarab style of the 12th and probably early 13th Dynasties (see Chapter 5C).

Period IV consists of the scarabs from Jericho Groups III-IV, Megiddo Phases E-F, and the lower levels of Tell el-^{c}Ajjûl as defined by Tufnell (1984). The latter is a particularly welcome addition to our knowledge of this key site which can now be used with more assurance than previously. The ^{c}Ajjûl scarabs used for Period IV are from blocks AC-AD-AJ-AQ, B-D and T below burning.[5] This phase dates to the later 13th and perhaps the early years of the 15th Dynasties.

Period V is made up of the scarabs from Jericho Group V, Megiddo Phase G, Fara cemetery 500,[6] and the later MB groups from ^{c}Ajjûl blocks T upper, A rooms, G Lower City, and G graves. Period V equates with the MB III in Canaan, the 15th Dynasty in Egypt.

Period VI has been added to give a general idea of scarab typology during the earlier New Kingdom. It consists of scarabs from the Maket tomb at Lahun, and a series of burials at Gurob and Sedment (Brunton 1927, pls. 21-28, 40-41; Petrie and Brunton 1924, pl. 58). While this group is only generally representative, it does give a fairly accurate picture of the changes which took place in scarab style at the beginning of the 18th Dynasty and, in any case, lies outside the framework of the present study.

Also incorporated into this scheme of seven Periods are the royal name scarabs of the 12th to 15th Dynasties. A departure from the initial study in this phase of the project (Ward, 1987) introduced the division into Early and Late for each dynasty as defined in Ward 1984: 173, rather than consider each dynasty as a whole. These divisions are not arbitrary, but reflect the actual scarabs and allow a somewhat more precise chronology as the resulting six royal name scarab groups are compared with the design scarab series.

It should be noted that this dating schema is supported by the sparse evidence of the royal name scarabs found in the archaeological deposits just mentioned:[7]

Period IIA: Sesostris I (Ruweisé), Sesostris II (Ruweisé), Amenemhat IV (^{c}Ajjûl)

Period III: no examples

Period IV: Sebekhotep V (Jericho), Neferhotep I (^{c}Ajjûl)

Period V: Mayibre Sheshi (Jericho, ^{c}Ajjul, Fara), Sekhaenre *YKBMW* (^{c}Ajjûl)

Period VI: the Thutmosids (Maket Tomb, Gurob)

An unfortunate drawback in the presentation of this material is that many publications do not illustrate scarab profiles so that almost a third of the side types are unknown. This is a particular problem with the material from ^{c}Ajjûl, Fara, Jericho Group V, and the Egyptian groups which make up Period VI. A group of the ^{c}Ajjûl scarabs have been fully illustrated by Giveon (1985: 61-100) so a few back and side types could be added to the statistics. There is a lesser problem with back types due primarily to the fact that the original classification for backs has been replaced by another. This seriously affects only the scarabs from Fara, many of which are missing, and from ᶜAjjûl which are too widely scattered to be seen and reclassified. Still, 86% of the backs in the main sample are known so this is a minor difficulty.

Several test groups not included in the main sample are examined in Chap. 7D. They indicate that the outline of scarab typological history as outlined here is substantially correct.

NOTES

1 These dates are only approximate though are sufficient in the present context. Egyptian chronology has been much discussed in recent years with little consensus among Egyptologists. For a recent survey of the current debate, see Ward 1992. For convenience' sake, we use here Kitchen's revised dates (1989: 152-53) for the 12th Dynasty as probably the most accurate that can be achieved at the present time. The problem is not settled, however, and some leeway must still be allowed.

The primary issue in the current debate is where in Egypt official sightings of the heliacal rising of Sirius were made, thus instituting the Lunar New Year. Long and complicated arguments have been presented in favor of Elephantine (Krauss 1985) and Memphis or Heliopolis (Leitz: 1989). Due to astronomical considerations, the location of such a national observatory has been thought vital to determining absolute chronology, hence, the wide disagreement on, for example, the absolute dates of the 12th Dynasty.

In reality, this debate is unnecessary since the Egyptian Lunar New Year could not possibly have begun at the same time throughout the country. No one involved in the debate has considered the practical matter of communicating an "official" sighting from a single observatory to the rest of the country which could take weeks. Simple logic demands that each district in Egypt kept its own local Lunar Calendar so that the Lunar New Year began on different days the length of the Nile; this event occurred seven days earlier at Elephantine than in the Delta (Ward 1992: 61-62; Helck: 1989: 41, though he says "later"). The confusion into which Egyptian chronology has been thrown in recent years thus revolves around an assumption which happens not to have any substance. The same assumption mars the otherwise excellent study of all the astronomical evidence from the Lahun archives, largely published for the first time by Luft (1992). Luft opts for Memphis, though Lahun itself would be more logical.

2 The oracle, dated to Hatshepsut's second year, describes retroactively a public scene in which the god Amon chooses her as the next ruler; Schott 1955: 212-13. This text has now been published in Lacau and Chevrier 1977: 97-104. For the birth scenes, cf. Porter and Moss, 1972: 348-49.

3 Some mention, at least, must be made of the two stelae of Kamose recording this king's advance on the Hyksos capitol of Avaris, though he did not actually take the city. The texts are collated in Helck (1975: 82-97; a translation and historical-literary analysis in Smith and Smith 1976, with the pertinent literature quoted there. In the present context, the interest of these stelae lies in the frequent reference to the Hyksos ruler Apophis as an Aamu-asiatic and the bellicose statements of Kamose emphasizing that fact. This has led to the general feeling among historians that Kamose saw Apophis

and his predecessors as foreigners who had overrun Egypt from *outside* that land, that is, as an invasion force much as Josephus describes.

However, one can read these stelae and the sparse textual material recounting the successful end of the war under Ahmose (Vandersleyen 1971) from a rather different viewpoint. Seen through Theban eyes, this was a civil war to unite the country. The rulers at Avaris indeed "overran," that is, occupied, the land down to Ashmunein (certainly not as far south as Gebelein as often asserted), the nature of this kingdom apparently being a loose confederation of vassal cities. The constant appeal to the "foreigness" of Apophis was an appropriate battle-cry allowing Kamose to rally his own followers who seem not to have wanted the war in the first place. The Hyksos kings were "foreign" only to the extent that Avaris had been settled by their ancestors, though by the 15th Dynasty it had become an Egyptian city. The personal names of the Hyksos rulers and some of their vassals were all that remained of this foreign heritage, but this was sufficient to warrant their villification as foreigners.

The whole "war of liberation" can thus be interpreted not as an "expulsion of the Hyksos" but as a purely internal affair -- Egyptian against Egyptian -- with the convenient excuse that the rulers of Avaris were, after all, of foreign extraction and therefore did not deserve to rule in Egypt. Throughout Kamose's stelae, this theme is hammered home: Apophis is a "vile Asiatic" and a "Chieftain (*wr*) of Retenu" who rules over "the land of the Aamu" in contrast to Kamose who rules "the land of Egypt." Here, "the land of the Aamu" means that part of Egypt ruled from Avaris and should not be taken to suggest that Apophis and his predecessors were themselves from Canaan. That he is further identified as a Chieftain of Canaan simply magnifies his supposed status as a foreigner, thus making a civil war more palatable.

[4] Phase 4 as defined there has been omitted in the present work since it is made up mostly of the Montet Jar scarabs which are here considered separately. Of the other 18 scarabs formerly assigned that date, 14 have been added to Phase 3, the final phase of Period I in the present work; cf., Ward 1987: 513, n. 25. The four scarabs from the tomb of Wah can now be dated to the early 12th Dynasty as this burial "dates most convincingly to the early years of Amenemhat I;" Arnold 1991: 34-35. Since these scarabs are unique in size and material and have not yet been fully published, they are omitted from all statistics in the present volume.

[5] Tufnell worked off and on for over ten years in a meticulous examination of the ᶜAjjûl material and was able to reconstruct a much more precise history of its occupation. The full extent of her research remains unpublished and Tufnell's account (1984: 8-23) only hints at the scope of her work. For this reason, only a few of the ᶜAjjûl groups are included here in Periods IV and V, less than Tufnell included in her volume.

[6] Now published by Price Williams (1977). Eight tomb groups which include a score of scarabs were missing at the time of this publication, though one has apparently been located (Tomb F568 with seven scarabs) and is to be published separately.

[7] This list omits a scarab naming Sesostris II from Period IV at Jericho (Tufnell 1984, no. 2325), obviously an heirloom, and a pair from Fara and Jericho with a problematic name. On the debate over the latter two, see Ward 1987: 521-22, and Bietak 1991: 56, who insists that Mayibre Sheshi is named even though both pieces show an overall typology quite different from the many known scarabs of that ruler.

CHAPTER 2

HISTORY OF SCARAB TYPOLOGICAL STUDIES

A. Early Research

More than a century ago, Petrie (1889) published the first attempt to arrange scarabs with royal and private names into chronological order. While this work was a valuable reference for the time and gave an overall view of scarab history, the emphasis was solely on the designs on the base. The backs and sides were ignored, a practise Petrie would subsequently follow in the publication of his many excavations where only the bases of scarabs are illustrated. In this work, Petrie accepted as contemporary scarabs naming rulers of the Old Kingdom and cataloged many "kings" who did not in fact exist. He further accepted as genuine royal names the so-called "abbreviations" by which a royal name was supposedly spelled in shortened form, often in a cartouche or oval, and proposed variations in the spelling of royal names whereby one or more signs were substituted for the correct one. While such "abbreviations" and variant spellings patently do not record genuine royal names, they are still proposed in the literature as genuine and contemporary (Giveon 1967).

Hall (1913) was the first to publish a real typology in his catalogue of royal name scarabs in the British Museum. He gives 13 main types based on an overall view of backs and sides, with sub-types accounting for details such as lined or plain backs, arched or high backs, striated (feathered) legs, legs represented by a single line, sides cut *à jour* (pierced), etc. While Hall insisted that scarabs naming Old Kingdom rulers were later reissues, he accepted as genuine the "abbreviations" and variant spellings. Hall's work is important in that he emphasized the value of scarab sides as chronologically important, though the dating of his general types is so vague it is of limited use.

Newberry, long considered an expert on scarabs, never produced more than a summary outline of his typology. His basic criteria consisted of general back types and whether or not details of the head, eyes and clypeus are well marked (Newberry 1906). These back types are based on royal name scarabs only and were then applied to design scarabs as in his catalogue of the Cairo collection (Newberry 1907). Newberry was less inclined to accept variants and abbreviations of royal names and, like Hall, believed that scarabs naming Old Kingdom rulers were reissues of the Empire period and later.

Some three decades after his initial work on scarabs, Petrie, returned to the subject in his catalogue of royal and private name scarabs in University College London, producing a more elaborate typology than those of Hall and Newberry. Petrie's primary division of scarabs into stylisitc groups was according to six genera of the live insect though this has since been shown to be incorrect (Petrie 1917: 4-5; Bishara 1978). In spite of major defects, this work became the standard reference on scarab typology for many years. Petrie still believed that at least some scarabs naming Old Kingdom rulers were contemporary and that later reissues can only be proposed if a given scarab also names a later king. He continued to include "kings" who did not exist and accepted the abbreviated or variant spellings as genuine. Petrie also used one general criterion of date which is highly questionable, the "continued degradation of work from the xiith dynasty onward" (Petrie 1917: 15). This principle was espoused by Petrie throughout his career, probably influenced by his early work on predynastic pottery (Petrie 1901: 4-12), though it does not generally apply to all classes of object as he maintained. Fig.

2:1 illustrates several scarabs of Mayibre Sheshi which run the gamut from a very naturalistic to a schematic summary style. Since there is no question of later reissues of scarabs of this king, we may assume that these examples are all contemporary and that the extremes in workmanship are due simply to engravers with varying degrees of ability.

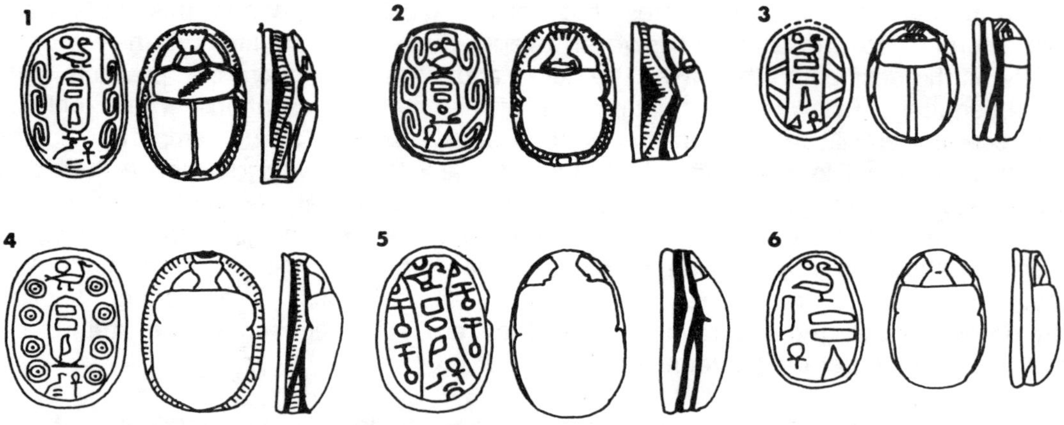

Fig. 2:1. Scarabs of Mayibre Sheshi carved with varying degrees of craftsmanship ranging from highly naturalistic (1) through naturalistic and schematic (2-5) and highly schematic (6). 1. Tufnell 1984, no. 3339; 2. *ibid.*, no. 3322; 3. *ibid.*, no. 3309; 4. *ibid.*, no. 3321; 5. *ibid.*, no. 3307; 6. *ibid.*, no. 3278

The next major typology to appear was that of Rowe (1936) whose material consisted of both design scarabs and scarabs with names in the Palestine Archaeological Museum, largely from excavations in Palestine. In this work, Rowe classified heads, backs, and sides separately so that for the first time the essential features of scarab style were all included in a scarab typology. No attempt was made at a general typological history, though each head, back, and side was assigned a chronological range. However, Rowe continued the mistakes of previous studies in that he accepted the abbreviations and variant spellings of royal names as genuine. His dating of individual scarabs is often vague or incorrect since the archaeological chronology of Canaanite deposits was still in its infancy at the time. Rowe's typology and dating have been used by others down to the present (e.g. Niccacci 1981).

During the next few years, two detailed studies on scarabs of the Middle Kingdom and Hyksos Period appeared, both within the framework of an attempt to clarify the historical problems of that age. Scarab typology was used as a key source of evidence though, again, the emphasis was on designs rather than the whole scarab.

Weill (1953) created a very general typology of design involving considerable subjectivity as to how this typology should be applied to individual scarabs. He defined three main styles of design -- classical, exotic, and degraded -- and attempted to prove through the use of these design categories on royal name scarabs that the Hyksos rulers immediately followed those of the 12th Dynasty in the north of Egypt, with the 13th Dynasty being contemporary to both and strictly confined to Thebes and the south. The full range of evidence, of course, proves otherwise and Weill's attempt to rearrange the chronology and history of the period has never been seriously considered by others. His typology is really one of design only and he falls into the same errors of accepting abbreviated names, spelling variations, and kings who never existed.

Stock (1955) offers a much more detailed analysis of scarabs of the 12th to 15th Dynasties, though again the emphasis is on design. While he does outline a very general chronology of scarab backs based on royal name scarabs, the main thrust of his argument concerns various borders around the design and a study of the *Neferzeichen* style. In general, Stock feels that spiral and rope borders were introduced in the later Middle Kingdom and that concentric circle borders belong in the Hyksos age. Scarabs naming kings of the 12th Dynasty which show these borders are thus, for the most part, of later origin. Dating to the Empire or later are royal name scarabs with only a name, done in deeply cut hieroglyphs, and with no cartouche, border, or other decoration. Stock does not really come to grips with the key problem in dating scarabs of the period, how to identify contemporary royal name scarabs of the 12th Dynasty. His criteria for contemporaneity are the use of a cartouche, the fineness of the engraving, correct spelling of the name, and comparison with scarabs found in Middle Kingdom contexts.

Allied to the problem of which scarabs actually portray royal names is the concept of *Neferzeichen* designs, groups of hieroglyphs representing "good luck" or magic, with paired signs forming a vertical framework for a central vertical row of signs. Frequently, the central panel of signs resembles a royal name or, as is often the case, these signs are considered to be misspellings or abbreviations of royal names. Stock shows that they are not royal names at all, but rather fortuitous groupings of "good luck" symbols which were not intended to reproduce part or all of a royal name (Stock 1955: 16-17; cf. Ward 1977). He thus corrects an error which has persisted from Petrie's first study on scarabs to the present: misspellings and abbreviations cannot be considered royal names. This eliminates a rather large number of "royal name" scarabs hitherto used as dating criteria and it is unfortunate that Stock's conclusions have sometimes been ignored by later writers. With regard to design scarabs, Stock asserts that the *Neferzeichen* style had its floruit in the 12th Dynasty and degenerated thereafter, and that the *anra* motifs, the tripartite division of the design by vertical lines, concentric circle borders, and large human and animal figures are all essentially of the Hyksos period (Stock 1955: 22-34).

The half century of research on scarabs represented by the studies surveyed above established patterns of methodology which have persisted to the present. The subject is so vast both in terms of the prodigious amount of material and the span of time it covers that most scholars are content to quote those who have specialized in the history of scarab style. This has meant that premature or questionable conclusions in the specialized studies have been multiplied many times throughout the literature. Aegean archaeologists, for example, who find scarabs in their excavations cannot be expected to devote the time or acquire the knowledge to evaluate small objects which are relatively unimportant within the context of a whole Aegean site. They must depend on the conclusions of those who have examined in detail a class of object that does not fall within their own expertise. Thus, basic errors in judgement or a faulty methodology on the part of the experts are quoted time and again by others. This constant repetition over a period of time brings to such errors the aura of truth.

Chief among the false assumptions of the past is that royal names could be spelled incorrectly or in an abbreviated form on scarabs made during the lifetimes of the kings supposedly named. This produced a vastly distorted corpus of primary material since it is to the royal name scarabs that we must turn to suggest approximate absolute dates. Stock was the first to point out this error though, while specialists have in general abandoned this idea, it can still be found in recent literature (e.g., Giveon 1967; Bietak 1984).

The other basic assumption which can now be shown to be faulty is that the designs engraved on the scarab base are second only to royal names as dating criteria., This led to a series of comfortable conclusions about the chronological range of individual designs which, in the light of much new material, have proved unreliable. It was this assumption which caused a major defect in almost all publications of scarabs in archaeological reports. Only the designs on the base were considered important enough to illustrate so that the vital dating criteria provided by details of the backs and sides has been lost. This can be regained only by an arduous, long-term search for the original objects in museums throughout the world.

This does not mean that the first fifty years of scarab research were without value. Pioneering works which organize a vast amount of material must of necessity deal in generalities and must depend on the corroborative evidence available at the time. Petrie, Hall, and others provided the essential first stage of scarab research, the collection of large amounts of material into a general corpus which still remains useful. In the initial phase of such a broad project, it is often hard to define what is or is not important. The early emphasis on design and the acceptance of "royal names" which are not royal names were unfortunate assumptions, but understandable in the context in which they were made.

B. RECENT STUDIES

1. Martin on Private-name Scarabs

Martin's (1971) useful corpus of scarabs engraved with private names and titles offers a detailed classification of backs, sides, and designs, as well as a general chronology of scarab style based on eleven back types. These back types -- each including the head, clypeus, and plates -- range in style from very naturalistic to highly stylized, depending on the engraver's degree of accuracy in portraying the features of the live beetle. Absolute dates are established by comparison with royal name scarabs which evidence these general back types.

Martin gives only a limited sample of royal name scarabs for the 12th Dynasty since he feels that for this period only examples from contemporary archaeological deposits are valid for dating. For the 13th and 15th Dynasties, this limitation is unnecessary since reissues, a very tiresome difficulty for the 12th Dynasty, are rarely a problem (below, note 3). Martin's back types 3 to 10 form "a fairly clear typological development from the naturalistic form of the Twelfth Dynasty to the debased, stylized form of the Second Intermediate Period."[1] This is not a hard and fast rule, however, as witness the scarabs of Sheshi illustrated in fig. 2:1 which show Martin's back types 3, 5, 6, and 10, that is, types which range from the naturalistic style of the 12th Dynasty (his type 3) to the highly stylized type of the 15th Dynasty (his type 10). But it should be emphasized that Martin did not intend his chronology of back types to form a typological history for scarabs in general. His purpose in this work is to classify his material and provide a summary chronology *for private name scarabs only.* Indeed, when applied solely to that category, Martin's chronology is a useful one.

2. O'Connor's Typology

The opposite is true for the scarab typology proposed by O'Connor for some years but only recently published in full.[2] While O'Connor is careful to omit reissues, abbreviated names, and variant spellings of royal names, his typology and resulting chronology of scarab style, based on a series of eleven back types, is applied to design scarabs as well as those with names. Since his methodology is faulty at many points and his overly simplified dating chart will have some appeal to the non-specialist, it is worth discussing this work in some detail. This is especially true since both Bietak and Kemp draw heavily on O'Connor's work and all three now propose a chronology for the Canaanite Middle Bronze Age, based on scarab style, that is quite unrealistic.

O'Connor's first step is to analyze the backs (which in his typology include the head, clypeus, and plates) of royal name scarabs which can be well dated. Again, this is not a problem for the 13th and 15th Dynasties since all agree there would be no reason to reissue scarabs naming rulers of either dynasty at a later date.[3] For the 12th Dynasty, O'Connor considers as contemporary only the 25 scarabs from the princesses' graves at Dahshur, securely dated to the reigns of Sesostris III and Amenemhat III (O'Connor 1987: 7; Newberry 1907, nos. 37400-37424). These consist of a mixture of royal name, private name, and design scarabs. For the 13th, 15th and 18th Dynasties, he utilizes the catalogues of Petrie (1917) and Hall (1913). From this material, O'Connor (19897: 3) defines eleven back types in several *modes* which he defines as

> the generalized but distinct visual impression that is conveyed by the combined effect of the principle attributes of the scarab back, this effect being dependent upon the way in which each attribute has been treated by the craftsman.

According to O'Connor, these modes -- ranging from highly naturalistic, through naturalistic, naturalistic-schematic, schematic, to highly schematic -- produce a convenient progression of back types from the highly naturalistic mode of the 12th Dynasty to the highly schematic mode of the 15th Dynasty, with the earlier naturalism reemerging in the 18th Dynasty. The resulting typology, described in fig. 2:2, is very similar to that of Martin, though the two schemes were developed independently.

O'Connor then tests his back type sequence, determined from royal name scarabs, against several collections of design scarabs. For the Middle Kingdom, he uses the FIP material from Qau, Matmar, and Mostagedda, a group of 17 scarabs from Harageh, and an unpublished group of 37 from Denderah. The 15th Dynasty is represented by Sedment Cemetery K and contemporary groups, the 18th Dynasty by the scarabs from three cemeteries at Buhen. According to O'Connor, this supplementary material confirms the chronological sequence of back types obtained from the royal name scarabs.

His system is then expanded by a seriation of twelve design classes, arranged according to the back types already established. The result is a chronology of the use of design from the 12th to the 18th Dynasties. Here, his basic series of backs and designs against which other groups are measured is taken from Petrie's catalogue of design scarabs in University College London (O'Connor 1987: 21-28; Petrie 1925).

Finally, the completed typology of backs and designs is applied to scarab groups from Canaanite sites. He concludes that the scarabs from Ruweisé tomb 66 date to the later 12th , preferably the 13th Dynasty, the Montet Jar scarabs to the later 13th Dynasty, the scarabs from the MB tombs at Jericho from the later 13th to the 15th Dynasties. In reaching these conclusions, O'Connor depends solely on the scarabs and totally disregards the considerable archaeological contexts in which they were discovered.

While ignoring the Canaanite archaeological contexts is sufficient to throw serious doubt on this whole approach, there are other errors. In his choice of contemporary 12th Dynasty royal name scarabs, O'Connor restricts his material to the 25 scarabs from the princesses' graves at Dahshur. But twenty of this group are made of hard stone and that particular kind of scarab tends to have a very high percentage of lined backs (Ward 1987: 512-13). By itself, then, this group cannot represent 12th Dynasty style since scarabs made of hard stone are in general atypical. O'Connor himself recognizes this problem and queries whether the Dahshur group is in fact representative of the 12th Dynasty. He concludes that this group with its high percentage of lined backs is indeed typical, based on a comparison with the FIP scarab groups from Qau and related

Modes	**Highly N**	**N**	**N-S**	**N-S**	**S**	**Highly S**
Lined Back types:	**3**	**4**	**4**	**6**	**8**	**9**
clypeus notched	yes	yes (no)	yes (no)	no	no	no
head	oval	T (L)	T (L)	T	T (L)	T (L)
plate	N	N (S)	N (S)	S	S	O
back	N	N	S	S	S	S
Plain Back types:		**5**	**5**	**7**	**10**	**10**
clypeus notched		yes	yes	no	no	no
head		T (L)	T (L)	T	T	T
plate		N	S	S	S (O)	S (O)
back		N	S	S	S	S

N = Naturalistic T = Trapezoidal ( ) = rare variant

S = Schematic L = Lunate O = absent

Fig. 2:2. Description of O'Connor's back types; after O'Connor 1987, fig. 2.

sites and Denderah (O'Connor 1987: 17-20). Lined backs, according to O'Connor, are thus the only style characteristic of the 12th Dynasty.

Since the Denderah group is as yet unpublished, it is not possible to comment on it except to note that O'Connor (1987: 19, n. 41) is somewhat vague about the date and that fourteen scarabs are omitted from this sample as they are made of hard stones which would make the results "less valid." This contradicts his view that the hard stone scarabs from Dahshur do represent valid evidence.

The appeal to the material from Qau, Matmar, and Mostagedda to validate the late 12th Dynasty back types from Dahshur is surprising. These scarabs belong rather to the FIP and early Middle Kingdom, having been found in those archaeological assemblages Brunton termed "dynasties VIII-IX" and "dynasties IX-XI , X-XI, XI." This dynastic numbering, of course, has no significance and was merely a convenient way to define the successive cultural phases at these sites; the two phases in question are termed FIP Periods 2 and 3 in Ward 1978: 15. O'Connor justifies his use of these scarabs as representative of the *late* 12th Dynasty by appealing to the rather offhand suggestion of Kemp and Merrillees that "there is probably room for allowing the latter end of G. Brunton's sequence to run some way into the Twelfth Dynasty, until the arrival of the El Harageh pottery repertoire" which event apparently occurred in the reign of Sesostris II.[4] Even if this were true, one can hardly justify using the bulk of the early scarabs from these sites to validate evidence of the much later Dahshur group, itself atypical.

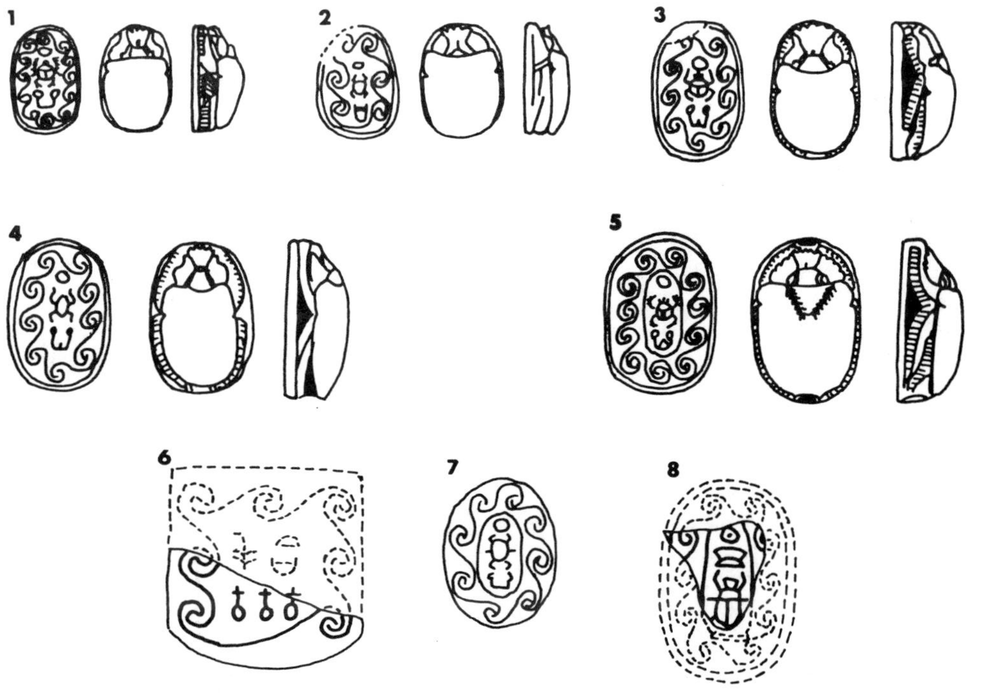

Fig. 2:3. Contemporary scarabs of Sesostris I and related material. (1) Tufnell 1984, no. 3016; (2) *ibid.*, no. 3017; (3) *ibid.*, no. 3019; (4) *ibid.*, no. 3020; (5) *ibid.*, no. 3021; (6) Ward 1971, fig. 26:1, impression of Queen Nefru, Lisht; (7) Macalister 1912, III, pl. 209:13, impression of Sesostris I; (8) Dunham 1967, Uronarti no. 13, impression of Sesostris II.

Furthermore, the entire repertoire of scarab style of the FIP is vastly different from that of the Middle Kingdom as shown in fig. 7:2; compare the Period I column with IIA and III. There is a minimal overlap, but these are essentially two different phases in the history of scarab manufacture. Note especially the side types where the early corpus is almost totally different from that of the Middle Kingdom. The same is generally true of head types and designs.[5] Fig. 7:3 also emphasizes that lined backs dominate in the FIP, plain backs in the Middle Kingdom (see further Chap. 9, Table 6). The Dahshur group is thus atypical and does not represent the back types current in the 12th Dynasty. It cannot be stated strongly enough that scarabs made of hard stones have a typology of their own and do not constitute what is "typical" in any period in scarab history.

That *plain* backs are also characteristic of the Middle Kingdom is shown by scarabs with plain backs naming kings of the 12th Dynasty that are contemporary on the basis of archaeological evidence. There are, for example, five scarabs naming Sesostris I, all with a round running scroll border and O'Connor's plain back type 5 naturalistic (fig. 2:3, nos. 1-5). This border is also found on contemporary seal impressions such as that of Nefru, Queen of Sesostris I and one of that king himself from Gezer (fig. 2:3, nos. 6-7). While the latter impression has no archaeological context, it can be assumed that seal impressions are in general contemporary to the king named. The only other contemporary example of this particular border in the royal name series appears on an impression from Uronarti naming Sesostris II (fig. 2:3, no. 8). While this border design is infrequently found on design scarabs into the 15th Dynasty, it does appear quite early (e.g., Kemp and Merrillees 1980: 216, fig. 58, from Qubbet el-Hawa) and is associated only with early 12th Dynasty kings on royal name scarabs.[6] This makes it more or less certain that O'Connor's plain back type 5 naturalistic is a 12th Dynasty style.

Corroborative evidence is found in impressions and scarabs naming Amenemhat III with borders of 3B paired signs. Two impressions from Lahun and Tel Michal, Israel (Tufnell 1975, fig. 12: 441; Giveon 1988, no. 110), with borders of five and six pairs of signs, respectively, indicate that this design was used on contemporary seals of that king. These impressions, in turn, carry with them three scarabs naming Amenemhat III with 3B borders of four or five pairs; these scarabs have plain backs (Tufnell 1984, nos. 3078-3080). It is true that 3B borders were also commonly used on scarabs naming Hyksos period kings, but these consist usually only of two pairs of signs, sometimes three, and very rarely four (Tufnell 1984, pls. 56-60).

Using O'Connor's own criteria, the 12th Dynasty royal name corpus can be even further expanded. He suggests (1987: 11, 21) that his back type 4 naturalistic is a marker of 12th Dynasty date and did not again become characteristic until the 18th Dynasty. It therefore follows that scarabs naming 12th Dynasty rulers which have this back can be considered contemporary as long as they do not show details indicating a later date. Some examples are illustrated in fig. 2:4, though only three of this group are included in O'Connor's source material. Fig. 2:4, no.1 is classified by O'Connor as back type 9; fig. 2:4, no.6 as back type 8; fig. 2:4, no.7 as back type 4 naturalistic-schematic.[7] The facsimile drawings given here, however, show that these are all of O'Connor's back type 4 naturalistic. The other scarabs in the group come from various collections. All conform to the requirements of O'Connor's back type 4 naturalistic (fig. 2:2).

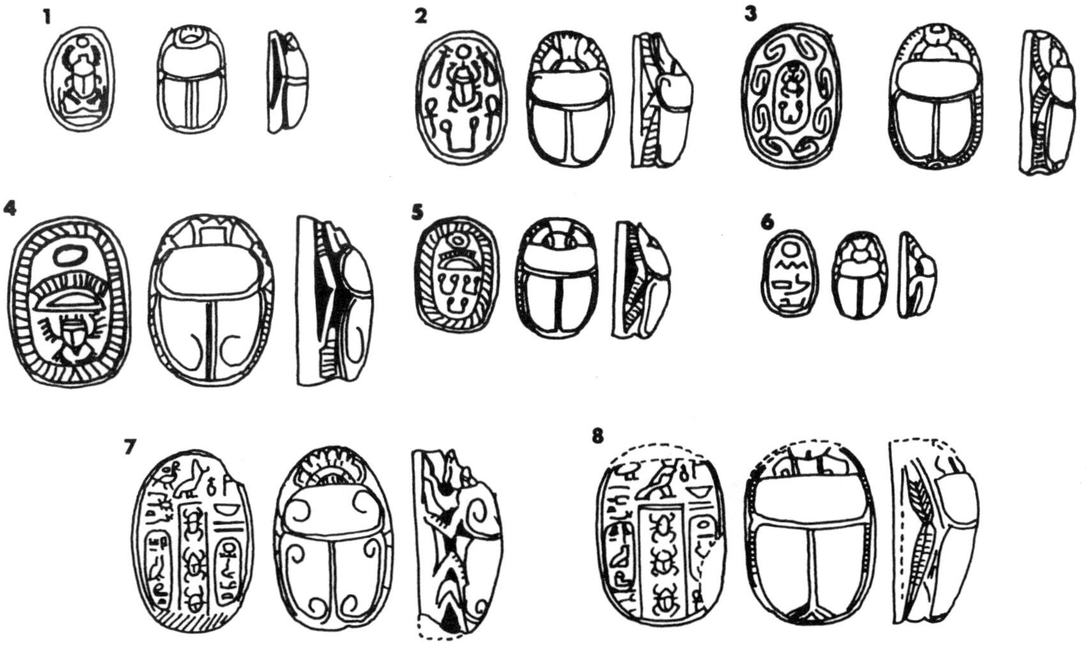

Fig. 2:4. Contemporary 12th Dynasty royal name scarabs.
(1) Sesostris I: Tufnell 1984, no. 3002; (2) Sesostris I: *ibid.*, no. 3010; (3) Sesostris I: *ibid.*, no. 3025; (4) Sesostris II: *ibid.*, no. 3048; (5) Sesostris III: *ibid.*, no. 3071; (6) Amenemhat III: *ibid.*, no. 3074; (7) Amenemhat IV: *ibid.*, no. 3091; (8) Amenemhat IV: *ibid.*, no., 3092.

This illustrates the basic defect in O'Connor's methodology, namely the use of type drawings in the publications of Petrie and Hall to establish the basic chronology of back types. In both works, a type drawing may represent as many as a dozen or more scarabs so that only a single object may actually conform to the drawing. For example, the scarabs illustrated in fig. 2:5, nos. 2-6 are all classified by Petrie as having his back type T.30 (fig. 2:5, no.1) and by O'Connor (1987: 7) as having his back type 6. That this is not true is shown by the following remarks which also emphasize the subjectivity involved in typing individual scarabs and the difficulties in classifying some examples according to O'Connor's scheme (fig. 2:2).

Fig. 2:5, no. 2 corresponds to O'Connor's back type 5 except for the back (pronotum + elytra) which is naturalistic, a mode emphasized by the profile. It is therefore a combination of his back types 5 and 7.

Fig. 2:5, no. 3 shows a clearly naturalistic back -- again, note the profile -- and is a combination of O'Connor's back types 4 naturalistic and 6.

Fig. 2:5, no. 4 is close to his back type 8, though the pronotum + elytra could be classified as 4 naturalistic. The head is neither trapezoidal nor lunate, but square, which is not considered in O'Connor's schema.

Fig. 2:5, no. 5 does fit the requirements of back type 6.

Fig. 2:5, no. 6 has the head and plates defaced so cannot be typed at all, though the pronotum + elytra are in a naturalistic mode.

Thus, only one of the five scarabs shown here conforms to O'Connor's back type 6 (= Petrie's back T.30), not all five as both scholars claim.

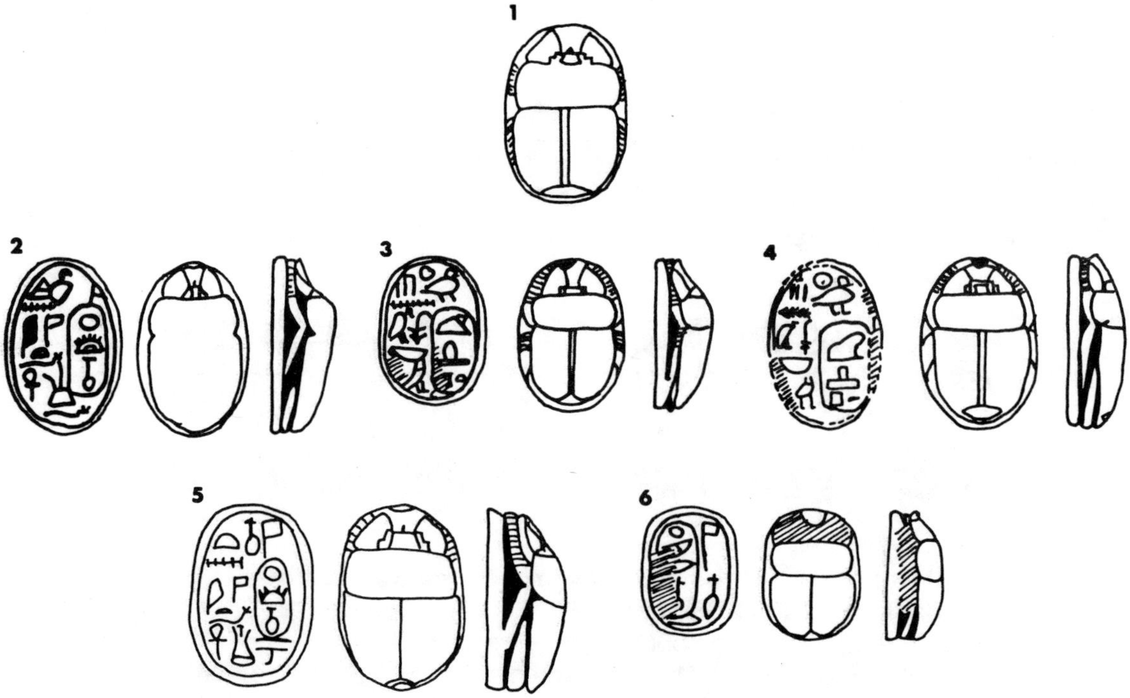

Fig. 2:5 Petrie's back T.30 (O'Connor's back type 6) and facsimile drawings of the five scarabs classified under this back type. (1) Petrie back T.30, Petrie 1917, pl. 69;
(2) Tufnell 1984, no. 3152; (3) *Ibid.*, no. 3133; (4) *ibid.*, no. 3150; (5) *ibid.*, no. 3157; (6) *ibid.*, no. 3184.

Another key problem in any typology, especially one based on back types, occurs with royal name scarabs of the 13th Dynasty. With a few exceptions naming kings of the beginning and end of that dynasty (Ward 1984: 159-61), the vast majority of scarabs of this period name the six kings from Sekhemre-Sewadjtawy Sebekhotep III to Merneferre Ay, the so-called "Sebekhotep-group" of ca. 1744-1690 B.C.[8] Scarabs of these kings comprise a unique group in scarab history on almost every count, as illustrated in fig. 2:6. Since these scarabs are of the "genealogical" style, there is no room in the design for borders of any kind so that with extremely rare exceptions the border designs (fig. 2:6, classes 3B to 8) are lacking.[9] Such border designs are frequent on royal name scarabs of the 12th and 15th Dynasties and appear throughout the design scarab series.

The Sebekhotep-group is dominated by square heads (type C) and one variety of trapezoidal heads (type D5); plain backs are very rare, most backs being LN or LS. The side types are the simple ones, especially d8 and e8 to e10, rarely the more detailed sides such as e6 with feathered legs. As a group, these scarabs are generally larger: the mid 50%[10] is 14-20mm for royal name scarabs of the 12th Dynasty, 18-24mm for the 13th, 16-22mm for the 15th.

		Dynasty 12	Dynasty 13	Dynasty 15
Length: ave.		17	21	19
mid-50%		14-20	18-24	16-22
Heads	A	37	8	5
	B	40	8	17
	C	6	44	1
	D5	4	25	7
	D7-9	2	1	40
Backs	LN	15	63	4
	LS	8	25	4
	PN	31	5	21
	PS	46	7	71
Sides	d5-6	34	18	63
	d9	-	23	-
	e6	24	3	3
	e8-10	12	28	7
	e11	2	-	20
Border designs	3B	18	-	6
	3E	2	-	66
	7A	16	-	-
	7B	9	1	4
	7C	5	-	16
	8	11	-	1

Fig. 2:6. Comparison of Royal name scarab groups by percent of use (except measurements)

In other words, the Sebekhotep-group represents a rather complete break in the stylistic history of royal name scarabs, which has incorrectly given rise to various theories about Upper and Lower Egyptian scarab styles in the later Middle Kingdom. The royal name scarabs of the 13th Dynasty therefore do not constitute a phase in the general evolution of scarab style, but a significant departure from that evolution as evidenced in the design scarab series. The Sebekhotep-group does not represent what is characteristic of the 13th Dynasty, but rather what is *not* characteristic. This conclusion can be reached on the basis of back types alone, but is clarified in much more detail by examining all aspects of the scarab. This group illustrates the typology of the Sebekhotep-group only; any typological system errs if it attempts to measure design scarabs against this group.[11] On these scarabs, see further Chap. 7C.2.

Finally, by using only the 15th Dynasty royal name scarabs catalogued by Petrie and Hall, O'Connor's sample for this dynasty is small and not representative. Fig. 2:7 gives O'Connor's percentages for his 15th Dynasty sample and those for the early and late 15th Dynasty as collected in Tufnell 1984, pls. 56-62.[12] Lined backs are rare in this period, of course, though the plain backs are more varied than in O'Connor's sample. Note especially the extensive use of O'Connor's back types 5 naturalistic and 5 naturalistic-schematic in Early 15, types used on most of the scarabs of Khyan and Meruserre Yaqubhar. While O'Connor allows none of his back type 7 for this dynasty, the facsimile drawings of Tufnell 1984 show it was used, though not in large numbers. Contrary to O'Connor's assertion (1987: 10) that his back types 5 naturalistic and 5 naturalistic-schematic "are statistically fairly evenly distributed throughout most periods and therefore do not provide good chronological markers," they *are* excellent markers for the early 15th Dynasty.

Back Type	O'Connor (49 exx.)	Ward E 15 (91 exx.)	Ward L 15 (94 exx.)
3		1	
4 nat		1	
4 nat-sch			
6	2	1	4
8	8	-	2
9	-	-	-
5 nat	4	17	-
5 nat-sch	6	14	4
7	-	13	12
10 sch	53	38	72
10 highly sch	25	15	6

Fig. 2:7. 15th Dynasty royal name scarabs: percent of use of back types in O'Connor 1987 and Tufnell 1984.

In general, then, O'Connor's source material is unreliable at many points, suggesting that the statistical analysis of this material is likewise unreliable. The consequent dating criteria evolved from the statistical analysis are thus erroneous since the core material on which they ultimately depend is so highly questionable. When such dating criteria are then applied to scarab groups from Canaan, the absolute dating which results must be incorrect since it rests on a typology that does not represent the actual history of scarab style.

3. The Tufnell-Ward Typology

The typology proposed by Tufnell (1984) and Ward, (1978, 1987) uses a different methodological approach. To begin with, the long accepted dating criteria proposed by Petrie, Stock, and others have been discarded as unreliable, especially where these criteria are concerned with the historical development of design patterns. A totally new typology has been created which considers the whole scarab and does not concentrate on one feature such as back types or designs. This is described in Chap. 9B and illustrated in figs. 9:1 to 9:5.

The typology developed by this project is admittedly very complex, but it has the flexibility needed to allow for the almost infinite variety of details in scarab style and for the addition of new details as they emerge. Scarab heads are classified separately from the backs (=pronotum+elytra only) and typed as lunate, open, square, and trapezoidal, each with several varieties. The numerous side types or profiles are emphasized as an important typological category which has generally been ignored. A very broad range of designs and their variations are used as well as details of design since the details are often chronologically significant. The typology of scarab backs used is based on plain or lined backs and variations such as decoration of one kind or another. However, this has now been abandoned in favor of a modified version of O'Connor's modal classification (see fig 9:2), used already in Ward 1987 and now in the present work.

Secondly, the source material for the Middle Bronze Age period (the 12th to 15th Dynasties) is quite different from that used by O'Connor. To develop a new typology leading to an acceptable chronology of scarab style, one must begin with a chronological sequence of dated archaeological deposits containing scarabs which yield a sequence of stages in scarab manufacture. The major scarab deposits from Egyptian excavations of the Middle Kingdom and Hyksos Period are largely unsatisfactory for this purpose since they cover long ranges of time and are, in most cases, only summarily published. Therefore, while this project uses some Egyptian material, it concentrates on a series of archaeological sites in Canaan, better stratified in terms of Canaanite archaeological phases. This series is then keyed in to the royal name scarab series for absolute dating. Applying these results to scarab groups from Canaan and studying these scarabs within their whole context, the absolute dating conforms more closely to that now generally preferred for the MB period by most archaeologists working in that field.

Third, wherever possible, the source material is based on an examination of the scarabs themselves, both royal name and design scarabs.[13] Since the Tufnell-Ward typology depends heavily on the details of engraving and since each scarab is unique if one considers all stylistic features, type drawings such as those of Petrie and Hall are insufficient. Furthermore, most earlier publications ignore scarab sides which can be significant chronological indicators. Study of the objects themselves is thus vital. As emphasized above, type drawings do not adequately illustrate the details of individual pieces and it has become clear that such details are often the key in establishing a typological chronology.

Fourth, there is the important problem of the 12th Dynasty royal name corpus, limited to the Dahshur group by O'Connor, but much larger in Tufnell 1984. The decision as to what constitutes valid examples of 12th Dynasty royal name scarabs is a difficult one since so few have been found in contemporary archaeological contexts. In this regard, it is important to correct O'Connor's repeated criticisms of Tufnell. He states that she "assumes that most known scarabs bearing the names of Dynasty XII kings are contemporary with the king named" and strongly implies that she was also unaware that the humeral callosity did not appear on scarab backs until the beginning of the 18th Dynasty. This is a false reading of two of Tufnell's earlier articles and disregards the principles, clearly stated in Ward 1984: 152, by which 12th Dynasty royal name scarabs were judged to be contemporary or not.[14] The criteria used in Tufnell 1984 to reject individual scarabs are based on (1) demonstrably later stylistic features, (2) incorrect spellings of royal names, and (3) proven reissues (also Hornung and Staehelin 1976: 49). The resulting catalogue of 12th Dynasty royal name scarabs is thus considerably larger than O'Connor's limited sample and covers the whole dynasty. This catalogue is the result of fifteen years of constant sifting through a large amount of material, about two-thirds of which was rejected on the criteria just noted.[15]

There is one aspect of the this project that was evident from the early stages of the project;[16] many typological features have little or no value in creating a chronology of scarab style. For example, from the beginning of the FIP to the end of the 15th Dynasty, considering both royal name and design scarabs, square heads (type C) are a dominant feature only in the later FIP, restricted then to one variant,[17] and with the royal name Sebekhotep-group of the 13th Dynasty when several variants were used on over a third of the total number of examples (Ward 1984: 158, 186, 189; here, Table 9). Elsewhere, square heads rarely appear and do not in general have any chronological value. This factor, one significant proof of the stylistic uniqueness of the Sebekhotep-group, would not have been clear had square heads been classified as trapezoidal, as O'Connor has done. There is thus an advantage in beginning with a typology which classifies all the details. Square heads have no general significance, but do play an important role at one point in scarab history. A simplified typology does not isolate such factors which are sometimes the key to a proper assessment of that history.

NOTES

[1] Martin 1971: 5. His back types 1 and 11 consist of unique or very rare examples of no use in dating. His back type 2 is really a miscellaneous collection of scarabs dating from the 12th to the 18th Dynasties, not before the 12th, as he suggests; cf. Ward 1978, Appendix B. O'Connor 1987: 3, ignores this fact and includes Martin's back type 2 in his back type 9.

[2] O'Connor 1987. The full typology was first presented in O'Connor 1969: 228-58 (not seen by the present authors). He has used this typology in summary form in subsequent articles and Weinstein, Kemp and Bietak have used O'Connor's conclusions to support their own arguments. None of these scholars have apparently examined the typology itself, hence were unaware of the faulty methodology.

[3] The one exception to this is Khaneferre Sebekhotep IV of the 13th Dynasty for whom there exists a series of scarabs giving his prenomen and nomen, but no other design, e.g., Petrie 1917: 13.23.5 to 23. Most of this group show the humeral callosity or other late features such as the head of no. 13.23.10. Since scarabs of this king are otherwise of the genealogical type, this and the late features prove a reissue in Empire times. O'Connor 1987: 14, omits this group, as does Tufnell 1984, pls. 54-55.

[4] Kemp and Merrillees 1980: 52, 54. O'Connor himself (1974: 26-27, came to a different conclusion. Since Brunton's analysis of the relative chronology of the Qau and related material "was not adequately documented," O'Connor reanalyzed this material confirming "the correctness of Brunton's conclusions." These cemeteries, he states, fall into three chronological periods from the later Old Kingdom to the early 11th Dynasty. This definite opinion, based on a rather detailed restudy of the material in question, cannot be reconciled with his later acceptance of Kemp's unsupported statement.

Another reassessment of the Qau and related cemeteries is given by Lilyquist 1979: 114-20. She argues that Brunton's pottery classification is faulty and that he did not include important grave material in his chronological scheme. Some material placed by Brunton in the Old Kingdom should be dated later and, by analogy to other sites, these cemeteries may well run into the early 12th Dynasty.

---

5 While fig. 7:2 shows that design class 3, Egyptian signs and symbols, is common to both periods, in reality, the FIP repertoire is substantially different. None of the class 3 designs typical of the Middle Kingdom are found in the FIP. For this reason, the earlier group is labelled Class 3 Early to distinguish it from the typical designs of the Middle Kingdom and later; cf. Ward 1978: 23.

6 A few apparent exceptions to this are shown in Petrie 1917; 12.4.2, a "variant" of the name of Sesostris II which is not contemporary; 12.5.11, a large scarab naming Sesostris III made of pottery, a material not associated with Middle Kingdom scarabs, but found in the Empire period and later; 14Y, 14AP, and 14AY, all "uncertain kings", but certainly not royal names

7 O'Connor 1987: 12. Fig. 2:5, no. 7 (= Petrie 1917: 12.7) is listed by O'Connor as having a corrupt writing of the Horus-name of Amenemhat IV. This king's Horus-name is normally spelled with four *ḫpr*-signs arranged in two horizontal pairs. A scarab surface, however, is oval and too small to easily accommodate the full spelling (*ḫpr-ḫprw*) ; the use of three *ḫpr*-signs suggests that the scarab itself represents the initial sign of the full spelling.

8 Omitting Sihathor (Turin Canon VI.26) for whom no scarabs are known; Ward 1984: 158, n. 46. See further, Chap. 6C.

9 One example each of 3B paired signs (Newberry 1906, pl. 10:7) and 7B scroll border (Tufnell 1984, no. 3201).

10 That is, one-quarter of the total scarabs subtracted from each end of the general size range, leaving 50% which constitute the more frequent sizes. This gives a more accurate picture since the less frequent smaller and larger sizes are omitted.

11 O'Connor's own statistics (1987: 20, Table 5) point to this conclusion. In his Middle Kingdom Denderah sample, over 32% have plain backs, 19% have lunate heads. This group is typologically quite different from the Sebekhotep-group scarabs. His small Harageh sample (1987: 15-16) does not apply since several of these are of FIP date; on this group, see Chap. 8B.

12 The division into early and late 15th Dynasty follows the sequence of rulers of the period established by scarab style as explained in Ward 1984: 164-68. See also Chap. 7, fig. 7:4. This style can be divided into early (Khyaranu [Khyan] to Mayibre Sheshi) and late (Khauserre Amu to Apophis) on the basis of the use of individual features in the Tufnell-Ward typology.

13 The bulk of the material was obtained by Tufnell who travelled widely over several years to work in museum collections. Ward copied the material in Beirut, Cairo, and helped in London. Practically all the royal name scarabs utilized were seen and drawn by one or the other. In the case of the numerous design scarabs from ^{c}Ajjûl, these are dispersed so widely that many could not be examined; several have been lost or misplaced.

14 O'Connor 1987: 37, and 1983: 167, 169. Since O'Connor had Tufnell 1984 in hand before he published his latest remarks (1987: 40-41), his continued blanket criticism

is out of place. From the very start of the project, Tufnell was well aware that 12th Dynasty royal name scarabs were sometimes issued later and that the humeral callosity was a late development. O'Connor writes as if neither point was known to the authors.

15 For example, two-thirds of the catalogue of 12th Dynasty royal name scarabs found in Canaan listed by Giveon 1967: 32-37, are not included in Tufnell 1984 because they do not meet the criteria stated here. Comparison with any published museum collection will show the same thing. If anything, the choice erred on the conservative side.

16 Here it should be noted that Tufnell already had the project under way when Ward began collaborating with her in 1962. She had by this time established the broad outlines of the study and begun classifying some of the material. In the ensuing years, the typology was altered, expanded, and clarified through a voluminous correspondence and reciprocal visits in Beirut and London. The numerous articles produced during this period by both authors were read and approved by both before publication.

17 Ward 1978: 27 (Table VI), 39 (Table XI), and 105. Sub-type C1 along with lunate heads A1 and A3 make up the bulk of the head types in FIP Period 3.

CHAPTER 3

ARCHAEOLOGY OF THE CANAANITE MIDDLE BRONZE AGE

A. STRATIGRAPHY OF THE MIDDLE BRONZE I-III SITES IN PALESTINE.

A satisfactory if somewhat skeletal historical-cultural framework for Middle Bronze Age Palestine is provided by half-dozen or so major excavated sites, filled out to some degree by several lesser sites with specific or unique features. We shall discuss the major sites first, moving from north to south, emphasizing the earlier phases of development in MB I.[1]

1. Hazor

Hazor, an impressive 180-acre mound in Upper Galilee on the eastern slopes of the Lebanon range overlooking the Huleh basin, was extensively excavated by an Israeli team under Yigael Yadin in 1955-1958. First mentioned in the later Execration Texts, and frequently referred to in the 18th cent. B.C. Mari letters, Hazor evidently grew from a modest Early Bronze Age town into the second largest Middle Bronze Age city-state in Palestine (after Kabri, perhaps 200 acres), by which time the entire Lower City was occupied and fortified.

The excavations, finally fully published in 1989 with the text volume of *Hazor III-IV*, present an enormous amount of material from three overall Middle Bronze Age strata and a number of tombs, reasonably well excavated and published.[2] Str. "Pre-XVII"-XVI (= Lower City IV-III) span mid MB I through late MB III, but the fortifications emerged only in MB II-III (cf. fig. 1). This defense system comprised a combination of massive *terre pisée* embankments; a dry fosse and counter-embankment along the west; cyclopean masonry and mudbrick walls; a section of casemate wall; and at least one triple-entryway gate (Area K). Other monumental architecture included several temples, of bipartite, broadroom, longroom, and "maze" types (Areas A, C, F, H); and a possible palatial structure (Area F). Among the other domestic remains were underground cisterns and tunnels (Area D), some filled with pottery, and some reused for burials; and tombs ranging from MB I through MB III (especially the 1971 tomb, and T. 1-33 in Area C).

2. Megiddo

Megiddo, a 32-acre mound at the mouth of the principal pass through the Coastal Plain and the Samaria Hills into the Jezreel Valley and northward, grew into a major city-state in the Middle Bronze Age, with Str. XV-X all belonging to this period. It was excavated in 1903-1905 by a German expedition; in 1925-1939 by the University of Chicago; and by Yadin and other Israeli archaeologists in 1960-1971.[3]

Str. XV-XIV (part) and XIII b-a span the MB I phase, already exhibiting a well laid-out town with courtyard houses; a city wall and gate; an enclosed sacred area; a large palace; and dozens of intramural tombs (fig. 1). Str. XII may begin in late MB I, but it belongs mainly to MB II, together with Str. XI. A new, more strongly urban city emerges, with enlarged fortifications consisting of a massive *glaçis* and (probably) a mudbrick city wall and a straight-axis gate. The sacred area continued in use, and a new palace was constructed. Str. X is MB III and represents the zenith of Megiddo's Middle Bronze Age urban development. Fortifications were augmented, and a new Syrian-style longroom fortress-temple was built, replacing the old sacred area. Many elaborate intramural tombs, some vaulted, continued from Str. XI and contained fine assemblages of pottery and other objects.

The Megiddo Middle Bronze stratigraphy, always troublesome, has been extensively reworked by several authorities, notably Kenyon (1958; 1969; 1973); Epstein (1965); Dunayevski and Kempinski (1973); Gerstenblith (1983); Kempinski (1992b); and others.

3. Shechem

Shechem, a 12-acre mound located in the strategic pass between Mt. Ebal and Mt. Gerazim 40 miles north of Jerusalem, was excavated by German scholars in 1913, 1914 and 1926-1934, and again by a large team of American archaeologists directed by G.E. Wright and others in 1957-1973.[4]

The town was first founded in MB I (Str. XXII-XXI) but remained unfortified initially. A large area in Field VI enclosed by a sort of "temenos" wall (Wall D) was interpreted by Wright as a "courtyard temple" (Temenos 1), but it now appears to be only a domestic area. The well known inscription of Khu-Sobek, an official of Sesostris III (*ca.* 1878-1843 B.C.), mentioning a campaign to the "mountainous area of Shechem," belongs here; but it does not require (as some think; cf. Kempinski 1992: 172) that Shechem itself was already a heavily fortified city.

Str. XX-XVIII (Temenos 2-5) see the continued growth of the town, probably overflowing the Wall D enclosure. It is Str. XVII-XV (Temenos 6, 7), however, that witnesses the development of Shechem into one of the most impressive city-states in Middle Bronze Age Palestine. A massive cyclopean wall (Wall A), still standing as much as 30 feet today, now surrounds the entire site. Inside this wall--essentially a retaining wall (Albright's "battered wall")--is a variegated earthen embankment and plastered *glaçis*, topped by Wall B, a solid wall converted late in MB III into a casemate wall in places. There is a unique East Gate with two entranceways, and also a more typical Northwest Gate of three-entry type. Adjoining the latter is a barracks-complex to the north, and a two-story palace-temple structure to the south (Field IV). Inside the gate area, in nearby Field V, was another sacred building for public use, a massive fortress-temple nearly identical to that at Megiddo.

Although some of the above defensive elements may go back to MB II, it is evident that most belong to MB III (contra Kempinski 1992b: 172). Toward the end of MB III and the transition to LB IA --between *ca.* 1530 and 1470 B.C.--three successive phases of massive destructions were observed in the Northwest Gate area, after which the Middle Bronze Age fortifications fell into disuse.

4. Jericho

Jericho, another strategically located mound, was excavated by Sellin and Watzinger in 1907, 1908; by Garstang in 1930-1936; and, most importantly, by Kenyon in 1952-1958. Kenyon's T. K3 and part of her "Tomb Group I" belong to MB I; but most of the tomb material is MB II-III (fig. 1).[5]

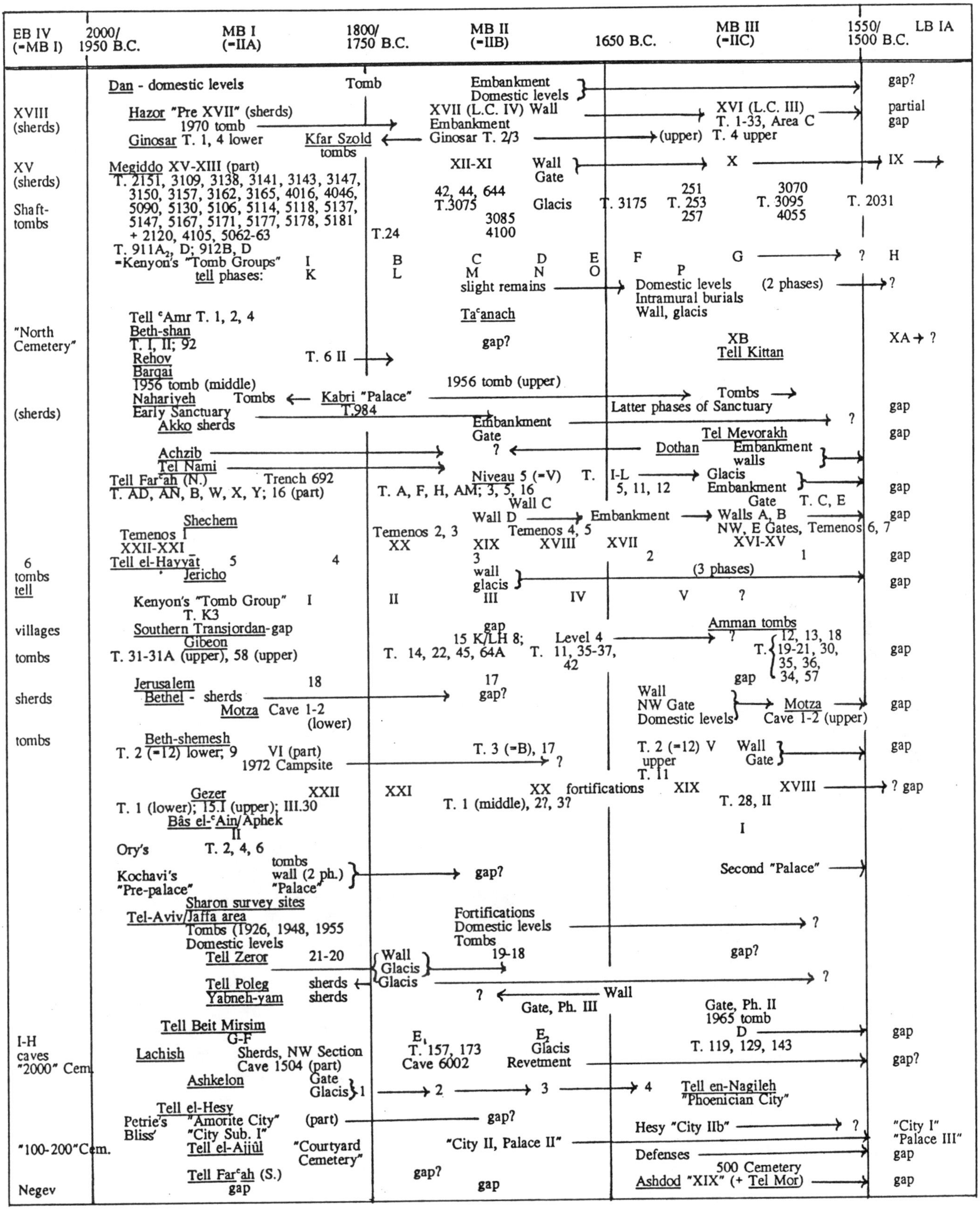

Fig. 3:1 Stratigraphic chart of Middle Bronze Age sites

The town was encircled by a massive earthen rampart, revetted at its base by a battered wall and crowned by a stone and mudbrick city wall. Garstang's "palace storerooms" were reinterpreted by Kenyon as a series of two-story shops and residences lining the street coming up the east slope from a gate area--rather like the *suqs* of medieval Middle Eastern cities. The several hundred reused EB IV shaft-tombs and newly cut MB II-III tombs (Kenyon's "Tomb Groups" II-V) yielded rich deposits of pottery, other objects, and unique, especially well preserved wooden furniture, mats, and even food and other organic materials. The 427 scarabs of Kenyon's "Tomb Groups," published by Kirkbride (1965), have often been used as a basis for establishing Syro-Palestinian and even Egyptian Middle Bronze Age chronologies (as Bietak; below); but, as we shall see, there are numerous pitfalls in this approach.

5. Aphek

Tel Aphek, located east of Tel Aviv in the Sharon Plain at the headwaters of the Yarkon River, has been excavated since 1972 by M. Kochavi, P. Beck, and others. Of particular importance are the "Pre-palace" and "Palace" phases, which belong to MB I. These phases have produced not only a large colonnaded courtyard palace (only partially excavated), but many tombs and by far the best stratigraphically controlled MB I ceramic sequence from any site in the country (Beck 1975; 1985). In addition, there are two phases of a heavy stone and mudbrick city wall that belong indisputably to MB I. MB II is not well represented, but private houses built over the early palace probably are to be assigned to this phase. In MB III a second palace was built and continued in use until the end of the period (fig. 1).[6]

6. Gezer

Gezer, a 33-acre mound at the juncture of the Shephelah and the Centrill Hills, near the mouth of the Ayalon Valley, was excavated by R.A.S. Macalister in 1902-1908; by A. Rowe in 1934; and by a large American project in 1964-1990 headed by G.E. Wright, W.G. Dever, J.D. Seger and others.[7] Although founded in the Late Chalcolithic and occupied in EB I-II, Gezer became a large city-state only in MB I-III.

To the MB I phase are to be assigned several of Macalister's tombs and the domestic levels of Str. XXII in Field VI, from a period before the site was fortified. MB II is attested by the continuation and development of the Field VI domestic installations (Str. XXI-XX) and, toward the end, the first phase of the great "Inner Wall" system. In MB III, however, this system was fully augmented and now featured some of the most impressive defensive constructions ever encountered in ancient Syria-Palestine. These included a steep, almost geometrically precise earthen embankment and tongued-plaster *glaçis* ; a cyclopean stone and mudbrick city wall running some 450 yards around the entire site, with at least a dozen rectangular towers; a classic three-entryway South Gate, still preserved nearly three stories high; and a massive multi-roomed citadel, Tower 5017, to the west of the gate, the stone foundations of which are 53 feet across and stand 9 courses high. Also belonging to MB III are another much-ruined citadel in Field VI on the acropolis, reached by a wide cobbled street; an area of private houses just inside the South Gate; and the famous Gezer "High Place" in Field V, an outdoor cultic installation with 10 large stelae (or Hebrew *mazzebôth*), a stone basin, and an extensive plastered pavement area. All these structures were violently destroyed at the very end of MB III, probably in the well known first Asiatic campaign of Thutmosis III in 1468 B.C., who includes Gezer among his conquered sites listed on the walls of the Karnak Temple.

7. Tell el-^{c}Ajjûl

Although excavated long ago by Petrie (1930-1934) and inadequately published, Tell el-^{c}Ajjûl has produced MB I-III material too important to ignore, including large and significant groups of scarabs.

To the initial MB I phase belong the "Courtyard Cemetery"; "City III" with its remains of a probable palace and some nearby domestic structures; and a relatively large quantity of Egyptian 12th-13th Dynasty materials. "City II" and "Palace II" are MB II and early-mid MB III, perhaps destroyed in the early campaigns of the renascent 18th Dynasty against the "Hyksos." The rampart, walls, and gate were probably constructed during this phase and identify the site as "Sharuhen" of the Egyptian campaigns. City I and "Palace/Citadel III" span the very end of MB III into LB IA.

Unfortunately, there are severe stratigraphic problems in trying to utilize the rich material of Tell el-^{c}Ajjûl, despite the efforts of scholars such as Albright (1938); Tufnell (1962); Weinstein (1975); Kempinski (1983; 1992b); and others. In particular the exact provenience of the diagnostic MB III/LB I Chocolate and Bichrome wares is difficult to specify.

8. Other Sites

A number of other MB I-III sites are important, not so much for overall chronological or cultural framework as for specific features. Thus the Ginosar, Kfar Szold, Kabri, and Barqai tombs provide a few chronological links; and Petrie's old Tell el-Far^{c}ah MB tombs, while problematic, still may yield some information (below). Smaller temples and sanctuaries are known from Nahariyeh on the coast; and from Tel Kittan and Tell el-Hayyat in the northern Jordan Valley (Falconer and Magness-Gardiner 1984; 1989). The recently discovered MB II Palace at Kabri, with its Aegean-style frescoes, is of major significance for cultural interconnections (Niemeier 1993). Tel Nami, on the coast near Athlit, seems to have been a seaport already in MB I (Artzy 1993). Much further information on fortifications will come from such recent excavations as Dan, Akko, Shiloh, Tel Sera', and Ashkelon, once they are more fully published. Finally, our first glimpses of village life and of rural areas, from sites like Giv'at Sharet and Tell el-Hayyat, should be supplemented by other excavations in future, filling out our picture of life in Middle Bronze Age Palestine.

B. Middle Bronze Age Settlement Types and Distribution.

1. The Middle Bronze I Period (*ca.* 2000-1750 B.C.)

Settlement types and patterns in the first phase of the Middle Bronze Age can only be appreciated fully by comparison with the preceding phase. The Early Bronze IV period, *ca.* 2300-2000 B.C., was a sort of "dark age," a non-urban interlude between the Early and Middle Bronze Ages. Urban life almost completely collapsed, the large mounds were all progressively deserted, and the population retreated to the rural areas and even the steppe-zones. While somewhat more than 1,200 EB IV sites are now known, almost all are small, unfortified one-period sites, the majority dispersed throughout the marginal zones noted above. In the latter area subsistence was obviously based on a decentralized, mixed economic strategy in which pastoral nomadism prevailed, sometimes accompanied by dry farming. The Early Bronze Age urban economy, based on intensive agriculture, industry, and trade, had collapsed along with the urban centers--large regional city-states that had served as administrative centers and market-towns. In "Central Place Theory" (below), each of the latter EB II-III urban centers had been the central hub in an interlocking network of lower-level sites. With the decline of the central places, the entire socio-economic structure collapsed by EB IV, and for several centuries Palestine remained at a level of integration probably less advanced than that of the Neolithic (Dever 1987; 1993a; 1993b; Palumbo 1991, and full references there).

By the beginning of the MB I period, *ca.* 2000 B.C., conditions in Palestine had improved, however, as Egypt emerged from its own "First Intermediate" period (Dynasties 6-11) and resumed international trade with Asia; and Syria also probably exerted a dynamic influence upon Palestine. (On the beginning of MB I, see Dever 1976; Gerstenblith 1983; Tubb 1983). The changes in Palestine are dramatically clear in settlement types and patterns. First, nearly all the hundreds of rural villages and pastoral nomadic sites in the marginal zones were abandoned, most of them permanently. The bulk of the population migrated back toward central Palestine, especially the more favorable sites with strategic locations, good water resources, and land suitable for intensive agriculture. The sites thus occupied in MB I were quite often large, centrally located *tells* that had formerly been settled in the Early Bronze Age. Indeed, almost all the several dozen such sites were now reoccupied, rapidly developing once again into urban centers. In addition, however, several hundred new sites were founded on virgin soil. Many of these were no more than hamlets and small villages at first, but by the end of MB I they were developing into towns and in some cases even cities. Broshi and Portugali's (1988:17) suggestion that MB I may be divided into an "MB IA" pre-urban phase, and an "MB IB" fully urban phase, has much to commend it, and we predict that future archaeological data will confirm this notion (see also Gerstenblith 1983: 101-23).

While there is a growing body of data on settlement history in MB I, only a few synthetic studies have been done, notably those of Gophna (1984), Broshi and Gophna (1986), Gophna and Portugali (1988), and Dever (1993d). In Broshi and Gophna (1986), some 130 MB I sites are listed, yielding an estimated total settled area of 426 hectares (or 164 acres), and a population of *ca.* 106,500 (using a figure of 250 persons per hectare). Broshi and Gophna, however, characterize individual sites only according to five, rather general categories:

1. Very small = 0.1-0.3 ha. (mean = .2 ha.)
2. Small = 0.4-1.0 ha. (mean = .7 ha.)
3. Medium = 1.1-4.9 ha. (mean = 3 ha.)
4. Large = 5-9.9 ha. (mean = 7 ha.)
5. Very large = 10 ha. up

Although Broshi and Gophna do not give the total number of sites for each category, apparently not considering that significant, an attempt to work out the numbers yields the rough statistics in fig. 3:2 (giving also MB II for comparisons).

It will be noted that the total number of sites in all five of the MB I categories above yields only 27 out of some 130 sites, and only 147 out of some 337 listed MB II sites. The discrepancy is due to the fact that many sites have been dated only by non-diagnostic

MB sherds from surface surveys and thus cannot be assigned confidently to a specific phase of MB I-IIII (listed by Broshi and Gophna simply as "x"; an MB I-II division was subsequently made by Gophna and Portugali [1988], but only for the Coastal Plain). To these must be added, of course, the 57 other "generic," or MB I-II, sites that are so listed.

Site Size	MB I	MB II	MB I & II
Very Small	17	83	14
Small	5	34	8
Medium	3	21	11
Large	- -	6	5
Very Large	2	3	14
Total	27	147	52

Fig. 3:2. Breakdown of MB I-II Sites; last column = sites where the two periods are undifferentiated.

Here one sees at once the pitfalls of settlement history and demographic projections based largely on data from surface surveys. Furthermore, it must be noted that *all* the size estimates are based on the largest extent of the *tells* as observed today, assuming both that (1) the present configuration of the mound is the *direct result* of the Middle Bronze occupation and use (and no other); and that (2) the *entire* mound was occupied in the period in question. Obviously both assumptions can easily be challenged--although it is likely that most of the large fortified *tells* were indeed products of the Middle Bronze period, as Gophna (1984) and others have argued. These "guesstimates" here for MB I-III, however, would not work as well for other periods in Palestine, where the current size of a site, or random sherd scatters, would probably not yield reliable figures (cf. Portugali 1982).

The above caveats notwithstanding, Broshi and Gophna's figures and the statistics we have derived from them, while inevitably flawed due to inadequate data, do perhaps yield *relative* percentages that have some heuristic value. The data suggest, I believe, two valid general conclusions. (1) From MB I to MB II-III there appears to be a nearly 160% increase in the total number of sites of all categories, but only a 30% increase in total population (see below for further discussion of MB II-III). (2) The MB I period already exhibits the "three-tier hierarchy" of site-types that is usually taken to be a classic example of an urban pattern of development (below). That is to say, the largest number of sites is in the small category, i.e., hamlets and villages widely distributed over the landscape (17); many fewer sites are in the medium category, or towns (8); and only a very few sites (2) could be classed as large cities or "central places." These tentative conclusions can in fact be substantiated by other studies.

A more sophisticated use of survey data, going well beyond Broshi and Gophna's early attempts at quantification and demographic projections, would employ a "rank-size" model (as, later, Gophna and Portugali, 1988, figs. 8, 10, 11; for orientation and bibliography see especially Paynter 1983; Grant 1986). This approach attempts to arrange all known sites along a curving graph on the basis of size, then breaks down sites into several groups based on relative size, and finally develops a hierarchy of site-types by groups. Where such statistical analyses have been done, as by Jonathan Mabry (1984; 1986) and Wade Kotter (1986), we can build upon Broshi and Gophna's results. Mabry (1986), for instance, has suggested that by the end of MB I some 65% percent of the population probably lived in a relatively few large cities of 15 acres or more. Nevertheless, almost half of the 400 or so settlements were still villages or hamlets of 2 acres or less. Such a breakdown of settlement-types into a hierarchy (not merely the presence of some of the first city walls, as Broshi and Gophna 1983: 86) indicates that already in MB I we are dealing with at least an early urban pattern of development, anticipating the fuller growth of urbanism in MB II-III (below).

It is not merely the type and distribution of settlements that point to the renascent urbanization of Palestine in MB I, but also several other factors that can be analyzed (on the following, see further Dever 1993c). Among these indicators of the growth of what is often called "social complexity"--an inevitable accompaniment of urban development--would be the following. (1) In the advancement of technology, MB I sees the development of two especially significant industries that had a profound effect on economy and society: the introduction of true tin-bronze technology (using imported tin from Anatolia or Mesopotamia) (Malamat 1989); and the first fast wheel-made pottery, resulting in a ceramic industry that could be based upon mass-production and trade (cf. Dever 1976; Gerstenblith 1983; Tubb 1983; Beck 1985). (2) Socio-political stratification, or specialization, as evidenced not only by the above crafts, but also by the architectural sophistication reflected in the early MB I defensive embankments and city walls; the presence of monumental "palaces" at Tel Aphek and elsewhere, almost certainly the residences of local rulers; evidence from burials that other elite social classes existed, including (to judge from weapons) perhaps a standing army or at least local militias; and sophisticated Canaanite-style temples, probably evidence of a priestly class. (3) International trade grew dramatically in MB I, bringing Palestine out of the isolation and poverty of EB IV, as shown by the "Execration Texts" in Egypt, as well as numerous Egyptian objects found in Syria-Palestine, including both luxury goods, like scarabs and alabasters, and even statuettes of high-ranking Egyptian officials, more likely commercial envoys than political officials (cf. Weinstein 1975). Egyptian trade may well account for the fact that the largest number of MB I sites in any region is the group along the coast and the coastal road from Egypt northward (55), including such large fortified cities as Tel Aphek, Burga, Tel Zeror, Tel Nami, Akko, and Achziv (Broshi and Gophna 1986: 86; cf. Gophna and Portugali 1988). Akko was almost certainly a seaport in this period, as was Tel Nami; and it has recently been suggested that seafaring placed a much larger role in the MB I economy and society than was previously suspected (Artzy 1993).

2. The Middle Bronze II Period (*ca.* 1750-1650 B.C.)

The Middle Bronze II-III periods, typically separated by American scholars, are usually lumped together by most Israeli and some European scholars (see Kempinski 1983; Bienkowski 1989; but cf. Finkelstein 1988-1989, agreeing with Dever 1987; 1992), but we shall retain the two-fold division in order to facilitate analysis, and also because we feel the analysis justifies it. The first phase, MB II, witnesses a further, continuous development of the urban settlement pattern outlined above for MB I. Repeating our statistical breakdown of Broshi and Gophna's figures above, we get the following picture (combining, however, our MB II *and* III):

Once again the total number of 199 MB II-III sites is much less than Broshi and Gophna's list of 337 sites, since scant survey pottery may not have allowed them to make a precise assignment to a specific phase of MB. Nevertheless, *relative* percentages may still be significant.

While Broshi and Gophna do not employ a "rank-size" model (only in Gophna and Portugali 1988), the hierarchy of MB I settlement types noted above as indicative or urbanization is even more apparent in MB II (and III). Here the "three-tier hierarchy" is even more strongly developed, and it now has the classic proportions of intensified urban centralization. Some 139 MB II-III settlements are in the Very small-Small

MB II	MB II, undifferentiated from MB I	Totals
VS = 83	14	97
S = 34	8	42
M = 21	11	32
L = 6	5	11
VL = 3	14	17
Total 147	52	199

Fig. 3:3. Breakdown of MB II sites.

range; 43 in the Medium-Large range; and only 16-17 in the Very Large range. Furthermore, if we re-do Broshi and Gophna's figures so as to list the 16 largest MB II-III sites together and calculate their settled area, we come up with the following (fig. 3:4):

Site	Size in ha./acres	Dates (Broshi and Gophna 1986)
Akko	20/50	MB I + II/III
Aphek	10/25	MB I + II/III
Ashkelon	10/25	MB I + II/III
Bira	15/37	MB I + II/III
Dan	16/40	MB I + II/III
Dor	10/25	MB I + II/III
Gezer	12/30	MB I + II/III
Hazor	80/200	MB I + II/III
Ibleam	9/22	MB II/III
Kabri	40/100	MB I + II/III
Kedesh	10/25	X
Lachish	12/30	MB II/III
Tell el-^{c}Ajjûl	12/30	MB I + II/III
Yavneh-Yam	64/160	MB I + II/III
Yoqneam	10/25	X
Zafit	15/37	MB I + II/III
Total occupied MB II/III area: 345/862		

Fig. 3:4. The 16 largest MB II-III Sites in Palestine.

If we compare the 345 ha. of occupied area in the 16 largest MB II/III sites with Broshi and Gophna's total of 660 ha. (1986: 86), it is evident that over half the population (52%) -- or some 73,000 out of *ca.* 140,000 people -- were concentrated in the 16 largest of the 337 known settlements. If we calculate not simply the 16 or more largest sites, but the largest *fortified* sites, as Broshi and Gophna do (1986: 88), we come up with an even larger percentage, or 80% of the population living in such cities.

Working with somewhat different figures, and attempting to apply a "Central Place Theory" model to Palestinian MB II-III, Kotter (1986) has come up with corroborative statistics. He also lists some 400 sites, showing that the "three-tier hierarchy" breaks down as shown in fig. 3:5.

Broshi and Gophna's 16 largest MB II-III centers noted above, while not necessarily identical to Kotter's list of those comprising his upper 5%, do constitute *ca.* 8% of their 199 datable sites. That is to say, either way we arrive at a figure of some 16-20 MB II-III sites that make up about 5-8% of the total. And in both calculations it appears that the majority of the population lived in these relatively few sites, the balance scattered over a somewhat larger number (Kotter = 10%; Broshi and Gophna = 22%) of medium-sized towns; and especially in very small sites (Kotter = 85%; Broshi and Gophna = 70%) in the rural areas.

Category	Size, ha./acres	% of total sites
Large urban centers	8-70/20-175	5%
Medium-sized towns	3-8/7-20	10%
Small villages, hamlets	.4-3/1-7	85%

Fig. 3:5. MB II-III Sites, following Kotter (1986).

Kotter (1986) goes on to analyze such statistics in terms of classic "Central Place Theory." A variant of locational analysis first developed by economic geographers in Europe, Central Place Theory attempts to design a model to explain how settlement hierarchies function and to determine demography within a modern market economy. The principal model assumes that a hexagon is the most efficient geometric form for the equal spatial division of an area among a number of points. Located at the hub of the hexagon will be the "central place" or market town; third-tier sites, villages and hamlets, will be at the far corners of the hexagon; and roughly equidistant in between, at the nodes of the network, will be the second-tier towns. Given the "three-tier hierarchy" of sites that we discern in Middle Bronze Age Palestine, it seems irresistible to use the analogy of modern "Central Place" models to analyze ancient urban development. Despite some success, however, Kotter's analysis is limited by the fact that the necessary components--an *even* distribution of terrain, population resources, and transportation--is prohibited by the unique landscape of Palestine (below). Some useful polygons can be drawn for MB II-III Palestine, but they are not classic "Thiessen polygons," and they vary widely from region to region (see further Paynter 1983; Grant 1986).

The data sketched above do not allow us to differentiate sufficiently to quantify many aspects of urban developments from MB II into MB III, and thus to characterize MB II separately. Nevertheless, I would argue that we can extrapolate from MB III back to MB II with some confidence, because of the *general continuity* between the two periods, observable at nearly all excavated sites. Indeed, as we have noted, it is precisely that phenomenon that leads Israelis and others to lump the two phases together. Thus the strongly urban "three-tier hierarchy" of settlement pattern that we have just analyzed as common to the generic MB II-III era must surely have characterized Palestine already by MB II, following the initial "proto-urban" MB I phase. Gophna and Portugali (1988: 19) speak of a "massive urban society" already in MB I. It would follow that many of the 16 largest MB sites listed above in fig. 3:4 had attained much of their size and importance, if not their zenith, already before the end of MB II. For instance, I would suggest that by MB II most of these sites that have been excavated were heavily fortified (Shechem and Gezer being notable exceptions).

Beyond theoretical postulates based on MB II-III continuity, however, there *are* some specifically MB II developments that we can discern, at least at those sites that have been excavated stratigraphically. Among the diagnostic features that we might note would be first (1) the increasing pace and complexity of defensive constructions. Not only are many more sites fortified in MB II, but the defenses now begin to incorporate elaborate *glaçis* systems that are more technologically advanced than the earlier earthen embankments or ramparts. In addition, multi-phase masonry and mudbrick city walls and standardized triple-entryway gates now proliferate--probably influenced by the spread of Syro-Anatolian and Hittite prototypes as Palestine became more internationalized (Naumann 1971; Matthiae 1984; Gregori 1986).

(2) The growth of many of these MB II fortified sites into true city-states undoubtedly intensified urban trends already underway, especially toward further social complexity and political centralization. A half-dozen or so of the principal urban sites could then be considered true "central places"--i.e., not only market towns for the second- and third-tier sites in the surrounding rural areas, but regional administrative centers that came increasingly to manage the overall economy (see further below, on definitions of "urban").

In spite of the evidence for such centralization, two cautions are in order. First, the existence of these large walled cities dominating the hinterland in Palestine should not be taken to reflect a sort of "feudal" society and economy, as Albright (1954: 91, 92) and others had suggested. Neither the archaeological data nor the scant textual evidence demonstrates the seigneurial system, the classes of military aristocracy, vassals, and landless peasantry, or any other of the basic institutions of medieval European feudalism. The latter is thus an unsuitable model for Middle Bronze Age Palestine.

Second, while centralization of administration and other functions is by common consensus among social theorists the hallmark of the "State," Palestine was only *regionally* (i.e., not "nationally") centralized in MB I. If nothing else, competition among the rival city-states fostered centrifugal, rather than centripetal, forces and precluded further centralization. Palestine may have been highly urbanized in MB II, as its neighbors Mesopotamia and Egypt had long been; but it did not attain statehood until the time of the Israelite monarchy 1500 years later (on state-formation processes, see Dever 1993e).

3. The Middle Bronze III Period (*ca.* 1650-1550 B.C.)

The final phase of the Middle Bronze Age, MB III, *ca.* 1650-1550/1500 B.C., represents the zenith of the urban Middle Bronze Age in Palestine (Dever 1987) and on that basis alone should be set off as a separate phase. There are, however, multi-phase stratigraphic sequences that justify the distinction, at least at mounds that have been excavated with more precise modern methods. Shechem, for instance, has five late MB occupational phases, separated by three destructions (Dever 1974). Gezer has three MB III phases (Dever et al. 1974: 4, 5). Other sites show the same complex stratification (fig. 1). Unless this phenomenon is the creation of archaeologists' imaginations, it must be taken to reflect an actual historical-cultural situation that is much too complex to be compressed within a few years and regarded as simply the last part of MB II (or late "MB IIB").

Against those who maintain the latter view (e.g., Kempinski 1983; Bienkowski 1989), I would point out a number of developments that occur only late in the Middle Bronze Age and more than justify the distinction of a separate MB III phase. Among these would be (1) the fact that by now (and only now) nearly *every* site in Palestine is heavily fortified -- even sites as small as Tel Mevorakh, less than four acres. The rest of the larger sites that had not been previously fortified, like Shechem and Gezer, now boast multi-phase, truly monumental fortifications. I have argued that these late MB III defense systems -- exactly contemporary with the 15th Dynasty/"Hyksos" interregnum in Egypt -- were intended as a backup for the Asiatic penetration into the Delta (Dever 1985; 1990; cf., however, Hoffmeier 1989; 1991; refuted by Weinstein 1991). But whatever the case, the phenomenon of these defenses, together with their dramatic destruction at the end of the period, is characteristic of MB III (below).

(2) It is not just augmented defenses, however, that characterize MB III. We also confront more sophisticated planning overall. The parade example is the Northwest Gate area at Shechem, comprising a deliberately laid out complex that includes a double city wall and *glaçis* with triple-entryway gate; a large barracks building adjoining the gate; a two-story colonnaded palace, with its own integral tripartite temple; a large plastered plaza; and a massive fortress (*migdal*) temple (Dever 1974). The Shechem "citadel" closely parallels that of Alalakh VII. Only *now*, in MB III, does Palestine rival the great Middle Bronze Age cities of Syria (cf. Dever 1974; 1987; Matthiae 1981).

(3) In other aspects, as well, we see novel developments in MB III. The sophistication of local tastes and the prosperity of the elites of the city-states are reflected in a proliferation of ceramic imports that are unique to (and diagnostic of) the period. Among imported wares are numerous Cypriot styles, such as White Painted III-VI ("Pendant" and "Cross Line" styles), Red-on-Black, Monochrome, Bichrome, White Slip I, and (possibly) Base Ring I, as well as wares like Chocolate-On-White that may be Cypriot-inspired. Syrian vessels also appear in MB III, like Gray Lustrous wares and Syrian Red-polished Bottles (Oren 1971; Gittlen 1981; Ilan 1993).

(4) The increased internationalism of MB III is also seen in the first well documented, large-scale ethnic movements of foreign peoples into Palestine. Thus Hurrians from Syria, who constituted a large minority by the subsequent Late Bronze Age (Egyptian New Kingdom texts speak of Canaan as "the Land of the Hurru"), are first attested in an MB III cuneiform text from Gezer (Dever, Lance, and Wright 1970: 111-13).

(5) In a related development, Palestine in MB III produces both the first written texts in its long history (several cuneiform documents), as well as one of humankind's most profound cultural advances, the first truly *alphabetic* script (Naveh 1982; Sass 1988). Writing and simplified writing systems alone, an innovation of MB III, would in my judgment justify seeing this period as a distinct phase--indeed the "zenith" of Middle Bronze Age Palestine.

Beyond these specific cultural developments, however, we can only point to the analysis of MB II and MB III urbanism above--assuming that much of the composite data as recovered by archaeology belongs to the last, uppermost, and usually best preserved phase of the MB sequence, or our MB III.

Such statistical analysis as we can confine to MB III suggests that, while a few large urban sites still predominate in the "three-tier hierarchy," medium sized or middle-tier sites now increase in number. Thus Broshi and Gophna (1986: 88, n. 1) conclude that the percentage of the population living in walled towns shrinks from 80%

in MB I to about 66% in their MB IIB, or our MB II plus MB III. Working on a somewhat different basis Mabry (1984: 4, 5) argues that in MB II-III the percentage of the total occupied area represented by very large sites declined by about 15%, while that represented by medium and large sites grew by about 12%. Some of this development toward large villages and towns that were becoming important rural networks within regional hierarchies (or "nodes" in "Central Place" parlance) probably began in MB II. The modest increase in population from Broshi and Gophna's 106,000 in MB I to 140,000 in MB II-III could then be accounted for mostly by growth in these larger villages and towns. I would propose that this development crested in MB III, as the process of urbanization reached its maximum expression.

This is not all speculative. Falconer and Magness-Gardiner (1984; 1989) have excavated a small MB II-III village at Tell el-Hayyat in the Jordan Valley (1.5 acres), which has quite surprisingly produced a series of temples, a potter's kiln, and other features that were formerly associated only with "urban" life. Indeed, Falconer's (1987) dissertation argued that archaeologists have skewed the picture by focussing too exclusively on large urban *tell*-sites; that, in contrast to Adam's (1981) Mesopotamia as "the heartland of cities," Palestine in MB I-III should be understood as "the heartland of villages" (see also Gophna and Beck 1981; Gophna and Portugali 1988; Gal 1991).

A final task remains, that of *defining* "urban," and here as well Falconer has advanced a provocative model. The term "urban," rarely defined in Palestinian archaeology, has been used indiscriminately to describe almost any site that is large, particularly if surrounded by defense walls--but *how* large? Falconer makes a laudable attempt to quantify size as a criterion of urbanism by taking the case of ancient Mesopotamia for comparison. Here, because of rich alluvial plains that surround a typical site, one can calculate average annual agricultural yields per acre. Then, working from the nutritional requirements for an individual for a year, one can arrive at the maximum population that a site could support on the land within a practical working radius (usually estimated on the basis of ethnographic data as 1-2 miles). Such a site would be a self-supporting village or town. Falconer argues, however, that a "city" may be defined as a population aggregate that has *outgrown* its capacity to feed itself, and thus must expand its domination to the agricultural hinterland in order to organize the means of production. Falconer demonstrates that the "threshold" at which this urban transformation normally takes place in Mesopotamia is at the level of an occupied area of 34 ha. (85 acres), or a population of some 8,500 (using a coefficient of a maximum of 100 persons per acre). By that rule-of-thumb, Mesopotamia had many true cities from the late 4th millennium onward. Palestine, however, with few sites even in the Middle Bronze Age exceeding 30 acres and 3,000 people, would have been almost entirely non-urban. According to this model, only three Palestinian Middle Bronze sites could possibly have qualified as "cities": Kabri (200 acres); Yabneh-yam (100 acres); and Hazor (200 acres).

Despite the general utility of Falconer's model, his criteria obviously lead to unacceptable conclusions when applied to Palestine. And the reason for the discrepancy is simple: the broken landscape and unpredictable rainfall of Palestine result in much lower agricultural yields per acre of available land--and thus a much *lower "threshold"* for a site's transformation into an urban configuration. I would suggest that a figure of *ca.* 25 acres, rather than 85, would be appropriate for Palestine (although even that figure might have to be reduced for sites in marginal areas). Such a figure, for instance, would allow us to classify many of the MB II-III sites discussed above as "cities," as indeed they must have been. In this revised definition then, Palestine was indeed urbanized throughout much of the Middle Bronze Age, as we have argued above.

C. URBANISM, SOCIO-ECONOMIC COMPLEXITY, AND POLITICAL STRUCTURE.

1. Defining the Terminology

Previous syntheses of the Middle Bronze Age in Palestine have sought to characterize the period's uniqueness in terms of ceramic and metallic typologies, urban renascence, trade and the Syrian connection, "Amorite" newcomers, and even the notion of an Egyptian empire in Asia. But no analysis thus far has focused on *social complexity* as an organizing principle. That might not seem so surprising if we consider that the term "complexity" itself remains ill-defined.

By general consensus in the past decade in the broader fields of archaeology, anthropology, and social theory, vague and moralistic concepts like "civilization" have been replaced by the notion of "complexity." This term is not only more precise and neutral, but it also allows us to focus on, and to begin to quantify, the single most basic and significant variant in cultural evolution--i.e., *not* "urbanism," or the development of a "state" level of organization, but rather *social stratification*, together with its implications for every aspect of culture and history (see further below). Palestinian archaeologists, however, fully a generation behind in social and anthropological theory, have clung to outworn and fuzzy notions of "the rise of civilization." As a single example, I cite Aharon Kempinski's *The Rise of an Urban Society: The Urbanization of Palestine in the Early Bronze Age, 3000-2150 B.C.* (1978), following the outdated approach of V. Gordan Childe (cf. however, Kempinski 1992a). We may begin to improve upon this situation by defining some basic terms. (1) "Urbanization." Clearly this term is superior to "civilization," even though both denote the process by which a society becomes "citified," as it were. But how are we to *specify* this process? Despite the fact that most scholars use the terms "urban/urbanization"--especially *à propos* for the Middle Bronze Age in Palestine--what precisely do we mean by this? Even a working definition is rare in the published literature (unless we accept rather simple-minded descriptions such as "large," "walled," etc.)

Above we have suggested several possible definitions of "urbanization" with reference to Middle Bronze Age Palestine. Whether or not one adopts any of the above or other models in attempting to define urbanism, we should keep in mind that the phenomenon of urbanization is neither an inevitable nor necessarily beneficial stage in cultural evolution. It is certainly not a prerequisite for the development of social complexity, much less for the attainment of a state-level of political organization. This is borne out by the fact that urbanization has never taken place in many parts of the world, although some of these so-called "primitive" societies are exceedingly complex. Moreover, others, like the Han Dynasty in China, or Old Kingdom Egypt, have created a true state on the basis of an almost entirely rural society. Finally, a number of recent studies, such as Yoffee and Cowgill, *The Collapse of Ancient States and Civilizations* (1988), suggest that urbanization itself is often something of an anomaly. Under certain conditions, such as those in ancient Palestine, urbanization is in fact an artificial form of socio-political organization, one that is inherently unstable and subject to periodic collapse. Any long-term settlement history of Palestine, using a model like *la longue durée* of Braudel and the *annales* school of historians, will reveal dramatically the recurring cycles of urbanism and ruralism, centralization and decentralization, specialization and despecialization, advance and abatement.[8] One has only to look at the country -- from the Bronze Age, through the Israelite monarchy, even into modern times -- to bear out the truth of the observation that urbanization always tends to be fragile and impermanent. In that sense, the phenomenon to be explained is not the collapse of the Middle Bronze Age around 1500 B.C., but rather its *rise* in the first place--especially after the first, disastrous experiment in urban living in the preceding Early Bronze Age, which ended with the abandonment of every urban site in the final centuries preceding the MB I period. In one sense, Falconer's (1987; above) intuition on the "heartland of villages" is correct: even though ancient Palestine may be considered as a parade example of Rowton's "dimorphic society," the village-pastoral morpheme is better suited to the natural conditions of this region and has tended to predominate throughout history at the expense of the urban morpheme. Leon Marfoe (1979) has made the same point with regard to parts of southern Syria in antiquity, and even for modern Lebanon.[10]

(2) "*Complexity.*" A second term that we must define further is "complexity." Obviously *all* societies are complex to some degree, since no truly "egalitarian" social system has ever been encountered, ancient or modern. For the purposes of our discussion, however, we may understand complexity to denote basically the phenomenon of stratification, or the process by which groups within a society become differentiated, become "elites" (see further Dever 1993c).

Ultimately, of course, the distinction of "elite" is based upon class, or inherited status, and to that extent the complex society may seem to resemble earlier stages of social evolution, such as the so-called "tribal" or "chiefdom" levels, which are lineage groups or kinship-based societies that confer privilege by birth, not achievement. But complexity differs not only in the fact that now only a relatively *few* members of society inherit privilege, but also in the origins of this privilege. In a complex society elites may not be born as such, but can *become* so through craft specialization, entrepreneurship, accumulation of capital, the wielding of power in a variety of ways, or through other means. Thus there emerges a minority ruling class that enjoys differential access to goods and services, and in turn manipulates the majority of the less privileged to maintain themselves, as well as social institutions like kingship and priesthood that serve to legitimize their special role and function.

Such an elite group, once established, may persevere not only through ideology, of course, but frequently through coercion, since the society at large may resist this funneling off of resources to the privileged few. As long as an approximate equilibrium can be maintained, peace and prosperity are the apparent result, although at an enormous price. When the balance shifts, however, as it inevitably does, the elites may be displaced, social institutions tend to fragment, urban centers are depopulated, and the economy reverts to a lower (i.e., simpler) level of integration and production (typically in Palestine, ruralism and pastoralism, rather than industry and trade). Thus there ensues what we call "collapse," even if temporary, or the *reversal* of the process that produced "complexity."

Finally, it must be noted that, in our current understanding, upheavals and even radical socio-cultural changes are not likely to be satisfactorily explained by positing invasions of new peoples, catastrophic natural disasters, or even the diffusion of new ideas, but rather by *indigenous* developments that lead to a shift in the competing demands of elements within the local society.

(3) "*City-State.*" A final definition is appropriate, namely that of "city-state," a term again much abused. One has the impression that the use of "city-state" by Palestinian archaeologists means little more than "beyond urban," but "not quite state." Yet we can easily be more precise. A city-state is simply a large, centrally located urban site that has gained autonomy by monopolizing its hinterland, up to the sphere of

influence of its nearest urban rival--in short, what economic geographers call a "Central Place" (above). It is a "state written small," a state in miniature; it possesses the centralized authority needed to command essential resources, but on a regional rather than national scale city-states, one stage short of true state-level development, such city-states seem ideally suited to marginal areas like Palestine, where in periods like the Middle Bronze Age they are particularly well documented.

2. A General Systems Theory Approach to Assessing Complexity in the Middle Bronze Age.

The growth of complexity in the Middle Bronze Age in Palestine may be best understood and compared with the preceding EB IV by analyzing the period in terms of General Systems Theory (GST; see further Dever 1987). This model is borrowed, of course, from the biological sciences; it applies the basic notion of "the organized state" in living organisms to the study of human culture and society. Although not always spelled out so specifically, the concept is often implicit in "holistic" or "systemic" approaches to culture-history, which are gradually making an impact on Syro-Palestinian archaeology.

The basic assumption is that society, like nature, is composed of numerous, interacting sub-systems. When these sub-systems maintain a proper balance, stability (or "homeostasis") is the result. Changes in any sub-system can occur, however, through a variety of causes, and these tend to affect the whole, either negatively or positively ("deviation amplifying mechanisms"). Thus, because of a series of mutual outputs and inputs of information and energy ("feedback loops"), social systems, like organisms, are not static, but are *dynamic* --subject constantly to a variety of internal and external forces that promote either growth or decay (the "complexity"-"collapse" syndrome noted above).

While there are obvious limitations to the use of models derived from biology in analyzing social systems, the attractions of General Systems Theory are such that in recent years it has become one of the most widely adopted models in anthropology and archaeology. The principal sub-systems that we may isolate in the Middle Bronze Age provide both the ideal categories of analysis and the means to move beyond generalities to specifics. Let us look in turn at: (1) settlement types and distribution patterns; (2) subsistence, including ecological setting, technology, and trade; (3) social structure; and (4) political organization. In each case, our assignment is to measure only *social complexity*, in particular the rise of elites, not the overall characteristics of the period, which have been amply discussed elsewhere. We shall also need to keep in mind the essential nature of the preceding EB IV period, in order to have some basis for comparison.

(1) *Settlement types and distribution.* Here the data are abundant and clear, and we have analyzed them above. With respect to "complexity," it would appear that it is present nearly from the beginning of the Middle Bronze Age, since complexity is both a necessary component of and an outgrowth of urbanism. Specifically, we must presume that cities (and soon, city-states) could not have developed without the emergence of an elite class that was capable of centralized planning, administration, and funding of collective activities such as food production, building projects, commerce and trade, and relations with neighboring cities and more distant regions and states. Such a complex society is not difficult to envision in Middle Bronze Age, for it had forerunners in third millennium Syria-Palestine, as shown by studies of numerous EB II-III sites. What we see, then, in MB I is simply the *re-emergence*, after a long gap in EB IV, of an older type of city-state social system that had prevailed for some six or seven hundred years. In

MB I, however, the level of complexity was higher and more intensified, as the following will show. Furthermore, it grew throughout MB II-III.

(2) *Ecological setting, technology, and trade.* These *subsistence* sub-categories, all having to do with the economy, cannot easily be separated. At first glance, the natural setting of the first phase, MB I, would seem to be the same as that for EB IV. There are those, however, who posit environmental deterioration, and even climatic shifts, as explanations for the "dark age" in EB IV; and if we accept that view, we could see the urban renascence in MB I as due to an amelioration of natural conditions. But, in any case, the study of "ecology" embraces not simply environmental conditions *per se*, but both culturally and technologically derived mechanisms for exploiting that environment (i.e. subsistence). And these clearly have changed from EB IV to MB I. But in particular, we see that the much less specialized, mixed economy of EB IV, combining pastoralism and dry-farming, has been eclipsed in MB I. It is replaced by a multi-faceted economy that is comprised of intensified, high-yield agriculture; industry (especially true tin-bronze metallurgy and wheel-made, mass-produced ceramics); and trade, some of it long-distance. Again, not only is the new economy evidence of urbanism, but also of growing social complexity. We cannot possibly imagine that an "egalitarian" or non-stratified society, without centralized management, could have produced either the quantity or the quality of the goods and services that we see reflected in the archaeological record in MB I. For example, an economy based on intensified agriculture requires skillful organization of both city and countryside so as to produce surplusses of food that can be stored and redistributed. Mass-production of metals and pottery requires not only sophisticated and specialized technology, but enforced standardization and the capital to develop markets. Long-distance trade, such as that needed to procure tin for bronze manufacture, requires an exceptionally high degree of centralized planning. The presence of all these activities in MB I strongly suggests that an elite, managerial class had already emerged in MB I.

In the MB II-III phases, the strong continuity that is evident from MB I means that the "urban" character of the economy overall--based on specialized agriculture, industry, and trade--changed little except for intensification of trends already begun. Technological improvements in metallurgy, however, included the introduction of bronze shaft-hole axes of several types; cast figurines in bronze, silver, and gold (mostly of deities); sheet-metal and gold-foil figurines and items of personal adornment; and soldered ("granulated") gold jewelry. Ceramics could not advance much beyond the superbly crafted and decorated MB I repertoire; but MB II-III innovations did include several classes of sharply carinated bowls, which require great skill of the potter in both wheelworking and firing. Superbly designed and crafted wooden furniture now appears, as in the Jericho tombs; and wooden tables, boxes, and other items often are embellished with inlaid ivory or bone carvings with both geometric and figural motifs. Imported Egyptian scarabs, alabasters, and various faience objects not only increase, but are no doubt manufactured locally. One aspect of technology that develops dramatically in MB II-III is architecture and urban planning, both domestic and monumental. Advances in domestic architecture are exemplified by multi-room patrician houses or villas at Megiddo, Ta^{c}anach, Tell Beit Mirsim, and Tell el-^{c}Ajjûl--all exceptionally well laid out, spacious, and skillfully constructed. Even more elaborate and luxurious residences of MB II-III are known that may be regarded as citadels or palaces of ruling elites (below), such as those at Hazor, Kabri, Megiddo, Shechem, Aphek, Gezer, and Tell el-^{c}Ajjûl.

The complex defense systems that are found now at almost every site, and which reach the zenith of their evolution by MB II-III, reveal considerable sophistication in concept, design, and construction. For example, *glaçis* such as those at Hazor, Shechem, Shiloh, Gezer, and elsewhere are really marvels of ancient engineering and the expert use of local materials--so much so that they almost defy explanation. Moreover, the sheer *size* of the earthworks and cyclopean masonry constructions presumes the ability to plan, organize, and carry out building projects that deserve the designation monumental (cf. Bonimovitz 1992).

A few MB II-III sites are so well arranged functionally--with separate areas for defense, administrative temple precincts, domestic quarters, industrial installations, and other operations --that we must consider this phenomenon as evidence not simply of technological advance but of true "urban planning." Especially noteworthy MB II-III examples are Megiddo, Shechem, and Gezer, all of which rival or even surpass most contemporary sites in Syria.

One aspect of the MB II-III economy deserves special mention, namely trade. Trade is assumed to be one important aspect of ancient Near Eastern economies and societies, yet definitions of trade vary widely. Often trade is taken simply to mean the exchange of commodities between individuals or groups. As Renfrew puts it, trade is "the reciprocal traffic, exchange, or movement of materials or goods through peaceful human agency" (1969: 151). Other scholars would broaden this somewhat materialistic definition of "exchange" to include non-material goods, services, or resources, which may yield data on rank, prestige, or power.

The term should retain its customary meaning of reciprocal transfer or exchange but may be expanded to include the asymmetrical and unequal exchanges of deference and obedience for prestige or protection, transactions which may be regarded as applications of power.

Above all, the larger *symbolic and social* context of trade, as with all aspects of the economy, must be considered. Yet the question is: to what extent is it possible to recognize trade in the archaeological record? To this point we shall return below.

It is now commonplace to refer to what may be called a relatively new sub-field of anthropology and archaeology, namely prehistoric economics, or economic archaeology. This branch of inquiry, simply put, focuses on the economic processes of production, distribution, and consumption, seeking to explain why changes in the economy take place and what their implications are for other aspects of social organization, settlement types and patterns, and material culture (Earle 1985; cf. Dalton 1967, 1969; Sahlins 1972; Schneider 1974; Webb 1974; Earle and Ericson 1977; Earle and Christianson 1980; Ericson and Earle 1982; Sheridan and Bailey 1981; Ortiz 1983; and Renfrew 1984). As Earle says of the newer approach:

> It is carefully non-reductionist inasmuch as it sees the economy as both determining and being determined by the broader cultural context. This general systems approach identifies the economic variables as basic to linking a human population to its environment and to linking population to population. The dynamics of the system, however, do not derive from any simple changes in the "infrastructure" but result from a complex set of feedback relationships that interlock environmental, economic, and cultural variables (1985: 106).

It is obvious that a fundamental task within economic archaeology is the study of ancient *trade*. Here several initial observations may be made. (1) Important as it is, the study of trade can contribute to the larger discipline of economic archaeology only as we come to understand particular regional patterns and local sequences more fully: these are the basic "building blocks" upon which any general theory must be built. For many regions of the eastern Mediterranean world, however, the detailed studies that we need are just beginning. It is true that Mesopotamia and its trading networks in Syria and Anatolia are relatively well known, at least in certain eras such as the Old Assyrian and Old Babylonian periods (Garelli 1963; Larsen 1976; Yoffee 1977). Egypt's trade with the Levant has been only sporadically documented; but the Early Bronze I-II, Middle Bronze, and Late Bronze Ages in Palestine have been the subjects of basic treatments (Ward 1971; Ahituv 1978; Kemp and Merrillees 1980; Na'aman 1981; Weinstein 1981; 1985; Ben-Tor 1982). Trade between Cyprus and the Levant has been studied in some detail, but principally for the Late Bronze Age (Gittlen 1981; Muhly 1982, 1986). Wider Aegean trade contacts with the Levant have been explored mostly with regard only to ceramics and copper-bronze production, but also in one recent treatment (Runnels and Van Andel 1988) with respect to the origins of agriculture in the Neolithic. Despite these studies, we need many more detailed treatments of *specific* sites and regions where trade can be shown to have been a major factor in the economy, such as Heltzer's (1971 and subsequently) analyses of Ugarit, based on both texts and artifacts.

For the area closer to our topic here, a collection of papers edited in 1985 by Knapp and Stech is noteworthy. This volume is one of the first *regionally* focused collections of studies in economic archaeology, but more are needed. For the larger region, one should note also the papers in the volumes edited by Gale (1991) and Hawkins (1977).

(2) A second initial observation is that despite the desirability of regional studies of ancient trade, and the growing sophistication of theoretical models, the archaeological data at our disposal thus far for the southern Levant are distressingly poor. At best, we can show that certain items are imports and can sometimes document their provenience. But what about the larger *exchange systems* that were operative in given instances? The data, even when fully exploited (which is rare), are scarcely capable of answering such questions.

(3) Third, it may be suggested that good evidence on ancient trade is scant not so much because the archaeological record is inadequate, but because our research designs (if any) have been badly flawed. Particularly in "Biblical" and Syro-Palestinian archaeology, we have focused on "political history"; cultural history has lagged behind, social history is just now being discovered, and economic history is non-existent. One can scarcely think of a single recent field or research project in Syro-Palestinian *historical* archaeology that has been designed specifically to address economic considerations. Eric Higgs' pioneering "Cambridge Environmental Project on the Early History of Agriculture" should have pointed the way. But then Palestinian archaeologists working in the Bronze Age, Iron Age, and Classical periods have never profited as much as they should have from the more sophisticated ecological and technological orientation of their colleagues in prehistory. Perhaps they think that having texts will solve all their problems. However, as Norman Yoffee, an Assyriologist who has dealt both with economics and the rise of social complexity, observes: "Even under the most optimum circumstances of preservation, recovery, and publication ... texts can offer only disparate and highly focused episodes in the structure of society" (Yoffee 1977: 140). We might add that a genuinely *systemic* approach to ancient trade is required, utilizing all the data at our disposal, including the textual facts, but also

artifacts and ecofacts. Even then, the paucity of really useful data will likely be disconcerting.

One promising project may be singled out, the "Madeba Plains Project" in Jordan, sponsored by Andrews University. There the cultural anthropologist on the Core Staff, Øystein LaBianca, has almost completely reconstructed what was originally a very conventional excavation around the central concept of "food systems," analyzed in the light of long-term oscillations in the economy and settlement-history on the Transjordanian plateau (LaBianca 1990). Food production is, of course, only one aspect of subsistence, but it is arguably the most basic aspect of the economy. It is also pertinent to the question of trade since, at least for Palestine, food was one of the most commonly traded commodities (albeit difficult to trace in the archaeological record).

(4) Finally, we might observe that if economic research designs are not to remain simply *ad hoc, post factum* improvisations in archaeology, we must educate ourselves to some degree in *economic theory*. It is a truism that in archaeology we see only what we are conditioned to see; and, unfortunately, our myopia usually means that what we fail to see is badly excavated and recorded, and therefore irrevocably destroyed. How can we sensitize ourselves to phenomena that may have implications for the economy and trade? How do we learn to observe not only isolated "exotic" artifacts, but also the ecological and social context that alone could give them cultural significance? In considering trade in its wider dimensions, do we really know what to *look* for archaeologically?

Specialists in economic anthropology and archaeology commonly identify two primary schools: (1) substantivism; and (2) formalism. (1) Substantivism is a *structural* approach that sees economic behavior, even that of individuals, as influenced primarily by the institutions of society. Economic behavior is "embedded" in the society as a whole. Thus there is a direct correlation between differing types of societies and forms of economic behavior, on a sort of ascending evolutionary scale: "tribes" are characterized by simple reciprocity; "chiefdoms" by more complex "redistribution"; and "states" by true "market economies." These categories derive principally from Polanyi's classic work (with Arensberg and Pearson), *Trade and Market in the Early Empires* (1957; see also Sahlins 1972). The logic of substantivist models, as Earle points out, generally appeals to archaeologists, because changing forms of production and exchange seem to be identifiable in the archaeological record and can even be reduced to convenient typological classifications. Thus Renfrew (1975) develops a sort of "trait-list" that should serve to identify various modes of exchange archaeologically. The goal of such substantivist approaches is "to describe different economic institutions as linked to specific social formations" (Earle 1985: 107).

(2) Formalism, derived from microeconomic theory, makes certain assumptions about *individual* decision-making and economic behavior that are held to be universal. Among these is the principle of "least effort," or the complementary notion that human beings always strive to "optimize" their returns by adopting the most efficient means of production and exchange. The formalist approach is less congenial to most archaeologists, if for no other reason than that it is exceedingly difficult, if not impossible, to isolate the individual in the archaeological record, much less to deal with ideological factors such as those implied by the presupposition of individual "choice." How can we *ever* know what an individual's economic options were in the past?

Finally, on recognizing and understanding trade in the archaeological record, several scholars have recently addressed the issues (Hodder 1974; 1978; Runnels and Van Andel 1988). Among many considerations, we might mention simply (1) that the most readily recognizable evidence will probably be that of simple down-the-line or long-distance trade in specific items such as a type of ceramics. (2) Exchange or trade in raw materials, in such commodities as foodstuffs, or in services, will likely be somewhat more difficult to isolate. (3) Exchange in items of symbolic or ideological significance may remain enigmatic, despite our best efforts at interpretation. (4) The actual *mechanisms* of trade--i.e., why and how items were exchanged, what containers may have contained and how their value was determined--will also remain somewhat elusive. That is, market systems are less amenable to archaeological investigation than simple redistribution. (5) Above all, it is in *systemic* analysis of trade items, that is in larger context, that our best hope of understanding exchange lies.

Despite these formidable obstacles to modelling MB II-III trading networks adequately, we can point to expanding international exchange systems. First, extensive trade with Egypt is documented by a growing number of Egyptian scarabs, faience vessels, alabasters, ivories (and their influence on local products), jewelry, and other imports into Palestine in MB II-III. From Syria, we have clear evidence of continuing influence on metals and ceramics, although perhaps decreasing somewhat from MB I into MB II-III. And if "exchange" includes the exchange of ideas, then the growing number of Palestinian city walls and gate systems are certainly evidence of the adoption of Anatolian-Syrian norms. Cypriote trade items have not been thought common in Palestine until the Late Bronze Age, but we may have increasing numbers of Cypriote ceramic styles, beginning already in MB I, such as Line-Pendent and Black-on-Red wares; and also, from Tell el-Hayyat, a miniature Cypriote-style oxhide ingot. Finally, an even wider sphere of MB II-III cultural influence is now seen in the astonishing Aegean-style frescoes in the palace at Kabri--linking Middle Bronze Age Palestine not only to the Aegean, but also to Crete, Cyprus, Syria, and the Egyptian Delta, where similar "international" decorative styles are also seen (Niemeier 1993).

(3) *Social structure*. It is sometimes said by skeptics that "archaeologists do not dig up social systems." Of course not; but they can and do bring to light material remains that are the *products* of social organization, some features of which we can indeed extrapolate. For the first phase of the Middle Bronze period we can isolate, as evidence for social stratification, two particular phenomena: (a) craft specialization; and (b) the emergence of a ruling class.

(a) In the first instance, developments in several areas yield clues: ceramic production; bronzeworking; and the replication of imported luxury items. The introduction of true tin-bronze, which with rare exceptions begins suddenly in Palestine in MB I, constituted a true technological revolution. It required not only imported tin (above), but a vastly more sophisticated process of controlled amalgamation, smelting, casting, tempering, and cold-hammering. The typical MB I bronze types--duckbill axes, notched chisel-axes, veined daggers, socketed spears, and elaborate toggle-pins--are a far cry from the simple copper implements of EB IV. They cannot have been produced any longer by itinerant metalsmiths, or even by a simple cottage-industry. They are certainly the product of highly skilled specialists, possibly organized in craft-guilds, and probably occupying a coveted niche in society, due to demand for their products. It may even be that the preponderance of weapons in the bronze repertoire of MB I constitutes evidence that some city-states maintained a standing army, or at least a militia.

The same observations may be made for ceramic production. The fast wheelmade, beautifully decorated pottery of MB I has, despite the objections of some, virtually nothing to do with the relatively crude pottery of EB IV. It is another world, not only much more advanced, but closely aligned with the cosmopolitan ceramics of Syria. The first fast potters' wheels, improved kilns and firing techniques, altogether new shapes, and vastly superior decorative designs--all point to craft specialization, as well as the first true mass-produced and widely traded pottery in the archaeological history of Palestine.

Finally, highly trained artists and craftsmen first learned in MB I how to imitate imported luxury goods, such as Egyptian alabasters (in local calcite), and particularly scarab seals, which are first attested in this period and soon become common.

In all the above (and possibly other) cases, we have evidence for at least one class of *specialists*, who no longer were hunters or farmers or the like, but now commanded sufficient leisure, skill, and markets that they could make a livelihood by pursuing an art or craft. It is likely, furthermore, that from these recent entrepreneurs and their accumulated capital there soon emerged a new elite class, who could maintain their status and even pass it on to their heirs, because their skills were necessary to preserve the new social order.

(b) An even more important elite class were those who ruled the new Middle Bronze Age city-states; but we shall treat some aspects separately (below), since they represent both social and political elites. Evidence of the growth of an elite ruling class in MB II-III, however, is seen in the growing number of villas and palaces that we have noted above.

4. *Political organization.* An MB I ruling class might not have been recognized solely from the archaeological record, but the presence of local "princes" in Palestine is abundantly clear from the Egyptian Execration texts. Indentifiable MB I sites in Palestine include ^{c}Elyon, Laish, Qadesh, Hazor, Achshaph (Tell Keisan?), Akko, Shechem, Rehov, Pella, Jerusalem, and Ashkelon. It is significant that those individual princes, all with Amorite- or Canaanite-style names and associated with specific city-states and major regions in both Syria and Palestine, were sufficiently prominent that they and their activities were intimately known to the far-off court of the Egyptian 12th Dynasty.

Surely these "princes" were elites, the products of a highly segregated social system; and their emergence must be dated before the end of MB I, not later than *ca.* 1850-1800 B.C., to judge from the Brussels texts. Whether or not we accept Albright's attempt to distinguish an earlier EB IV/MB I "tribal" political organization, with several rulers for each site named (based on the earlier Berlin texts), it is nonetheless clear that by the time of the later Brussels texts we are dealing not only with single rulers who were elite "princes," but also with highly integrated, centralized *city-states*, powerful enough to be the subject of Egyptian international intelligence in the 12th Dynasty.

At this point, we might note not only textual but artifactual evidence of ruling elites, such as the well-documented MB I "palace" at Tel Aphek, a splendidly constructed building, comparable to anything in MB I Syria; and several rich tombs that certainly reflect a wealthy and privileged class. (As archaeologists in other branches of our discipline have always recognized, burials are especially significant for distinguishing elites, not only in the evidence of luxury grave goods, but also in traces of differential treatment of certain of the dead.)

A final (although not necessarily crucial) aspect of a city-state level of political organization is the existence of massive city wall systems already in MB I at many sites.

This is evidence not only of inter-urban rivalry, but also of the ability of local rulers to command impressive resources in men and material, as well as the engineering skills and organization necessary to construct such defenses (above).

By MB II-III, the best evidence of increasing urbanization and political centralization is the phenomenon of the full-fledged growth of the city-states themselves. Three aspects are especially significant.

(1) The largest of these regional city-states (above) are really "states-in-miniature," encompassing as they do all the essential functions of state-level organization: centralized administrative, economic, juridical, religious, and other functions. Such a city-state level of political integration--one step short, as it were, of a true state-level of evolution--constitutes a polity that is especially well suited to the distinctive, small-scale ecological and socio-economic landscape of the Southern Levant, in contrast to Mesopotamia and Egypt. Indeed, the city-state system, which reaches the zenith of its development precisely in MB II-III, characterizes Palestine until the first true state emerges in the Israelite Monarchy of the 10th cent. B.C.

(2) Second, the maturation of a distinctly Levantine form of socio-economic and political organization in the typical Syro-Palestinian city-state marks the full flowering of what may now be aptly characterized as "Canaanite" civilization. Justification for such terminology is found not only in highly-evolved, homogeneous aspects of material culture, such as ceramic and metallic repertoires and architectural norms, but also in certain canons of art, religion, and ideology. "Canaanite" culture now apparently includes even literature, to judge from the several Middle Bronze archives that we possess from Syria, and even in a few hints of Akkadian texts from Palestine at Hazor, Shechem, Gezer, and Hebron. Furthermore, the world's first truly alphabetic script, the "Proto-Sinaitic," or better "Proto-Canaanite," system of writing appears in both Canaan and Egypt late in MB III (Naveh 1982; Sass 1988).

Finally, the term "Canaanite" itself appears in nearly contemporary texts and thus may be used legitimately as an ethnic and linguistic designation. It should be noted, however, that despite the homogeneity of Palestinian MB II-III *material* culture, there were clearly "non-Canaanite" elements among the population, as attested by some Hurrian (Indo-Iranian) personal names in texts from Gezer and Hebron. And, of course, alongside the local newly-emerged Canaanite alphabet, Akkadian continued in use as the language of international economic usage and diplomatic correspondence (as it did still in the Late Bronze Age).

(3) A final witness to the cultural vitality of the Middle Bronze Age Canaanite civilization of Palestine was the first expansion of this culture into neighboring areas -- virtually the only such instance in Palestine's entire ancient history. As is well known, Canaanites -- specifically *Palestinians*, we would argue (above) -- not only infiltrated the Delta of Egypt as early as the 12th Dynasty, but rose to power in the 15th or "Hyksos" Dynasty and ruled Lower (and perhaps even parts of Middle) Egypt for roughly a century, *ca.* 1650-1550 B.C., until expelled by New Kingdom kings of the early 18th Dynasty. The strongly "Canaanite" character of the material culture of earlier levels (H-E) of Tell el-Dab^{c}a, the ancient "Hyksos" capital of Avaris in the Delta, would in itself attest to the remarkable *floruit* of the Palestinian Middle Bronze Age culture, economy, society, and political order.

D. CERAMIC CRITERIA FOR DEFINING THE MIDDLE BRONZE I AND "TRANSITIONAL MIDDLE BRONZE I/II" PHASES.

1. Stratigraphy and Chronology

Over the past 25 years the pottery and chronology of the MBI I period in Syria-Palestine have been analyzed in increasing detail. The major studies in ceramics have been those of Tufnell (1969; 1975-76; 1980; 1984); Dever (1976); Gerstenblith (1983); Beck (1975; 1985); Cole (1984); Tubb (1983); and Kempinski (1983). Additional studies concerned with larger chronological issues--based not only on pottery, but also on scarabs, textual evidence, international synchronisms, and other supposed means of establishing "absolute" chronology -- would include those of Mazar (1968); Oren (1971); Yadin (1972); Kenyon (1973), Epstein (1974); Bietak (1979; 1984; 1989; 1991); Kempinski (1983); Ward (1978; 1984); Weinstein (1981; 1992); Tufnell (1984); and Dever (1985; 1991; 1992).

One of the most difficult and controversial issues that has emerged from the foregoing studies is the nature and date of the transition from Middle Bronze I to Middle Bronze II. This obviously has significant implications for the comparative ceramic phasing and scarab typology being discussed here. The major differences may be simplified for our purposes here in chart-form (fig. 3:6), classifying the "range" primarily with regard to the position taken on the MB I/II transition.

Range	MB I (=IIA)	Trans MB I/II	MB II	Authority
Ultra-high	1950-1850	1850-1825	1825-1659	Ward
High	2000-1800	- - -	1800 --	Mazar
	1950-1800	1800-1780	1780 --	Epstein
Middle	1950/1960-1780/1750	- - -	1780/1750 --	Yadin
	2000-1750	- - -	1750 --	Gerstenblith
	2000-1800	1800-1750	1750 --	Kempinski
	2000/1950-1775	1775-1750	1750-1650	Dever
Low	1900/1875-1740/1730	1740/1730-1720/1710	1720/1710-1625	Weinstein
Ultra-low	1800-1700	- - -	1750-1575	Albright
	? -1700	- - -	1700 --	Kenyon
	1875/1850-1710	1710-1680	1680-1590	Bietak

Fig. 3:6. Dates for MB I/II and MB II proposed by various scholars.

It is noteworthy that as a way out of the apparent impasse a number of scholars have proposed a brief "transitional MB I/II" phase, beginning with the suggestion of Epstein (1974) and continuing with Furshpan (1975; = Walker) and Kempinski (1983), a view espoused recently and explicitly by Dever (1991; 1992) and Weinstein (1992), and followed apparently independently by Bietak (1991). Proposing such a transitional MB I/II phase is convenient, perhaps even necessary, in some ways; but the archaeological assemblages to be assigned to such a phase have not been generally specified. It may be suggested that "MB I/II" might include such Palestinian groups as the latter part of Gerstenblith's "MB IC"; several tombs at Dan; Hazor "pre-XVIII" and the 1971 tomb; several tombs at Munatta; tombs at Kfar Szold; Tomb 6 II at Tel Rehov; Jericho Tomb B 48; perhaps Aphek "Post-Palace II" and several infant burials; and certain Gezer materials (Dever 1992: 10). Comparably dated groups in Egypt would be Tell el-Dab^{c}a F=h/3 (Dever 1992: 9), and perhaps Dahshur complexes 4, 6 (Weinstein 1992: 29-33). In Syria, material corresponding to the transitional MB I/II horizon would include the later Byblian Royal Tomb deposits; T. 66 (and perhaps T. 73) at Ruweisé; and possibly the "Tomb of the Lord of Goats" at Tell Mardikh (cf. Dever 1992: 4-8; Weinstein 1992: 36-38). In terms of Egyptian synchronisms, and thus in absolute dates, all the above materials would be late 12th/early 13th Dynasty in date (i.e., in the "Middle" chronology preferred here).

Preceding these deposits, and serving to define MB I proper in Palestine, would be a number of more or less homogeneous tomb groups, all correlating with the 12th Dynasty in Egypt. These would include T. 1 and 4 lower at Ginosar; the Tel Amr tomb; T. AD, AN, B, W, Y, and 16 (part) at Tell el-Far^{c}ah N.; many Str. XIV-XII tombs at Megiddo; Beth-shan T. I, II, 92; tombs at Gesher; the 1956 Barqai tomb (middle); the Tel Aviv Harbor and Dhahrat el-Humraiya tombs; Beth-shemesh T. 2, 9; many tombs at Tel Aphek; Macalister's T. 1 Lower, 15: I Middle, and several intramural burials of the 1964-1973 excavations at Gezer; T. K3 at Jericho; and Petrie's Tell el-^{c}Ajjûl "Courtyard Cemetery." Coeval with these, but often less homogeneous or well dated stratigraphically, are occupational deposits at the above and a dozen or more other MB I sites (Fig. 3:1). Among the most secure of these MB I *tell* groups, reasonably well published, would be Megiddo Str. XIV-XIII (plus possibly some Str. XII), and Kenyon's Ph. K; Kenyon's several Jericho *tell* phases; Gezer XXII; especially the Tel Aphek "Pre-Palace" and "Palace" phases; and, of less significance today, Tell Beit Mirsim G-F (Fig. 3:1). In Syria, Tell Mardikh-Ebla should be of considerable value, but until the material is more fully published it will remain uncertain.

2. The Ceramic Sequences of MB I and MB I/II.

In the past several years, a reasonably good working consensus has emerged on the ceramic assemblages that should be diagnostic for MB I and MB I/II. The typological essentials may be derived from Dever (1976); Beck (1975; 1985); Gerstenblith (1983); Cole (1984); and Kempinski (1992b). For illustrations of the principal types, see fig. 3:7.

a. MB I; *ca.* 2000-1775 B.C.

(i). Overall characteristics.

Storejars: pronounced ovoid form, with deliberately flattened base, simple but elegant rim, sometimes handleless; ware is red to pink, wet-smoothed, often band-combed on upper shoulder; many quite small, handleless examples.

Platter bowls: rather small in diameter but deep, either inverted simple or slightly pointed rim or collar-rim (often red-slipped), tendency toward flat or disc-base; some have four handles at rim; ware wet-smoothed; may have interior red-cross paint.

3:7.1. Storejar; Kh. Kufin; R.H. Smith 1962, Pl. XIV:3 (T. 3).

3:7.2. Ovoid jar; Loud 1948, Pl. 12:16 (T. 3143, Str. XIV).

3:7.3. Krater; Aphek; Beck 1985, Fig. 16:2 (Area B, Str. B IV).

3:7.4. Cooking pot; Aphek; Beck 1985, Fig. 2:10 (Str. X20-X19).

3:7.5. Cooking pot; Aphek; Beck 1985, Fig. 2:11 (Str. A VI).

3:7.6. Cooking pot; Aphek; Beck 1985, Fig. 2:13 (Str. A VI).

3:7.7. Jug; Loud 1948, Pl. 10:6 (T. 4016, Str. XIV).

3:7.8. Dipper juglet; Loud 1948, Pl. 17:19 (T. 5088, Str. XV-XIIIA).

3:7.9. Piriform juglet; Aphek; Beck 1985, Fig. 9:2 (T. 490, Str. A IVa).

3:7.10. Cup; Aphek; Beck 1985, Fig. 14:5 (T. 43).

3:7.11. Carinated bowl; Aphek; Beck 1985, Fig. 14.1 (T. 7).

3:7.12. Globular bowl; Loud 1948, Pl. 14:27 (T. 4046, Str. XIV).

3:7.13. Painted juglet; Aphek; Beck 1985, Fig. 14:8 (T. 43).

3:7.14. Tell el-Yehudiyeh juglet; Affuleh; Amiran 1969, Pl. 36:3.

3:7.15. Cylindrical juglet; Aphek; Beck 1985, Fig. 10:8 (T. 272, Str. A II).

3:7.16. Painted jug; Aphek; Amiran 1969, Pl. 35:7 (T. 4).

3:7.17. Flask; Aphek; Amiran 1969, Pl. 33:8.

3:7.18. Beaker; Aphek; Amiran 1969, Pl. 28:1.

3:7.19. Platter bowl; Loud 1948, Pl. 14:17 (T. 3148, Str. XIV-XIII).

3:7.20. Four-handled bowl; Aphek; Beck 1985, Fig. 15:1 (Str. X17).

Fig. 3:7. Selected diagnostic ceramic types of MB I.

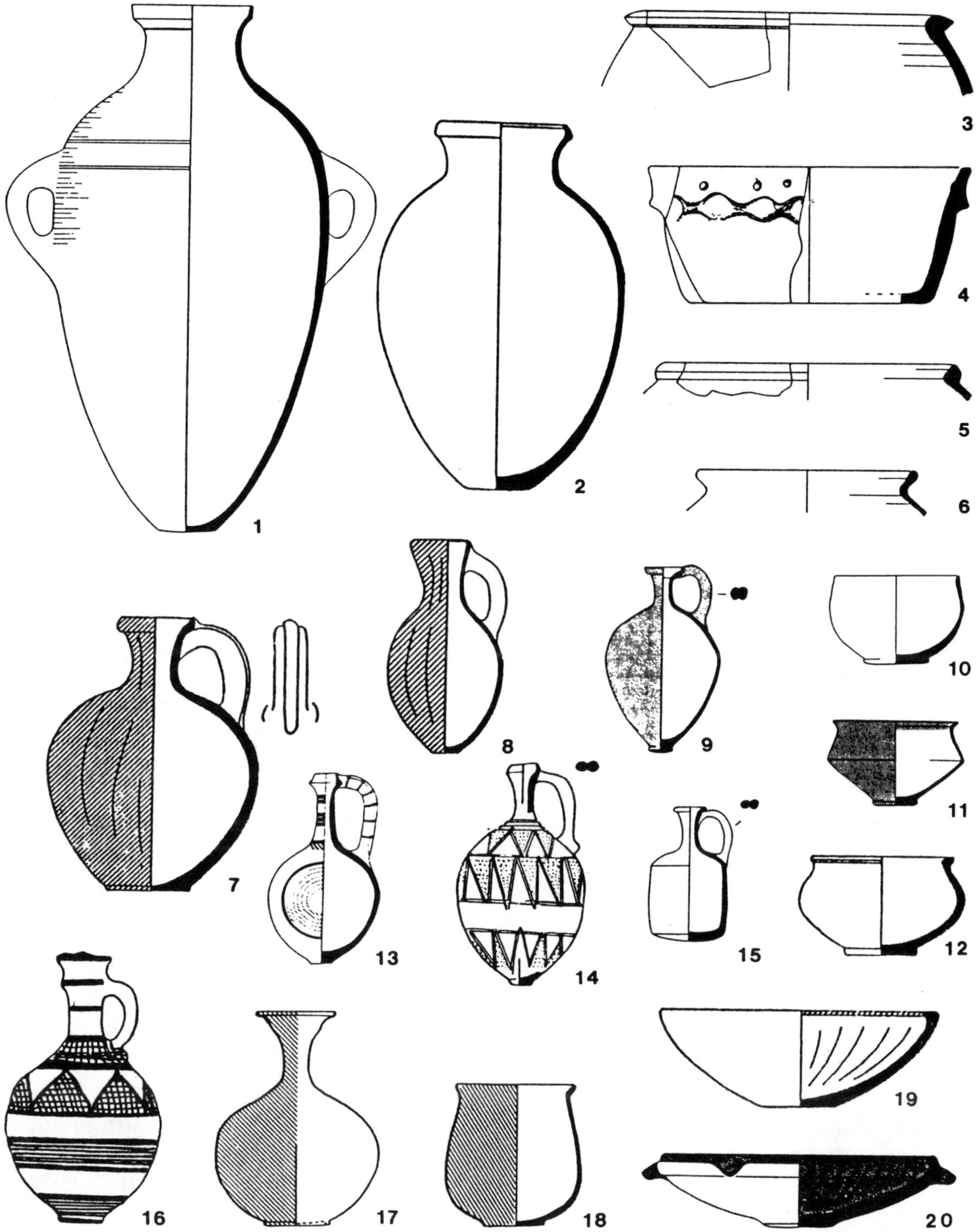

Fig. 3:7. Selected diagnostic ceramic types of MB I. Scale = 1:6.

Biconical bowls: tend to be almost as deep as wide, with slightly rounded rather than sharp carination, simple slightly everted rim but may have "gutter", flat or disc-base; may be red-slipped and burnished; rare until late in the period.

Globular bowls: similar to above, but with rounded, more globular or cyma profile; also late in MB I.

Carinated bowls: similar to biconical and globular bowls, but shallower and with more pronounced carination; many have everted "gutter" rim; tend to have thin ware, dark red slip and burnish.

Cups: small, with simple globular shape, curving upper body, no neck, simple or slightly beaded rim; usually flat base; fine, wet-smoothed ware; may have band of red paint around rim.

Mugs: larger cups, with baggy shape, one small loop-handle near rim; may be slipped and burnished; not common; a few miniatures are known.

Beakers or goblets: similar to mugs, but more straight-sided; handleless.

Flasks: tall globular body, flat or disc base, constricted neck, flaring rim, handleless; may be red slipped and burnished; relatively rare.

Jugs: globular, everted profiled rim, flat base, simple or multiple-strand handle well placed on upper shoulder; many are red-slipped and burnished, some may have bands of red paint ("Habur"-style) or more elaborate geometric ("North Syrian Simple Ware" style) on upper shoulder.

Dipper juglets: elongated and graceful, small flattened base, often pinched mouth; many are red-slipped and burnished. Some may be band-painted.

Tell el-Yehudiyeh juglets: similar to piriform juglets, but gray-black ware with elaborate chalk-filled punctate geometric designs; clearly begin in MB I, but relatively rare.

Cylindrical juglets: small squat straight-sided body, with pronounced flat base; may be red-slipped and burnished; a few miniatures known; quite rare in MB I (more a MB III type).

Kraters: large globular handleless jars, flat base, inverted thickened or "flanged" rim; relatively rare until recently, but now well known.

Cooking pots: three types. (1) wide, shallow, straight-sided, flat base, rope-molding below rim; may have completely or partially pierced "steam holes" below rim; coarse, handmade. (2) deep, globular, simple everted (or slightly flanged) rim; no handles; wheelmade. (3) similar to no. 2, but with well everted, folded-over rim.

Miscellaneous: small basket-handled vessels; trefoil-rim jugs.

Imported vessels: Cypriote White Painted IV-V, Line Pendant and Cross Line style jugs and juglets; previously thought to begin in MB II, are now known from secure late MB I contexts; Red on Black wares are also attested, but rare.

(ii). Inner MB I phasing.

Within MB I, we now have the beginning of a stratigraphic basis for subdividing the pottery of the period, which is only to be expected if this phase extends over some 200 years. The best evidence at present comes from as many as six phases recognized by Kochavi and Beck (1975; 1985) at Tel Aphek. These can be set forth as in fig. 3:8.

Although the excavators state that there are no external data that would yield an absolute chronology for the several MB I phases at Tel Aphek (Beck 1985: 199), there are some useful typological observations that provide the basis for a relative ceramic chronology. Based on Beck (1985), reducing the six Aphek phases to four general MB I horizons (somewhat as Gerstenblith had attempted; 1983: 105, 106), and attaching rough dates, one might posit the following developments.

1. MB I, Ph. 1, Str. XVII-XVI (*ca.* 2000-1950 B.C.): Diagnostic forms include: bulbous-rim kraters, often with coarse ware, impressed decoration; simple storejar rims, not elongated; straight-sided flat bottom cooking pots, with only a few globular wheelmade examples; deep thick-rim bowls; in decoration, *no* red slip/burnish, but some white slip, frequent band-combing.

2. MB I, Ph. 2, Str. XV (*ca.* 1950-1900 B.C.): Many forms continue, reach their full development; more profiled storejar rims; carinated bowls more globular; red slip/burnish *begins*, as also painted decoration.

Str.	Area A	Area B	Area X
XVII	"Pre-Palace" I; Ory, T. 2 A VII; T. 473, 478, 494	B VI (pre-wall)	X 20-19
XVI	A VI; T. 409 A V		
XV	"Pre-Palace" II Ory, T. 2		
XIVb-a	"Palace" I-II A IVb-a; T. 468, 490	B V (city wall)	X 18-17
XIII	"Post-Palace" I A II; T. 427, 428, 436, 499, 501; plus child burials	---	---
XII	"Post-Palace" II	---	---

Fig. 3:8. Stratigraphic phases of MB I at Tel Aphek.

3:9.1. Ovoid jar; Tel Rehov; Yogev 1985, Fig. 3:1 (T. 6 II).

3:9.2. Ovoid jar; Tel Rehov; Yogev 1985, Fig. 3:9 (T. 6 II).

3:9.3. Globular bowl, high-neck; Tel Rehov; Yogev 1985, Fig. 3:5 (T. 6 II).

3:9.4. Globular bowl, low-neck; Aphek; Beck 1975, Fig. 11:2 (T. 427, Str. A II, "Post-Palace").

3:9.5. Globular bowl, neckless; Albright 1933, Pl. 4:5 (Str. G-F).

3:9.6. Biconical bowl; Kenyon 1965, Fig. 95:12 (T. B 48, Group II).

3:9.7. Carinated bowl; Kenyon 1965, Fig. 95:18 (T. B 48, Group II).

3:9.8. Krater; Shechem; Cole 1984, Pl. 10C (Str. XVIII).

3:9.9. Cooking pot; Aphek; Beck 1975, Fig. 16:5 (Area B, Str. V-IV, "Post-Palace").

3:9.10. Platter bowl; Ginosar; Epstein 1974, Fig. 9:10 (T. 2/3).

Fig. 3:9. Diagnostic ceramic types for a transitional "MB I/II" phase.

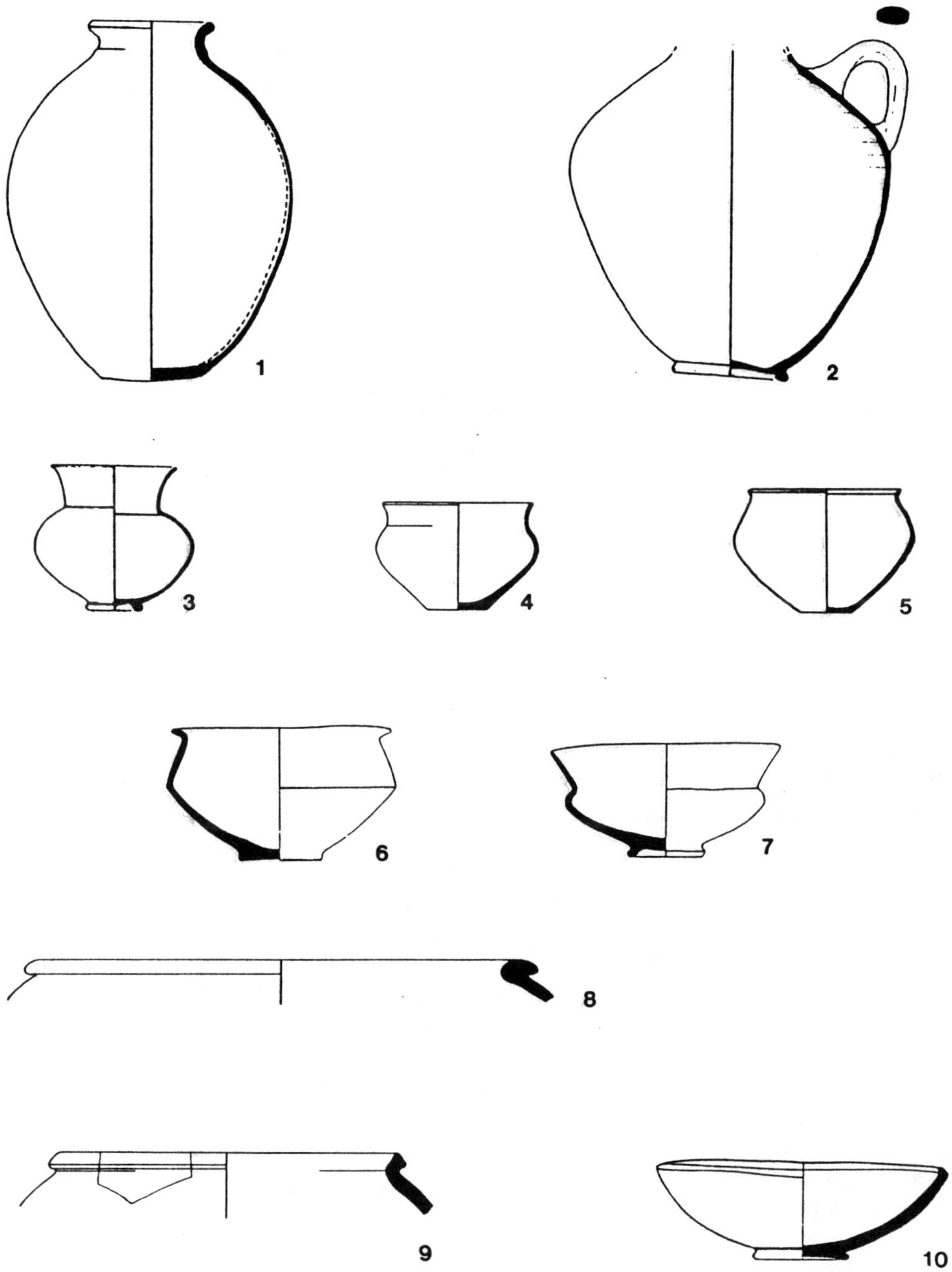

Fig. 3:9. Diagnostic ceramic types for a transitional "MB I/II" phase. Scale = 1:6.

3. MB I, Ph. 3, Str. XIV (*ca.* 1900-1850 B.C.): "Classic" expression of MB I repertoire now, in "Palace" I-II phase; best red slip/burnish; diagnostic forms include handless storejars, with elongated or profiled rims; deep bowls with knobs at rim; biconical jugs; burnished dipper juglets; button-base piriform juglets; burnished carinated bowls; more ring-bases. Best parallels are from Megiddo XIV, into XIII.

4. MB I, Ph. 4, Str. XIII-XII (*ca.* 1850-1800/1775 B.C.): Red slip/burnish continue, but incision or paint very rare; kraters disappear; hemispheric bowls rare, but high globular bowls begin; also new are piriform juglets with stepped rim. Best parallels are from Megiddo XII (?), possibly also Tell ed-Dab^{c}a H-G.

b. Transitional MB I/II; *ca.* 1775-1750 B.C.

Obviously it is difficult to distinguish a putative "transitional" ceramic assemblage with precision, much less to assign it confidently to a time-period as short as 25-50 years. In practice, what one does is to lump together in an "MB I/II" phase those ceramic forms that do not seem to fit comfortably in either MB I or MB II as classically defined. The advantage of such a procedure, while speculative, is that it allows us to *reconsider* tomb groups that have been regarded as "mixed" (and therefore stratigraphically useless), or else have been moved back and forth between MB I and MB II by various authorities. It must be cautioned that our attempt to discern a "transitional MB I/II" *ceramic* phase is simply a heuristic device. It is not assumed here that such a phase would have had an empirical basis in actual historical-cultural developments--at least not in any that we are capable of discerning on the basis of our present knowledge of the archaeological record. And, of course, its dating will remain relative to the absolute chronology that one prefers for MB I and MB II.

A preliminary attempt to assign certain ceramic assemblages to the MB I/II phase has been made above. Assuming that this is valid, what ceramic developments can be seen in these groups--especially those that might characterize a logical, next-step typological evolution immediately beyond Tel Aphek, Ph. 4, worked out above? If consistent developments can be discerned, and if they can be shown to precede the major typological developments of the full-blown MB II phase as generally defined, then we may have a working "diagnostic assemblage" for MB I/II.

To facilitate our discussion it will be necessary at the outset to posit several ceramic forms and hypothetical developments that may be "diagnostic"--to be tested, of course, against actual typological developments in the key assemblages. The best forms - - i.e., those that span late MB I into early MB II - - would seem to be: (1) wide shallow platter bowls with inverted rim (Cole's Type Bp 21, 41, 51, 61); (2) globular necked bowls (Cole's Bn A, low neck; Bn B. 1, high neck); (3) biconical bowls (Cole's Bg B. 21, 22, 23); and (4) kraters (Cole's Bd C.32). Obviously other forms, such as ovoid storejars, cooking pots, juglets, etc., also extend over this time-span; but their typological evolution is less pronounced or certain, and they may not occur as frequently in whole examples in tomb groups that are homogeneous or well-dated. In addition, it is worth noting that while the presence of the above forms may be diagnostic, their *absence* is not, since that may be merely fortuitous. For illustrations, see fig. 3:9.

E. THE ABSOLUTE CHRONOLOGY OF SYRIA- PALESTINE IN MB I.

However reliable the relative sequence of archaeological deposits put forward here may prove--and only further excavation will judge--it is desirable to anchor the whole sequence with fixed dates wherever possible. That is particularly necessary for the transitional MB I/II phase proposed here, upon which so much depends.

1. The Beginning of MB I.

An absolute chronology for MB I is, however, difficult, and some would say it is impossible. First, we cannot fix the beginning of MB I in Syria-Palestine except in relation to the end of EB IV (Albright's MB I). For that, we have only a handful of radiocarbon dates for the period as a whole, yielding a range of *ca.* 2300-2000 B.C. (Dever 1992: 1, 2, with references to the dates published thus far), and none of these pertain especially to the end of the period. There is, however, a radiocarbon date that may give a general indication for the beginning of MB I, namely a date of 2138-1907 B.C. from the wooden handle of a socketed spearhead in T. 13 at Gesher (Garfinkel and Bonfil 1990: 132-147, Figs. 1-6; English summary 106*; the date is an Oxford date, calibrated). The sample is unlikely to be from old wood, such as a large beam, and ought to be roughly contemporary with the spearhead. The material from T. 13 (Garfinkel and Bonfil 1990: fig. 5: 1-4) includes the spear; a duckbill axe; a very simple flat-based platter bowl; and, in particular, a classic MB I small handleless ovoid jar with a geometric painted design on the upper body. Garfinkel and Bonfil (1990: 106*) regard this and the other 13 Gesher MB I tombs at Gesher as very early in the period, contemporary with the "Pre-Palace" phase at Aphek and Tell el-Hayyat 5-4, and they are almost assuredly correct. Particularly important are toggle-pins still clearly in the EB IV tradition (1990: fig. 2: 8; 142); rather crude platter bowls with simple or knobby rim (fig. 1: 1, 3; 2: 2, 3; 3: 4, 7; 4: 2; 5:1); clumsy, shapeless carinated bowls (fig. 1: 7; 2: 3: 8; 4: 3, 4); and squat ovoid jars with simple knobby rim (fig. 1: 4; 2: 7, 9; 3: 1, 6; 4: 7-9). The assemblage also includes typical MB I bronzes: two socketed spearheads (fig. 1: 5; 5: 4); three duckbill axes (fig. 1: 6; 4: 10; 5: 3); a notched chisel-axe (fig. 5: 10); and the two toggle-pins mentioned above. Especially significant is the complete absence of such fully developed MB I traits as red slip and burnish; and of the typical carinated bowls, globular necked bowls, Tell el-Yehudiyeh juglets, and piriform juglets (only one rather crude example; fig. 3: 2).

Such a demonstrably early MB I assemblage would have been unique a few years ago; but it is now paralleled very closely in the *stratified* sequence at Tel Aphek (Beck 1985: 194-196; for the platter bowls, cf. fig. 2: 2; 4: 3; for the simple carinated bowls, see fig. 2: 3--all Phase 1). This early phase of MB I is perhaps also present at Tel Ifshar, which exhibits some 7 MB I phases (A-G; earliest to latest). A Phase C vessel is an Upper Egyptian import, dated by Dorothea Arnold to *ca.* 1900-1850 on the basis of Egyptian parallels (Weinstein 1992: 34). The local ceramics of Phase C include painted wares, with burnished wares beginning in Phase E. Bietak (1989a: 96, n. 98; 1991: 54) takes the Phase C Egyptian jar at Tel Ifshar as support for his own date of *ca.* 1900 B.C., and Weinstein concurs (cf. Weinstein 1992: 35). The point, however, is that preceding this phase are Phases A-B, which surely would fall in the mid-late 20th cent. B.C. *at latest*. Similar evidence, not yet fully published, suggest that Akko and Kabri also begin very early in MB I, probably in the early 20th cent. B.C. (Kempinski 1992: 166, 167). Also, Ph. 5 at Tell el-Hayyat (Falconer and Magness-Gardiner 1984; 1989), in the Jordan Valley, is very early.

The evidence from Gesher, Tel Aphek, and Tel Ifshar, together with that from Akko, Kabri, and Tell el-Hayyat, suggests that despite the skepticism of some, the beginning of Levantine MB I and the renascence of urbanism in Palestine coincides roughly with the end of the First Intermediate and the shift to the 12th Dynasty in Egypt, as previously thought (see also Kempinski 1992: 107). The earlier citation of a scarab of Sesostris I (Kitchen: *ca.* 1943-1898) in T. 66 at Ruweisé by Tufnell and Ward to support their high chronology (Tufnell 1975-76: 24; 1984: 3, 53-56, 199; Ward, in Tufnell 1984: 152) may not be far off the mark, after all.

Weinstein (1992: 37) is doubtful; but he is simply following Gerstenblith's (1983: 43) opinion of the pottery, some of which she thinks may have MB II parallels--a view that is, as we shall see, now outdated. As for Weinstein's comment (1992: 37) that the scarabs in T. 66 cannot be related to specific groups of pottery or to individuals, it should be noted that there are only two intact burials in T. 66, and the scarabs were found near the hands of the adult. The Sesostris I scarab is *not* then necessarily an heirloom.

2. The Floruit of MB I.

By 1900 B.C., even on the lowest possible chronology (i.e., Bietak), the Levantine MB I phase is well underway. This is indicated perhaps by the scarab of Sesostris II (*ca.* 1897-1878 B.C.) in T. 73 at Ruweisé. There is also the evidence of the well known tomb painting at Beni Hasan, *ca.* 1875 B.C., depicting a party of Asiatics in the Delta, one of whom carries an MB I duckbill axe with a curved wooden handle exactly like those preserved in the MB I burials at Baghouz near Mari, and now in T. 990 at Kabri in Israel (Dever 1992: 6-8; Weinstein 1992: 34; for Kabri, Kempinski 1989: 14, fig. 14: 2; contra Bietak, 1989a: 99; 1991: 49, n. 25).

3. The End of MB I.

The precise end of MB I and the transition to MB II in Syria-Palestine is one of the thorniest problems in current discussions of Levantine chronology in the second millennium B.C. (see most recently Dever 1992; Weinstein 1992, and references there). The only royal name scarab anywhere in a clear Palestinian MB I context is one of Amenemhat IV (*ca.* 1798-1789 B.C.) in Tomb 303A at Tell el-^{c}Ajjûl. Following Tufnell's (1980) restudy of this tomb, we regard T. 303A as a homogeneous deposit of our "transitional MB I/II," *ca.* 1800-1750 B.C. (below), which would mean that this scarab is in proper context, not an heirloom. That would then suggest an approximate *terminus ante quem* of 1800-1775 B.C. for the end of MB I proper.

Another pertinent datum for the MB I-II transition is a ceremonial scepter handle from a tomb in the Royal Necropolis at Tell Mardikh near Aleppo, inscribed with the royal name "Hetepibre" (*Htp-ib-r*^{c} ; Matthiae 1984: 25; Scandone Matthiae 1979; 1982: 16, 17, fig. 33). The tomb in which this scepter handle was found is "The Tomb of the Lord of the Goats," which Matthiae (1979) dates *ca.* 1750 B.C. (Early Mardikh IIIB). He bases this date partly on the pottery, which he thinks advanced somewhat beyond the classic MB I repertoire; and partly on the name "Hetepibre," possibly the same individual as the ninth pharaoh of the 13th Dynasty, *ca.* 1770 B.C.

The identification of this minor king, however, is not certain (Weinstein 1992: 38); and even the reading is contested. It is not always noted that the inscription is overwritten, making its reading somewhat unclear (Scandone Matthiae 1979). Kempinski (oral communication) insists on reading *(s)htp-ib-R*^{c}, or Amenemhat I (*ca.*

1979-1950 B.C.; high chronology), a possibility that Scandone Matthiae herself had considered, and one that even Bietak (1991: 63, n. 22) does not necessarily reject.

It should be noted that the "Tomb of the Lord of the Goats" is one lobe of a bilobate tomb, sharing a single *dromos* with the "Tomb of the Princess." Matthiae dates the latter chamber somewhat earlier, to his late MB I, *ca.* 1825-1800 B.C. (Early Mardikh IIIA). However, the presence of such classic MB I forms as "eye-juglets" in the "North Syrian Painted Ware" tradition would allow a date for the "Princess Tomb" even earlier, in mid-MB I, or *ca.* 1850 B.C., as we argue here.

Furthermore, the "Tomb of the Lord of the Goats" contained three samples of fenestrated axeheads, one of the broad eye type, and two of the narrow, elongated duckbill variety. Matthiae argues that the two types overlap, and that they are in proper place in the "early MB II" context in which he would place the tomb (1980). Yet he overlooks the clear evidence elsewhere in Syria-Palestine that these two types are mutually exclusive, the broad axe confined to EB IV, and the duckbill axe to MB I, wherever there are controlled contexts. Furthermore, even the advanced duckbill variety does not occur later than MB I (unless occasionally in the transitional MB I/II phase, *ca.* 1775-1750 B.C.E.; below), being replaced by the narrow shaft-hole variety at the beginning of MB II. This evidence has been amply documented (cf. Oren 1971; Dever 1975: 30, 31; Tubb 1983; Philip 1989: 51-53). Further confirmation comes from the well known Beni Hasan wall painting, dated *ca.* 1875 B.C., which despite Bietak's skepticism does depict just such an axe, complete with the odd curving wooden handle that has actually been found preserved in the contemporary MB I tombs at Baghouz, near Mari (du Mesnil du Buisson 1948: pls. 47, 54, 56). All this evidence is ignored not only by Matthiae but also by Bietak (1989: 94; 1991: 49). Either the axes are heirlooms (the eye axe is certainly so); the "Tomb of the Lord of the Goats" should be dated earlier, *ca.* late 19th century B.C.; or the date for the end of MB I must be lowered to *ca.* 1750 B.C. Although present evidence is inconclusive, I prefer the second option. Nevertheless, the date of the tomb, even if it could be determined absolutely, would not help us to decide definitely between the "middle" and the "low" chronologies for Palestine (as Bietak supposes: 1989: 94; see further Weinstein 1992).

Kempinski (1992b: 167; 168; 177) has approached the problem of the end of MB I and the transition to MB II via two other lines of evidence. The first is the presence of four cylinder seals of derivative Old Babylonian style in tombs of Group II at Jericho, which he attributes to the Age of Hammurabi (1792-1750 B.C.; middle chronology). Since these seals occur together with ceramic forms that Kempinski thinks characterize the MB I/II transition, he dates that transition *ca.* 1750 B.C. Two of these seals occur in T. D9; and there is one each in T. B3 and J54 (Kenyon 1965: 656-661). Kempinski credits Porada, in Appendix F of *Jericho* II, with the early-mid 18th cent. B.C. date for the four seals. In fact, Porada only opts for an Old Babylonian date *generally*, concluding that "we must rely on Miss Kenyon's dating of her tombs for a more precise date" (1965: 658, 659). Thus accepting Kempinski's date for Tomb Group II (a bit earlier than Kenyon's, 1758-1730 B.C.) is simply arguing in circular fashion. Furthermore, Kempinski adopts the Babylonian Middle Chronology, so one could easily raise his dates to 1898-1806 B.C., or lower them to 1728-1686 B.C. (cf. Dever 1992: 11). I tend to agree with him regarding the Tomb Group II pottery (at least some of it) as transitional to early MB I; and my own preference for beginning MB II proper *ca.* 1750 B.C. is the same as his. But neither the cylinder seals from Jericho or the relative typological sequence of Kenyon's Tomb Groups yield an absolute chronology (as Bietak seems to think; cf. Dever 1991: 76).

Kempinski's second line of reasoning (1992b: 167; 177) leads him into the morass of the well known Royal Tombs at Byblos, especially T. III and IV, which contained objects bearing the names of Amenemhat III and IV, the last kings of the 12th Dynasty, *ca.* 1828-1798 B.C. (high chronology). He believes that the associated pottery is characteristic of the latest phase of MB I, and should thus be placed *ca.* 1800 B.C. Again, I tend to agree on the absolute date, but *not* on the basis of ceramic parallels between the Byblian Royal Tombs and the typical MB I pottery of Palestine.

All chronological arguments based on the Byblos Royal Tombs suffer from deficiencies. Albright, from visual inspection of the material (and memory?), had argued that the pottery was closely comparable to his Palestinian MB IIA. He had then proposed ingeniously to restore the name on an alabaster from Tomb IV inscribed *['I]ntn* as "Yantin," and then to identify this individual with "Yantin-ᶜAmmu" of Byblos, a known contemporary of Zimri-lim of Mari and thus also of both Hammurabi of Babylon and Neferhotep I of Egypt -- all to be dated roughly within the 18th century B.C. on Albright's preferred "low chronology." Thus Albright lowered the date of all four Royal Tombs to *ca.* 1800-1720 B.C., and accordingly revised his original date of 1900-1750 B.C. for MB I (his MB IIA) to *ca.* 1800-1700 B.C. (cf. 1966 and references there).

This "ultra-low" chronology was followed by Kenyon (1973), although for somewhat different reasons. Moreover, despite the fact that it remains idiosyncratic, it has recently been taken up and vigorously championed by Bietak, since he believes that it best fits his Palestinian material (*sic*) at Tell el-Dabᶜa in the Delta (below). Bietak, however, had originally (1981) overlooked the refutation of Albright's use of the Royal Tombs by Kitchen (1967) and myself (1976; cf. later, Gerstenblith 1983: 102, 103). Only in his later treatments (as 1989: 97) does Bietak acknowledge that Albright's use of the Byblian Royal Tomb evidence is not unassailable; and even then he seems unaware that no Palestinian archaeologist today follows Albright's arguments or his low chronology. Not only was the linguistic argument weak all along (see Kitchen 1967), but now the full publication of the material by Tufnell (1969) makes it clear that the pottery was probably mixed by the excavators and may well span MB I and MB II, and in any case is not "typical" of Palestinian MB I pottery at all. The latter point was suggested by Tufnell (1966), made even more explicit by me (1976: 11), and followed by others like Gerstenblith (1983: 102, 103). Even if Albright's several assumptions were granted, this would only date the end of MB I, not the beginning. Bietak has recently (1989: 97) responded to these points, but simply to restate Albright's argument, adding his own opinion that the small bowls and cooking pots, perhaps from Tomb I (with inscribed objects from the period of Amenemhat III), could now be compared with those from Tel Aphek in Phases 1 and 2. Perhaps so, but how does that yield a "fixed chronology" -- especially one like Bietak's "ultra-low" chronology of *ca.* 1850-1700 B.C. for MB I? Bietak simply ignores the opinion of Palestinian specialists that the Royal Tombs are too atypical to provide a firm synchronism with Palestinian MB I, and too uncertain in date themselves to offer chronological precision for any phase in MB I or MB II. It is time that the supposed chronological evidence derived from both the Byblian Montet Jar and the Royal Tombs be recognized for what it is, i.e., largely irrelevant and insignificant, except possibly for the former's implication for scarab dates (see further Weinstein 1992: 30, 37).

Finally, in a very valuable recent survey of the data, Weinstein (1992) has assessed not only Tell el-Dabᶜa, but several other sites where MB I Levantine material occurs, in order to see whether the Egyptian context offers any hope for a fixed date for Syro-Palestinian MB I and the MB I/II transition. Weinstein's critical evaluation of Bietak's published data and their bearing on Levantine Middle Bronze chronology is similar to ours here, except that he adopts a "moderately low" chronology, somewhat between our "middle" and Bietak's "ultra-low" chronologies (below; cf. Dever 1992: 10). Concerning the handful of MB I "Levantine Painted Ware" vessels at Kahun, he concludes that it is not well enough stratified to be dated (although it is said by the excavators to have come from "12th Dynasty dumps"). He concludes that MB occupation at the site extended from the time of Sesostris I into the Hyksos period. Weinstein's opinion is that "such vague contextual assignments (for the pottery) mean that the finds from Kahun cannot be given a more precise dating than the town as a whole" (1992: 33). Yet he argues that "the MB IIA (our MB I) pottery at Kahun probably fits somewhere between the second quarter of the 19th century and third quarter of the 18th century B.C.E." (1992: 32). On what basis does he *reach* such a conclusion, given his own evaluation of the data? Why not put the Levantine ware in the reign of Sesostris I, which is attested by scarabs and sealings? Such arbitrary assignments get us nowhere.

Beck (in Arnold 1982: 41, 42; fig. 13) has discussed several MB I and early MB II Syro-Palestinian vessels in Complexes 4-6 at Dahshur. But Weinstein (1992: 33) regards the temporal ranges the Arnolds give the Dahshur complexes as too broad to choose between the late 12th or 13th Dynasty as a context for the Levantine ware.

Holladay's (1982) important excavations at Tell el-Maskhuta in the Delta have revealed a large Asiatic settlement with a history parallel to that at nearby Tell el-Dab^{c}a. Having studied the 33 scarabs, Weinstein dates them all to the 13th and the 15th Dynasty. He states that "the earliest deposits containing scarabs date to the first half of the MB IIB (our MB II) period." Since these are 13th Dynasty scarabs, Weinstein concludes that the scarabs "indicate that the early MB IIB (our MB I) period at that site does not predate the late 18th century B.C.E." (1992: 33). Again, how does he make such a leap? As I can attest from close examination of the Maskhuta pottery, there are late MB I and MB I/II forms in the corpus; so there is likely to be a *pre*-scarab, *pre*-13th Dynasty, *pre*-MB II occupation at the site. Weinstein's logic for beginning MB II late in the 18th cent. B.C. would hold only if he could prove (1) that there is no MB I or MB I/II occupation at Maskhuta; (2) that the scarabs are late, not early, 13th Dynasty; and (3) that the pottery associated with these levels was pure MB II, with no admixture of MB I traditions. The final publication by Carole Redmount may, of course, vindicate Weinstein; but until then one must be cautious about accepting his dates for MB I and MB I/II, as far as they utilize the Maskhuta data.

As for Weinstein's review of the Syro-Palestinian pottery, weapons, and other materials, he is obviously dependent upon other authorities who are specialists. He would need to demonstrate his moderately low chronology by showing that Egyptian Royal Name scarabs (or other historically dated objects) are associated with MB I and MB I/II deposits--and provide a *terminus post* (*sic*) *quem*. As he acknowledges, however (1992: 34), there are no such scarabs -- except that of Amenemhat IV in T. 303A at Tell el-^{c}Ajjûl, which he initially denied, but which fits our chronology and not his. All in all, I cannot see how Weinstein can substantiate his conclusion that the end of MB I "substantially overlaps" (1992: 32) the 13th Dynasty and falls in the late 18th cent. B.C.

To sum up, suggested dates for the end of MB I in Syria-Palestine are still disputed. The chart of fig. 3:10 may be helpful.

High	Tufnell and Ward (1966)	1850 B.C.
Middle	Mazar (1968) Yadin (1972) Gerstenblith (1983) Dever (1992; with "MB I/II," 1800-1750 B.C.)	1800 B.C. 1800 B.C. 1800 B.C. 1800 B.C.
Moderately Low	Wright (1971) Kempinski (1992) Weinstein (1965)	1750 B.C. 1750 B.C. 1700 B.C.
Ultra-Low	Albright (1965) Kenyon (1973) Bietak (1991; with "MB I/II," 1710-1680 B.C.)	1700 B.C. 1700 B.C. 1710 B.C.

Fig. 3:10. Various schemes for dating the end of the Syro-Palestinian MB I and the transition to MB II.

F. A Comparative Analysis of MB I and MB I/II Ceramic Groups in Syria-Palestine and Egypt.

1. Hazor, Cistern 9024

Tufnell discussed Cistern 9024 at Hazor, with its 10 scarabs, only briefly (1984: 56), concluding that the Str. 5-4 pottery was best paralleled by Ruweisé T. 66 and the tombs at Kfar Szold and Ginosar. Thus she put the scarabs early, in MB I. In the light of comparative material available today, these views are no longer valid.

Cistern 9024 at Hazor had a long period of use, possibly from late MB I (only a very few pieces, such as *Hazor* I, pl. CXXI: 23-25), through LB II. Str. 5 and 4 represent the Middle Bronze Age deposits. Str. 5 (= V) is not given a precise date in the publication; but Str. 4 (= IV), from whose burials the 10 scarabs almost certainly come, was dated by the excavators to *ca*. 1750-1650 B.C., or MB II (Yadin *et al.* 1958: 134).

A careful re-examination of the pottery in the light of more recent material bears out this date in general, but it also suggests that the pottery of Str. 5-4 as published is somewhat mixed--which is not surprising, considering the admitted difficulties of stratifying something like a long-used cistern deposit (cf. *Hazor* I: 127, 128). We are fortunate now to have Cole's (1984) exhaustive analysis of MB II pottery, based on the four phases of stratified materials from the 1957-1968 excavations at Shechem. Cole (1984: 88), however, did not discuss Hazor Cistern 9024 in any detail. He simply regarded Str. 5 as MB II, with mixed materials; and he presumably thought Str. 4 more MB III (cf. Cole 1984: 84, 88). Yet when we carefully separate out the pottery of Str. 5-4 (*Hazor* I: Pls. CXIV-CXXI), it turns out that "Str. 5" consists mostly of MB II forms, some fairly early, with a few possibly anticipating early MB III; and Str. 4 (with the scarabs) is surprisingly quite homogenously MB II - - possibly mid-late in the period (i.e., *ca.* 1700-1650 B.C.).

The clue to adequate separation lies especially in the platter bowls, globular bowls, and carinated bowls. Cole, however, does not discuss Hazor Cistern 9024 Str. 5-4 with these in mind, as he might have done. To take the platter bowls first, most of those of Str. 5 are early in the MB sequence, with simple rim, only slightly concave disc-base, and sometimes still with red slip and burnish (*Hazor* I: pl. CXIV: 1-4). An early MB II date would suit these platter bowls perfectly, based on Cole's own comparative discussion (1984: 41-46). In Str. 4, the platter bowls have the more incurved, slightly pointed rims and tendency toward ring-bases that are hallmarks of developed MB II (cf. *Hazor* I: pl. CXIX: 1-12). These are paralleled very closely by Cole's Bp. 21 forms (Cole 1984: pl. 2).

Globular neckless or low-necked bowls of the late MB I and MB I/II horizon are conspicuously absent in Cistern 9024. Only two examples, with the high neck typical of early-mid MB II, are present, in Str. 5 (*Hazor* I: pl. CXIV: 14, 15). By Str. 4, the few examples of these bowls have a relatively high neck, typical of developed MB II (*Hazor* I: pl. CXIX: 21-25). These vessels are paralleled closely by Cole's Types Bg B.11 (globular bowl; 1984: pl. 13; cf. *Hazor* I: pl. XIX: 25) and Bn A and Bn B.1 (globular necked bowls; 1984: pl. 14; cf. *Hazor* I: pl. CXIX: 22, 23).

Most of the Str. 5 carinated bowls have the low disc-base and moderate cyma-profile that is typical of early MB II vessels (*Hazor* I: pl. CXIV: 8, 9, 12). All those of Str. 4, however, display the definite ring-base and sharper carination of fully developed MB II (*Hazor* I: pl. CXIX: 17-20). These carinated bowls are nearly identical to Cole's Type Bf A.1 (1984: pl. 17).

Other Str. 5-4 forms, such as the storejars, kraters, piriform juglets, and dipper juglets, are not of much help. Three Str. 5 fragmentary storejars with combed upper body (*Hazor* I: pl. CXVII: 6-8) are in the MB I tradition and would fall in early MB II at latest. A few Str. 4 piriform juglets have degenerate "candlestick" rims (*Hazor* I: pl. CXXI: 1, 3, 6); but these are now known from the sequence of tombs at Tel Dan to extend from MB I into early MB III (Ilan 1991). Several Str. 4 piriform juglets in cream ware with burnished surface and brown geometric decoration (*Hazor* I: pl. CXXI: 14-21) look superficially like MB III "chocolate ware." This decoration, however, is rarely, if ever, found on piriform or cylindrical juglets. It is attested now and then on late MB I or MB II juglets.

In the light of comparisons available today, it can safely be said that the bulk of the Str. 4 material in Hazor Cistern 9024 falls in the MB II period, extending perhaps to the end of the period *ca.* 1650 B.C. The 10 scarabs confirm that date nicely.

2. Nahariyeh

The temple/sanctuary at Nahariyeh has never been published in any detail, but the scant material known shows that the installation extends from MB I through MB III (see, provisionally, Ben-Dor 1950; Dothan 1956; 1981). Dothan's work at the site suggests that the various phasing schemes can best be collapsed into Phases A-C (A being the earliest). Some of the earliest material at the site belongs to MB I, such as a painted piriform juglet (Dothan 1960: fig. 8). Some scholars (i.e., Kempinski 1992: 174) are even inclined to regard MB I as the main period of use. The scarab in question is not attributed, however, to any specific locus, only to "the early temple" (Dothan 1960: 20). Thus the scarab might be from an MB I context, but this cannot be confirmed in the light of the current state of the publication.

3. Ginosar and Kfar Szold Tombs.

Of the MB I/II deposits noted above, several tombs at Ginosar and Kfar Szold have been cited as typical of our "transitional MB I/II" group, since they were first published as such by Epstein (1974; cf. Kaplan 1980: 108; Gerstenblith 1983: 35, 36; Tufnell 1984: 59; Beck 1985: 190). T. 4 at Ginosar was regarded by Epstein as having no MB I pottery, but mixed burials of MB I/II and MB II (1974: 4*-6*). A number of painted piriform juglets, however (fig. 14: 1-5, 9), are classic MB I forms, paralleled at many MB I sites, as are the typical socketed spears (fig. 18: 1, 2). There are certainly MB II vessels from a later burial, such as a disc-base platter bowl (fig. 16: 6) and several high flaring carinated bowls (fig. 16: 12-14, 16), and probably a high-necked globular bowl (fig. 16: 7). Among these clear MB I and MB II forms, however, there are several examples of the "transitional" forms that we are positing here, as Epstein also thought. These would include form 1 above, i.e., globular necked bowls (fig. 16: 9-11). All in all, a range of MB I-II is suggested.

Tomb 2/3 at Ginosar was published by Epstein (1974: 4*) as belonging entirely to MB II, although extending over a considerable time-span. In fact, some of the material is pure MB I, such as the painted piriform juglets (fig. 8: 21, 22; 9: 8; 13: 15); several of the burnished piriform juglets (fig. 8: *passim*); two socketed spears (fig. 11: 23, 24); and especially the two notched chisel-axes (fig. 12: 1, 2), which do not extend past MB I (Oren 1971; Dever 1975: 29, 30; Philip 1989: 37-40, 266-71). Probably to be assigned to our transitional MB I/II phase are some of the platter bowls still exhibiting a disc-case but tending toward incurved or bulbous rims (fig. 9: 10, 11, 15, 16); and several intermediate forms of deep globular necked and carinated bowls (fig. 10: 1-10). On the other hand, several high, "trumpet"-footed carinated bowls (fig. 10: 23-25) should be at least as late as MB II. Thus a range of MB I-II seems best for this tomb as well.

Tomb 1 at Ginosar, assigned to our MB I and MB I/II phase by Epstein (1974: 3*), is on the contrary pure MB I. Indeed, it is a classic MB I assemblage, including painted piriform juglets, four-handled bowls, and even a notched chisel-axe and a socketed spear (Figs. 5-7).

The collection of published pottery from several tombs at Kfar Szold (figs. 1-4) was all regarded by Epstein (1974: 2*-3*) as transitional MB I/II. However, the fine burnished and painted juglets (fig. 1: 1-14) could easily be assigned to MB I, as could the combed storejars (fig. 2: 1-7), the cooking pots (fig. 4: 7, 9, 12), and the socketed spear (fig. 4: 10). On the other hand, several of the platter bowls, one with four knob-handles (fig. 4: 1, 3-5), are transitional in form, as are many of the globular necked bowls (fig. 3: 5-13); and these could easily be assigned to MB I/II. The single scarab (fig. 4: 13) cannot be assigned to any specific burial or assemblage at that site.

Gerstenblith (1984: 35, 36) did not treat the Ginosar tombs in detail, but largely on the basis of the juglets with candlestick rim she assigned T. 1 and 4 to a date toward the end of MB I and the transition to MB II. More recently, however, it has been shown that candlestick rims continue well into MB II, and even MB III (Ilan 1991).

4. Middle Bronze Age Tombs at Tel ^{c}Amr

Three MB tombs were excavated at Tel ^{c}Amr (Druks 1982). Tomb 2 contained an early scarab, in Chamber I. The pottery from Chambers I-III was published together, without adequate separation, but seven vessels were said to have been found with the scarab in Chamber I (cf. Druks 1982: 1*; Figs. 2, 3). These are apparently the seven platter bowls published together by Druks (1982: fig. 2: 4-10). All are classic MB I in form and decoration, most with characteristic flat base and simple or slightly inverted rim, and five of them are red-slipped. These platter bowls cannot be dated other than

MB I. For that matter, neither can the remaining vessels from T. 1, 2, and 4. These include typical MB I red-slipped and burnished carinated bowls (fig. 2: 11-15); and similarly decorated cups (fig. 2: 16), beakers (fig. 2: 17), piriform juglets (fig. 2: 20, 22, 23, 26, 27; 3: 5), and jugs (fig. 3: 6-9). The storejars (fig. 3: 10-13) are indisputably MB I. Of significance is the presence of both piriform juglets (fig. 2: 22) and Tell el-Yehudiyeh juglets (fig. 3: 2-4) in this classic MB I assemblage. The single scarab was dated by Leibovitch to the early Second Intermediate period in an unpublished report (Druks 1982: 1*); but the date of T. 2 cannot possibly be later than the 12th Dynasty, or the very early years of the 13th Dynasty *at latest*.

5. Early MB Tombs at Megiddo

T. 3109 at Megiddo has been assessed by several scholars. Beck (1975: 68, 69) and Gerstenblith (1983: 27) thought it MB I. Only Kenyon (1969: 31) and Cole (1984: 88) placed it later, in early MB II. Cole did so on the basis of two vessels, a carinated bowl and a cooking pot. The carinated bowl (*Megiddo* II: pl. 21: 8), with gently rounded carination and a perfectly flat base, in wet-smoothed ware, is, despite Cole, a typical MB I form. Nearly identical forms are now known from the "Palace" phase at Aphek (cf. Beck 1975: fig. 4: 1). Similarly, the cooking pot with rim folded over and down, often wheel-worked to create a slight "gutter" around the inside (*Megiddo* II: pl. 22: 7), is indeed more typical of MB II. Again, however, there are clear examples at Aphek, as early as the "Pre-Palace" phase (Beck 1975: fig. 2: 11; 52), and in good MB I assemblages at Tel Qashish (Ben-Tor, Portugali, and Avissar 1981: fig. 13: 14-15); and the form has long been known from Tell Beit Mirsim G (*Tell Beit Mirsim* I: pl. 6: 20). These (and other) parallels remove Cole's only reasons for positing an MB II date for T. 3109. The remaining vessels in T. 3109 are so typically MB I that they require little comment. They include a large flat-based burnished jug (*Megiddo* II: pl. 19: 21); a button-base burnished piriform juglet (pl. 19: 28); a typical dipper juglet (pl. 20: 8); a trefoil-mouth jug (pl. 20: 17); and a classic storejar (pl. 21: 1). There is no reason to place any of these vessels any later than late MB I, much less in our transitional MB I/II phase.

T. 5090 produced only two pieces of pottery, a red-burnished juglet (*Megiddo II*, pl 17:14) and a red-burnished flat-based platter bowl (pl. 19:9. Both are classic MB I types; Gerstenblith (1983: 27) agrees in placing T. 5090 in MB I, in her phase 3/4.

T. 5106 produced three vessels, all red-slipped and burnished: a jug (*Megiddo II*, pl. 25:12); a dipper juglet (pl. 25:17); and a flat-based platter bowl (pl. 29:13). These vessels are all diagnostic MB I types (cf. also Gerstenblith 1983: 27, her phase 4).

T. 5137 at Megiddo produced only two pieces of pottery, a button-base burnished piriform juglet (*Megiddo* II: pl. 24: 20), and a large ovoid jug (pl. 25: 6). The jug is somewhat nondescript, but the juglet is a classic MB I form. Gerstenblith (1983: 27) also dated this tomb to MB I.

6. Tomb 92 at Beth-Shan

T. 92, one of the tombs excavated by Fisher as part of the "Northern Cemetery" at Beth-Shan, but left unpublished, was shown by E. D. Oren (1971) to contain a classic MB I assemblage. There is no pottery reported, but the weapons include the familiar combination of a duckbill axe, a veined dagger and a socketed spearhead -- all types that can be shown (Dever 1975) to belong exclusively to MB I. The single scarab in T. 92 thus comes from a pure MB I context.

7. Tomb 6 II at Tel Rehov

Of the several tombs excavated near Tel Rehov, just south of Beth-shan in the Jordan Valley, T. 2, 8, and 6 II belong to MB I or MB I/II, although T. 6 II was dated by the excavator to early MB II, *ca.* 1750 B.C. (Yogev 1985: 104). T. 6 is significant here, since level II produced two scarabs between the fingers of the left hand of a flexed young female burial, together with six pottery vessels and a toggle pin. The two large one-handled jugs (Yogev 1985: fig. 3: 8, 9) are missing their necks, but the globular form of the body, the placement of the handle, and the disc-base would place them probably in late MB I or early MB II. The button-base piriform juglet (fig. 3: 6) and cylindrical juglet (fig. 3: 7) could be MB II, but they are not especially diagnostic. The most helpful piece is a high-necked globular jar with ring-base of Cole's Type Bn B. 1 (cf. Cole 1984: pl. 14: d), which has good early MB II parallels, among them Ginosar T. 2/3, which we have assigned above to a considerable range within MB II. Nevertheless, the globular jar with *low* neck is a good transitional MB I/II *fossile directeur* (as in the Kfar Szold tombs; above), so a date of MB I/II would seem to suit Tel Rehov I and II quite well, i.e., late 12th/early 13th Dynasty. The fact that Level II of T. 6 contained only four intact vessels and a single flexed burial (Yogev 1985: 92) means that it is certainly homogeneous. One of the scarabs (No. 68) is closely paralleled by a scarab in T. D 6 at Jericho, which belongs early in Kenyon's Group II, the pottery of which would be dated by us to *ca.* 1750 B.C.--a date that corresponds closely to our transitional MB I/II attribution of Rehov T. 6 II.

8. MB I Tombs at Tell el-Farah (N)

A number of the tombs excavated by de Vaux at Tell el-Farah (N) belong to MB I, including T. AD, AN, B, W, X, and Y. Here, however, we shall treat only T. AN, with an early scarab. This tomb (Mallet 1973: pl. 17, 18) contained little pottery, but some beads, two rings, and two toggle pins. One of the pins (1973: 6) has a nail-head, which could be either EB IV or MB I; the other (1973: 7) has the decorated head more typical of MB I. The two storejars (1973: pl. 17: 1, 5) would fit very well in MB I, as would the two red-burnished juglets with button-base (1973: 2, 3). The globular neckless jar (1973: 4) is especially diagnostic for late MB I. All in all, the latter date suits this tomb well, i.e., *ca.* 1850-1800 B.C. Mallet (1973: 94, 95) dated T. AN, along with T. AD, B, W, X, and Y to mid-late MB I. Gerstenblith (1983: 35, 50) also dated these tombs to MB I, along with T. D and 16.

9. Tel Aviv Harbor Cemetery.

The Tel Aviv harbor tombs published by Kaplan (1955) belong generally to MB I or MB I/II, as I first pointed out in 1976 (Dever 1976: 18). Since there are some 24 scarabs from these tombs, however, a closer examination of the date of individual tombs may be helpful.

T. 1, with Scarab 1, is not illustrated. T. 2, with Scarab 11, produced two MB I juglets (fig. 4: 1, 2); a classic MB I red-cross platter bowl; and one MB I toggle-pin (fig. 5: 6). T. 3A, with Scarab 3, has a carinated burnished bowl (fig. 2: 8) and a disc-base platter bowl (fig. 4: 7), both MB I. T. 3 B, with Scarab 23, has a squat storejar (fig. 1: 5); a classic MB I red-cross bowl (fig. 4: 11); an intermediate form of carinated bowl (fig. 2: 6); and a drop-shaped juglet that has MB I parallels. A date of MB I/II at latest is suggested. T. 4A, with Scarabs 4, 9, 10, and 24, has several unillustrated vessels, but also an intermediate carinated bowl (fig. 2: 5) and a transitional EB IV/MB I style toggle-pin (fig. 5: 3); a date in MB I or at latest MB I/II may be suggested. T. 5, with Scarab 8, has an MB storejar of indeterminate date (fig. 1: 6); a platter bowl (fig. 4: 9) that would fit our criteria above for MB I/II; a good MB I dipper juglet (fig. 4: 4); and a button-base piriform juglet (fig. 4: 13) of good MB I type. All in all, a date of MB I is best, or possibly MB I/II. T. 7A, with Scarab 16, has a classic MB I burnished open bowl (fig. 2: 7). T. 8, with Scarab 20, is certainly MB I, with a disc-base platter bowl (fig. 3: 12); a burnished dipper juglet (fig. 3: 15); a button-base piriform juglet (fig. 3: 5); and a typical toggle-pin (fig. 5: 4). T. 10A, with Scarab 17, has only two illustrated finds, a burnished-rim platter bowl (fig. 3: 11) and a toggle-pin (fig. 5: 7), both certainly MB I. T. 10 C, with Scarab 13, is illustrated only by an indeterminate MB storejar (fig. 1: 4) and a Tell el-Yehudiyeh juglet (fig. 3: 4). A precise date is impossible, but this tomb could be MB I or MB II. T. 11A, with Scarab 14, is illustrated only by a carinated bowl (fig. 2: 13) that looks more MB II than MB I, and a miniature (fig. 3: 7) that cannot be closely dated. T. 11B, with Scarabs 2, 6, is illustrated only by a button-base piriform juglet (fig. 3: 3) that is probably MB I. T. 12, with Scarab 5, is not illustrated. T. 14, with Scarabs 19, 22, is illustrated by an indeterminate dipper juglet (fig. 3: 16); a biconical juglet (fig. 3: 1) of MB I type; a jug of either MB I or early MB II (fig. 2: 11); and a classic MB I toggle-pin (fig. 5: 5). A date in MB I is preferable, or MB I/II at latest. T. 15, with Scarab 7, is illustrated by a carinated bowl (fig. 2: 12) and a button-base juglet (fig. 3: 6), both of which could be MB I/II or MB II. T. 16, with Scarab 12, is illustrated by a classic combed MB I storejar (fig. 1: 1); an equally classic burnished-rim platter bowl (fig. 3: 10); and an MB I or MB I/II carinated bowl (fig. 2: 14). A date late in MB I is preferable. T. 18, with Scarabs 15, 18, 21, is illustrated by an incurved-rim platter bowl (fig. 3: 9) that is MB I/II or possibly early MB II, and a broken MB I toggle-pin (fig. 5: 8).

It should be noted that the Tel Aviv harbor burials were all shallow pit-graves, most (13 of 18) for single individuals. They are thus homogeneous, do not extend over a long time-span, and cannot be regarded as containing mixed contents (except perhaps T. 6, which seems to have both MB I/II and MB II material). Kaplan (1955: 7, 8) dated all these tombs to MB III, or the "Hyksos" period, even as late as Megiddo IX. This date seemed confirmed by Leibovitch's (1955) opinion that many of the scarabs were of "18th Dynasty" type. In 1976, however, I pointed out that nearly all of the neglected Tel Aviv Harbor tombs, along with those at nearby Dhahrat el-Humraiya and the Wadi Rubin, should be redated to MB I or MB I/II. That dating was followed by Weinstein (1975: 5, 6) and others, among them Gophna and Beck (1981: 47; Gerstenblith, 1983, does not date the material at all; and Tufnell, 1989: 56, dates them only to MB generally). My date is now confirmed by Ward's redating of the scarabs to the 12th Dynasty.

10. The Dhahrat el-Humraiya Cemetery

A cemetery at Dhahrat el-Humraiya, some 8 miles south of Tel Aviv on the north bank of the Nahal Rubin, was excavated in 1942 by J. Ory (1948). However, the early date of some of the Middle Bronze Age tombs went generally unnoticed until pointed out by myself (Dever 1976: 18; followed by Gerstenblith 1983: 50). Tombs of clear MB I date are T. 2, 21, 38, and 55. T. 15 (with a scarab) is not well illustrated but is probably MB I; and T. 49 (with a scarab) may well be early MB II.

11. Râs el-ᶜAin 6

We have treated the stratified MB I material from recent excavations of Kochavi and others in some detail above. In addition, these excavations have published a few tombs of the period, although none with scarabs. The older soundings of Iliffe and Ory in the 1930's produced a number of classic cist-burials of MB I, in addition to a pit (No. 15) with some MB I pottery and a scarab originally dated by Rowe to the 13th Dynasty. Ory gives only the sketchiest description of Pit 15, however; and Iliffe publishes quite a bit of classic MB I pottery, but says only that it was found "in loose association" with the scarab in question (cf. Ory 1936: 111, 112; Iliffe 1936: 119). The pottery *may* simply have come from the so-called "reservoir" site some 60 m. from the find-spot of the scarab, but at approximately the same depth below the surface (cf. Ory 1936: 112), in which case the scarab is undatable stratigraphically.

12. The Earliest MB Tombs at Jericho

Kenyon's division of the many rich Middle Bronze Age tombs at Jericho into her "Groups I-V" has been widely accepted, both by specialists in Syro-Palestinian archaeology as well as those in other fields. Kenyon eschewed absolute dates for these groups in the original publication (1960; 1965); but in her synthesis in the *Cambridge Ancient History*[3] (1973: 94) she suggested the following scheme (fig. 3:11); dates in parentheses my estimates):

Kenyon	"MB I"				"MB II"							
		1800	(1750)		(1716)			(1675)		(1625)	1567	
	T. K3	Group I	II		III				IV		V	
Here	T. K3	I	II		III				IV		V	
		1800	1750			1650						1550
Phase	MB I		I/II	MB II			MB III					

Fig. 3:11. Jericho Tomb Groups I-V.

Kenyon's absolute dates are still workable in general, except for Group I, which can be dated to late MB I rather than early MB II. Manfred Bietak, however, has misunderstood the Jericho Tomb Groups and their scarabs as supporting his ultra-low chronology for the Egypto-Levantine Middle Bronze Age (cf. below).

It is not sufficiently noted that Kenyon's scheme, while based partly on careful separation of layers within the Jericho multiple burials, derives finally from typological presuppositions regarding the pottery, which are always somewhat subjective (cf. Lapp 1961: 70). Furthermore, Kenyon in her 1960 and 1965 treatments neither sets forth the basis for her typological presuppositions in any detail, nor justifies her assignment of tombs to groups on the basis of exhaustive comparisons with well dated materials elsewhere. These deficiencies cannot be compensated for merely by taking Kenyon as an "authority." We must re-examine the Jericho tombs and up-date the discussion to see which, if any, really belong early in MB. Here we must take into account also Kirkbride's use of the scarabs for chronology in the original publications (1960; 1965), as well as Tufnell's reworking of some of the material in *Studies on Scarab Seals II* (1984).

Tomb K 3 was regarded by Kenyon as unique, so she placed it alone in MB I, slightly preceding her Group I (Kenyon 1965: 203-206). Others have generally accepted this date (cf. Gerstenblith 1983: 50; Cole 1984: 84; Tufnell 1984: 62). In 1965 Kenyon was able only to note the generally globular forms, the lack of red slip and burnish, and a few parallels from Ory's tombs at Ras el-^{c}Ain and the Megiddo tombs. Today it is possible to go much further. In particular, the neckless globular jars taken above as diagnostic for late MB I and our MB I/II are present in T. K 3 (Kenyon 1965: fig. 93: 6-8). Together with the flat and disc-base platter bowls (fig. 93: 1-4) and the button-base juglets (fig. 93: 16, 17), these globular jars fix the date of T. K 3 nicely in late MB I.

Kenyon dated her next tombs, Group I, to early MB II generally (presumably *ca.* 1800-1750 B.C.); but only T. A 1, A 34 phases 1-2, B 48 phases 1-3, and J 3 were assigned to this group. T. B 48 is critical to our discussion here, since seven scarabs came from this tomb.

Kenyon's discussion (1965: 206-211) is not altogether clear. She distinguishes only 2 "layers" in this tomb, the lower burials assigned to her Group I, the upper to her early Group II. She publishes the pottery together, however, "for stratification in tombs of this nature does not have the certainty of stratification on the Tell, and other interpretations are possible" (1965: 208). In addition to two "layers," Kenyon speaks of "phases," apparently individual burials (Tufnell's "deposits"). Here "phases 1-3" and the "repository" thus should belong to "layer 2" and the earlier burials that she assigns to Group I, which would place these deposits -- together with the seven scarabs found in phase 3 -- in her early MB II, *ca.* 1800-1750 B.C., or our transitional MB I/II of the same horizon. Tufnell's remarks (1984: 59, 62) on the date and the scarabs in phase 3 are somewhat enigmatic, except that she thinks that while phase 3 belongs in Tomb Group I, some of these scarabs might be later and would fit better with the later burials in Group II, or our early MB II.

If one goes carefully through all the pottery of T. B 48 (*Jericho* II: figs. 95-99), separating it by phases, it becomes apparent that the earlier burials in layer 2/phases 1-3 can readily be dated to the *floruit* of MB I, somewhat earlier than Kenyon (and apparently Tufnell) thought. The classic MB I forms are present: flat-based storejars (fig. 99: 2); combed flat-based jugs (fig. 97: 3); disc-base platter bowls (fig. 95: 1-7); burnished button-base juglets (fig. 97: 6-9, 11, 12); slipped biconical bowls with flat base (fig. 95: 11); and especially the neckless globular jars with flat base (fig. 95: 11, 19; 96: 12). The one cylindrical juglet (fig. 98: 9) had been taken by Kenyon and others to be more MB II; but there are now well documented appearances of this ceramic form in MB I, including red-slipped and burnished examples (Beck 1975: fig. 12: 12; Tel Aphek, "Post-Palace" phase). Thus the earliest use of T. B 48 should be redated to MB I, i.e., pre-Group I or contemporary with T. K 3. That means that the four scarabs in phase 3 should be 12th Dynasty in date--in any case not later than *ca.* 1750 B.C. on the *lowest possible* chronology.

Kenyon also dated the "repository" in T. B 48 to her layer 2/phases 1-3, or early Group I, our early MB II; and that date seems generally sound. It is significant that here the critical diagnostic forms are later than layer 2/phases 1-3. Among these are neckless globular jars with ring rather than disc-base (fig. 96: 2, 4, 7-9); similarly, a platter bowl in buff ware with a ring-base (fig. 95: 9). Thus a date in early MB II is suggested here, *ca.* 1750-1725 B.C.

Layer 1/Phase 4 of T. B 48 was dated by Kenyon to her early Group II, or our early MB II. To this layer apparently belongs the final intact Burial A, near which was found Scarab 25 (Kenyon 1965: 206-208). The pottery most closely associated with the skeleton is fig. 95: 14, 14, two carinated globular bowls in buff ware with distinct ring-bases; and fig. 98: 10, a dipper juglet in pink-buff wet-smoothed ware. Both forms have good parallels in early MB II, but they cannot be specified further in our opinion. The other pottery in layer 1/phase 4, not so closely associated with this particular burial but presumably roughly contemporary, consists of typical MB II forms well advanced beyond the MB I repertoire. Especially noteworthy are the large storejars (fig. 99: 1, 3, 4); inverted-rim, ring-base platter bowls (fig. 95: 8-10); rather sharply carinated bowls (fig. 95: 17, 18); piriform juglets in buff ware with no red slip and less flattened button base (fig. 97: 4, 15, 16; 98: 1-8); and more squat dipper juglets (fig. 98: 11, 12). The only problematic forms are the globular jars with higher flaring rim and higher pedestal-base (fig. 96: 14-19, nos. 14, 16, 17 with bands of red paint on the upper shoulder). The form itself is more typical of developments in MB III; but the ware, slip, and especially the paint on several examples (above), all point to a date in MB II, probably early in the period. To return, then, to the archaeological context of Scarab 25, it could be (1) an heirloom; (2) originally *in situ* in layer 2, mistakenly attributed in digging to layer 1; or (3) taken as belonging properly to the final burial in layer 1, and thus dated to early MB II, *ca.* 1750-1725 B.C. Unfortunately, the archaeological context in this case is not decisive.

T. A 34, with four phases, was assigned to Group I by Kenyon, although she suggested that phase 1 might be "slightly earlier than the main range of Group I" (1960: 355), a date followed by Tufnell (1984: 59). That would place phase 1 in our late MB I. The four vessels assigned to phase 1 (1960: fig. 140: 3, 24; 142: 14) would fit well enough in MB I, although rather late in the period. Phase 2 includes piriform juglets with small ring-base (fig. 141: 7, 10-12, 167) and open carinated bowls with concave base (fig. 140: 11, 12) that would place this phase either in late MB I or MB I/II. Phase 3 seems generally somewhat later typologically, as shown by platter bowls with incurved rim (fig. 140: 2) and a fairly sharply carinated bowl form with ring-base (fig. 140: 16). However, the diagnostic MB I/II neckless globular jar is present (fig. 140: 25), as is a classic MB I painted piriform juglet (fig. 142: 6). Thus phase 3, if *homogeneous*, can hardly be dated later than our MB I/II, *ca.* 1800-1750 B.C. (Phase 4, not especially pertinent here, would date to mid-late MB II; below). As noted, Kenyon hinted at an MB I date for phase 1, but dated phases 2-4 to her Group I, or early MB II. Tufnell (1984: 59, 62), however, argued cogently that phase 1, as well as 2-3, all predated Kenyon's Group I, citing as we have here the painted piriform juglet and some of its well known MB I parallels. The revised dates here would place the two scarabs (Tufnell 1984: nos. 1918, 2801) assigned to phase 3 by Kenyon well within the late 12th Dynasty. Tufnell (1984: 62, 70, 71), however, thinks that no. 1918 is earlier than the deposit itself; and that no. 2801 may belong rather with phase 4, i.e., in MB II. She gives no *stratigraphic* reasons for the latter assumption; and if the scarab can be 12th Dynasty typologically, our ceramic date for phase 3 would fit well.

The other 13 scarabs in T. A 34 are in phase 4, which we have redated to mid-late MB II (above), *ca.* 1700-1650 B.C. Tufnell's preference (1984: 71) for phase 4 in Kenyon's Groups I-III, rather than Group I, would fall within this range. Her date is based on the increasing number of cylindrical juglets in phase 4 (as 1965: fig. 142: 8-10), as well as pedestal-base goblets (fig. 140: 32), a view that is generally still sound.

Another tomb assigned by Kenyon to her Group I was J3. It is a single intact burial of a young male, with only a few ceramic vessels of early MB II; a classic shaft-hole axe of MB II; and Scarab 44. The early platter bowls (fig. 115: 6) with incurved rim, and the globular necked bowls still in the MB I disc-base tradition (fig. 116: 3, 4), together with the fairly sharply carinated bowl (fig. 115: 6), would suggest a date in early-mid MB II, *ca.* 1750-1700 B.C. for T. J 3, i.e., Group II rather than Kenyon's Group I. That would provide a similar date for Scarab 44.

Kenyon's final tomb in her Group I is T. A 1. This tomb had eight or nine burials and may cover a considerable time-span. It need not detain us here, since it produced no scarabs. The platter bowls (1960: fig. 112: 1, 2) and globular neckless jars with disc-base (fig. 112: 3, 67, 7, 10, 11) would suggest a date in early MB II, i.e., not in Kenyon's Group I but in II.

Before leaving the discussion of Kenyon's Tomb Group I, we must summarize the results of our redating of the several tombs above. If we are correct, based on more recent comparisons than were available to Kenyon (or, for that matter, Tufnell 1984), T. A 1 and J 3 would now be moved *later*, to early MB II, or her Group II. Likewise, T. B 48 phase 4 would belong to Group II or even III. At the *other* end of the spectrum, T. A 34 phases 1-2 would be moved earlier, to pre-Group I, contemporary with MB I tomb K 3. That would leave only T. A 34 phases 3-4 and B 48 phases 1-3 in Kenyon's Tomb Group I, equivalent to our MB I/II. It should be noted, however, that despite our rearrangement of individual tomb groups, Kenyon's instinct that Tomb Group I belonged to the MB I/II horizon was essentially correct, as were her absolute dates of *ca.* 1800-1750 B.C.

Tufnell, to her credit, also moved T. A 34 phase 3 earlier, to a "pre-group I" (1984: 59), i.e., to an MB I date even earlier than our MB I/II. Tufnell (1984: 63) then proposed adding T. B 3, the earliest phases, to Kenyon's Group I, in line with Kenyon's own hints based on the presence of piriform juglets with ring-base (*Jericho* I: 395). The 12 scarabs in T. B 3 (*Jericho* II: fig. 293: 1-12), which may have had a very long life-span (*Jericho* I: 393-395), cannot be related to particular levels, and their archaeological content could range anywhere from late MB I to late MB II.

Finally, despite their obvious importance, Kenyon's Jericho Tomb Groups I-V were not analyzed in any detail by either Gerstenblith or Cole. Gerstenblith (1983: 35) only commented on T. K 3, regarding it with Kenyon and us as MB I. She does not mention Kenyon's Groups I-II otherwise. Cole (1984: 84, 85) does not comment on any of Kenyon's individual tombs, concluding only that Tomb Group I belongs to MB I, Groups II-IV to MB II.

13. The Tell el-^{c}Ajjûl "Courtyard Cemetery"

The "Courtyard Cemetery" or "Palace Yard" cemetery at Tell el-^{c}Ajjûl, excavated by Petrie in 1930-1931 and published in *Ancient Gaza* II (1932), has often been singled out for its rich collection of MB I tombs. The 24 tombs are numbered in the 1400 series, but a few others, like Cave 303 A-B, belong also to MB I or MB I/II, practically speaking, to the 12th Dynasty.

The materials from the "Courtyard Cemetery" were published sketchily, in Petrie's usual fashion, and the pottery was presented only by "type" in Petrie's *Corpus*. The "Courtyard Cemetery" has been reworked several times, most recently by Tufnell in an exceedingly important treatment (1962) based on first-hand re-examination of the material that can now be located. In addition, *Studies in Scarab Seals* II (1984) treats the hundreds of scarabs from the mound and their context. Here, however, we need be concerned only with the few tombs that produced early scarabs, namely T. 303 A-B, 1406, and 1410 B-C.

T. (= "Cave") 303 A-B has recently been reworked by Tufnell (1980), who re-examined the original material and published much better drawings of the pottery, the weapons, and the two scarabs. The lower burial (B) is dated securely to MB I by two characteristic platter bowls (*Ancient Gaza* II: fig. 3: 7, 8); a classic red burnished bowl (fig. 3: 9); an early Tell el-Yehudiyeh juglet (fig. 3: 11); two red-slipped dipper juglets (fig. 3: 12, 13); a typical large ovoid storejar with flanged rim (fig. 4); and especially by a rilled dagger and a socketed spear (fig. 5: 16, 17). Tufnell rightly compares this assemblage with other MB I burials, such as Gibeon T. 31, Kh. Kufin T. 3, the Kfar Szold tombs, and T. K 3 at Jericho, as well as T. 66 at Ruweisé (1980: 42-46). She dates Burial B accordingly to early-mid MB I, *ca.* 1900 B.C.

The upper (A) burial in T. 303 was dated by Tufnell about a century later, *ca.* 1800 B.C. -- partly on the basis of one of two scarabs in this tomb, a royal name scarab commemorating Amenemhat IV, *ca.* 1798-1789 B.C. (fig. 3: 5). This was attributed by both Petrie and Tufnell to Burial A and is paralleled closely by scarabs of Amenemhat IV elsewhere (Tufnell 1980: 38). Petrie had attributed the other scarab, of the *rdi-R*^{c} type, to Burial B (followed, for example, by Weinstein 1975: 4, 10; but cf. now 1992: 40, n. 24); but Tufnell's reallocation to Burial A may be preferable.

Re-examining Tufnell's ceramic date for Burial A does not, unfortunately, yield a firm chronology. There are only four vessels. The cylindrical Tell el-Yehudiyeh and dipper juglets (*Ancient Gaza* II: fig. 3: 3, 4) are not especially diagnostic, although Tufnell compares the Yehudiyeh juglet with Tomb Group III at Jericho. The carinated bowl (fig. 3: 1) could be either later MB I or early MB II, as is the case with the large cordon-neck jug (fig. 3: 2). All in all, Burial A in T. 303 would fall nicely with our transitional MB I/II, *ca.* 1775-1750 B.C. That would contradict Tufnell's Jericho Tomb Group III comparisons, and it would favor comparisons rather with Tomb Group II, more in line with current scholarship (above). In this case, the large scarab of Amenemhat IV type would be roughly *in situ*, while the smaller formula scarab provides an early context for a type generally thought to be of the Hyksos period, or just before.

T. 1406, with an adult and a child burial, contained scarabs 103 and 104 on the adult's left wrist. It is almost certainly MB I in date, to judge from those items that are well enough illustrated in *Ancient Gaza* II. These include a classic MB I storejar (pl. XXXI: 38 C^{2}); two large flat-based juglets (pl. XXX: 35 R; XXXIV: 51 G^{3}); a flat-based piriform juglet (pl. XXIV: 60 N^{5}); and a button-base Tell el-Yehudiyeh juglet (pl. XXXIV: 60 M^{5}). Another storejar (43 D^{6}), two carinated bowls (23 J^{7}); 25 G^{1}) and a toggle-pin (202) are illustrated in *Ancient Gaza* II by several good MB I forms. These include two flat-based ovoid storejars (pl. XXXII: 43 E^{4}; 43 E^{5}); a baggy-shaped jug with trefoil mouth (pl. XXX: 34 B^{9}); and two Tell el-Yehudiyeh juglets of early type (pl. XXXIV: 60 M^{5}; 60 M^{6}). A globular carinated bowl (26 C^{2}) is not illustrated in *Ancient Gaza* II. A flat-based carinated bowl (pl. XXVIII: 25 S) and a diagnostic late MB I globular neckless jar (pl. XXVIII: 28 P^{3}) are not listed in the register but are attributed to T. 1410 in the plates (not, however, specifying which chamber, A, B, or C). The one toggle-pin illustrated (pl. XVIII: 2-6) is, like that in T. 1410 B, a classic MB I example.

Tufnell (1962; 1984: 8-10) had dated all her Groups I-V in the "Courtyard Cemetery" to MB I, in which I have concurred (1976: Chart 2), as well as Cole (1984: 84, 92). Group 5 may, however, belong to our transitional MB I/II phase (as also Cole 1984: 92). Gerstenblith's opinion (1984: 32) that only Groups I-II are MB I, and that Groups III-V are MB I/II or MB II, is unsubstantiated. In any case, the exact overall assignment of groups does not affect T. 1406, 1410 B, and 1410 C, which stand on their own as pure MB I assemblages.

14. Ruweisé, T. 66 and 73.

Tomb 66 at Ruweisé (= Kafer Djarra), on the Lebanese coast, is especially significant for chronological purposes, since it contained 24 scarabs. Originally published by Guigues (1937; 1938), this tomb has been much discussed (cf. Tufnell 1975-1976; 1989: 53-56; Epstein 1974: 2*; Dever 1976: 13; Gerstenblith 1983: 42, 43; Beck 1985: 196). Nevertheless, only Tufnell (1975-1976) undertook a detailed analysis, based upon first-hand examination of the pottery, which has been published only in rather poor photographs. But Tufnell's early study, while undoubtedly still valuable, must now be re-worked in the light of much MB I and MB I/II material that has since accumulated. In particular, it is clear that both Tufnell (1975-1976; 1984) and Ward (in Tufnell 1984: 152) preferred an early-mid MB I date--i.e., 20th-19th cent. B.C.--because of a scarab of Sesostris I in T. 66, and another of Sesostris II in T. 73, as well as because of their high date at that time for the Montet Jar and its scarabs. A thorough and independent examination of the pottery (and other objects) in T. 66 and T. 73 at Ruweisé thus becomes a necessity.

Tomb 66 had only two burials and therefore should be roughly homogeneous, or at least should have but two phases (cf. Guigues 1938: figs. 66-73 for the material). Despite the misgivings of some (i.e., Gerstenblith 1983: 43, on grounds unspecified, followed by Weinstein 1992: 37), the pottery of T. 66 is *overwhelmingly* of MB I date. Gerstenblith (1983: 43) is able to cite as evidence for a mixed MB I-II date only several globular bowls and carinated bowls. Yet the illustrated examples of such vessels (figs. 67, 68: *passim*) can now be shown to belong either to MB I or, at latest, to the types that we have proposed above as diagnostic for transitional MB I/II. Thus figs. 67: 3; 68: bottom left; pl. IV: bottom right are all globular necked bowls that are paralleled very closely in the Kfar Szold and Rehov tombs classified above as MB I/II. The same is true for the several carinated bowls on figs. 67: a, b; 68: bottom right; pl. IV: bottom center. Furthermore, the recent definitive work on MB II pottery by Cole (1984) has shown that these globular necked bowls -- his Types Bg B. 11 and Bn A (low neck) and Bn B. 1 (high neck) --clearly *begin* in late MB I in both Syria and Palestine (1984: 51-54). Furthermore, even fairly sharply carinated bowls, formerly thought continued to MB II or even MB III, are now known to have begun in late MB I in Syria-Palestine. These would include Cole's Types Bn A. 11, Bc B. 13, and Bf B. 1-3 (1984: 55-59, citing many parallels). Thus there is no *a priori* reason to assign these two vessel types -- admittedly the latest in T. 66 -- to MB II, or for that matter even to our MB I/II. Indeed, MB I/II would be the *latest possible* date for T. 66 on current evidence.

If there were any doubt, it would be removed by an examination of the other items in T. 66, i.e., the bulk of the material. This includes classic examples of painted piriform juglets similar to those at Kfar Szold and elsewhere; other juglets, jugs, and cups typical of MB I; platter bowls; painted elongated dipper juglets; and, especially, two notched chisel-axes and two veined daggers, both types that do not extend beyond MB I, or at latest MB I/II (above; cf. Guigues 1938: figs. 66-73; pl. IV). Thus the Sesostris I scarab, *ca.* 1943-1898 B.C., is roughly *in situ* in T. 66, since this tomb does not need to date after 1800 B.C., and could easily be considerably earlier. It is worth noting that its best parallels in Palestine are now found in the Ph. 2-3 or "Palace" levels at Tel Aphek (so also Beck 1985: 196), well before the "Post-Palace" levels and the end of MB I; that would not rule out a date as early as *ca.* 1900 B.C.

Virtually the same, or even stronger, arguments can be made for an MB I or MB I/II date for T. 73 at Ruweisé (cf. Guigues 1938: figs. 77-85). Here there was one adult and one infant burial, which need not (contra Weinstein 1992: 37) imply that this tomb has a long life-span, i.e., has both MB I and MB II burials. If anything, the pottery of T. 73 is even more homogeneously MB I than that of T. 66. There is certainly no basis for Gerstenblith's statement (1983: 43) that this tomb should be dated to MB II; again, she is basing herself erroneously on the presence of globular necked jars and certain carinated bowls, forms that we now know began well before the end of MB I. All in all, Tufnell and Ward's original date of 20th-19th cent. B.C. is quite acceptable.

15. Sin el-Fil

Sin el-Fil, on the right bank of the Nahr Beyrouth, produced a find that M. Chéhab (1939) published as a "Phoenician" tomb, but it contains a classic assemblage of MB I ceramic vessels; bronze implements including two duckbill axes, four spearheads, three daggers, and two toggle pins; and several scarabs. The pottery is poorly illustrated in photograph only, but the assemblage includes red-slipped and burnished juglets, low-necked globular jars, Tell el-Yehudiyeh juglets, and painted jugs. The pottery is very similar to that of T. 66 and 73 at nearby Ruweisé, which we have dated above to MB I, or MB I/II at the latest. That general horizon would serve admirably for the Sin el-Fil tomb; Gerstenblith (1983: 51) even places it in her earliest MB I phase. Indeed, only the single low-necked globular jar (Chéhab 1939: fig. 3a) inclines us to a slightly later date within MB I.

16. Tell el-Dab^{c}a in the Egyptian Delta.

Since the appearance of the first preliminary reports of Manfred Bietak's excavations from 1966 on at Tell el-Dab^{c}a in the Eastern Delta, now identified certainly as the long-lost Hyksos capital of Avaris, the site has increasingly been recognized as being of major significance for Levantine interconnections (see Bietak 1981; 1984; 1989; 1991). It has been clear almost from the beginning that the material culture of the lower levels--Strata H, G, and F--is "Canaanite" in character and represents an early Asiatic settlement in the Delta that is fascinating because it is "pre-Hyksos." Specialists have pointed out that in archaeological terms the material ranges from Palestinian early MB I through an intermediate phase that we are calling here "transitional MB I/II." Bietak himself has acknowledged that this relative assignment of the material is correct. In most treatments, however, he has drastically lowered the absolute dates of Dab^{c}a Stratum E 3 and on that basis has sought to adjust the entire Syro-Palestinian archaeological-chronological framework downward by as much as 125 years (especially for MB I).

Bietak's view in several synthetic works (1979; 1984b; and especially 1984a) have been received with some skepticism, pending fuller publication of the data upon which he bases his dating; meanwhile I have challenged his "ultra-low" chronology (Dever 1985; 1991; 1992). In what follows I shall try to update the discussion, with specific reference to Bietak's latest and fullest publication (1984a; 1991). The most efficient way to grasp the essential problem may be to outline our respective views in chart form (fig. 3:12).

Bietak's current absolute dates (1984a; 1991) differ from his previous dating scheme (Bietak 1979) only by giving what is apparently a "median date," rather than a chronological range, for each stratum; and by having a stronger tendency to prefer the "low" absolute Egyptian chronologies of Helck, von Beckerath, and Hornung, or of Krauss (see also Dever 1985; Dever 1992; Bietak 1984a: 472-73, references; Ward 1992). Since we have already challenged the evidence for those dates as presented in Bietak's earlier treatments, (Ward 1987; Dever 1985; 1991) here we can concentrate on any newer data that have been published, as well as on a summary of the evidence *in toto*.

There are two classes of chronological evidence to be considered from Tell el-Dab^{c}a: (1) the local Egyptian material, some of which Bietak thinks yields an absolute chronology, which he then wishes to impose on Syria-Palestine; and (2) the imported and locally made "Canaanite" material, much of which we will argue is from Palestine, which can yield at least a reliable *relative* chronology, for both the Southern Levant and Egypt.

In the first category, Bietak (1984: Table 2) recently listed nine "datable" objects that can be correlated with Tell el-Dab^{c}a Str. H through D/2. He has now (1991) added a few other items of chronological significance. Of the "Canaanite" or Levantine material that can be compared with the Syro-Palestinian sequence that we are treating here, Bietak has consistently promised fuller treatments but has published very scant data. Almost all the illustrated material is found in his first synthesis (1979) and in a paper (1991) presented in a symposium organized in 1988 by the American Schools of Oriental Research, in which the present authors also participated (cf. Dever 1991; Ward 1991).

In the following we shall attempt to synthesize the two classes of chronological data from Tell el-Dab^{c}a--virtually all the evidence published thus far --and correlate it with the current archaeological phasing of Syria-Palestine. This has been acknowledged all along as a desideratum, but it has not heretofore been undertaken.

<u>Str. H = d/2</u>.

The only published Egyptian object from this stratum is a cylinder seal depicting apparently a duckbill axe, attributed by Bietak (1984a: 479) to d/1, "contemporary with or earlier than stratum H." Bietak adopts Porada's (1984) preferred date of "18th century B.C.," supported by R.H. Boehmer (Bietak 1984a: 478, n. 1). But comparative art-historical considerations, even when advanced by as great an authority as Porada, do not yield a fixed chronology without external controls. Porada's argument rests largely upon the familiar "duckbill" axe of Syro-Palestinian type portrayed on the seal, for which she cites as parallels a miniature from pre-Hammurabi destruction levels at Mari; an example on a seal in the British Museum, dated by Dominique Collon on stylistic grounds to the 18th century B.C.; and finally on two examples of "duck-bill" axes in the "Tomb of the Lord of Goats" at Ebla, which she apparently would date to the 18th century B.C., our MB II. Yet Porada ignores the overwhelming evidence of specialists that wherever we have controlled contexts in Palestine this type of "duck-bill" axe is confined exclusively to the MB I (or the transitional MB I/II phase at latest), being replaced in MB II by the socketed or "shaft-hole" axe (see Oren 1971; Dever 1975; Gerstenblith 1983; Porada cites none of these). As for the "Tomb of the Lord of Goats" at Ebla, Matthiae dates it to his early Mardikh IIIB, which he thinks begins *ca.* 1800 B.C., although he places the tomb itself in mid-MB IIIB, ca 1750 B.C. However, the pottery in that tomb is largely reminiscent of MB I styles, as Matthiae himself acknowledges, and thus it need not fall later than *ca.* 1800 B.C.; some of the metals are even earlier. Even if one could document "duck-bill" axes in the early to mid-18th century B.C., their main *floruit* is earlier, in the classic MB I period,

Dab^{c}a (Tell A)	Character	Palestine	Bietak (1984)	Dever
H	Open Settlement, Eg. MK Material; ruined at end	Early MB IIA (12th Dynasty)	1750 B.C 1720 B.C.	*ca.* 1950-1875 B.C.
G/4-2	Dense settlement; cist-tombs; Palestinian material	Late MB IIA (12th Dynasty)	1710 B.C. 1690 B.C.	*ca.* 1875-1825 B.C.
F	New town plan, numerous tombs; Palestinian material dominates; tr. to "Hyksos"	Transitional MB IIA/B (13th Dynasty)	1680 B.C. 1660 B.C.	*ca.* 1825-1775 B.C.
E/3	Consolidation of "Hyksos" town; Canaanite temples; first Asiatic rulers?	Early MB II (13th Dynasty)	1640 B.C. 1620 B.C.	*ca.* 1775-1725 B.C.
E/2	Large settlement; temples continue; major "Hyksos" period	Late MB IIB (13th Dynasty)		*ca.* 1725-1675 B.C.
E/1	Houses overflow; cemeteries and sacred area continue; = "Hyksos" 15th Dynasty	Transitional MB IIB/C (15th Dynasty)	1600 B.C. 1590 B.C.	*ca.* 1675-1625 B.C.
D/3	Increased occupation; burials below houses; = mid. "Hyksos" rule	Early MB IIC (15th Dynasty)	1570 B.C. 1560 B.C.	*ca.* 1625-1575 B.C.
D/2	Little Yehudiyeh ware; tombs with Eg. material; wholesale disruption at end	Late MB IIC (late 15th Dynasty)	1540 B.C. 1530 B.C.	*ca.* 1575-1525 B.C.
D/1	Erosion during gap; 18th Dynasty retaining wall	Transitional MB IIC/LB I	Post-1540 B.C.	*ca.* 1525-1475 B.C.
B	Temple refortifications of 18th-20th Dynasties; Ramesside "Per-Ramesses"		*ca.* 1310-1080 B.C.	
A	Small Ptolemaic settlement		3rd cent. B.C.	

Fig. 3:12. Strata of Tell el-Dab^{c}a, with comparative phases and chronology.

contemporary with 12th Dynasty contexts in Syria-Palestine. In any case, the example of the axe on the Tell el-Dab^{c}a seal offers no help. It does not itself yield an absolute date (certainly not 13th Dynasty, as Bietak's use of it would require); and at best it gives only a *terminus post quem* of *ca.* 2000-1800 B.C. since that seal, like so many others, may be an heirloom. On present evidence, while the seal would fit better with my date of *ca.* 1950-1875 B.C. for Stratum H than with Bietak's *ca.* 1750-1720 B.C. (1984: 478; cf. 1800-1770 B.C. in 1991: 32), it does not help very much.

As for the relative date of Str. H -- i.e., in comparison with the Syro-Palestinian sequence -- Bietak equates it with Albright's MB IIA, our MB I. However, he has published only a large jug in "Levantine Painted Ware" (1991: fig. 4). As has been shown by several authorities, and is now generally accepted, this distinctive style of painted ware characterizes Syria and northern Palestine in MB I, especially the middle (and later) phases (cf. Dever 1976: 13-15; Tubb 1983; Gerstenblith 1984: 59-77; Beck 1985: 196-198).

In addition, we have only a duckbill axe from T. Fl-0/19, no. 8 (Bietak 1991: fig. 3), a distinctive type of axe that can be shown not only to be typical of MB I in Syria-Palestine, but confined almost exclusively to that phase, or the transitional MB I/II phase at latest (above). Thus Str. H., with its typical Palestinian (*sic*) material, appears to be early-mid MB I; only its *absolute* date (especially its beginning) remains in dispute. Bietak has dated Str. H to 1750-1720 B.C. (1984: 479), or 1800-1775 B.C. (1991: 32); our date is *ca.* 2000/1950-1875 B.C. (Dever 1991: 75).

Str. G/4 = d/1.

This dating of Str. H well before the end of MB I, is confirmed by the little material published thus far from succeeding Str. G/4 (= d/1). This includes the metals from T. Fl-m/18, no. 3, a typical MB I assemblage consisting of a notched chisel-axe, a rilled dagger, and two socketed spears (Bietak 1991: 36). No pottery from Str. G/4 is published; but Bietak (1991: 36) states that there are no red-burnished carinated bowls present, although there are sherds of Middle Minoan IIA Kamares ware (see further Walberg 1993). In any case, Str. G/4 would seem to fall within Palestinian mid-MB I (in agreement with Bietak's *relative* assignment; cf. 1991: 32). Bietak's dates are 1710/1690 (1984: 479), or 1770-1750 B.C. (1991: 32); ours are *ca.* 1875-1800 B.C.

The only Egyptian items published thus far from Str. G/4 = d/1 are a serpentine statuette of an official found in the palace garden in T. F/I-1/19, no. 1 (Bietak 1991: 49, fig. 15); and fragments of a colossal seated statue of an Asiatic dignity, from the chapel of T. F/I-1/19, no. 1 (1991: 49, 50). Bietak says simply that the first statue "is dated stylistically to the 13th Dynasty," citing B.V. Bothmer (1991: 49). The other fragments are said to be "unthinkable in the time of the 12th Dynasty" (Bietak 1991: 50), on the presumption that Asiatics could not have risen to prominence (and be portrayed thus), until the 13th Dynasty. Methodologically, it is difficult to see how these observations can carry much chronological confidence.

It may be worth noting in passing that Bietak now (1991: 49) assigns the cylinder seal discussed above, with the representation of a duckbill axe, to Str. G/4 = d/1. In 1984, however, he attributed this cylinder seal to Str. d/1, but regarded that as "contemporary with or earlier than Str. H" (1984: 478). In either case, however, duckbill axes are MB I in date and could thus fit with either Str. H or G/4 in *relative* dates. For absolute chronology, however, this cylinder seal is largely irrelevant, as we have pointed out.

<u>**Str. G/1-3 = C.**</u>

No pottery has yet been published from this stratum. Bietak (1991: 38) comments, however, on the variety of classic late MB I Syro-Palestinian types: ovoid storejars; red-cross platter bowls; and red slipped and burnished carinated bowls, jugs, and juglets. Beck (1985: 199) has compared the latter with very similar wares and vessels from "Palace II/Ph. 3 and "Post-Palace"/Ph. 4 at Tel Aphek, which would fall late in MB I.

In addition, there is an assemblage of weapons of MB I types from T. m/15, no. 9 (Bietak 1979: fig. 4; cf. 1991: 38), which includes a ribbed dagger, notched chisel-axes, and socketed spears.

The only Egyptian items published thus far from this stratum are several lotus-back scarabs (Bietak 1984b: 333; 1989: 95, n. 80) Bietak, following Tufnell, O'Connor and Weinstein, dates these scarabs to the 13th Dynasty; but we show here that such scarabs are found in good MB I tomb contexts in Palestine and can predate the 13th Dynasty.

Another line of Bietak's reasoning in support of his low date for Str. G/1-3 = C is its alleged contemporaneity with the Valley Temple of Amenemhat III in Complex 7 at Dahshur, dated *ca.* mid-13th Dynasty (Bietak 1991: 51; cf. Arnold 1977; 1982: 39-42; Arnold and Stadelmann 1977: 15-20, pl. 46). There are several flaws in this reasoning. First, the link is admittedly formed only by means of Bietak's seriation of local Egyptian vessels, such as cups, beer jars, and bag-shaped jars, along with his Tell el-Yehudiyeh juglets of Type 1a. That is, the basis of argument rests on purely *typological* assumptions, which are notoriously subjective, and even at best can yield only a relative, not a fixed, chronology. In any case, Bietak's seriation is not published except in simplified graphs (such as 1991: figs. 13, 14), which do not actually illustrate vessel types and cannot be used with any confidence.

Only in the case of the Tell el-Yehudiyeh juglets has Bietak been more forthcoming with his much-vaunted seriation. Here he has indeed shown a progression of changes in punctate decoration from Str. G/4 through D/2. Yet several caveats must be entered.

(1) Such changes are largely in decorative style--in this case, from rather ornate to progressively simpler designs. They may be purely local, and if so they have little or no comparative value, even for *relative* chronology. For instance, some of the earliest, MB I Palestinian Yehudiyeh juglets are also more ornate, such as the example in T. 303B at Tell el-^{c}Ajjûl (Tufnell 1980: fig. 3: 11), similar to Bietak's Type 1a vessels from Str. G (1991: 38; fig. 12). Yet there are *simpler* styles of decoration right alongside these elaborate styles at Affuleh and other sites (below).

(2) Even if a consistent, fully comparable, reliable relative sequence of Yehudiyeh juglets could be worked out on typological grounds, it would still not be "anchored" anywhere without *historical* dates, such as those provided by literary sources. Bietak presents no such evidence. He can only fall back on the Dahshur Complex 7 dates. Yet Weinstein (1992: 32) cautions that the Dahshur pottery comes from "complexes" or sectors that are not derived from superimposed stratigraphic

levels, but are horizontally distributed assemblages. Not only can the pottery not be divided into neat sub-phases, but the dates ascribed by the Arnolds to these Dahshur complexes are much too broad to offer chronological precision. Finally, Bietak's frequent comparisons (Bietak 1984a: 480; 1991: 51) of Tell el-Dab^{c}a with Dahshur imply that the Arnolds have seen his pottery and concur that it is similar; in fact, there is no indication in any of the Dahshur publications that such is the case, or that they agree with the absolute dates Bietak gives to the Tell el-Dab^{c}a pottery. He dates Str. G/1-3 1750-1710 B.C. (1991: 32); we prefer 1800-1775 B.C.

Str. F = b/3.

In many ways Str. F = b/3, which both Bietak and we now agree to designate "transitional MB I/II" (his "MB IIA/B"; cf. Bietak 1991: 40, Dever 1992: 8, 9), is the critical horizon at Tell el-Dab^{c}a. Several Str. F vessels have been published: a large flat-based storejar (Bietak 1979: fig. 6B: 39); a red-cross platter bowl (1981: fig. 7; T. A/II, m/15, no. 8); and red-slipped and burnished button-based piriform juglets (pl. XXVI: b, c). In addition, two valuable tomb groups are published. T. A/II-m/10, no. 8 was first attributed by Bietak to either Str. F or E/3 (1979: fig. 6A; 244); but he now (1991: 40) regards it as belonging to Str. F, and quite properly so. The material (1981: fig. 6A; 6B) consists of early elaborate Yehudiyeh juglets; button-based red-slipped and burnished piriform juglets, some with candlestick rim; a large, flat-based ovoid storejar; two flat-based platter bowls; and an Egyptian cup. In addition, there is a classic MB I rilled dagger, together with the first appearance of the typical MB II shaft-hole axe. The latter *combination* would suit our transitional MB I/II horizon perfectly. T. A/II - m/15, no. 8 (1979: fig. 7) contains similar piriform juglets and an Egyptian cup, plus several small burnished biconical juglets and a red-cross platter bowl; a nearly identical example of the biconical juglets come from the "Post-Palace" phase of Tel Aphek (Beck 1975: fig. 12: 5), which falls late in MB I. Such a horizon for Dab^{c}a Str. F is confirmed by Bietak's observations (1991: 39) that by the time of Str. F carinated bowls are rare and the last of the handmade straight-sided cooking pots appear. Bietak compares the Str. F material to Jericho Tomb Group I and regards it as equivalent to Syro-Palestinian "transitional" MB I/II (Bietak 1984a: 484; cf. 1991: 110)--a view with which we agree entirely. Only on absolute chronology do we differ (below).

The Str. F Egyptian material consists of two fragments of different stone door jambs inscribed with the name of King Nehsy (Bietak 1991: 51), found in the area of the Str. F Temple III. Bietak proposes that the blocks came from this temple, and thus he dates Str. H to the late 18th cent. B.C. (1725-1700 B.C.) on the basis of Nehsy's dates. Yet he acknowledges that these blocks were actually *found* in pits of Str. A/2 and B, which are Ramesside and Ptolemaic in date (1991: 51). As Weinstein (1992: 30, 31) has pointed out, Bietak originally attributed these jambs to Str. G; but in any case they were not found *in situ* and thus have little or no chronological significance. Furthermore, Nehsy's dates are uncertain. They probably fall at the beginning of the 14th Dynasty; but that date depends in turn upon which of the several dates for the end of the 12th Dynasty is chosen. Even Bietak (1987: 50) has suggested only "approximately 1730-1720 B.C." for "a King Nehsy (or perhaps his father)."

Even if the jambs had come originally from the Str. H Temple III, dates for a King Nehesy or his father would not necessarily contradict our date of *ca.* 1775-1750 B.C. (in contrast to Bietak's 1725-1700 B.C.; Bietak 1991: 40).

In addition to the door jambs, the Str. H Egyptian material published thus far includes a scarab of "Deputy of the Treasurer, Aam" ("the Asiatic") from T. A/II-1/12, no. 5, which is said by Bietak (1991: 51) to have been a large donkey burial and to have contained typical MB I bronzes (cf. 1989a: 95; a notched chisel-axe and rilled dagger). Bietak follows Martin (1971: 29) in dating this seal to the 13th or 14th Dynasty, without, however, giving any reasons. As we have shown, what is known of its typology would allow for a 12th or 13th Dynasty date, so it is of no chronological value in Str. F.

A second Str. F scarab is one with a deeply incised human figure. Bietak (1984: 478) has argued that it has a corrupt inscription that could be read *rḫ-ny-nṯr*, and he dates it, without giving reasons, to *ca.* 1700-1650 B.C. Such speculations can hardly be taken as chronological evidence. In any case, Str. F marks the end of the long MB I tradition. Bietak (1991: 32) now dates it *ca.* 1710-1680 B.C.; we prefer 1775-1750, or our "transitional MB I/II horizon."

Str. E/3 = b/2.

Few pottery vessels or objects seem to have been published from Str. E/3. Bietak notes (1991: 40, 41) that the juglets are still in the button-base, candlestick rim tradition, but that most of the MB I types are now gone. The few published juglets (Bietak 1981: pl. XXVI: d; pl. XXVIII) include a Yehudiyeh juglet that would seem to belong to Bietak's Piriform Type 1 (cf. 1991: 45, fig. 12). There were few bronzes, none so far published.

The only item of Egyptian material thus far published is a scarab bearing the name "Sebekhotep." This scarab, first published in a photograph in 1970, was later read as "Sebekhotep IV" by Bietak (1979: 254), whose date of *ca.* 1720 B.C. would suit his own current date of *ca.* 1700-1660 B.C. for Str. E/3 (1991: 32; but in 1984: 477, no number given; and Str. E/3 now dated *ca.* 1640/1620 B.C.). Weinstein (1992: 31) has pointed out that this scarab could belong to any of several kings with the nomen Sebekhotep. And Ward suggests that its unique design -- unlike those of any known of the King Sebekhoteps -- makes it highly unlikely that it is even a royal name scarab. Thus, while a 13th Dynasty date is likely, this scarab has little if any bearing on the date of Str. F/3. Bietak dates this stratum 1680-1640 B.C. (1991: 32); we prefer 1750-1760 B.C., or precisely in Syro-Palestinian early MB IIB, following the transitional horizon in Str. F (above).

Str. E/2 = b/1.

Very little pottery has been published from Str. E/2. There is one red-cross platter bowl (Bietak 1979: pl. XXXII: a). Bietak comments (1991: 41) that by now candlestick rims have given way to folded rims on piriform juglets, and double handles are now succeeded by strap handles. These traits are not, of course, very diagnostic, but they would fit in MB II. Bietak (1989: 484) compares Str. E/2 with Jericho Tomb Group II, but comparisons are better with Tomb Group III. (Bietak's low chronology, of course, pulls down not only his own sequence, but also the Jericho tombs.) Str. E/2 is mid MB II in date. Bietak (1991: 32) dates it 1640-1620 B.C.; we prefer 1700-1675 B.C.

Str. E/1 = b/1-a/2.

The few Str. E/1 juglets published (Bietak 1979: pl. XXIX, T. M/11, no. 7; XXXI: c, d; 1990: 14, T. A/II-N/12, no. 7) include both simpler Yehudiyeh and red-burnished piriform types, neither closely datable. The same is true of a Cypriot White Pendent

Line jug (1981: pl. XXXIIIb), since these imports are now known to begin in Palestine as early as MB I (Dever 1976: 34; n. 104; Salz 1977; Johnson 1982). Another such Cypriot jug is published from T. m/11, no. 7 (Bietak 1981: fig. 13), along with Tell el-Yehudiyeh juglets of Piriform Type 2 (cf. Bietak 1991: fig. 12). A tomb attributed to the E/1-D/3 range (T. I/12, no. 1; Bietak 1981: fig. 14) cannot be used with precision. Another plate of general pottery from Str. E/ - D/2 (Bietak 1991: fig. 11) includes many good MB II and MB III Palestinian forms, but none are specified as to context. Bietak (1991: 43) states that there is now much less "metallic" burnish (characteristic of MB I and early MB I); an increase in imported Cypriot wares; and no longer any of the "warrior graves." He dates Str. 1620-1590 B.C. and compares it in part with Jericho Tomb Group II (plus Some III?). He, of course, places the Jericho tombs too late (above). However, his comparison -- if correct, and if correlated with the *proper* Palestinian chronology of Tomb Group II-III *ca.* 1750-1675 B.C. -- would tend to support our higher chronology of 1675-1625 B.C., rather than Bietak's 1620-1590 B.C. (1991: 32). In any case, Str. E/2 is late MB II.

Of significance is the fact that the *rdi-R*^{c} scarabs begin here, extending into Str. D/3 (Bietak 1991: 52). Traditionally considered a hallmark of the "Hyksos" 15th Dynasty (although they begin earlier), these scarabs would fit easily with this late MB II or transitional MB I/II stratum on either Bietak's dates of 1620-1590 B.C. (1991: 32), or our date of 1675-1625 B.C. Another scarab, of Sesostris I, is, of course, an heirloom.

<u>Str. D/3 = a/2</u>.

Little pottery is published from this stratum, although Bietak (1991: 44) states that there are no longer any red-cross bowls, and carinated bowls are rare. No Middle Bronze Age bronzes are said to have been found, although an earlier treatment (Bietak 1979: 263) describes a "warrior tomb" with knives, battle-axes, and daggers. Bietak (1991: 55) cites Jericho Tomb Group III for comparisons, but that clearly pulls this group down too late, to suit his low chronology. He thinks (1989a: 483) that a scarab in T. H 13, reading the name of the 15th Dynasty king "Sheshi/Meyibre," justifies this down-dating. He also cites (1984: 483) a scarab of a king "Nubkheperre" in Tomb Group II, and thus he argues that Tomb Group II, which falls early in MB II, must be lowered in date to the 17th Dynasty--thus supporting his low chronology for Tell el-Dab^{c}a. If Bietak were correct in his understanding, then Tomb Groups II and III would have to be dated some 75 years later. Ward, however (1984), has shown that the readings of these two scarabs (and one other) are simply *erroneous*, so Bietak's argument falls apart (cf. his retort, 1991: 55, 56, hardly persuasive). In any case, the "Sheshi" scarab does not belong with Tomb Group III, as Bietak states, but rather with *Tomb Group V* (*Jericho* II): 583), which on everyone's reckoning is "Hyksos"/15th Dynasty, which adds nothing to our knowledge of chronology.

A scarab of an unknown Hyksos king (?) was discovered in Str. D/3, as were *rdi-R*^{c} and ^{c}*n r*^{c} scarabs; but these belong easily to the "Hyksos" era and would agree both with Bietak's (1991: 32) date of 1590-1560 B.C. for Str. D/3, or ours of 1625-1575 B.C. Two bronze plates of Neferhotep I, *ca.* 1725 B.C. (1991: 53), intentionally destroyed, are from an earlier context than Str. D/3 and thus are insignificant for purposes of chronology.

<u>Str. D/2</u>.

The final Middle Bronze Age stratum, D/2, is not represented by any published

Levantine pottery. The first Late Cypriot I wares appear here, however, including a White Painted V bowl from T. m/11, no. 1 (Bietak 1979: pl. XXXIII:a); and White Slip I ware (cf. Åström 1989: 58). The latter ware also occurs sporadically at the very end of MB III and the transition to LB IA in Palestine, *ca.* 1550-1500 B.C. (Dever 1992: 14-16). In any case, Bietak's date for the end of Str. D/2--coinciding with the fall of Avaris and the expulsion of the "Hyksos"--is 1560-1530 B.C. (1991: 32), and ours of 1575-1530 B.C. is virtually identical.

Bietak (1991: 53) states that there are no 18th Dynasty scarabs, as should be the case. A tripartite pattern scarab of the "chancellor" Har is a common "Hyksos" type and would be in place in Str. D/2. The remainder of the Str. D/2 scarabs are typical of the "Hyksos" period, such as scarabs with twisted-rope and tripartite patterns, $^{c}n\ r^{c}$ signs, and deeply cut figures.

In conclusion, there is absolutely nothing at Tell el-Dab^{c}a *published thus far*, in either the Levantine imports or the local Egyptian material, that would give unqualified support to Bietak's low chronology, *or* his attempt to lower the dates of the Middle Bronze phases of Syria-Palestine. His often-promised presentations of the material in full, when published, may of course change the present picture (such as Christine Mlinar's work on the scarabs). In the meantime, however, the middle chronology proposed here still represents the overwhelming consensus among Syro-Palestinian specialists. And the lower range of dates proposed by Bietak and O'Connor for certain types of scarabs -- based on a faulty understanding of comparable scarabs in Syro-Palestinian archaeological contexts -- must yield to the higher dates proposed here.

17. Tell el-Dab^{c}a and the Seriation of Tell el-Yehudiyeh Juglets.

From early preliminary reports on, Bietak (cf. 1979: 234; 1984a: 474, 480; 484, 485; 1989: 81-87; 1991: 38-45, 55, 59-61) has made much of this seriation of Tell el-Yehudiyeh juglets at Tell el-Dab^{c}a, adopting the typological scheme of Kaplan (1980). As time goes on, his confidence in the value of such sequences for determining chronology seems to grow. Lately he has promised an elaborately worked out seriation of local Egyptian hemispherical drinking cups, based largely on size and proportion, and attempting a correlation with the Arnolds' sequence at Dahshur (1991: 49-53). He concludes (1984: 481) that "this system seems to be a very fine tool for relative and absolute dating in Egypt." It may eventually become such a tool for relative dating, even though there are many pitfalls here; but how so for Egyptian *absolute* dating (much less for Syria-Palestine)?

Bietak's rather simplistic use of his Yehudiyeh juglet series raises a number of fundamental questions about typological methods, questions that he has not adequately addressed.

(1) First, it is axiomatic in typological analysis that one must develop and spell out explicitly the diagnostic criteria that one is using. If the exercise is not to be entirely subjective, these criteria should constitute a pattern of a *cluster* of traits, which can be shown to be essential to, and characteristic of, the basic "type" that one is seeking to discern. The difficulty in doing this has to do with the long-standing controversy in general archaeology about whether ideal "types" are discovered or designed--i.e., whether the postulation of a type has any empirical basis, or is merely invented for the convenience of the cataloger of individual artifacts.

Bietak's chief criterion for seriating Tell el-Yehudiyeh juglets is elaborateness of design. His assumption that the design becomes simpler over time is unstated; but it is indeed similar to assumptions that most Palestinian specialists make in their own typological analyses of many ceramic forms. Such assumptions, however, must be proven in stratigraphic contexts and sequences--i.e., one must show both overlapping sequences (the familiar "battleship curve" that Bietak employs, not very convincingly; 1991: fig. 14, 15), and finally in mutually exclusive temporal distributions.

To illustrate the problem, a chart of Bietak (1991: fig. 12) shows the occurrence of Tell el-Yehudiyeh juglet forms at Tell el-Dab^{c}a by type and stratum. Here it does appear that the more elaborately decorated "Piriform 1" juglets with triangular decoration occur only in Str. G - E/2, while simpler band-motif juglets of "Piriform 2" type span Str. E/1 - D/2. That scheme is "logical" enough, and it seems to confirm Bietak's relative chronology -- *given* his beginning assumption. It is worth noting in passing that Bietak seems to think that his notion of progressively simpler decoration is implicit in Kaplan's original typology, but it is not necessarily so as Kaplan (1980: 70-72) had dated her Piriform 1 juglets to MB I and MB I/II, and Piriform 2 juglets to MB I/II through late MB II, i.e., with a chronological overlap that Bietak's scheme (1991: fig. 12) does not allow for at all.

In Palestine, however -- which, contrary to Kaplan (1980: 66; 74; 121-123), we now know to be (with Syria) the home of this ceramic type -- Bietak's typological assumptions can be shown to be false. A potter's workshop at Affuleh excavated in 1950, but only recently published (Zevulun 1990), confirms what some of us have long suspected: Tell el-Yehudiyeh vessels of various "subtypes" that are based largely on *decoration* are often contemporary, i.e., not chronologically valid or useful types at all. The 36 Tell el-Yehudiyeh juglets from Affuleh are not only from a homogenous deposit in a single potter's refuse pit, but they occur together with ordinary local MB I sherds that date them precisely (Zevulun 1990: 107*). The essential point is that the range of decorative designs in the assemblage of juglets includes Bietak's (and Kaplan's) elaborate "Type I" piriform juglets with triangle-design (1990: 180-182) *together with* "Type 2" piriform juglets with horizontal or vertical band-design (1990: 183, 184). Indeed, a close examination shows that the homogeneous Affuleh group of Tell el-Yehudiyeh juglets embraces *all* of Bietak's "types" from Tell el-Dab^{c}a Str. H through Str. D/2 (compare Zevulun: 180-184 *passim*, with Bietak 1991: fig. 12), a time-span of at least 250 years. It should be noted that Tufnell's recent (1985) restudy of the Yehudiyeh juglets from Tell el-Yehudiyeh itself shows a similar mixture of decorative design "types" side by side--"earlier and later"--in graves that must all be confined to the 15th Dynasty. These facts completely vitiate Bietak's (and also Kaplan's more modest) attempt to base even a relative chronology on the design (or, for that matter, simply on the form) of Tell el-Yehudiyeh juglets of Syro-Palestinian or local Egyptian derivation. The matter is much more complicated than that.

2. That brings us to the second caveat, the problem of stratigraphic control. All of Bietak's published examples of Tell el-Yehudiyeh juglets are from tombs. There is a problem here. Bietak (1991: 55) does recognize the difficulty of using pottery from the Jericho tombs, due to their long period of use (although he seems to accept the chronological arrangement of Kenyon's "Groups" at face value). But it is noteworthy that his own tombs, although mostly individual burials and thus much more homogeneous, cannot always be securely assigned to a particular stratum. Thus T. A/II-m/10, no. 8 was originally assigned to Str. F or E/3, but it is now regarded as belonging to Str. F (cf. Bietak 1981: 244; 1991: 40). Such vacillation is understandable, as every experienced field archaeologist knows, since even intramural tombs are often difficult to stratify precisely. Whatever the reasons, Bietak's tomb groups may not be

as closely stratified as he suggests.

Furthermore, both Kerma and the Dahshur sequence of "complexes," on which Bietak depends so heavily (cf. Bietak 1984: 475-482; 1991: 49-51), lack good stratigraphic controls. Bietak's confident citation of material from these sites, as though it confirms his own chronological framework at Tell el-Dab^{c}a, is quite misleading. Elsewhere (Dever 1991: 76) we have treated the Dahshur material and its significance; and for Kerma, Bietak is dependent upon the highly idiosyncratic chronology of Bruce Williams (Bietak 1981: 234; 1984: 475). Finally, even if the Kerma and Dahshur dates for assemblages there *were* historically anchored, Bietak's Tell el-Dab^{c}a link with those assemblages is purely by means of typological comparisons. And even if the material from all three sites were published (it is not), the stylistic comparisons would remain subjective at best; and even under optimum conditions such comparisons could not possibly yield a date precise enough to decide between Bietak's chronological preferences and ours. His insistence that his comparisons will carry the day (i.e., 1991: 27, 28)--and, moreover, will force a revision of *Levantine* chronology -- betrays a fundamental misunderstanding of what typology is and how it can contribute to absolute chronology. Again, Bietak has been misled in part by Kaplan's early attempt at typology (to which few Syro-Palestinian archaeologists have lent credence). A close examination of her "Piriform" and "Ovoid" types, based ostensibly on form, will show that the shapes are often indistinguishable, so this particular distinction is too subjective to be useful.

(3) Next there is the problem of correlating relative sequences with absolute historical dates, i.e., with events in political history that can be dated by written evidence such as texts or Royal Name scarabs (for Egypt, preferably those corroborated by astronomical calculations). It cannot be stressed too strongly that Bietak's entire list of "datable objects" published thus far (as 1984: 478; cf. 1991: 47-53) fails to meet this fundamental criterion for absolute chronology (Dever 1991). In fact, apart from the dubious Egyptian connections at Kerma and Dahshur (above), it is obvious that Bietak's dates for his Tell el-Dab^{c}a sequence are dependent upon synchronisms with Syro-Palestinian materials and their historical-cultural context -- exactly the reverse of his claim that Levantine chronology must be dependent upon Egypt! (Bietak, who earlier looked to Syria for almost all his Levantine imports, now accepts the clear evidence of neutron activation analysis that much of this ware is from Palestine, as I have long insisted; see Dever 1975: 29, 30; 1985; cf. Bietak 1991: 33-41). Egyptian dates *might* take precedence, but only if historically fixed dates can be directly correlated with archaeological assemblages in both areas, in a way that Bietak has yet to show.

(4) Finally, even a valid and securely anchored typological sequence may have only local significance, since typological developments do not proceed according to universal laws (if any at all). Thus even if Bietak's seriation of Tell el-Yehudiyeh juglets at Tell el-Dab^{c}a is valid for Egypt, it may not necessarily correspond to ceramic developments in Syria-Palestine. Bietak does now acknowledge, of course, that many of the Tell el-Dab^{c}a juglets are Levantine imports and therefore should reflect ceramic developments in both their homeland and Egypt quite faithfully. The Affuleh potter's workshop, however, demonstrates that it is precisely these Yehudiyeh juglets that are "specialty items," i.e., luxury goods manufactured primarily for trade and export. As such, they may be especially made for certain markets, including Egypt. However that may be, it does seem to be a fact that the Syro-Palestinian and Delta sequences of these unique juglets are different, demonstrably so. Thus the typology of "Levantine" wares in

Egypt cannot be determinative for Syro-Palestinian ceramic chronology. If anything, it must be the other way around. That, in essence, is why Syro-Palestinian archaeologists have staunchly resisted Bietak's unilateral attempt to lower Levantine dates for the Middle Bronze Age by a century or more (cf. Dever, 1985; 1991 and references there).

As a postscript on the typology of the Tell el-Yehudiyeh juglets, we should note that Bietak's chronological starting point -- on which the rest of his relative and absolute sequence hangs -- is apparently his adoption of Kaplan's early (1980) formulation, explicit from 1989, if not earlier (cf. 1989: 100, n. 9). Kaplan argued that (1) these juglets originated in Egypt, and were then imported into Syria-Palestine (and Cyprus); and (2) thus they occur somewhat later in the latter areas, i.e., mostly in MB I/II and especially in MB II (1980: 66; 71-73; 121-123). Of Kaplan's 11 sub-types, she regarded only 3 as beginning in Syria-Palestine in MB I, and placed these late in the period: her Ovoid 2, 3, and 5. Even in Egypt, she thought that the Yehudiyeh juglets began only in the late 12th/early 13th Dynasty (1980: 74). These conclusions suit Bietak's view that the Tell el-Yehudiyeh juglets, which begin at Tell el-Dab^{c}a only in Str. G/4, are later than the Levantine Painted Ware that begins in Str. H, i.e., they do not precede the 13th Dynasty (cf. 1984: 432; 1991: 33, 36). But this is obviously an argument from silence; and the argument compounds the error in assuming from Tell el-Dab^{c}a that Tell el-Yehudiyeh juglets do not precede the 13th Dynasty in *Syria-Palestine*. (Bietak does acknowledge MB I origins for this ware; but his low absolute chronology forces him nevertheless to date it mid-late MB I to the 13th Dynasty).

Today, Kaplan's conclusions are no longer valid; nor is Bietak's continued reliance upon them, revealed in such statements as "knowledge about the relative chronology of the Tell el-Yehudiyeh ware can be used for a chronological plotting of the different styles represented in Tell el-Dab^{c}a" (1989: 91).

(1) First, we now know a number of early examples of Tell el-Yehudiyeh juglets from good MB I contexts in Palestine, clearly antedating the 13th Dynasty, as well as Bietak's earliest occurrences in Dab^{c}a Str. G/3 (his dates for G/3-1 are 1750-1710 B.C., ours 1800-1775 B.C.). These examples predate Dab^{c}a G/3 even on our higher chronology. The MB I examples include, among others, Tell el-Yehudiyeh juglets of Kaplan's Piriform 1-2 type at Affuleh, discussed above; in Tombs 911 A1, 5137, 5171, and 5177 at Megiddo; sherds at Tell Qashish; the Tel ^{c}Amr tomb; and T. 303A at Tell el-^{c}Ajjûl, as well as T. 1406, 1407, and 1410a. Furthermore, in Syria, older tomb groups with Tell el-Yehudiyeh juglets, such as T. 62 at Ruweisé and the Sin el-Fil tomb, can now be dated more confidently to MB I, or to MB I/II at the latest (above).

(2) Recent evidence for Syro-Palestinian dates earlier than those in Egypt for the appearance of Tell el-Yehudiyeh juglets suggests a Levantine origin, contra Kaplan. This is now confirmed by neutron activation analysis, which Kaplan herself first undertook (1980: 47-66), although at the time she did not see the full implications. She was able to take only limited samples, from both Egypt and Syria-Palestine, but only a few from Tell el-Dab^{c}a. She observed that juglets of Egyptian provenience were found in Egypt and Syria-Palestine; but she had only one juglet of Palestinian provenience from Egypt, an Ovoid from Tell el-Dab^{c}a Str. F, T. a/II - m/15, no. 8. Since her presumption was (cf. 1980: 66) that the origin of Yehudiyeh ware was in Egypt, she was "surprised" at even this one Palestinian juglet (1980: 100). She concluded:

> In summary, then, we have seen that the chemical proveniences for the different types of Tel el Yehudiyeh ware correspond highly to the geographic pattern of the findspots. The evidence is sufficient to say that there are Egyptian types manufactured in Egypt and exported elsewhere. There are also Syro-Palestinian types, but the only example of their being found outside Syro-Palestine is the one vessel from Tell el-Dab^{c}a (1980: 66).

Here one sees starkly the dangers of statistical statements and far-reaching historical-cultural conclusions reached on the basis of very small and often unrepresentative samples. Now that a much more extensive sample from Tell el-Dab^{c}a (1700 sherds) is being tested, in a systematic program at the Museum of Applied Science Center for Archaeology (MASCA) at the University of Pennsylvania (Bietak 1989: 101, n. 11), Kaplan's picture is completely overturned. With some groups of Dab^{c}a ceramics, as much as 90% of the wares come from the Levant -- and from *Palestine*, not Syria. Bietak has thus far only hinted at these results (as 1991: 33, 36, 38, 39); but they effectively dispose of his earlier view that the Delta Middle Bronze Age/Levantine culture stemmed from "coastal Syria" (1981: 272), or was brought to Egypt by "a major migration of Byblites by sea to the Eastern Delta, where their kinsmen had already established themselves" (1984: 474). It is only the latter clause that has any claim to historical and archaeological validity; and how did these "kinsmen" arrive in Egypt, if not by the most logical process, i.e., overland migrations from central and southern Palestine? Here is where virtually all of Bietak's Levantine material has its best, more frequent, and most closely dated parallels -- as pointed out long ago by some (e.g., de Vaux 1971: 80, 81; Dever 1975: 19, 30; 1985). To be sure, Bietak has referred, rather obliquely, to "Syro-Palestinian culture" at Tell el-Dab^{c}a (1984: 474); to extensive "Syro-Palestinian trade" with Egypt (1991: 28); or to an "Asiatic community" that had established itself in the Delta (1979: 273). But he has been reluctant to draw the appropriate conclusion -- especially *chronological* -- from his own excavation and research. The earlier Egyptian Middle Bronze Age levels at Tell el-Dab^{c}a, Str. H-G-F, must be understood and dated from Palestine, not *vice versa*. In particular, the *earlier* manifestation of this culture in Syria-Palestine--in early MB I, shortly after *ca.* 2000 B.C., and certainly within the 12th Dynasty -- must not be underestimated, simply because it did not appear until somewhat later in the Delta.

NOTES

[1] For general orientation to the Palestinian Middle Bronze Age, see Mazar 1968; Kenyon 1973; Dever 1976, 1987b; Gerstenblith 1983; Kempinski 1983, 1992b; and Ilan 1993. For the MB I-III framework that we adopt here -- rather than Albright's MB IIA-C -- see Dever 1987b, 1992; this simpler, more rational terminology is gradually being adopted (Gerstenblith 1983; cf. Ilan 1993: 229). See further fig. 3:1. Details on individual sites discussed below will be found conveniently in the four-volume *Encyclopedia of Archaeological Excavations in the Holy Land,* edited by E. Stern (New York: Simon & Schuster, 1993; = *EAEHL*).

[2] On Hazor, see Yadin 1972; Yadin *et al.* 1958; 1960; Malamat 1989; Kempinski 1992b: 169, 184-88.

---

[3]On Megiddo, see Kenyon 1958; Epstein 1965; Dunayevsky and Kempinski 1973; Tufnell 1973; Kempinski 1992b: 168, 186, 187.

[4]On Shechem, see principally Wright 1965; Dever 1974.

[5]On Jericho, see Kenyon 1957; 1960; 1965; 1973; Kempinski 1992b: 188, 189.

[6]On Aphek, see Kochavi 1975; Beck 1975; 1985; Kempinski 1992b: 169

[7]On Gezer, see Dever *EAEHL* ; Dever, Lance, and Wright 1970; Dever *et al.* 1974; 1984.

[8]See further Coote and Whitelam 1987; Joffe 1991; LaBianca 1990; Knapp 1992.

CHAPTER 4

THE MONTET JAR SCARABS

The well-known Montet Jar deposit was discovered by Pierre Montet during the first official excavations at Byblos (ancient *Gubla*) in the early 1920's (Montet 1928: 111-25, pls. 60-71). Found within the precinct of what later came to be known as the Baalat Gubla temple, this large storage jar containing some one thousand objects has been an enigma from the start. It is generally agreed that this deposit is the earliest of over 40 such jar deposits in the temple compounds at Byblos[1] though its contents are markedly different from the others. The Montet Jar was filled with a mixed collection of objects, both foreign and local, which do not fit into the category of votive offerings that characterize the contents of all the other jar deposits from this site.

Numerically, the contents of the jar deposits are strongly dominated by small male figurines, probably Reshep, and weapons -- daggers, spearheads, and fenestrated axes. Animal figurines are also found and there are many miscellaneous objects of metal, rarely ivory or bone. The figurines and weapons, however, are so prominent that one can hardly escape the conclusion that this material originally constituted votive offerings. There was an apparent plan in collecting these objects as some jars contained mostly weapons (Dunand 1954-58: 8287, 8359, 9614, 10107, 10653, etc.) while others contained mostly figurines (Dunand 1939: 2000, 2064; 1954-58: 7852, 9673, 9686, 10237, etc.). Some jars combine both types of objects. The number of objects in individual jars ranges from half a dozen to several hundred.

Torque-wearer material, so prominent in the Montet Jar, is only common in one other deposit (Dunand 1939: 2131 from the Baalat Gubla temple) with isolated pieces appearing in other jars. Egyptian objects, again a hallmark of the Montet Jar, are restricted to a few scarabs (mostly from Dunand 1939: 2285) and a cylindrical pendant (Dunand 1939: 2314). The overall character of these jar deposits is thus overwhelmingly local in sharp contrast to the Montet Jar collection with its strong foreign connections. The latter also lacks the figurines and weapons which characterize the other jar deposits as a group. It thus seems proper to assume that the Montet Jar collection was assembled for a reason which does not apply to the rest of these deposits.

In the Montet Jar, there were Egyptian figurines, amulets, bits of jewelry, a complete bead collar, and the controversial group of 68 scarabs. There are pieces with Mesopotamian connections as well as Syrian, the most important being the large collection of bangles, torques, and toggle pins associated with the "torque-wearers" prominent at Ugarit and other sites.[2] The collection as a whole is dominated by the Egyptian and "torque-wearer" material, neither of which appears -- with isolated exceptions -- in any of the other jar deposits. The Montet Jar is thus unique among these storage jars with regard to contents.

One can only speculate on the overall nature of the Montet Jar deposit and the reasons for its being collected and buried in the first place. The contents differ so markedly from that of the other jars that this deposit cannot consist of votive offerings cleared away from a temple altar to make room for new ones. Nor do the contents suggest the jar represents a foundation deposit. The idea that these objects form a jeweler's stock in trade (Tufnell and Ward 1966: 217) accounts for the unique character of the collection, but why would a craftsman's private stock be buried in a temple precinct?

Such craftsmen were associated with temples or even belonged to the temple personnel[3] though this cannot be proved in the present case.

It is now generally accepted that this composite hoard covers the EB IV - MB I periods[4] and that this range in date precludes the use of this deposit as a fixed point in absolute chronology. Since the detailed discussion of this material by Tufnell and Ward in 1966, new studies have appeared bearing on the general problem of the date when the jar was buried that indicate a time somewhat later than the Heracleopolitan age as suggested at that time (Saghieh 1983; Ward 1987). More information about individual objects in the jar has been published, for example, the gold medallion with granulation and inlays,[5] the gold head from a *psš-kf* amulet,[6] the bronze flask,[7] and more can be said concerning the Old Kingdom inscribed ivory label.[8] All in all, it now seems certain that the deposit was buried during the MB I Age, that is, sometime during the period of the Egyptian 12th Dynasty. This gives a general context for the scarabs from the Montet Jar and it is argued here, as elsewhere, that, on typological grounds, the scarabs must date to the early 12th Dynasty.

The Montet Jar scarabs have presented a problem with regard to their date ever since their discovery. Montet himself suggested they are close to Hyksos style, a date which has been adopted by many down to the present (Montet 1928: 129; Negbi and Moskowitz 1966: 24, n. 19; O'Connor 1987: 36-37; Kemp and Merrillees 1980: 45; Giveon 1973: 88) An alternative date has been proposed by Tufnell and Ward, though their original chronology of these scarabs is too high. As their scarab project has evolved over the past quarter century, it has become evident that the Heracleopolitan date suggested in 1966 is much too early and that the late 11th Dynasty date proposed by Ward (1978) is still somewhat early. The continuing study of this group and the publication of additional pertinent material has rather indicated that this collection belongs in the early 12th Dynasty (Ward 1987: 512). This is the date generally preferred by specialists on Canaan for the deposit as a whole (see Chap. 1). While, as Weinstein (1992: 36) argues, these scarabs do not contribute to the larger problem of MB chronology, they do have importance in the historical chronology of scarab style. When examined without preconceptions as to how early or late they *ought* to be, this group presents a near ironclad typological argument as to just where they must be placed in the design scarab series.

Overall, the Montet Jar scarabs can be characterized as dominated by typological features carried over from the FIP, Period I, and totally lacking in several typological features dominant in the 12th to 15th Dynasties, Periods IIA-V. This group shows a predominance of lined backs (91%), A1 and A3 heads (48%), and design classes 1 and 3 Early (31%), all of which are major components of Period I scarab style. Missing are heads A4, A6, D5, D6, sides d5, e8 to e10, and designs 3B and 7 to 10; at least some of these features are found in any group of scarabs made at any time during the 12th to 15th Dynasties. This is a crucial point which has not been sufficiently taken into account by those who prefer a date later than the first decades of the 12th Dynasty. Even small groups of three or four scarabs from Middle Kingdom or Hyksos age contexts will evidence some of the features just enumerated. What is missing in the typological profile of this group is just as important as what is included.[9]

Other stylistic features fit into this pattern. The a, b, and c sides which account for 87% of the side corpus in the FIP, are still notably present in the Montet Jar group (16%), but appear in the 12th to 15th Dynasties only as rare and isolated examples. Scarab length, not a decisive but certainly a secondary argument, shows an average length of 12.5 mm in the FIP, 13.7 mm in the Montet Jar group, and 15-17 mm in the 12th to 15th Dynasties. The Montet Jar group fits where it should in the steady average increase of design scarab size; see Chap. 9, Table 13. Other side types are also of some importance here. The Montet Jar group has no d sides at all other than a few examples of d1, a carryover from the FIP. It rather emphasizes e sides, especially e5 and e6; e5 is especially prominent only in this group, e6 only here and in the 12th Dynasty.

None of these factors in themselves is decisive for dating, but their collective weight leaves no alternative to a position in the stylistic history of design scarabs immediately following the FIP, but preceding the classical style of the 12th Dynasty (Chap. 5).

For the sake of argument, it should be pointed out that lined backs, heads A1 and A3, and sides a, b, and c -- all of which characterize the FIP and Montet Jar scarabs -- are again found as common typological features of New Kingdom scarabs. Such a late date, of course, is out of the question for the Montet Jar deposit. Also important to note is the faulty argument that since lined backs dominate the 13th Dynasty royal name scarabs, the Montet Jar scarabs must date to that period (O'Connor 1985: 33). Here one must keep in mind that the 13th Dynasty royal name scarabs have a unique and atypical typology on all counts and in no way represent a valid stage in the development of scarab style (see Chap. 2).

It is not necessary to answer in detail the other basic argument against an early date: the Montet Jar scarabs are dominated by design class 4, concentric circles, and the only other group which compares in terms of frequency of use is that from Sedment Cemetery K of the 15th Dynasty. This argument has been taken up in detail elsewhere (Ward 1987: 515-16) and it need only be remarked here that the two groups are totally different in all typological categories, including design class 4. The class 4 designs in the Montet Jar, on the scarabs as well as on several ovoids, belong to the early stages in the evolution of this design; the Sedment scarabs show only the latest stage of class 4 designs (4E) which is the one that continues into the New Kingdom. This is a clear example in which the details of style are important, in this case the historical sequence of varieties of a rather simple design. Furthermore, it is not true, as often stated, that concentric circle designs were not used on seals and scarabs as early as the date proposed for the Montet Jar group. There are six round seals of early Middle Kingdom date with concentric circle designs that parallel those in the Montet Jar collection.[10]

While the Montet Jar itself, its stratigraphic position, and its contents all suggest a date for the burial of this deposit in the early second millennium B.C.,[11] in the present context it is unnecessary to go beyond the broader view that the jar was deposited at some time during the MB I Age. The pertinent question here is where the collection of scarabs in the deposit fit in the typological history of this class of object. It seems quite possible that the final phase of the Period I scarabs may last into the early years of the 12th Dynasty. The Montet Jar group cannot be far removed from Period I and must therefore fall somewhere in the reigns of Amenemhat I and Sesostris I which, by the absolute chronology used here would be *ca.* 1963-1898 B.C., very probably toward the beginning of that period.[12]

NOTES

1 Conveniently listed by Negbi and Moscowitz 1966, though their conclusion as to when all these jars were buried -- the late 18th century B.C. -- is incorrect.

2 The so-called "torque-wearers" represent a probably new ethnic element at Ugarit, Byblos, and several other sites on the coast and inland Syria. This group is characterized by a metallurgical industry using molds in which were cast torques, fenestrated axes, toggle-pins, bracelets, and other objects. At Ugarit, their burials contain a wide variety of these metal objects, but no pottery; inland, their burials have ample pottery, but the metal objects are mostly toggle-pins with the rare torque or weapon. It is generally agreed that the torque-wearers, as represented by their metalwork, arrived in the coastal towns at the end of the Early Bronze Age and the very beginning of the Middle Bronze. The major discussion of this group remains that of Schaeffer 1939: 49-120; see also Kenyon 1966: 39-42, and 1971: 585-87. On the stratigraphy of Ugarit which establishes that of coastal Syria, see Ward 1971: 11-17; North 1973; Courtois 1974.

3 Note, for example, the artisans' workshop within the precinct of the Temple of the Obelisks at Byblos; Dunand 1954-58: 651. This, however, seems to have been primarily for the manufacture of votive objects.

4 E.g, Gerstenblith 1983: 40; Tubb 1983: 49; Bietak 1991:54; Dever 1992: 5; Weinstein 1992: 36. The latter points out that the three small metal vessels in the deposit may carry over into the MB II Age. However, they do have parallels in Hama H pottery vessels. Weinstein further notes that such carinated vessels with ring bases appear earlier in Syria than in Palestine which simply gives support to the MB I date; Byblian connections should be sought in Syria rather than Palestine.

5 Maxwell-Hyslop (1971: 102-03) regards this medallion as unique and made by a local craftsman imitating Sumerian metalwork. Lilyquist (1993: 38-39), on the other hand, sees this object within the framework of a "Byblos style" of granulation closely connected to the metalwork of Trialeti in Georgia.

6 Tufnell and Ward 1966, fig. 4: 87. Two FIP examples similar to the Byblos piece have recently been published in D'Auria, Lacovara, and Roehrig 1988: 244, nos. 177a-b; both are from unpublished burials at Mesheikh and Sheikh Farag. On the ritual use of the *pss-kf* and its meaning "fish-tailed knife (made of) flint (or obsidian?)," see Van Walsem 1978-79; Helck 1969; Graefe 1971.

7 Tufnell and Ward 1966, fig. 9: 208. This little vessel was unique until the discovery of the "Tomb of the Princess" at Tell Mardikh of the MB I Age. Among the objects in the tomb is a small sardonyx jar which is a near-perfect parallel to the Byblos piece; Matthiae 1980: 8.

8 Tufnell and Ward 1966, fig. 4: 89. The reference in Tufnell and Ward 1966: 193, n. 8, to a "Treasurer of Horus" is incorrect; cf. Fischer 1961: 24. The plural spelling, as if *sḏ3tiw Ḥr Sṯḥ*, on the ivory label is paralleled in Epron, *et al.* 1939, pl. 17. The Byblos title is perhaps best rendered "Treasurer of the King (Horus-Seth)."

---

[9]Weinstein 1992: 36, argues that the Montet Jar scarabs are "dominated by a few designs that are absent or poorly represented at Middle Kingdom type sites like Kahun and Uronarti," a circumstance which may "be more a function of the nonrandom nature and possible origin of the group than a useful chronological indicator." But he deals here only with the designs and his comment would be well taken were designs the only issue. In reality, there are also head and side types missing, notably sides d5 and e9 which are characteristic from Scarab Period IIA onward.

Weinstein's other reservation (1992:42, n. 33) concerns the use of carnelian and quartz for a dozen of the Montet Jar scarabs, materials which "are out of place in a pre-12th Dynasty setting." For some reason, Weinstein here quotes the now discarded dating of this group in Tufnell and Ward 1966 rather than the revised early 12th Dynasty date established in Ward 1987.

[10]Brunton and Engelbach 1927, pl. 12:3; Brunton 1930, pl. 6:18; two from early Middle Kingdom burials at Mesheikh (Boston MFA 12.1381, 12.1382, unpublished; two from contemporary burials at Sheikh Farag (Berkeley, Hearst Museum of Anthropology 6-13144, 6-13821, unpublished). The archaeological contexts in which the unpublished objects were found assures this date. These six examples are sufficient to show that concentric circle designs were firmly fixed in the design repertoire by the 11th Dynasty.

[11]On the stratigraphy, see Saghieh 1983: 51-52, 110-16, who suggests the Montet Jar was buried in the 20th century B.C. While this is disputed by some, Saghieh spent 20 years investigating the stratigraphy of Byblos and her opinion should not be taken lightly even though she admits that "the exact level is still and will remain a surmise" (1983: 40).

[12]It now seems likely that the scarab group from Ruweisé tomb 66, among which is a scarab naming Sesostris I, dates very close to the reign of that king; cf. Chap. 3F.14. Since this group belongs to the classical Middle Kingdom style (Chap. 5C), the Montet Jar group which must precede it on typological grounds would come early in the 12th Dynasty.

CHAPTER 5

PERIOD IIA: SCARABS FROM CANAANITE MB I AND I/II CONTEXTS

A. THE SCARABS: CLASSIFICATION

In this chapter, we collect those scarabs found in Syria-Palestine in archaeological contexts of the MB I and transitional MB I/II periods. For the sake of convenience, this group will be henceforth referred to as the IIA group, or Period IIA. Other than the few FIP scarabs from Byblos and those from the Montet Jar, this group represents the earliest collection of scarabs from datable archaeological deposits. As such, it should provide a reasonably well fixed point in the development of scarab style which, to anticipate the chronological discussion below and in Chap. 8, falls within the range of the 12th Dynasty.

In the following pages, the scarabs are described site by site following the system used in Tufnell 1984 with the new classification of back-types as explained in Chaps. 1C and 9B. The scarabs are numbered after fig. 5:1. Discussions of the individual archaeological contexts are found in Chap. 3.

TELL EL- ᶜAJJUL COURTYARD CEMETERY

CONTEXT: MB I. Chap. 3F.13
SCARABS:

No.	Length	Description	Design	Reference
1	18	D6 LSd e10	10C1a	Tufnell 1962, fig. 7:1, tomb 1406
2	16	A6 PS d6	2A	*ibid.*, fig. 7:2, tomb 1406
3	17	D4 LSd e10	3A3	*ibid.*, fig. 7:3, tomb 1410B
4	19	D5 PS e9	1E3, 3A1	*ibid.*, fig. 7:4, tomb 1410C
5	17	C5 PN e6	2B, 11A	Tufnell 1980, fig. 3:5, tomb 303A
6	9	- - -	3C	*ibid.*, fig. 3:6, tomb 303A

REHOV

CONTEXT: MB I/II. Chap. 3F.7
SCARABS:

No.	Length	Description	Design	Reference
7	14	D4 PN d6	3A3	Yogev 1985, fig. 3:1, tomb 6 II
8	20	D5 PS e10	4B3	*ibid.*, fig. 3:2, tomb 6 II

TEL AVIV, HARBOR CEMETERY

CONTEXT: MB I-I/II. Chap. 3F.9
SCARABS:

No.	Length	Description	Design	Reference
9	16	B3 PS e9	3B3b,3C, 3D1	Liebovitch 1955, fig. 6:2, tomb 11B
10	16	D5 PSd e10	3B1c, 3B3b	*ibid.*, fig. 6:3, tomb 3A
11	18	D3 PN e9	3B3b, 3C, 3D1	*ibid.*, fig. 6:4, tomb 4A
12	18	B6 LN d6	1E3, 3C	*ibid.*, fig. 6:6, tomb 11B
13	15	D3 PN e10	3C	*ibid.*, fig. 6:8, tomb 5
14	16	D6 PN e9	3A4, 10C1b	*ibid.*, fig. 6:9, tomb 4A
15	15	A5 LN d6	3B3e	*ibid.*, fig. 6: 10, tomb 4A
16	14	B2 LS e9	3B3b	*ibid.*, fig. 6:11, tomb 2
17	15	D6 PS e9	10A1b	*ibid.*, fig. 6:12, tomb 16
18	14	B2 LS e9	3A3	*ibid.*, fig. 6:16, tomb 7A
19	17	A4 PN e9	3A4	*ibid.*, fig. 6:17, tomb 10A
20	15	A6 LN e9	4B2	*ibid.*, fig. 6:19, tomb 14
21	13	D3 PSd e9	4B2, 5	*ibid.*, fig. 6:20, tomb 8
22	15	B2 xxx e10	4B2	*ibid.*, fig. 6:22, tomb 14
23	13	B2 PSd e11	4B3	*ibid.*, fig. 6:23, tomb 38
24	17	D8 LS o	12B	*ibid.*, fig. 6:24, tomb 4A

JERICHO

CONTEXT: MB I/II. Chap. 3F.12
SCARABS:

No.	Length	Description	Design	Reference
25	17	B3 LN e6	4A2	Kirkbride 1965, fig. 282:10, tomb A 34
26	14	A1 LN e9	3B3a	*ibid.*, fig. 282:4, tomb B 48
27	14	B2 PS e9	5	*ibid.*, fig. 282:2, tomb B 48
28	14	B2 PS e9	3A4, 3B1a	*ibid.*, fig. 282:6, tomb B 48
29	15	B2 PSd e9	3A4	*ibid.*, fig. 282:7, tomb B 48
30	15	B2 PS e10	3A4	*ibid.*, fig. 282:5, tomb B 48
31	23	D5 PS e10	10C1a	*ibid.*, fig. 282:11, tomb A 34
32	18	D3 PS e10	3B1b, 3B3a, 3C, 3D5	*ibid.*, fig. 282:8, tomb B 48
33	19	- LN e6	3A1, 6A	*ibid.*, fig. 282:3, tomb B 48

MEGIDDO

CONTEXT: MB I-I/II. Chap. 3F.5
SCARABS:

No.	Length	Description	Design	Reference
34	13	A? LN e6	2B2	Tufnell 1973, fig. 1:6, tomb 5106
35	16	A6 PN d6	7B2a	*ibid.*, fig. 1:19, tomb 5137
36	12	- LS -	1B	*ibid.*, fig. 1:28, tomb 5090
37	15	A6 PN d7	3B5, 3E1	*ibid.*, fig. 1:37, tomb 3109
38	15	B2 PS d5	2B1	*ibid.*, fig. 1:38, tomb 5090

RUWEISÉ TOMB 66

CONTEXT: MB I. Chap. 3F.14
SCARABS:

No.	Length	Description	Design	Reference
39	11	B2 PN e5	1B	Tufnell 1975-1976, fig. 1:1
40	14	B2 PN e5	3A3	*ibid.*, fig. 1:2
41	15	A4 LN e2	2B1	*ibid.*, fig. 1:3
42	14	- LN d5	1E3	*ibid.*, fig. 1:4
43	15	A1 LN d5	3A2	*ibid.*, fig. 1:5
44	16	A4 PN d5	3B5	*ibid.*, fig. 1:6
45	16	D1 LN e6	3B4, 3B7	*ibid.*, fig. 1:7
46	19	C4 LN d15	3B3b, 3B4, 3B7	*ibid.*, fig. 1:8
47	15	C1 PN e4	11A	*ibid.*, fig. 1:9
48	19	A5 LNd e9	4D3	*ibid.*, fig. 1:10
49	16	B1 PN e6	2B2, 5	*ibid.*, fig. 1:11
50	15	B2 PS e9	5	*ibid.*, fig. 1:12
51	12	B3 PS e8	6C3	*ibid.*, fig. 1:13
52	21	A4 PN d5	6B3	*ibid.*, fig. 1:14
53	18	C6 PN e6	2B1	*ibid.*, fig. 1:15
54	19	C4 PN e6	2B1	*ibid.*, fig. 1:16
55	20	A4 LN d8	2B1	*ibid.*, fig. 1:17
56	16	B2 LSd e9	3A4	*ibid.*, fig. 1:18
57	14	D8 PS e9	3A4	*ibid.*, fig. 1:19

RUWEISÉ TOMB 73

CONTEXT: MB I. Chap. 3F.14.
SCARABS:

No.	Length	Description	Design	Reference
58	16	- - -	3A3	Guigues 1938, fig. 84
59	15	- - -	3B3a, 3B4, 3B7, 11A	*ibid.*, fig. 84
60	18	- - -	2B2, 5	*ibid.*, fig. 84
61	21	- - -	2B2	*ibid.*, fig. 84
62	20	- - -	7B4	*ibid.*, fig. 84
63	21	- - -	2B2	*ibid.*, fig. 84
64	15	- - -	2B1	*ibid.*, fig. 85

TELL 'AMR

CONTEXT: MB I. Chap. 3F.4.
SCARAB:

No.	Length	Description	Design	Reference
65	20	D5 PS e6	3A1	Druks 1982, fig. 3:1.

BETH SHAN

CONTEXT: MB I. Chap. 3F.6.
SCARAB:

No.	Length	Description	Design	Reference
66	21	- LS -	3A3	Oren 1971: 112, no. 5

KFAR SZOLD

CONTEXT: MB I/II. Chap. 3F.3.
SCARAB:

No.	Length	Description	Design	Reference
67	21	B2 PS d5	6B3	Epstein 1974: 3, fig. 4:13

TELL EL-FAR'AH (N)

CONTEXT: MB I. Chap. 3F.8
SCARAB:

No.	Length	Description	Design	Reference
68	12	D7 LN e6	3A3	Mallet 1973, fig. 18:8, pl. 24:8

NAHARIYAH

CONTEXT: MB I? Chap. 3F. 2
SCARAB:

No.	Length	Description	Design	Reference
69	24 (?)	- - -	3A3	Dothan 1965, pl. 3D

DHAHRAT EL-HUMRAIYA

CONTEXT: MB I. Chap. 3F.10.
SCARAB:

No.	Length	Description	Design	Reference
70	11	- - -	3B1a, 10D2	Ory 1948, pl. 33:11

RAS EL-'AIN (APHEK)

CONTEXT: MB I?. Chap. 3F.11.
SCARABS:

No.	Length	Description	Design	Reference
71	15	B5 PS	3B6	Ory 1936: 112; 6; 1937: 100, pl. 32A:5
72	22	D6 LN d9	11B	Giveon 1988, no. 37
73	14	A1 LN d5	1D	*Ibid*, no. 38

SIN EL-FIL

CONTEXT: MB I. Chap. 3F.15.
SCARABS:

No.	Length	Description	Design	Reference
74	20	- - -	2A, 3B3e	Chéhab 1939, fig. 11;1
75	20	A5 LN	3B7	*ibid.*, fig. 11:2
76	18	- - -	2B1	*ibid.*, fig. 11:3
77	13	- - -	1E3, 3A3	*ibid.*, fig. 11:4
78	14	- - -	1E3	*ibid.*, fig. 11:5
79	16	B2 PS -	5	*ibid.*, fig. 12

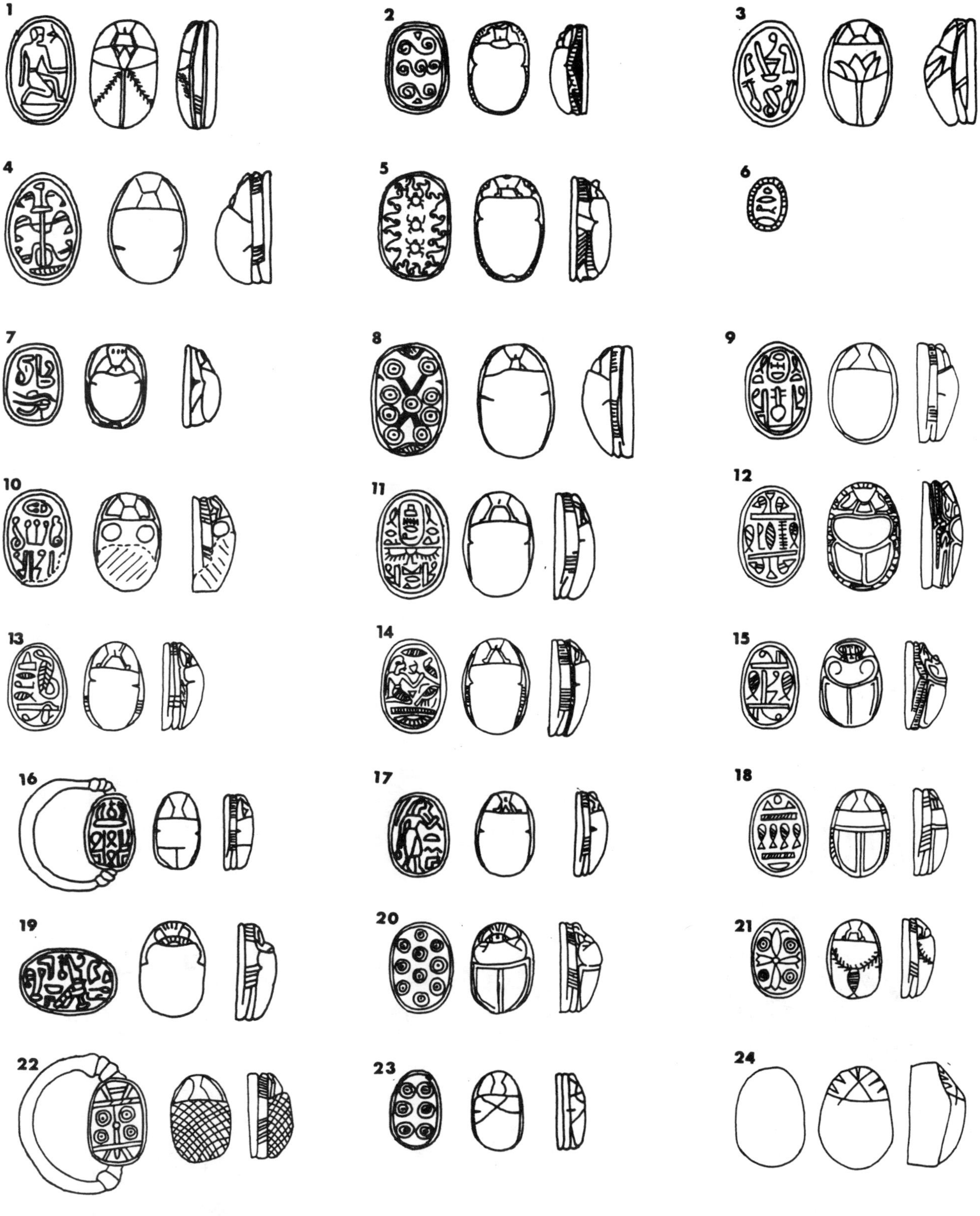

Fig. 5:1a. Period IIA: scarabs from MB I and MB I/II contexts.
Tell el-^{C}Ajjûl (1-6); Rehov (7-8); Tel Aviv (9-24)

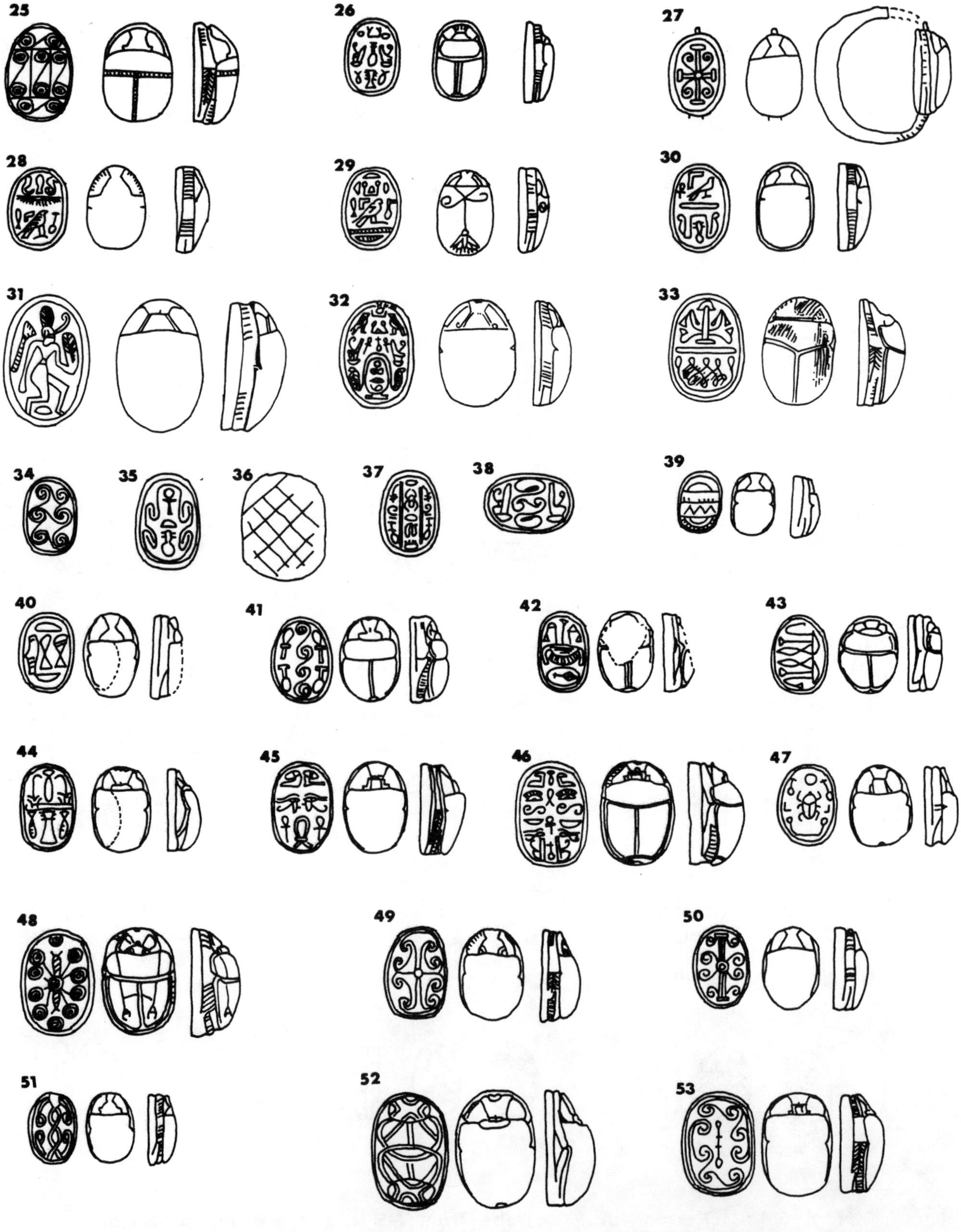

Fig. 5:1b. Period IIA: scarabs from MB I and MB I/II contexts (cont.). Jericho (25-33); Megiddo (34-38); Ruweisé tomb 66 (39-53)

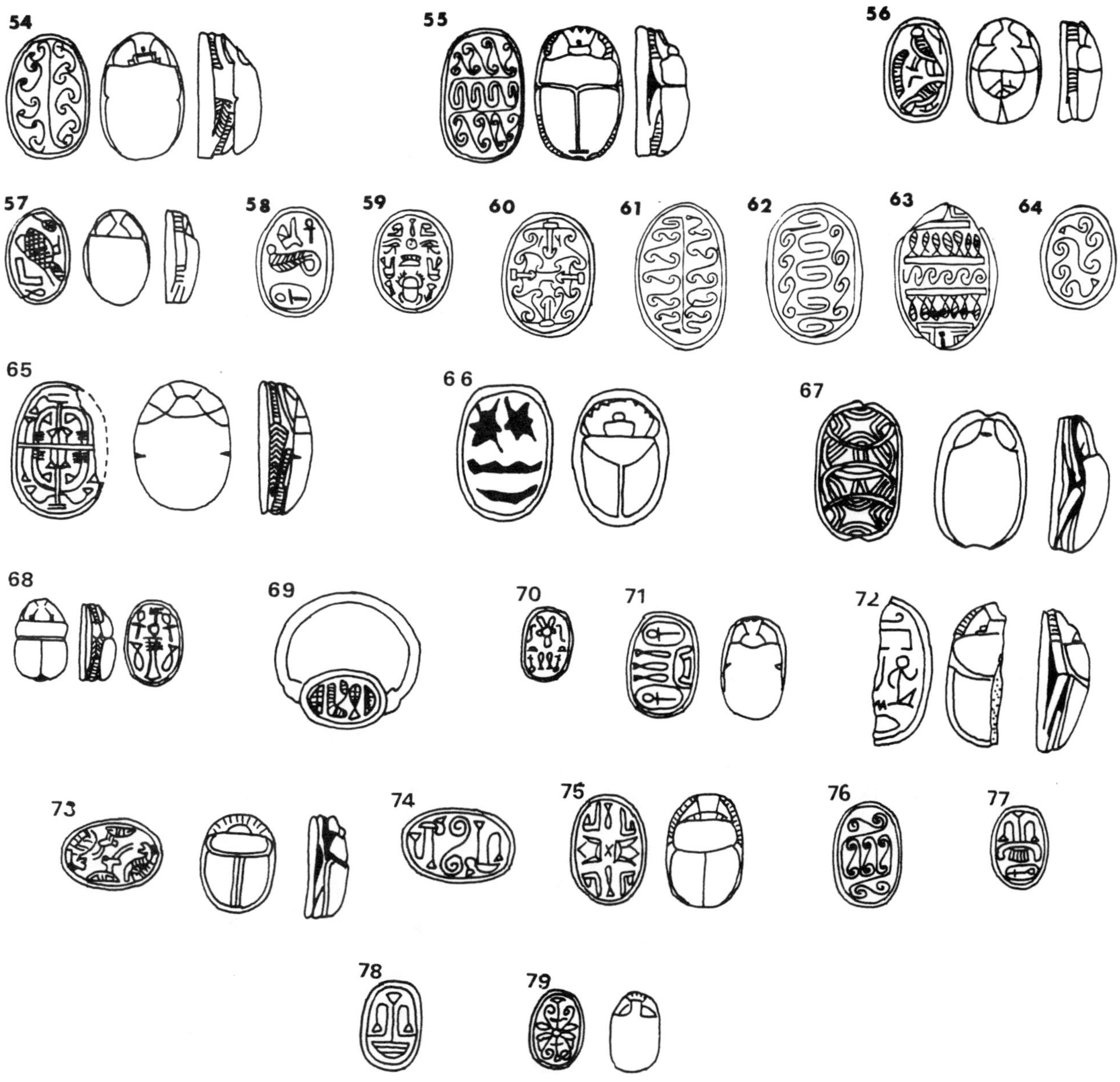

Fig. 5:1c. Period IIA: scarabs from MB I and MB I/II contexts (cont.). Ruweisé tomb 66 (54-57); Ruweisé tomb 73 (58-64); Tell ^{c}Amr (65); Beth Shan (66); Kfar Szold (67); Tell el-Far^{c}ah (68); Nahariyah (69); Dhahrat el-Humraiya (70); Ras el-^{c}Ain (71-73); Sin el-Fil (74-79).

B. TYPOLOGICAL PROFILE: THE IIA GROUP

For a tabular summary of the following discussion, see fig. 5:2, The Classical Middle Kingdom Style; for details on individual typological varieties, see Chap. 9, Tables 5-8 (design scarabs) and Tables 9-12 (royal name scarabs).

Heads (Table 5): A and B heads are found on 60% of this group, D heads on 32%. Of individual varieties of heads, A1 and A3, characteristic of the FIP and the Montet Jar, have all but disappeared and are replaced by types A4 to A6. Type B2 is now dominant and remains so in Periods III and IV; B3, B5, and B6 are new. These varieties of A and B heads thus represent the characteristic head corpus of the group.

Backs (Table 6): PN and PS backs constitute almost two-thirds of the total, back LN making up a quarter, back LS being the least common. This is in sharp contrast to the preceding periods where LN and LS constitute almost the whole back corpus.

Sides (Table 7): the early side types (a, b, c, d1-2), already much diminished in Period II, are now completely replaced in the design scarab series by varieties of sides d and e. Of these, types d5, d6, a few rare d types, e9, and e10 are new. The most common sides are d5, e6, e9 and e10.

Designs (Table 8): a few examples of the early corpus are found (classes 1 and 2), though the designs of this group are all essentially new. The emphasis is on 2B, 3A and 3B; classes 4 to 7, 10 and 11 are represented in small numbers, classes 8 and 9 not at all.

Length (Table 13): the size and average length of scarab groups shows a steady increase from the beginning of the FIP (average length 9.5 mm) to the later 15th Dynasty (17 mm). The IIA group fits precisely where it should with an average length of 16 mm, mid-50% at 14-18 mm, about the same as the scarabs of Period III. Note that Period VI reverts to a smaller size range and shorter average length in conformance to the general tendency of New Kingdom scarabs to revive at least some elements of earlier scarab style.

C. THE IIA AND RELATED GROUPS: THE "CLASSICAL" MIDDLE KINGDOM STYLE.

The typological profile of the IIA group just described fits into a broader spectrum of contemporary scarab groups. On archaeological grounds, the IIA group is from an archaeological context preceding that of Period III, the latter consisting of the earlier MB II burials from Jericho and Megiddo. This is reflected in the scarab typology of these periods in terms of the relative frequency of usage of individual categories of scarab style.

In terms of percent of use, the IIA group compares with Period II only in a few general categories: head C, side e, designs 1 and 2 (Summary Table One). The two groups roughly conform only with side e6, and in the lack of heads B7 and B8, side a, designs 7 to 9. What is lacking is often as important a chronological indicator as what is most frequent. Otherwise, the IIA group conforms closely to Period III, for example, heads A6, B2, B3, all back types, the mix of sides d and e, and most design classes. This emphasizes that, as with pottery sequences, there is bound to be some overlap in varieties of types within a gradually developing general style. However, Periods IIA and III form a relatively homogeneous group indicating they must belong to the same general stage in scarab manufacture.

The key issue, of course, is how the IIA group relates to the royal name series. Here it must be emphasized again that we cannot expect clear-cut comparisons in all typological categories. While there are many categories that do compare favorably, a few do not due to the differences between the typology of design scarabs and that of royal name scarabs, particularly in the relative emphasis placed on side and design types. In general, and this is fully substantiated by the facts at hand; the IIA and III design scarab groups show the same typological pattern. This pattern is quite distinct from what precedes and follows so that it is evident, as will now be shown, that the four groups in question -- Periods IIA and III, Early 12, Late 12 -- belong to the same major stage in the history of scarab style. Their collective typological profile is unique to these groups and appears at no other stage in scarab history.

In fig. 5:2, it is clear that all four groups are in general agreement in the relative use of the five main head types (X, A, B, C, D), the four back types (LN, LS, PN, PS), and the main side types (a, b, c, d, e). With the various classes of design, the relationships among these groups are less strong since royal name scarabs are necessarily restricted to those design classes that form frames or borders around the names andtitles, namely: 3B paired signs, 3E panels, 4 concentric circles, 7 spiral borders, and 8 rope borders. Of these design classes, 3B is the most significant since in all four groups 3B patterns are the most common and it is only with these four groups that this is true. After Period III in the design scarab series, 3B designs are greatly reduced in use; after Late 12 in the royal name series they appear hardly at all. Design class 3B, symmetric patterns, is thus one of the chief features of the classical Middle Kingdom style.

In general terms, Period IIA is related to both Early 12 and Late 12, though in different typological categories. Of those features which are most common at this time, the IIA group is closest to Early 12 in its overall use of heads A and D, heads A5, A6, B2, D5, D6, back LS, and the mix of sides d and e. It is closest to Late 12 in its use of B heads, head A4, backs LN and PS, sides d5, d6, e6. Period III, which is very similar to IIA (see supra),is slightly more oriented toward Late 12: note backs PS and PN, designs 7 and 8, side e6.

There are very few points in the typology of these four groups at which there is a fairly large discrepancy between the design scarabs and the royal name scarabs: for example, the overall use of sides d and e. Such differences in the style of the two groups should be expected, though it is remarkable that there are few of any importance. It should be recalled that, on the basis of presently known evidence, royal name scarabs were not manufactured prior to the beginning of the 12th Dynasty whether they were intended to be seals or amulets (Ward 1984: 151). A second point of no small significance is that a whole new scarab style was introduced at about the same time (see Chap. 7). Since the design scarab tradition was already a fairly old one by the beginning of the 2d millennium B.C., it is evident that scarabs bearing royal names copied that tradition with such alterations as were considered appropriate.

The emphasis on d sides in the royal name group and the emphasis on e heads on the contemporary design scarabs is simply a matter of using a more complicated technique for objects of more importance. The d sides are chip-carved, a technique which required more skill on the part of the engraver and produced a more realistic representation of the beetle. The e sides are scored, a much simpler technique which was more suitable for the ordinary design scarabs which were, after all, produced in considerably more bulk. This is particularly true with sides e9 and e10, of very elementary engraving technique, which dominate the design scarab side repertoire from Periods IIA to V.

Fig. 5:2. The Classical Middle Kingdom Style. Major typological categories.

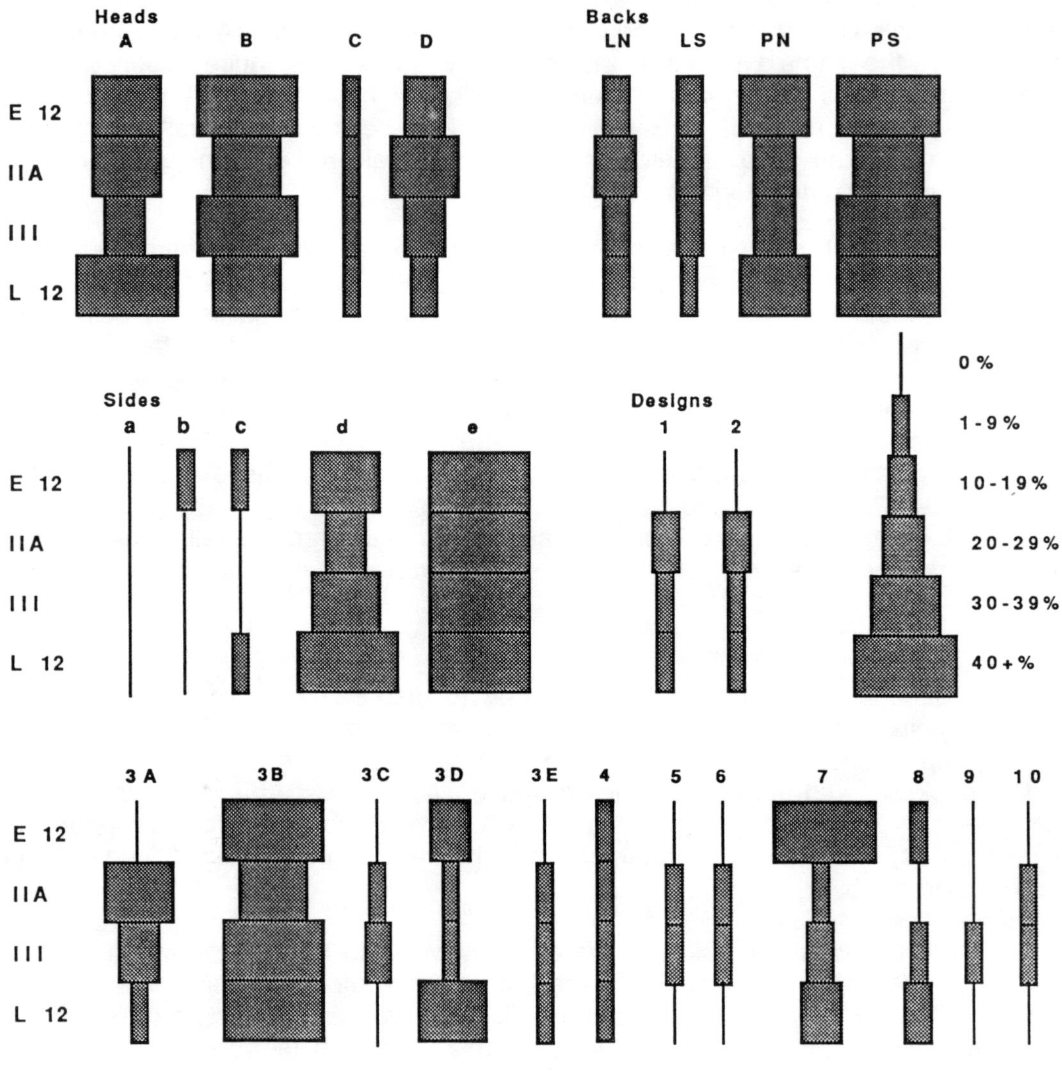

The extensive use of scroll and rope borders on royal name scarabs, especially in the Early 12 group, is in accord with the overall use of design classes on these objects. The royal name, titles, and epithets were usually placed longitudinally in the center of the scarab so that, as noted above, the only designs that could be added were those that formed decorative borders for the name. The same is true of private name scarabs where scroll borders are extremely common (Martin 1971, pls. 48-49). We must keep in mind that royal name scarabs were a new type of object at the beginning of the 12th Dynasty so it is in keeping with their newness and relative importance that scroll and rope borders should figure so prominently in the Early 12 group. These are essentially new designs in a very restricted design repertoire limited to the space available around a royal name. While scroll and rope borders are found on design scarabs, such scarabs did not have the limitation of space. The design repertoire is therefore much more complex and scroll and rope borders play a minor role.

	E 12	IIA	III	L 12
Heads				
X	-	-	2	-
A	30	25	27	42
B	42	35	42	38
C	5	8	3	8
D	23	32	25	12
Backs				
LN	10	28	17	19
LS	10	12	13	7
PN	31	25	28	30
PS	49	34	42	44
Sides				
a	-	-	-	-
b	5	-	-	-
c	5	-	-	6
d	36	27	31	47
e	50	63	69	47
Designs				
1	-	10	5	2
2	-	18	3	2
3A	-	30	25	2
3B	52	30	42	50
3C	-	8	12	-
3D	26	4	4	30
3E	-	1	6	4
4	4	8	9	8
5	-	8	7	-
6	-	4	7	-
7	40	2	16	20
8	4	-	8	18
9	-	-	1	-
10	-	6	3	-

Fig.5:2. The Classical Middle Kingdom Style: Periods IIA and III, E 12, and L 12. Percent of use, major typological categories.

The scarab evidence summarized in the preceding paragraphs strongly suggests that the MB I and I/II phases of Canaanite archaeological history were roughly contemporary to the Egyptian 12th Dynasty and that the Canaanite MB II Age was partially contemporary to that dynasty. The latter, of course, must overlap somewhat into the 13th Dynasty. While the chronology is more closely defined in Chap. 8, a preliminary conclusion may be recorded at this point: the Canaanite archaeological deposits in which the scarabs discussed here were found would appear to date from the later 20th into the early 18th centuries B.C. On the one hand. the contexts of Ruweisé tombs 66 and 73 put them rather early in the MB I (Chap. 3F. 14). On the other, the MB I contexts from Megiddo and Jericho, for example, are rather late in that period and the following Scarab Period III represents the earliest stage of the Canaanite MB II. As a working hypothesis, then, the scarab evidence indicates that the MB I was well under way in the 20th century B.C. and the transition from MB I to MB II took place in the early decades of the 18th century.

CHAPTER 6

THE SCARABS FROM TELL EL-DAB^{C}A AND JERICHO

A. THE PROBLEM DEFINED

Prof. Manfred Bietak (1984, 1989, 1991) has published a series of detailed studies on the chronology of the important Delta site of Tell el-Dab^{c}a, now generally accepted as being Avaris, the Hyksos period capitol in Lower Egypt. Originally an Egyptian town, Tell el-Dab^{c}a was settled by "already-Egyptianized newcomers" (Bietak 1991: 31, Stratum H) in the Middle Kingdom at which time it became partially Canaanite in character. Whatever the original intention for this Asiatic settlement, the archaeological record indicates a gradual shift from a Canaanite-Egyptian assemblage, with the Canaanite pottery mostly locally made, to an Egyptian assemblage which retained some of its earlier Canaanite background (Bietak 1991:31-47). Interestingly enough, there is no evidence of a destruction of the Canaanite settlement "which stops abruptly with the early 18th Dynasty" (Bietak 1991: 47). The overall impression is of a Canaanite colony strongly influenced throughout its history by the local Egyptian culture. The time-span covers much of the Middle Bronze period; the Canaanite settlement originated in the later MB II period and was abandoned by the end of the MB III (Bietak 1984: 476-77).

The archaeological record of the site has been explored in Chap. 3F.16-17, along with the reasons why we feel Bietak's absolute dating of his strata is untenable. His absolute chronology depends partly on scarab evidence from Tell el-Dab^{c}a itself and an analysis of the scarabs from the MB tombs at Jericho. The result is to greatly shorten the MB II-III phases at Jericho and, by extension, of all Canaan. The purpose of the present discussion is to examine Bietak's arguments relative to the scarab evidence.

While the scarabs from Tell el-Dab^{c}a have yet to be fully published, Bietak proposes that some of them provide absolute dates for the strata of the town (1984: 478).[1] From these scarabs, Bietak concludes that "The MB series [of scarabs] in Tell el-Dab^{c}a can only have started after 1800 B.C. with stratum d/2-1 [=Stratum H]. The subsequent strata G, F, and E/3 have to be placed within Dynasty XIII and not before. The traditional Hyksos scarabs came from strata E/1, D/3 and D/2" (Bietak 1984: 475). At this point, Bietak makes it clear that he is assigning absolute dates to the MB strata at Tell el-Dab^{c}a, not Canaan, and that the resulting lower chronology at this site may be due to a kind of cultural lag (Bietak 1984: 482). However, the scarab evidence from Tell el-Dab^{c}a is then correlated with the scarabs from the Jericho MB tombs which does bring Canaan very much into the picture.

B. THE JERICHO MATERIAL

While it was perhaps not intended to be so, the large collection of scarabs from the MB Jericho tombs is indeed one of Bietak's major arguments in favor of a low chronology for Tell el-Dab^{c}a. This falls into two categories, a series of six alleged royal name scarabs and a general assessment of the Jericho design scarabs. Bietak's basic argument is that (1) throughout the Jericho MB tomb groups there appear scarabs with "typical" designs of the Hyksos period and (2) that there are six royal name scarabs which establish a low chronology at Jericho. The Jericho evidence, in turn, supports the low chronology assigned to the Tell el-Dab^{c}a strata. It can be shown, however, that the initial step in the argument -- the dating of the Jericho scarabs -- is faulty so that the rest of the argument fails and the scarab evidence both from Jericho and Tell el-Dab^{c}a does not support the lower chronology.

In the first place, there are only three, not six, royal name scarabs from the Jericho tombs[2] (Ward 1987:521-23). But it is the three which are not royal name scarabs by which Bietak supports his lower chronology for Jericho. These are:

Nubkheperre (Inyotef V)	Jericho tomb Group II
Mayibre (Sheshi)	Jericho tomb Group III
Khaneferre (Sebekhotep IV)	Jericho tomb Group V

In other words, Jericho MB tomb Group II, which begins the Canaanite MB II phase at that site, should date to the 17th Dynasty on the basis of the "Nubkheperre" scarab, and Group III should date to the contemporary 15th Dynasty because of the "Mayibre" scarab. However, the scarab of "Nubkheperre" does not name a king, but belongs instead to a large class of design scarabs. The "Mayibre" scarab is really a late misspelling of Nimaatre (Amenemhat III) and does not conform to the typology of the more than one hundred scarabs of Mayibre Sheshi, a key factor overlooked by Bietak (1991: 56). The "Khaneferre" scarab is again a design scarab which, on all counts, bears no resemblance to the typology of the known scarabs of that ruler. Since the first two of these three scarabs are the key to Bietak's argument, his absolute dates for the Jericho tombs are not supported by these scarabs.

Once this chronological restriction is removed, the other evidence from the Jericho scarabs can be treated more realistically. Bietak suggests that throughout the Jericho tomb groups there are examples of eleven scarab designs which are "typical of Dynasty XV" (Bietak 1984: 83, with Ill. 6), here fig. 6:1 Since some of these designs begin already in Jericho Group I and many are well represented in Groups II-V, Bietak concludes that the Jericho scarabs, hence the archaeological phases they represent, must be mostly contemporary to the 15th Dynasty. But while some of these eleven designs are indeed common in the 15th Dynasty, most have a long history so that, collectively, they do not support a low chronology.

<u>Fig 6:1, no.1</u>, according to Bietak a "design like a bovine head flanked by two spiral patterns," is really the common cross pattern with a long history in Egypt (Tufnell 1984: 125, pl. 23, design class 5). The origin of this motif would appear to be the flower-rosette pattern of the Old Kingdom represented on the furniture from the tomb of Queen Hetepheres (Reisner and Smith 1955, figs. 32, 40) and a cylinder seal of Neferkare (Kaplony 1981, pl. 112). This motif is rare before the Middle Kingdom on scarabs, appearing on two examples of the FIP[3] and five in the Montet Jar group (Ward 1978, nos. 368-69, 371-73; the motif continued in use from that time until the New Kingdom.[4] It is typical of the Middle Kingdom (Table 8, design class 5), *not* the Hyksos age. Contra Bietak, this motif appears throughout the Jericho tomb series, not just the beginning.

<u>Fig. 6:1, no. 2</u> is a geometric design classified in Tufnell 1984 among the coiled and woven patterns (design class 6C), but which originates in the geometric patterns of the FIP (Ward 1978, Nos. 85, 87; Tufnell 1984: 126, pl. 25). The early form of the motif is found in the Montet Jar group (Ward 1978, nos. 86, 88) and was used

thereafter in relatively small numbers (Table 8, design class 6C), though it did find its most extensive use in Period V.

Fig. 6:1, no. 3, following Bietak's drawing, evidently indicates vertical rows of miscellaneous signs, the so-called *Neferzeichen* pattern consisting of paired signs for borders with other signs, sometimes a royal name, running down the middle. These patterns are classified in Tufnell 1984 as design class 3B with its numerous varieties. As a group, these designs are characteristic of the Period IIA scarab group assembled in Chap. 5, of scarabs naming 12th Dynasty rulers, and of Jericho tomb Group II and Megiddo MB tomb Phases A-D. They are certainly not typical of the 15th Dynasty but, as has long been recognized, of the Middle Kingdom (see Table 8 and Stock 1955: 18-23).

Fig. 6:1, nos. 4a-b are supposed variants of the tripartite pattern, all said by Bietak to be typical of the 15th Dynasty. Fig. 6:1, no. 4a is not a tripartite pattern at all, but rather one variant of the paired cobras motif which is far less frequent in Hyksos times than in the Middle Kingdom (Tufnell 1984: 118, pls. 9-10; Chap. 9, Tables 4 and 8, design 3B1). This particular variant appears already on two scarabs naming Amenemhat III (Tufnell 1974, nos. 3082-83). Fig. 6:1, no. 4b is likewise not a tripartite pattern since it never divides the design into three parts as fig. 6:1, no. 4c-d, but normally appears only in the lower half of the design.[5] This motif appears mostly on Middle Kingdom scarabs and on two examples naming Amenemhat III and IV[6] but never with later kings. It is more typical of the Middle Kingdom than the Hyksos age.

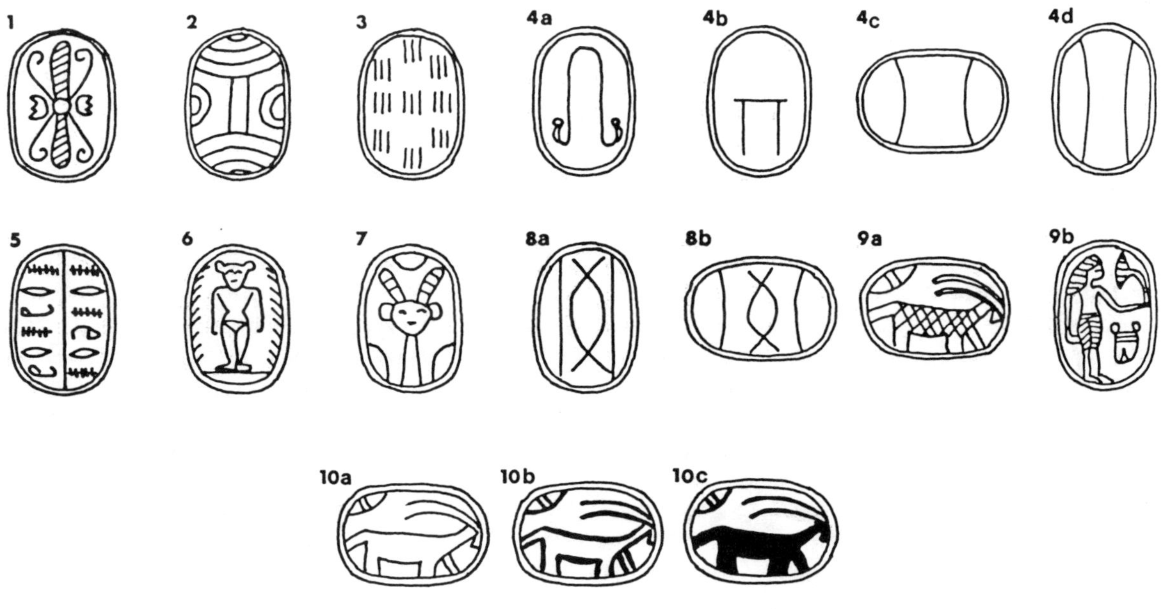

Fig. 6:1. Scarab designs "typical of Dynasty XV," after Bietak.

Fig 6:1, nos. 4c-d represent the true tripartite pattern in which two curved or straight lines -- incised from border to border, either vertically or horizontally -- divide the design surface into three parts. In the design scarab series, this is a rare pattern: while Bietak lists 29 examples from the Jericho tombs, there are really only eight.[7] This tripartite scheme is a characteristic feature only of 15th Dynasty *royal name* scarabs from whence comes the long-held but false assumption that it is a "Hyksos" design. While this is true for royal name scarabs, the tripartite pattern was little used on design scarabs. It is found already in a MB I burial at Megiddo (fig. 5:1, no. 37; cf. Chap. 3F.5, tomb 3109) and then appears very rarely through Periods III-V, after which it went out of use.

Fig. 6:1, no. 5, the so-called $^{c}n\ r^{c}$ pattern, presents a unique problem which as yet has no solution. This motif, with its endless variations, is certainly typical of the Hyksos age and it has been customary to assume that scarabs with this design date to that period. However, a new discovery at Memphis will force a complete re-evaluation of the chronology of this design; two $^{c}n\ r^{c}$ seal impressions have been found and "the deposits to which they belong are clearly contexted and date from the mid to late XIIth Dynasty."[8] Two examples occur in MB I-I/II burials at Tel Aviv (fig. 5:1, nos. 11-12) and continue on throughout the design scarab series in enough numbers to show that such patterns were common before the Hyksos Age (Ward 1987: 525). Stock (1955: 24) has proposed that this large category of designs developed out of the common *Neferzeichen* patterns of the Middle Kingdom and others have suggested that many of the $^{c}n\ r^{c}$ designs can be translated (Niccacci 1980: 26-31; Murray 1949). A main characteristic of this design is that after their earliest appearance there is a gradual increase in the number and variety of supplementary signs used so that by Hyksos times the original character of the design is often lost.[9]

Fig. 6:1, no. 6, the "naked goddess" motif, has now been studied in detail by Schroer (Keel, Keel-Leu and Schroer 1989: 89-138). The motif is characteristic of the MB II-III periods and, where the find-spot is known, scarabs portraying this figure are generally from Canaan. While the motif does show some Egyptian influence, it is essentially Canaanite. The naked goddess shown *en face*, an un-Egyptian way of portraying human and divine figures, appears as a secondary figure on Syrian cylinder seals of the first half of the 2d millennium B.C. and this must surely be the origin for the scarab motif. Schroer suggests that this figure was particularly important in Canaanite "folk religion" in the MB II and III periods (Keel, Keel-Leu and Schroer 1989: 198). though it disappeared as a motif on scarabs after that time.

Fig. 6:1, no. 7 is the very common Hathor head motif, again studied by Schroer (Keel, Keel-Leu and Schroer 1989: 139-97). This is of Egyptian origin, going back to archaic art and portrayed on scarabs as early as the FIP (Ward 1978: 63) at which time the symbol may have represented Bat rather than Hathor. While it may be true, as Schroer suggests (Keel, Keel-Leu and Schroer 1989: 196) that in Middle Bronze Canaan the symbol was used for an indigenous goddess, in terms of its use on scarabs in general, the Bat/Hathor head emblem appears on Egyptian examples from the FIP into post-Empire times.

Fig. 6:1, no. 8a, a panel or tripartite design with a loop down the center, is said by Bietak to occur four times at Jericho. In reality, there is only one example at Jericho though others appear at Fara and ^{c}Ajjûl (Tufnell 1984, pl. 20, design 3E4). Bietak must include here examples like Fig. 6:1, no. 8b which is not the same design, but a degenerated woven pattern (Tufnell 1984, nos. 2159-62, design 6C2) also found at Fara and ^{c}Ajjûl. In any case, he is correct in that both motifs are relatively late so that, while this pattern begins shortly before the Hyksos age, it is more common in that period.

Fig. 6:1, no. 9 represents a large and varied series of designs portraying animal and human figures which take up most or all of the scarab base. Bietak follows the traditional view that examples of this category of design which are "deeply cut" into the surface are characteristic of the Hyksos period. While the traditional view is correct to a point, it is impossible to clearly distinguish the various engraving techniques used for these designs unless one has access to photographs or the scarabs themselves. Throughout this large class of designs, three basic techniques can be seen:

(1) normal engraving on the surface (fig. 6:1, no. 10a);

(2) surface engraving but with wider and sometimes slightly deeper cutting (fig. 6:1, no. 10b);

(3) the entire figure is deeply cut into the surface, that is, hollowed out (fig. 6:1, no. 10c).

All three techniques may or may not include partial or complete cross-hatching, as fig. 6:1, no. 9a. Publications of scarabs in line drawings rarely show these various techniques clearly nor are writers always clear as to what they mean by "deeply cut'; Bietak includes the second and third techniques,[10] Kemp and Merrillees only the latter.[11]

The three engraving techniques for these animal and human figures may be roughly chronological as listed above. It is really only the third, with completely hollowed out figures, that can be called typical of the Hyksos period. Taken as a group, these motifs have a long history. Human and animal figures are prominent on design-amulets and scarabs of the FIP[12] though these are engraved mostly in a linear style which, with rare exceptions, was not carried on after the early 12th Dynasty (the Montet Jar). Three examples occur in the Period IIA group (fig. 5:1, nos. 14, 17, 31). All are human figures so it is evident, on the evidence now known, that the human figures (design class 10) done in the new lapidary style precede those of animals in time (design class 9)

Large animal figures occur in FIP graves at Sedment, Matmar and Hu and there is one example in the Montet Jar (Ward 1978: 51-52, nos. 172-74). Again, the earlier linear tradition does not reproduce animals in the later style which occur first in Megiddo A-D and Jericho III. Tufnell also compared the use of large cobras on Middle Kingdom scarabs (1984: 139) and we might also consider the large Horus falcon on a scarab from Ruweisé tomb 66 (fig. 5:1, no. 57). Such animals are also found among the Kahun impressions dating from Sesostris II to Neferhotep I (Tufnell 1975, fig. 11: 430). Thus, while one can show that large animal and human figures appear long before the 15th Dynasty, those done in the later techniques begin to appear in the later 12th Dynasty. Bietak is correct in calling them typical of the Hyksos period, but they do appear before that time so their presence does not automatically assume the later date.

As the preceding paragraphs show, the collection of designs supposedly typical of the Hyksos age do not, in fact, delineate the main design corpus of that period. Several are already evidenced in Period IIA, others are characteristic of the Middle Kingdom rather than the Hyksos age. Of these designs and their variants, very few are characteristic of the Hyksos period and even these have earlier origins. The fact that these designs appear throughout the Jericho tomb series is not, therefore, an indication that this tomb series is practically confined to the period of the 15th Dynasty.

C. The Key Scarabs from Tell el-Dab^ca

We may now turn to the individual scarabs from Tell el-Dab^ca used by Bietak (1984: 478) to help establish his absolute dating for that site. Here it must be again cautioned that the total scarab evidence from the site has yet to be published so it is not possible in the present context to compare this material in detail with that from other excavated sites. The following remarks are therefore necessarily restrictive and any fuller analysis of the material must await its full publication. The scarabs in question are:

scarab	stratum	Bietak's approx. date	MB Phase at Tell el-Dab^{c}a
1. with lotus on back	G 1/2	1725-1700	MB II A/3
2. of "Deputy Treasurer, Aam"	F	1700-1675	MB IIA/B
3. with deeply cut human figure	F	1700-1675	MB IIA/B
4. with name "Sebekhotep"	E/3	1675-1650	MB IIB/1-2
5. *Rdi-R*^{c}, ^{c}*n r*^{c}, deeply cut figures, tripartite designs	E/1-D/3	1625-1600	MB IIB/3
6. naming Sesostris I	E/1-D/3	1625-1600	MB II/3
7. with tripartite pattern, ^{c}*n r*^{c}, no division line	D/2	1575-1550	MB IIC

a. The first in the series, a scarab with a lotus design engraved on the back, is used as a chronological marker dating Stratum G 1/2 on Tell A to the late 18th century B.C. The treatment of this scarab highlights once again a common error in the literature, the notion that a single scarab can date an archaeological deposit. In the present case, the error is compounded since the premise on which scarabs with this type of decoration have been dated is incorrect. Bietak and others (e.g., Weinstein 1975: 10) quote without comment Tufnell's conclusions (1970: 95) regarding scarabs with decorated backs

> The date is established beyond doubt by a scarab naming Sa-Hathor, son and possibly ephemeral successor of Khasekhemre Neferhotep (I). The fact that figures of Taurt, goddess of childbirth, are prominent on the back of the seal suggests that it was in the nature of a commemorative issue to celebrate the prince's birth. In that case, it would have been made during the reign of the father, which lasted eleven years, estimated to be between c. 1740-1730 B.C.

Noting other scarabs in this group supposedly engraved with the prenomens of Khaneferre Sebekhotep IV and Djedneferre Dudimose I, she further concludes:

> The chronological range for the scarabs assembled in fig. 1 is therefore likely to fall between 1740 and 1720 B.C., with a possible extension in time for Djedneferre.

These conclusions are wrong and were later corrected (Ward 1984; 159, n. 51). The Sihathor of the scarab in question was the son of the Lady-in-Waiting Seket,[13] hence was not the Crown Prince. Indeed, there were several "King's Sons" named Sihathor in this period and it is not possible to determine which, if any, was the Sihathor who, according to the Turin King List (and *only* there), ruled for a short time (Dewachter 1976). The supposed scarabs of "Khaneferre" and "Djedneferre" are design scarabs, not royal name scarabs; that of "Khaneferre" is not of the genealogical style used on *all* scarabs of this king.[14] The close dating suggested by Tufnell therefore has no basis since none of the three scarabs in question bear royal names of the 13th Dynasty.

Finally, decoration engraved on scarab backs is already found on eight examples from the Period IIA group (fig. 5:1) and such decoration continues into the later 15th Dynasty. Decorated backs in general are more common with the classical Middle Kingdom style than later; Table 6. In the royal name series, they hardly exist prior to the 15th Dynasty; Table 10. All in all, the scarab from Tell el-Dab^{c}a level G 1/2 has no value in itself for dating that level.

b. The scarab naming the "Deputy of the Treasurer, Amu" is from a tomb in Stratum F, no. A/II-l/12 (Bietak 1991, fig. 17: 809) The tomb has a vaulted roof of mud bricks over a single chamber containing a limestone coffin. Inside the coffin was the skeleton of a young male, the grave goods consisting of a ribbed dagger, shafthole chisel axe, some small Tell el-Yehudiyeh jugs, and the scarab; outside the coffin were ca. 40 pottery vessels (Van den Brink 1982: 38; Bietak 1991a: 51-58) The scarab cannot be typologically dated since the head (type C4) is extremely rare and the back PN and side e6 were used throughout the 12th to 15th Dynasties. A Middle Kingdom date is most probable, though where in that period is not possible to determine.

Bietak does not state why this scarab is a significant dating criterion nor why he places it in the 13th Dynasty. As just noted, its typology would allow a 12th Dynasty date as well as 13th. Nor is the personal name any help. The Semitic personal name *^{c}m* is fairly common in Egyptian texts from the 12th to 15th Dynasties (Ranke 1935: 59, 2-3; 1952: 269: 21). This is a hypocoristicon and represents Semitic *^{c}Ammu*, either a divine name or the common term "uncle."[15]

c. The scarab of "King Sebekhotep" is from Stratum E3, tomb A II-n/13 (Bietak 1991, fig. 17: 1840). The design on the base shows an incorrect spelling of the name Sebekhotep surmounting a *nwb*-sign; none of the many known scarabs of any of the Sebekhotep kings shows such an arrangement; they are almost exclusively of the genealogical type (Tufnell 1984, pls. 54-55). While this might be a royal name scarab, that is, one that names a specific king, royal names were most frequently used on scarabs as a protective talisman and/or for the actual meaning of the name, in this case, "Sobk satisfies; is pleased," thereby calling on the protection of the deity. One can assume correctly that this scarab shows a garbled spelling of the royal name, but it could recall any of the seven Sebekhoteps who ruled from the beginning to the end of the 13th Dynasty. Thus, while a late 13th Dynasty date is possible, as Bietak suggests, this is not as definite as he states. The *nwb* - sign at the base likewise does not particularly point to that date (Bietak 1991: 51) as it appears on several royal name scarabs of the 12th Dynasty.[16]

d. The *rdi-R^{c}* scarab; this type has traditionally been considered a mark of 15th Dynasty date. While it is true that many of the known examples date to this time,[17] there is one from the ^{c}Ajjûl Courtyard Cemetery (fig.5:1, no. 6), another from a Middle Kingdom burial at Harageh (Chap. 8B, tomb A40).

e. The remainder of the Tell el-Dab^{c}a scarabs listed by Bietak (see supra) consist of examples of the so-called "Hyksos designs" which have all been treated in the preceding section. A few others have now been fully illustrated: a scarab from Stratum E/1-D/3, a re-issue with the name of Sesostris I,[18] one of the well-known Chancellor Har, and one with the strange name *Snsk* (Bietak 1991, fig. 18), plausibly argued as a unique garbled version of the common *Ssy.* The latter two were found in 15th Dynasty contexts.

Some 22 scarabs from burials at Tell el-Dab^{c}a (excluding a few of hard stones) have been fully presented in Bietak 1991a: *passim.* While it is premature to offer conclusions on only part of the scarab collection from this site, following the procedure used to date the small group from Harageh in Chap. 8B, the results are suggestive:

Stratum	No. Scarabs	Dynasty Bietak (1991:32)	Present work Per.	Dynasty
F	4	late 13	IIA	late 12-early 13
E3-E2	3	late 13 -early 15	III	early to mid 13
E1	11	early 15	IV	late 13
D3-D2	4	late 15	V	15

The 11 scarabs from Stratum E1 are especially instructive since none of the designs characteristic of Period V = !5th Dynasty are represented (fig. 7:3). Indeed, some of the designs in this group had all but disappeared by Period V. The mix of head, back, and side types conforms to a 13th rather than a 15th Dynasty date.

D. CONCLUSIONS

a. The differences in opinion between Bietak and the present writers with regard to the scarabs from Tell el-Dab^{c}a have arisen because two opposing methodologies are involved. Bietak has adopted that of O'Connor, we support the one developed originally by Tufnell. As these two ways of looking at scarab typology and history are totally different (Chap. 2B), any conclusions drawn from them are bound to clash.

b. Since the Tell el-Dab^{c}a scarabs as a group have not yet been fully published, in all fairness to Bietak, a proper evaluation of the scarabs from this site will have to await full presentation of the material. In the meantime, a controversial chronological scheme for one of the most important sites in Egypt has become rather rigidly fixed in the voluminous literature on the excavation. Since this chronology, at least in part, depends on the scarab evidence, it would have been far more useful to present that evidence in full.

c. It is clear once again that individual scarabs are far less reliable as dating criteria than groups of scarabs. Through their collective typological features, groups of scarabs found in the same archaeological context will always give a closer dating than individual examples selected for some outstanding feature. In each of the individual cases noted above, the possible range of date is too broad to be of chronological value. The group of 22 from the burials, on the other hand, produces a much larger set of typological features and is therefore more easily integrated into the typological history set forth in the present work.

d. To date, the Tell el-Dab^{c}a scarabs have been analyzed on the basis of dating criteria which, simply put, are invalid. The whole range of "Hyksos designs" has been a key factor in the chronology of scarabs for decades, yet almost none can be considered indicators of that period only. These "Hyksos designs" plus plain schematic backs and trapezoidal heads have long been felt to be hallmarks of scarab manufacture of the later MB Age. But all these features have a long history so that even a scarab showing all of them cannot automatically be dated to the Hyksos period as has been the custom in scarab studies.

e. From what has so far been published, Bietak's scarab evidence for a low chronology does not support that chronology. One must assume that in defending his low chronology he has produced whatever scarab evidence there is so that, with the full publication of this material, there will be no surprises. It may or may not be significant that, with the exception of a single mis-spelled royal name scarab, there have been no others noted naming a 15th Dynasty ruler found at Tell el-Dab[c]a, now recognized as the ancient Hyksos capitol of Avaris.

NOTES

[1] It should be noted that the analysis of the Tell el-Dab[c]a scarabs is not the work of Bietak himself, but rather a member of his team, Christine Mlinar, who will eventually publish the collection as a whole. Throughout his many studies on his excavation, Bietak constantly defers to Mlinar's research which is based on that of O'Connor 1969 and 1987 since his results support Bietak's lower chronology.

[2] Ward 1987: 521-23. Bietak's reply (1991: 55-56) re-asserts his original position on these "royal name" scarabs and interested scholars can compare the two arguments which need not be repeated here.

[3] Ward 1978, nos. 370, 374, both from the former Matouk Collection (Beirut). Both scarabs have head A3 and side c which are characteristic only in the FIP; Ward 1978: 65-58, 75-76, and fig. 7:2 of the present work.

[4] E.g., Petrie and Brunton 1924, pl. 58:39; Brunton 1930, pl. 34: 65-66; Brunton 1948, pl. 53:144 (post-Empire). This motif is evidently the same as that of a painted pattern in a tomb at Meir of the 12th Dynasty; Blackman 1915, pl. 9. While this has generally been considered to be of Aegean or Anatolian origin, the single proof offered for this is the pattern on the kilt of an Aegean offering-bearer in an 18th Dynasty tomb: Vercoutter 1956, pl. 26:188. However, Kantor 1947: 43, warns that many "Aegean" objects and artistic motifs, especially those on kilts, in 18th Dynasty representations of Aegeans bearing offerings are really Egyptian. In light of the long history of the motif in question within Egyptian art, this is a case in point. Note, however, that Vercoutter 1956: 241, disagrees with Kantor.

[5] Tufnell 1984, pl. 20, design class 3E5. This is not a true panel design (class 3E) with which it is grouped for convenience' sake. It is sometimes referred to as "serekh-like" or as a "shrine," neither of which seems appropriate.

[6] Tufnell 1984, nos. 3091-2. Both are without archaeological context though scarabs apparently commemorating a coregency of these two kings would hardly be issued later. No. 3091 is of a particularly detailed naturalistic style, complete with a rare realistic rendering of the legs. No. 3092 is again very naturalistic though the clypeus is broken so one cannot tell if it was notched; the side is type e6, characteristic on both 12th Dynasty design and royal names scarabs; Chap. 9, Tables 7, 11.

[7] He does not state what "varieties" he has included to reach his larger figure. The criterion used in the present work is that the dividing line must reach from border to border and not be part of a different design (e.g., the paired cobras and "shrine"). Bietak evidently includes many designs which *seem* to be tripartite, e.g., red crowns addorsed, but which are really quite different patterns.

[8] Richards 1992: 32. This is a caution to all who write about scarabs that definitive statements such as "[c]*n r*[c]-signs have not been found in any context before the Hyksos period" (Bietak 1991:56) should be somewhat tempered. Richards is currently engaged

in a thorough study of this design pattern and will hopefully resolve many of the problems it poses.

[9]Ward 1987: 524-26. While some have proposed an asiatic origin for this motif due to the more common occurrence in Canaan and the peculiarities of the orthography, this need not be the case. It is just as likely that these patterns derive from the *Neferzeichen* tradition and orthographic peculiarities exist already on scarabs from FIP deposits. The new finds at Memphis may well point to the latter explanation.

[10]Bietak 1984: 483, says simply "deeply cut human or animal representations," by which he evidently means both the second and third engraving techniques (fig. 6:1, nos. 10b-c). The 48 examples given in his Ill. 6 far outnumber the total of only three which are drawn as if completely hollowed out; Kirkbride 1965, Figs. 288:14, 290:22, 300:4.

[11]Kemp and Merrillees, p. 49, speak of "designs based on human and animal figures, deeply hollowed out, sometimes with cross-hatching over the hollowed out parts," which describes only the third engraving technique. This is the correct descriptive approach.

[12] Ward 1978, fig. 10, pls. 5-6. One does get the rare hollowed out example (*Ibid.*, fig. 10:1, and nos. 165, 177), but the early linear character is still evident. Such objects carry on a tradition of deeply cut designs in the earlier design-amulet groups. The engraving is crude and the representations are often difficult to recognize which is not generally true of the later work.

[13]*ẖkr.t-nsw Skt;* on the title, see Drenkhahn 1976 who has conclusively done away with the meaning "concubine," unfortunately still found in the literature. For the Middle Kingdom evidence, see Ward 1986: 24-27

[14]Tufnell 1970, fig. 1:4; Tufnell 1984, nos. 3131-3161. The scarab in question (BM 25554) is omitted in the latter work. The third "royal" scarab supposedly bearing the name of Djedneferre of the 13th Dynasty is likewise placed in the design scarab series in Tufnell 1984, no. 2889.

[15] Ward 1976: 360-61, on the Hyksos period ruler, probably Khauserre Amu (Ward 1984: 164). It is just possible that this name could be read *Qm3w*, abbreviated spellings of which are written the same way. In this case, the name would be Egyptian. It seems best, however, to retain Bietak's reading.

[16]Tufnell 1984, nos. 3011, 3063, 3077, 3083. To maintain a late 13th Dynasty date for this object, it would have to be shown that all four of the 12th Dynasty examples are later re-issues, a convenient argument too often used but rarely proved.

[17]A large number of references to Egyptian and Nubian material in Kemp and Merrillees 1980: 49, nn. 111-116. Weinstein 1975: 10, commenting on the example from the [c]Ajjûl Courtyard cemetery, and following O'Connor, states: "The hieroglyphic group on this scarab from the late MB IIA or transitional MB IIA/B tomb 303B at Tell el-[c]Ajjûl clearly marks this scarab as a Second Intermediate Period product.... (It) is not attested in the Middle Kingdom and only rarely in Dynasty XIII." Since O'Connor used outdated chronological criteria and dubious evidence, this conclusion no longer stands.

[18]Bietak 1991, fig. 17: 2191; certainly, as Bietak suggests, not a contemporary product, but of much later date; Bietak 1989: 104-5, n. 89.

CHAPTER 7

THE CHRONOLOGY OF SCARAB TYPOLOGY

A. PROBLEMS IN A TYPOLOGICAL HISTORY

1. Limitations of the Sample Used in this Study

Perhaps the single most troublesome aspect of any typological history, and the one most subject to criticism, is the size and origin of the sample used to establish both the typology itself and its historical development. While it is true that the present project is centered on scarab groups found in datable archaeological contexts which thus offer some exterior control, questions do remain. Chief among these is the size of the sample. In the first volume (Ward 1978), the total number of scarabs used is a mere 391: 220 from well dated excavations, 171 from vaguely dated excavations and unprovenanced examples in collections. But for this stage of the project, this is the material available; scarabs had not yet become the extremely common class of object they became in later years. The sample in that volume is therefore as complete as it can presently be.

This is not true, of course, in the second volume (Tufnell 1984) which utilizes some 2,100 scarabs and the present work where the sample is 2,500. Given the vast numbers of scarabs produced during the centuries covered here, a total of 2,500 in a sample intended to establish a working typological history from the FIP to the 15th Dynasty may seem rather small. This is especially true when that typological history is used to address such basic and important problems as the chronology of Middle Bronze Canaan.

These are justifiable reservations for which there is probably no entirely satisfactory rebuttal. It must suffice to note that of the prodigious production of scarabs during the period concerned, a relatively small number have come from controlled excavations and it is, after all, the latter upon which the typological history proposed here must be founded. A partial response, at least, is given below in Sect. D where a series of excavated groups not included in the main design scarab series is tested against that series. That they all conform to the typological history as reconstructed from the main sample indicates that the basic thrust of that typological history is correct.

One more point needs to be emphasized, the much larger number of scarabs which, on archaeological grounds, can be assigned to Period V, the Hyksos Age. It seems apparent from the overall picture of scarab production that this period was the floruit of the industry up to that point in time. While many scarabs and groups of scarabs originally dated to this period in the literature must in reality be earlier, it remains clear that, for sheer bulk, Period V saw the production of more scarabs than at any time previously. Not only do the archaeological contexts attest to this, but the widespread use of such features as clumsy D7 to D9 heads, PS backs and e11a sides help create a very stylized class of object which one associates with mass, perhaps hasty, production. Another supporting factor is the number of royal name scarabs produced during the 15th Dynasty which far outweighs that of the contemporary production of such pieces during the Middle Kingdom. All in all, for whatever reason, there are more datable scarabs in Period V than at any previous time. Also to be considered here, of course, is the growth of Canaanite cities in both size and wealth (Chap. 3B.3) so that the demand for scarabs and other Egyptian objects such as amulets would have been greater.

2. Local Traditions and Workshops

A second major problem not addressed as such in the present work is the question of different workshops which presumably would produce scarabs emphasizing different stylistic features. Scholars have long wondered if it is possible to define such centers of production and isolate their products in terms of scarabs from one workshop which show marked preferences in style over those of another workshop. Certainly, such workshops can be identified as shown in recent studies by Keel. He describes two scarab groups and offers a convincing case for local manufacture in Canaan during the MB II Age:

1. The "Omega group," all made of glazed composition and characterized by their small size, highly schematic typology, and the use of raised relief in the design which consists of symbols related to the Mesopotamian goddess Ishtar. Keel suggests a North Syrian origin for this group (Keel, *et al.* 1989: 39-87).

2. The "Jasper group" made of hard stones and with egyptianizing designs engraved in "stick figure" style. This group perhaps originated in the Megiddo region and is closely related in both material and design to a group of cylinders from a workshop somewhere on the Syrian coast (Keel, *et al.* 1989: 213-42).

In both cases, the designs are influenced by contemporary cylinder seals of North Syria, a key factor in identifying these two groups as being of local manufacture and not Egyptian imports. These are easily recognizable local traditions, restricted in number and distribution, and, above all, characterized by the techniques and materials used and the obvious connection to Syrian glyptic art.

The broader issue concerns scarabs made of steatite with an Egyptian typology and Egyptian designs. Such scarabs form the vast majority at Canaanite sites, exclusively so at some, and it is with this type of scarab that defining local workshops becomes extremely difficult. A case in point is Period I, the FIP and early Middle Kingdom, where the bulk of the excavated scarabs come from three neighboring sites in Middle Egypt: Qau, Matmar, and Mostagedda. Yet, the nine scarabs from contemporary burials at distant Mesheikh and Abydos conform precisely in all respects to those from the Middle Egyptian sites.[1] They show nothing which sets them apart as being from another workshop and, indeed, might almost be considered imports from an engraver's stock in Middle Egypt. This at a time when Egypt was not unified and one might expect regional differences to emerge as a result of local artisans working in relative isolation.

The situation is similar during the 12th to 15th Dynasties, though in dealing with a much larger sample some differences are bound to appear. We can, for example, look at four southern Canaanite sites and examine the scarabs found there in contemporary levels: the MB III phase at Lachish, Jericho, Fara Cemetery 500, and the upper levels at ^{c}Ajjûl. 40 typological categories are distributed in terms of general usage as in fig.7:1.

The distribution pattern that emerges shows that of the 40 typological categories, 15 show the same usage at all four sites, 17 at three sites. For the latter, no pattern is discernible in that any three of the four sites may agree in their use of any given category. The surprise is that in several categories there is a consistent division in distribution: all are rare or lacking at Lachish and Fara, but characteristic at Jericho and ^{c}Ajjûl. It is of interest that if we look at other contemporary sites such as Megiddo Phase G and the contemporary scarabs from Mostagedda, the typological profile is very similar to those of Jericho and ^{c}Ajjûl. The implication is that Jericho, ^{c}Ajjûl, and

Megiddo in Canaan, and Mostagedda in Egypt, have some common bond between them with respect to their scarabs.

	missing or rare	equally common
Four sites agree on:		
Heads	C, A1- A3	
Backs	lined	plain
Sides		d, e, d5, d6
Designs	1, 4, 5	2, 6
Three sites agree on:		
Heads	B1, D1-D6, D9	B, D, B2-B4
Sides	e4, e5, e7	e8-e10
Designs	8, 10, 11, 12	3, 9
Pairs of sites agree on:		
Heads A, A4-A6, B5-B8, D7-D8	Lachish and Fara	Jericho and ^{c}Ajjûl
Sides e11, e11a	Lachish and Fara	Jericho and ^{c}Ajjûl
Design 7	Lachish and Fara	Jericho and ^{c}Ajjûl

Fig. 7:1. Distribution of key typological features at MB III Canaanite sites.

This need not involve individual workshops at the Canaanite sites as sometimes proposed. Certainly, there were many workshops in Egypt and their products can be identified to a limited degree, more easily in the royal name series. One example is noted below -- scarabs of Amenemhat IV, Queen Sobknefru, and King Amenemhat-Senbef -- where one can suggest the work of a single engraver. Similarly, there are six scarabs of Neferhotep I which probably came from the same workshop.[2] One can also suggest different workshops for groups of design scarabs. The collections of Hyksos period scarabs from Sedment Cemetery K and Mostagedda, for example, are fairly well matched in their general typology. However, the Sedment scarabs do show an emphasis on X heads and class 4 designs not found at Mostagedda, or anywhere else for that matter, and the workmanship of the Sedment group is often inferior. Separate workshops in the Fayum and middle Egypt were obviously responsible for local production which illustrates different emphases at the two sites including different degrees of artistic competence. But identifying workshops and even individual engravers is a problem of some magnitude and is not a primary goal of the present work.

One matter which should be considered at this point is the source of supply for the extraordinary number of scarabs discovered at Canaanite sites. Here, of course, one must speculate at certain points, but a reasonable hypothesis seems to be as follows. It can be suggested with some justification that the great bulk of the scarabs found at Canaanite sites were imported from Egypt. The general typological profile, for example in Period V, is much the same everywhere and there is no way of isolating an "Egyptian" as opposed to a "Canaanite" style except in the case of a few individual pieces. Indeed, there is a general "sameness" in scarab production which, allowing for local differences such as pointed out above for Sedment and Mostagedda, almost forces the conclusion that scarabs as a class of object were made in Egypt and distributed from there.

It may all come down, then, to Canaanite merchants in different cities obtaining scarabs from various Egyptian sources of supply. This would readily account for the fact that A6 heads are far more common at Jericho, D6 heads and e9 sides at Lachish, and so on. Within the overall framework of the general typological profile of Period V, Egyptian workshops emphasized different features and this is reflected in their products exported to Canaan. This is not to say that we should discount local imitations for such were surely made. But these are usually easily identified; the great bulk of the scarabs found in Canaan came from Egyptian sources of supply. It would be reading too much into the vague evidence available to attempt to link individual Canaanite cities with specific Egyptian sources of manufacture. However, one can say with a degree of assurance that the differences in typology shown at different Canaanite sites may have arisen because local merchants purchased their stocks from different Egyptian producers.

All this, however, merely suggests that there seems to have been a single tradition of scarab manufacture represented by contemporary groups throughout Canaan that, allowing for minor local differences, shows the same general typology. That scarabs found in Egypt also conform to this typology suggests that scarabs in general were Egyptian imports.

This does not mean that local Canaanite workshops should be discounted. The Omega- and Jasper-groups noted above are proof enough that such workshops existed and certain motifs examined by Schroer such as the "toga wearers" (Keel and Schroer 1985: 52-115) and the "naked goddess" (Keel, *et al.* 1989: 92-138) are certainly of Canaanite origin. If, as now universally recognized, the Phoenician, Greek, and Etruscan scarab styles of the 1st millennium B.C. were produced in workshops around the Mediterranean, it is reasonable to expect that there was a Canaanite scarab tradition produced in that region in the 2d millennium B.C. The techniques and motifs noted here are sufficient to illustrate this, though there have some overly-enthusiastic conclusions drawn which one should expect in a relatively new field of research.[3] This is not an easy subject since, unlike the Mediterranean traditions just mentioned which are easily recognized both by their typology and corpus of designs, it is far more difficult to isolate Canaanite workshops since the overall character of scarabs found in Canaan and Egypt is very much the same.

B. THE DESIGN SCARAB SERIES

As a point of departure for a discussion of the evolution of design scarab typology, we can begin with Summary Table One (Chap. 9) which shows the percent of use of the general typological categories throughout the time-range covered here. It is quite clear that in each of the major typological categories, with few exceptions, a pronounced change in use occurred. This rather consistent change offers a basic general pattern for the history of scarab style.

Heads (fig. 9:1). Type X, a crude rendering of the head and clypeus in which the head is usually not even represented, is a common feature only in Period I. Type A, lunate heads, comprises 3/4 of the scarab heads in Period I and then shows a steady decline down to Period V, after which A heads again emerge in New Kingdom times (Period VI) as the dominant type. Type B, open heads, is rare at the beginning of the series and is then common from Periods IIA to V; B heads were much less used in the New Kingdom. Type C, square heads, are rare throughout the design scarab series and therefore offer no chronological criteria. Type D, trapezoidal heads, are rare in Periods

I-II and then increase until they appear on almost half the scarabs of Period V; in the New Kingdom, they become much less frequent.

Backs (fig. 9:2). Almost the entire repertoire of Periods I-II consists of LN, lined naturalistic, and LS, lined schematic, backs. In IIA they begin a decline, being replaced by PN, plain naturalistic, and PS, plain schematic backs. By Periods IV and V, the latter (PS) has become the dominant type. Once again, this steady evolution is reversed in the New Kingdom when LN and LS backs assume a more dominant role. Both lined and plain backs are sometimes decorated with various designs, the most common being a lotus, curl, or branch. Rarely, other designs may appear such as *ʿnḫ* or *m* hieroglyphs (Kirkbride 1965, fig. 293:10; Tufnell 1984, no. 3109). Such decorative elements appear throughout Periods IIA to VI, though are more frequent in IIA-III.[4] A very rare back is the so-called "hedgehog" type where the entire back is covered with a criss-cross design; this appears so seldom that it has no value for dating.[5]

Sides (fig. 9:3). Types a, grooved only and legs not shown, b, chip carved with head and tail clearly shown in profile, and c, pierced or hollowed, are distinctly early sides, common only in Period I; types b and c emerge again in the New Kingdom. Type d, chip carved with squared profile, and Type e, scored only, represent the full repertoire of sides from Periods IIA to V, with Type e making up two-thirds of the sides in IIA and III, the two types about evenly matched in IV and V. Both were less used in the New Kingdom.

Designs (figs. 9:4, 9:5). Class 1, geometric, is characteristic only of Period I, was still fairly common in II and IIA, but rare thereafter. Class 2, scrolls and spirals, is again an early type, rare from Period III on. 3 Early is a distinctly early design class, not used after Period II. Class 3 is basically of the Middle Kingdom and less used in Periods IV-V. 3A, monograms and varia, and 3B, symmetric patterns, represent the characteristic design repertoire of the Middle Kingdom and appear less frequently later on. The other class 3 designs are much less prominent. Design classes 4, concentric circles, 5, cross patterns, and 6, coiled and woven patterns, are generally of little chronological value though class 5 is more common in the earlier periods, class 6 in the later ones. Class 4 is generally rare; the extensive use in Period II cannot be considered typical since this is a singular feature of the Montet Jar collection and this very high percentage is shown nowhere else. Class 7, scroll borders, was most frequently used in Periods III-IV, Class 8, rope borders, are about evenly distributed in III to V, Classes 9, animals, and 10, human and mythical figures, are most common in Periods IV-V. The latter continue into the New Kingdom as relatively frequent.

This brief overview of the evolution of scarab style sets out the main stages in that evolution, each of which is distinct from the others in terms of which general typological categories are most frequent. These stages and their rough chronology may be listed as follows:

Period I	FIP and early Middle Kingdom
Period II	early 12th Dynasty
Periods IIA-III	12th and earlier 13th Dynasties
Period IV	later 13th Dynasty
Period V	15th Dynasty
Period VI	earlier 18th Dynasty

It now remains to verify this scheme and discuss the varieties of the general typological categories as they apply to the chronological evolution of scarab style. In this more detailed analysis, the basis for discussion are Figures 7:3, showing the characteristic features of each Period, and Tables 5-8 (Chap. 9) where the statistical information is assembled on the design scarab scarab series.

The most outstanding feature of any typology is its continuous development and change: each chronological stage will share some characteristics with the stages that precede and follow. This is especially true of general typological categories which tend to last and be characteristic over long periods of time. One must therefore examine the varieties within general categories which tend to be prominent for shorter periods. It is the combined weight of the shorter lived varieties and details of scarab style which offer the best evidence for typological history.

As an example, we may consider side type e (scored). Scored sides are very common from Period II on; as a general category, then, they are not helpful in dating. However, the varieties of side type e show a much more clearly defined chronology as illustrated in fig. 7:2. Side e6 is found most in Period II, then gradually declines in use until Period IV, after which it begins to be more common. Side e9 does not occur until IIA, is most common in III and then gradually goes out of use. Side e11 shows a gradual increase in use from Periods I to VI. In other words, e6 is most likely to occur in Periods II, IIA, V, and VI; e9 in IIA and III; e11 in IV, V, VI.

Even the smallest details may be significant. Fig. 7:2 illustrates that head A3, with single lines denoting the eyes and a flat base line, is clearly an early type which is not found from Periods IIA to V; it becomes characteristic again in VI. Head A6, with single lines denoting the eyes but with a "sausage" shape, shows the opposite. Head A6 was used during that span of time when A3 was not used.

Fig. 7:2 illustrates another important feature of the methodology used here. If one is dealing with a group of scarabs from the same context, the relative use of varieties comes into play. A group with a high percent of e9 sides and A6 heads, and with few e11 sides and no A3 heads, is most likely of Period III, the later 12th Dynasty. A group with about the same percent of use for all three sides and a low percent of use for both heads will date to Period V, the 15th Dynasty. One must, of course, assess the use of all heads and sides as well as backs and designs. It is a somewhat laborious process but does lead to fairly accurate dating.

It must be emphasized that it is not primarily *when* a given typological feature appears, but rather its frequency of use. That is, a scarab made at any time from the early FIP to the New Kingdom may have head A4 or A6, but it is most likely to have one of these heads if it was made during the 12th Dynasty. This is why it is essential to study the whole scarab and why the Tufnell-Ward typology is of necessity as complicated as it is. The more general typological features such as a back type or design class are not accurate criteria in themselves. One must look at all categories, varieties, and details to determine their collective evidence. Back type LN can appear on a scarab at any time, but it is least likely to occur during the 13th and 15th Dynasties. It is only when Back type LN is used in conjunction with head, side and design that a reasonable date can be suggested.

Periods I and II, the beginning and early phases of scarab manufacture, are characterized by a rather restricted typology. This is especially true of Period I, the FIP and early MK, when head types X, A1, and A3 are the overwhelming majority (84%), the early sides a, b, and c account for 87% of the side corpus, lined backs make up 99% of the back corpus, and designs 1 and 3 Early (as opposed to class 3 of the

Middle Kingdom and later)[6] comprise most of the design corpus. This is therefore a distinct and homogeneous stage in scarab style.

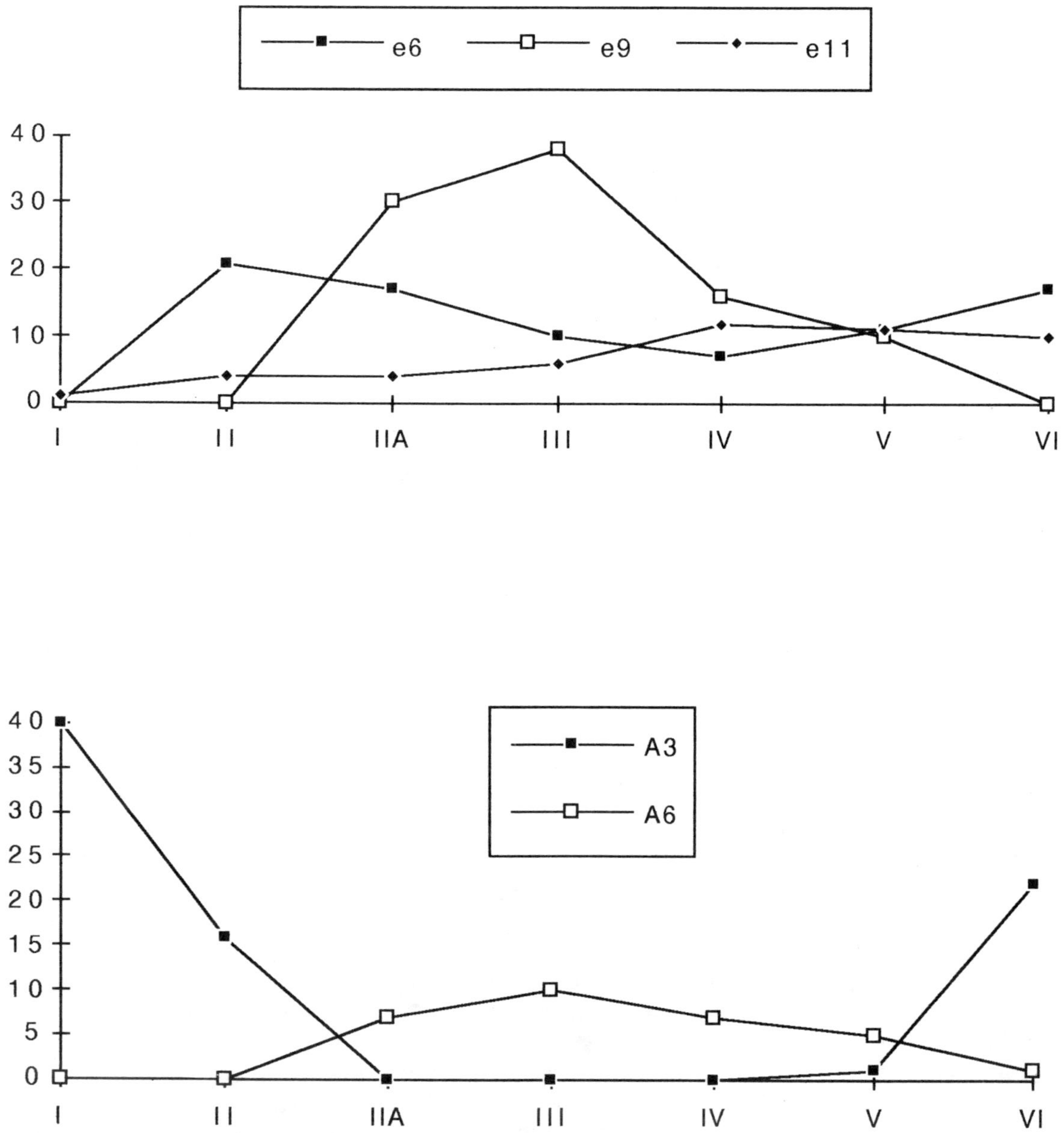

Fig. 7:2. Varieties of Side e and Head A, percent of use.

Period II, the Montet Jar group, carries on the older tradition in terms of heads, backs, and designs, but has generally dropped the early side types in favor of the new 12th Dynasty scored sides (type e) on 81% of the group, mostly e4 to e6. Again, it should be emphasized that the Montet Jar scarabs fit nowhere else in that they bridge the gap between Periods I and IIA, sharing basic typological features with both; see Chapter 4. On the details of these scarabs, see Ward 1978a, though the date suggested there is too early.

The IIA group introduces what may be called the classic 12th Dynasty style, with emphasis on heads A4 and B2, plain backs, sides d5, e9 and e10, and design class 3B paired signs. Elements of this 12th Dynasty style can be seen already in the Montet Jar group in its use of head B2. The IIA group is further tied to the Montet Jar in its continued use of lined backs (though less in number) and the emphasis that both place on side e6. Otherwise, the IIA scarabs have added several new characteristic features, indicating it represents a new stage in scarab style.

Period III follows very closely the typological profile of the IIA group with some slight differences in emphasis. The Period III scarabs thus carry on the classical 12th Dynasty style and, as already noted (Chap. 5), are contemporary to the late 12th and early 13th Dynasties.

Periods IV and V also go together in general terms: emphasis on plain backs, less use of lined backs, an increase in the use of side d5, and a new dominance of design classes 6, 9, and 10, and heads D7-9. Period V is distinguished from IV by, among other things, its extensive use of head D9 and side e11a, two of the few typological features which are more or less restricted to the 15th Dynasty and later.

Period VI, added here for comparative purposes only, shows an abrupt reappearance of old stylistic features such as the simple lunate heads A1 and A3, sides a and b, and lined backs. These head and side types were characteristic of Period I and hardly used thereafter. Lined backs were characteristic from Periods I to III and then became less common except for the royal name scarabs of the 13th Dynasty with their own unique style. It is of interest that some important categories of Period V continue as characteristic into the New Kingdom, though there are several new features which indicate yet another new stage in scarab history. Among these are the extensive use of the humeral callosity,[7] the portrayal of deities and kings in various poses, divine names, and a few new head types.

The gradual evolution of design scarab typology is shown in fig.7:3 which lists those features that appear on 10% or more of the scarabs in each Period. Many of these features, of course, were used in lesser numbers before and after their appearance in fig.7:3. The significant factor here is that in each Period there is a group of typological features which becomes characteristic even though there may be a few previous examples. Thus, each Period is distinguished from those before and after by the emphasis placed on individual features. For example, while isolated cases of design 1 are known after Periods I-II, it is only in these early stages of scarab history that this design can be termed characteristic. Sides d6 and e11 may be found sporadically before Periods IV-V, but it is only in these later stages that they are characteristic. There are, of course, a few features which are common throughout the series. In short, the evolution of scarab typology is exactly like that of any other common archaeological object such as pottery, jewelry, weapons, and the like.

While scarab length is only a supporting feature in scarab history, it does play a minor role. It must be cautioned, however, that the criterion of scarab length has only limited value with groups of scarabs , probably none when applied to individual examples. Table 13 (Chap. 9) summarizes the significant factors involved, showing that from Periods I to V scarab length gradually increased from an average of 12.5 to 17.5 mm. Again, note that Periods IIA-III are very close as are Periods IV-V. In the 18th Dynasty, or Period VI, as with so many other features of scarab style, the scarabs are generally smaller and the average length reverts to that of the 12th Dynasty. On the whole, the major contribution of the tabulation of scarab length is to add one more argument in support of the historical evolution of scarab style as represented by other general categories such as heads and sides. Again, it should be emphasized that the criterion of scarab length is of no value in dating individual pieces.

C. Comparison of Royal Name and Design Scarabs

Scarabs engraved with royal names first appear at the beginning of the 12th Dynasty (Ward 1984:151), some two centuries after the introduction of design scarabs. The designation "royal name scarab" is more appropriate than the customary "royal scarab" which implies the use and ownership of these objects by kings and high officials deputized to seal official documents and the like with the reigning king's name. In reality, there are very few such scarabs. Most of the known examples were rather used as amulets granting the protection and influence of the royal name to the individuals who owned them.[8] This raises the question of which royal name scarabs are contemporary to the kings whose names they bear and which were made later, for example, as talismans to be sold within the precinct of a royal funerary temple, perhaps centuries after a given ruler had died.[9] In the present context, this problem is only troublesome for scarabs naming 12th Dynasty kings, not those of the 13th and 15th Dynasties; the solution adopted here has been explained in Chap. 2B.3.

In its chronological evolution, the royal name series differs from the design scarab series in two respects. First, it does not show a continuous and unbroken development, but is interrupted in the 13th Dynasty by the new and temporary scarab style of the Sebekhotep group (see infra). Second, while the two series have many typological categories in common, the royal name scarabs are characterized by features which may be little used on design scarabs. It is primarily for the latter reason that royal name scarabs must be considered a class separate from design scarabs, and why the two kinds of scarabs should be examined by themselves.

The general history of royal name scarabs is seen in fig. 7:4 and Summary Table Two, Royal Name Series (Chap. 9). The most evident factor here is that on the basis of all major typological categories, there are three clearly defined groupings in the royal name series -- the 12th, 13th, and 15th Dynasties. Each of these is further subdivided into Early and Late as discussed in Ward 1984: 173-76. A break in the typological sequence occurs with the 13th Dynasty, a second break with the 15th Dynasty. This does not conform to the design scarab series where the typological sequence is constant and unbroken from the 12th to the 15th Dynasties (Periods IIA to V). The reason for this three-fold separation in the royal name series is the very different scarab style introduced by the "Sebekhotep group" which accounts for all but a few royal name scarabs dating to the 13th Dynasty.

As with the design scarab series (fig. 7:3), a listing of the characteristic typological features of royal name scarabs (fig. 7:4) shows a similar pattern of evolution. Each stage in the royal name series emphasizes certain features, though the sequence is disrupted by the unique 13th Dynasty style, characterized by many features common only at that time (C heads, sides d9, e9, e10, etc.). Still, the same gradual pattern of change is evident so that the beginning and end of the series are vastly different from each other and one moves from Early 12 to Late 15 though a series of distinct stylistic stages. Comparison between figs. 7:3 and 7:4 shows that design scarabs

Feature Per.	I	II	IIA	III	IV	V	VI
Head X	X						
Side a	O						
Sides b1-b2	X						
Side c2	O						
Side d1	O						
Side c3	O						O
Head A1	X	X					X
Head A3	X	O					X
Design 3 Early	X	O					
Design 1	X	O					
Back LN	X	X	X				
Back LS	X	X	O	O			X
Head A2		O					
Side e4		O					
Side e5		X					
Design 2		X	O				
Head B2		O	X	X	X	O	
Side e6		X	O	O		O	O
Design 3A3			O	O			O
Design 3B3			O	O			
Side e9			X	X	O	O	
Back PN			X	X	X	X	
Back PS			X	X	X	X	X
Side d5			O	O	X	X	X
Head A6				O			
Design 3B1				O			
Design 3C				O	O		
Design 7B				O	O		
Design 8					O		
Side d6					O	O	O
Side e11					O	O	O
Design 6					O	O	
Design 9					O	O	
Design 10					O	O	
Hewad D9						O	
Side e11a						O	
Head A5							O
Design 11D							O

Fig. 7:3. Characteristic typological features: design scarabs. O = 10%, X=20%

Feature Per.	E 12	L 12	E 13	L 13	E15	L 15
Head B2	O					
Head B6	O					
Design 3B3	O					
Design 3D1	O					
Design 7A	X					
Design 7B	O					
Head A4	O	O				
Side e6	O	X				
Back LN	O	O	X	X		
Back LS	O		X	X		
Back PN	X	X			X	
Side d6	X	O			X	
Back PS	X	X			X	X
Side d5	O	O	X		X	X
Head A6		O				
Head B3		O				
Head B4		O				
Side e8		O				
Design 3B4		O				
Design 8		O				
Design 7C		O			X	
Head C2			O			
Side d9			X			
Head C7			O	X		
Head D5			X	X		
Design 3D2			X		O	
Design 3D4			X	X	O	
Side d8				O		
Side d10				O		
Side e9				X		
Side e10				O		
Design 3D3					O	
Design 3E1					O	
Design 3E2					O	
Head D6					O	O
Head D9					X	O
Design 3E3					O	O
Head D3					X	O
Head D7						X
Head D8						O
Side e11						O
Side e11a						O
Design 3E4						X

Fig. 7:4. Characteristic typological features: royal name scarabs. 0=10% X=20%

and those with royal names each have their own distinctive evolution. While there are individual features emphasized at the same time in both classes of scarab, there are substantial differences which collectively illustrate why these two types of scarabs should be studied and classified independently.

The general history of royal name scarabs as they relate to design scarabs would appear to be as follows.

1. The 12th Dynasty.

When scarabs engraved with royal names first appeared, artisans used the obvious as their typological model, the design scarabs with which they had by then long been accustomed.. This accounts for the similarities between 12th Dynasty royal name scarabs and the contemporary design scarabs of Periods IIA and III; for the details, see Chap. 5C. It can be no coincidence that the introduction of royal name scarabs occurred roughly at the same time a major change took place in the typology of design scarabs evidenced first in Period IIA. It has been argued elsewhere (Ward 1984: 151) that the move of the Egyptian capitol from Thebes to Lisht, accompanied by active and widespread bureaucratic growth, was responsible for the appearance of scarabs with both royal and private names.[10] Such scarabs introduced basic stylistic alterations which were bound to affect design scarabs manufactured at the same time, probably in the same workshops.

Just how much this new class of scarabs with names is responsible for the changes in style in the design scarab tradition at this time is hard to say. One basic change was in the design repertoire. Since the vertical space of the scarab plinth on scarabs with names was reserved for names, titles, and epithets, there was room left only for border designs. The new royal name scarabs are thus replete with design classes 3B (paired signs), 7 (spirals), 8 (ropes), and 4D (concentric circles).[11] Such border designs were then adapted to contemporary design scarabs in which tradition there is very little to anticipate the extensive use of these design patterns in the 12th Dynasty groups.[12] While all these border designs eventually appear on design scarabs, it was a gradual process. Only 3B designs, a hallmark of the 12th Dynasty style, occur commonly in Period IIA; of the other border designs, there is only one example each of 7B (paired scrolls) from Megiddo and 4D from Ruweisé tomb 66; cf. fig. 5:1, nos. 26, 40. Borders 7B and 4D became more common in Period III, and 8 appears for the first time, but of all these border designs, only 3B, 7B and 8 became characteristic on design scarabs.

The more precise relationships between royal name scarabs of the 12th Dynasty and Periods IIA-III have been discussed in Chap. 5C and need not be repeated here.

2. The 13th Dynasty

Scarab studies generally emphasize the so-called "Sebekhotep group" when discussing royal name scarabs of the 13th Dynasty. However, there are several scarabs naming other rulers of this dynasty which fall before and after the Sebekhotep kings. While there are only a half dozen before this group and a like number after the Sebekhotep rulers, these few scarabs are instructive for an overall view of the history of royal name scarabs.

The half dozen from the early years of the 13th Dynasty (Ward 1984:159-60), insofar as their typological features are known, carry on the stylistic tradition of the 12th Dynasty. There is, for example, an emphasis on 7B scroll borders which allies this group to the Late XII royal name scarabs. To these may be added a recently published scarab of Amenemhat-Senbef, second ruler of the 13th Dynasty (Beste 1979: 158-60). It is of the finest Middle Kingdom work and its typology (A4 PN c3) plus the 7C scroll border ending in cobra heads exactly reproduces that of a scarab of Queen Sobknefru (these two scarabs may well have been produced by the same craftsman) and is very similar to that of one of Amenemhat IV (Tufnell 1984, nos. 3094-95). The 7C scroll border with cobra heads is further paralleled by a scarab naming Sesostris III from the Dahshur group (Tufnell 1984, no. 3065). The half dozen from the latter part of the 13th Dynasty (Ward 1984:160-61) show a typological pattern which allies them to both the Sebekhotep group (emphasis on C heads) and the Early 15 royal name scarabs (use of 7B scroll borders). In other words, these two groups of scarabs from the beginning and end of the 13th Dynasty preserve vestiges of what the 13th Dynasty royal name scarabs would have looked like had there been the same uninterrupted stylistic development in the royal name series as there was in the design scarab series.

But what of the abrupt break in the stylistic development of royal name scarabs with the so-called Sebekhotep group (Ward 1984: 156-59)? This consists of six kings from Sebekhotep III to Merneferre, placed by von Beckerath ca. 1744-1690 B.C., by Stock a few years earlier. This group is characterized by larger sizes, square heads (type C), a near-universal use of lined backs, sides d8 and d9, and an almost complete absence of ancillary designs on the base, the emphasis here being on "genealogical" inscriptions; see discussion of fig. 2:6.

One cannot easily explain this abrupt departure from an artistic tradition that had been slowly developing for some four centuries. It is highly unlikely that we are faced here with a "southern" scarab tradition as opposed to a "northern" one represented by royal name scarabs of the 12th Dynasty. No such distinction is discernable in contemporary design scarabs which, as already noted, continue in an unbroken and gradual stylistic development. And since the kings of the Sebekhotep group ruled from the Middle Kingdom capitol of Itj-towy (Ward 1984: 155, with n. 34), if anything, they would have continued the royal name scarab style of the 12th Dynasty. Since the earliest rulers of the 13th Dynasty did precisely that (see above), there seems no immediately obvious historical reason why Sebekhotep III would suddenly introduce a new and quite different scarab style.

The answer probably lies with the family itself, or rather, the general nature of "royalty" during this dynasty. By whatever means the sixty-odd kings of the 13th Dynasty attained the throne -- appointment or election by state officials is the usual suggestion -- they were not "royal" in the sense that they belonged to a ruling family or founded one. They were only "royal" for the short period they actually sat on the throne, having been promoted for a while from relative obscurity and then receding back into the more ordinary world from whence they had come. Fortunately, enough is known of the Sebekhotep family to outline its middle or lower class origins at Aswân. Whatever the method by which they achieved the kingship, this group, at least, established a short dynasty which was, according to available evidence, the most influential group of the period both in Egypt and abroad (Habachi 1951, 1981; Laming Macadam 1951). The sudden appearance of the new scarab style must thus surely be thought of as introducing a new commemorative style announcing the accession of Sebekhotep III to the throne, a practise then followed by his successors.

3. The 15th Dynasty

Royal name scarabs in the period of the 15th Dynasty are, as they were in the 12th Dynasty, typologically similar to contemporary design scarabs. The latter had continued in an unbroken development, not at all influenced by the radical stylistic changes of the Sebekhotep group. The few 13th Dynasty royal name scarabs following the Sebekhotep group show a mixture of features left over from that group -- e.g., an emphasis on square (C) heads -- and some from the contemporary design scarabs, e.g., scroll borders (Ward 1984: 161). The design scarab influence returns in full force with the royal name scarabs of the 15th Dynasty. In the following paragraphs, the general sequence of the many rulers of the period as proposed in Ward 1984 will be assumed (fig. 7:5).[13]

Main Sequence	Supplementary Sequence
Seuserenre Khayaranu (Khyan)	Semqen
Ynss-idn	
Meruserre Yakubhar	
	Anathar
Mayibre Sheshi	Sekheperenre
	Wadjed
Khauserre Amu	Nehsy
Sekhaenre *Ykbmw*	Seket
Nubuserre *Y*^{c}*mw*	Qar
	Šwb
Ahetepre	*Ykb*^{c}*l*
Auserre Apophis	Nikare
Khamudy	

Fig. 7:5. Tentative Order of Kings, 15th Dynasty Period. After Ward 1984: 172.

As in the 12th Dynasty, the design repertoire of the 15th Dynasty royal name scarabs is limited to borders since the central space of the plinth is taken up by names, titles, and epithets. 3B borders (paired signs) now appear on only 10% of both royal name and design scarabs, far less frequently than in the 12th Dynasty. What is new in the 15th Dynasty are the characteristic 3E3 and 3E4 borders, the so-called "Hyksos sides," which are a late degraded variety of 3B (Ward 1984: 165). These, however, are quite rare on the design scarabs of this period. The other border designs -- 4 concentric circles, 7 scrolls, 8 rope borders -- are all rare on both royal name and design scarabs. The single exception is 7C spirals which is a characteristic border in Early 15, but with only a single example in Late 15. This border is very rare on the contemporary design scarabs.

Other typological categories also show that royal name and design scarabs were again engraved in a similar style. In both classes of scarabs, the earlier characteristic features have all but disappeared, e.g., lined backs, side e6, and heads A4 and A6. Both classes are now characterized by, among other things, plain schematic backs, sides e11 and e11a, and heads D7 to D9.

4. Summary: Royal name and design scarabs

The most salient feature of a comparison between royal name and design scarabs of the 12th to 15th Dynasties is that while design scarabs underwent a continuous unbroken pattern of stylistic development, royal name scarabs did not. In the most general comparative terms, 12th Dynasty royal name scarabs show a typology very similar to that of Periods IIA and III; 15th Dynasty royal name scarabs compare favorably with those of Periods IV and V. There is no comparable typological similarity between the scarabs of the 13th Dynasty Sebekhotep group and any stage in the history of design scarabs. That is, one would expect to find some connections between this large group of royal name scarabs, representing the bulk of the known examples naming 13th Dynasty kings, and design scarabs of Periods III and IV.

This is not the case. The Sebekhotep group bears little similarity to the design scarab series in any typological category. It is as stylistically different from design scarabs as it is from 12th Dynasty royal name scarabs. Indeed, the Sebekhotep group shows a unique scarab style which shows only minimal relationship to the scarab tradition of the whole period. It is therefore obvious that, contrary to most scarab studies (Petrie 1917; Martin 1971; O'Connor 1987; etc.), the Sebekhotep group is not representative of 13th Dynasty scarabs, royal name or design, and has no value in establishing a history of scarab style.

D. TEST GROUPS

In order to confirm the general results of the typological system presented here, several test groups have been analyzed statistically and compared with the main sample. These test groups are as follows. Their full typological classification is given in Sect. E, below.

<u>Supplementary Group 1:</u> Canaanite contexts, MB III period

<u>1.</u> Lachish: 72 scarabs from MB III deposits -- Tufnell 1958: pls. 30-32; tombs 119, 153, 1502; caves 1542, 6002, 6027, 6028.

<u>2.</u> Barqai, Plain of Sharon: 14 scarabs from the latest MB layer in a tomb -- Gophna and Sussman 1969: 1-13, fig. 10. This group includes a scarab naming Mayibre Sheshi.

<u>3.</u> Shechem: 15 scarabs and 5 impressions from MB IIC strata -- Horn 1962: 6-14, nos. 22-27, 30; 1966: 48-56, nos. 46, 48, 50, 51; 1973: 281-89, nos. 57, 59-62, 66, 72-74.

<u>4.</u> Amman: 30 scarabs from two tombs discovered on the acropolis; Ward 1966: 5-18. The pottery from these tombs, subsequently studied by Piccirillo 1978: 73-86, is basically MB III though a few vessels may be early LB I. The scarabs, including one naming Mayibre Sheshi, belong mainly to Period V; three or four may be of the earlier 18th Dynasty. The classification of the scarabs used here is based on the original drawings which are somewhat blurred in the publication.

Supplementary Group 2: Egyptian contexts, 13th to 15th Dynasties.

5. 97 scarabs from the middle Egyptian sites in the Qau district -- Brunton 1930, pl. 19; 1937: pl.69; 1948: pl. 43. Brunton's use of "Second Intermediate Period" embraces the whole period between the 12th and 18th Dynasties. In these publications, the sides are generally not illustrated.

Supplementary Group 3: miscellaneous.

6. Megiddo: 28 scarabs from tomb 24; Guy 1938: 48-50, pls. 23 (pottery) and 105-06 (scarabs). The pottery from this tomb is of MB II date.

7. Mirgissa: 31 scarabs from Tomb KT.2 and Cemetery M.X; Vercoutter 1970; 1976; late 13th to early 15th Dynasty. Sides are not illustrated.

8. Sedment: 45 scarabs from Cemetery K; Petrie and Brunton 1924: pl. 43; 15th Dynasty. Sides generally not illustrated.

Discussion

Four of these test groups (Lachish, Barqai, Shechem, Amman) are considered together as "Supplementary Group 1" since they can all be placed by their context in Period V. The Qau, Mostagedda and Matmar scarabs make up "Supplementary Group 2"; the date here is less restricted and covers both Periods IV and V. The Mostagedda and Matmar groups belong in the latter period, but the context at Qau apparently begins in the 13th Dynasty. Unfortunately, the scarab sides of the Mostagedda and Matmar scarabs have not been published so one important dating criterion is missing. The miscellaneous groups (Megiddo Tomb 24, Mirgissa, and Sedment Cemetery K) are taken up separately below.

The actual number count of the typological features used on these groups is shown in Tables A to D in order to present the basic facts, though the important reference at this point is Table E. The latter shows the percent of use in all major typological categories in Periods IV and V and Supplementary Groups 1 and 2.

It is clear from Table E that Supplementary Group 1 and Period V of the main series are very similar in their typological profiles. This is to be expected since three of the four collections which make up this group have datable archaeological contexts (MB III) and the fourth (Amman) dates to MB III with a slight overlap into LB I. In terms of back and side types, Supplementary Group 1 conforms precisely to the percent of use in Period V. There is also general agreement in the use of head types, though the percentage is somewhat lower for B heads, higher for D heads. With the design classes, the only difference lies in 3A and 3B designs, both of which are less frequent in Period V of the main series, and class 8 which is missing in Supplementary Group 1. On the whole, however, the use of design is consistently the same as Period V. The significant point in the present context is that four additional scarab collections, when compared with those that make up Period V, have a very similar typological profile. This is sufficient to show that for Period V, at least, the main sample is probably representative of scarab production at that time.

Supplementary Group 2 is worth including here even though it presents problems which only a complete analysis of the archaeological contexts might resolve. Also, it illustrates the disadvantage in not knowing the full typology; in this case, most of the side types are unknown. The scarabs from Mostagedda, where most of the sides *are* known, generally conforms to Period V. The Qau group is close to Period IV in its use of head and back types, but to Periods IV and V in terms of design classes.[14] The group from Matmar is too small to be of value here though, since archaeologically it falls at the end of the series (Brunton 1948: 57), it goes with Mostagedda rather than Qau. As a whole, then, Supplementary Group 2 covers a substantial period of time, perhaps most of the 13th and 15th Dynasties with the main emphasis on the latter period. This conforms to the Period IV-V date suggested by the typology of the scarabs.

The remaining supplementary groups date to various periods. The 28 scarabs from Megiddo Tomb 24 conform in general to Period III, in particular the mix of back and side types. The head types of this group do not, as a whole, fit any single period though the mix of heads A and B is closest to Period IIA. The large percentage of D heads is more oriented toward Period V. The absence of X and C heads is meaningless since this is the general situation throughout the series after Periods I-II. The mix of design classes indicates the IIA-III range, with a few more akin to Period V. Since the pottery from this tomb dates to MB II, the scarabs fall typologically where they should.

The scarabs from Mirgissa come from late 13th to early 15th Dynasty contexts. The mix of head types is very close to that of Supplementary Group 1 (see supra), the mix of back types is what is expected in Period V. The scarab sides have not been published so that, as with Qau and Matmar, an important criterion is missing. Since the designs are dominated by classes 9 (animals) and 11 (names), several ancillary designs such as class 1 are less used or missing. This group thus conforms generally to its archaeological context (cf. Ward 1984: 176-78).

The last supplementary group is that from Sedment Cemetery K, the context of which is the 15th Dynasty. This collection is included here to illustrate one of the difficulties in dating groups of scarabs which may be dominated by typological features that are quite out of place in the period to which they belong. In this case, the Sedment scarabs are characterized by a rather crude style with class 4E designs as well as a large number of X heads. These two features set the Sedment group apart from all those examined in the present project. The large number of X heads is seen only in Period 1, the high percentage of design 4E is found nowhere else. The oft-repeated parallel between the concentric circle designs of the Sedment scarabs and those of the Montet Jar group of Period II is invalid; the Sedment group is wholly of class 4E, the latest stage in the history of that design which is not found in the large design 4 repertoire of the Montet Jar (Ward 1987, fig. 3). The extensive use of head X and design 4E is undoubtedly what lowers the high percentage of D heads and designs 9-10 one expects in a Period V group.

In summary, the testing of ten scarab groups against the typological history obtained from the main design scarab series has produced satisfactory results. These, of course, are not complete since the sides of four of these groups (Qau, Matmar, Mirgissa, Sedment) are unknown and in dating groups of scarabs the mix of side types is a significant factor. On the whole, however, the supplementary material presented here does fit chronologically where its archaeological context indicates it should.

Table A. Heads. Supplementary Groups. Actual numbers.

	Suppl. Group 1				Suppl. Group 2			Misc. Groups		
	Lach	Barq	Shech	Amm	Qau	Most	Matm	Meg	Mirg	Sedm
X1	-	-	1	-	2	-	-	-	1	1
X2	-	-	-	1	-	2	-	-	-	4
X3	-	-	-	-	-	-	-	-	-	1
X4	-	-	-	-	-	-	-	-	-	2
X5	-	-	-	-	-	-	-	-	-	-
A1	-	2	-	1	3	-	2	-	-	-
A2	-	-	-	-	-	-	1	-	-	-
A3	2	-	-	-	-	2	-	-	-	1
A4	2	-	-	-	-	1	-	6	-	2
A5	-	-	2	-	1	-	-	2	-	-
A6	3	1	-	-	1	-	-	1	2	-
A7	1	-	-	-	-	-	-	-	-	-
A8	-	-	-	-	-	1	-	-	-	-
B1	-	-	-	-	1	3	1	-	1	-
B2	8	-	3	1	7	3	3	6	2	10
B3	3	1	-	1	-	-	-	-	1	1
B4	1	-	-	-	-	-	-	-	1	-
B5	-	-	-	-	-	-	-	-	-	-
B6	1	-	-	-	-	-	-	-	-	1
B7	6	-	-	-	-	-	-	-	-	1
B8	-	-	-	-	-	-	-	-	1	-
B9	-	-	-	-	-	-	-	-	-	-
C1	-	-	-	-	1	-	-	-	-	-
C2	-	-	-	-	1	2	-	-	-	-
C3	-	-	-	1	-	-	-	-	-	-
C4	-	-	-	-	-	-	-	-	-	-
C5	-	-	-	-	-	-	-	-	1	-
C6	-	-	-	-	-	-	-	-	-	-
C7	-	-	-	-	-	1	-	-	-	-
D1	5	4	1	-	2	2	-	-	-	1
D2	1	-	-	2	1	-	-	3	-	-
D3	5	-	-	1	-	-	2	-	-	-
D4	1	-	-	-	-	-	-	1	-	-
D5	8	-	1	3	2	5	-	1	1	2
D6	14	2	2	13	1	1	1	6	3	-
D7	4	1	-	2	-	1	-	-	2	-
D8	1	-	2	3	3	8	2	2	11	9
D9	3	2	3	-	1	1	1	-	2	3

Table B. Backs. Supplementary Groups. Actual Numbers.

	Suppl. Group 1				Suppl. Group 2			Misc. Groups		
	Lach	Barq	Shech	Amm	Qau	Most	Matm	Meg	Mirg	Sedm
LN	2	2	2	2	2	1	-	6	3	1
LS	9	1	2	-	5	8	2	2	4	4
PN	17	5	1	3	6	1	3	7	6	5
PS	43	6	10	25	12	23	8	11	17	32
xx	-	-	-	-	-	-	-	2	-	1
MSc	-	-	-	-	3	2	-	-	-	1
d	10	-	3	-	-	2	-	-	2	1
v	-	2	-	-	-	1	-	-	-	-

xx = hedgehog back
MSc = multiple scarab back
d = decorated
v = incipient humeral callosity

(scarabs with d and v are counted with regular back types)

Table C. Sides. Supplementary Groups. Actual numbers. (Side types are mostly unknown for Qau, Matmar, Mirgissa and Sedment.)

	Suppl. Group 1				Suppl. Group 2			Misc. Groups		
	Lach	Barq	Shech	Amm	Qau	Most	Matm	Meg	Mirg	Sedm
d5	18	6	1	9	-	6	-	4	-	-
d6	6	1	-	4	-	1	-	4	1	-
d7	1	-	-	-	-	-	-	-	-	-
d8	-	-	-	-	-	-	-	-	-	-
d9	-	-	-	-	-	-	-	-	-	-
d10	-	-	-	-	-	-	-	-	-	-
d11	-	-	-	-	-	1	-	-	-	1
d12	-	-	-	-	-	1	-	-	-	-
d13	-	-	-	-	-	-	-	-	-	-
d14	-	-	-	-	-	-	-	-	-	-
d15	1	-	-	-	-	-	-	-	-	-
e2	1	-	-	-	-	-	-	-	-	-
e4	-	-	-	-	-	1	-	-	-	-
e5	-	-	-	2	2	5	-	5	-	-
e6	6	1	-	1	-	-	-	1	-	-
e7	-	-	-	-	-	-	-	-	-	2
e8	-	-	2	-	-	-	-	-	-	-
e9	8	1	-	-	-	2	-	10	-	1
e10	18	3	1	7	-	-	-	2	-	-
e11	1	-	-	1	-	2	-	2	-	-
e11a	7	1	2	6	-	10	1	-	-	-

Table D. Designs. Supplementary Groups. Actual numbers.

	Suppl. Group				Suppl. Group 2			Misc. Groups		
	Lach	Barq	Shech	Amm	Qau	Most	Matm	Meg	Mirg	Sedm
1A	-	-	-	-	-	-	-	-	-	-
1B	2	-	-	-	-	-	-	-	-	-
1C	-	-	-	-	-	-	-	-	-	-
1D	-	-	-	-	-	-	-	-	-	-
1E	2	-	1	1	-	3	-	-	-	1
2A	5	-	1	-	4	1	-	1	3	-
2B	3	-	-	-	1	-	2	-	-	1
3A1	1	-	-	-	1	-	-	2	1	-
3A2	-	-	-	1	2	-	-	-	-	-
3A3	16	-	3	4	10	10	4	9	2	8
3A4	2	-	1	-	-	-	-	-	-	1
3B1	2	1	-	3	1	1	1	3	-	1
3B2	3	-	-	1	1	-	-	-	-	-
3B3	3	-	-	1	3	-	-	3	1	-
3B4	1	-	-	2	1	-	-	2	-	-
3B5	5	1	-	2	3	2	1	3	1	3
3B6	6	2	1	-	-	-	-	3	2	2
3B7	-	-	-	-	-	-	-	-	-	-
3C	11	3	-	3	6	7	1	4	4	4
3D	2	1	-	1	-	-	-	2	-	-
3E1	2	-	2	-	-	-	-	-	-	-
3E2	-	2	-	-	-	-	-	-	1	-
3E3	-	-	-	-	-	-	-	-	-	-
3E4	1	-	1	-	2	-	-	-	-	-
3E5	-	-	-	1	-	-	-	1	-	-
3E6	-	-	-	-	-	-	-	-	-	-
3E7	-	-	-	-	-	-	-	-	-	-
4A	-	-	1	-	-	-	-	-	-	-
4B	1	-	1	-	-	-	-	1	-	-
4C	-	-	-	-	-	-	-	-	-	-
4D	1	-	-	-	-	-	-	-	1	-
4E	1	1	-	-	4	2	-	-	2	13
5	2	2	-	2	-	-	-	2	1	1

Table D (Cont)

	Suppl Group 1				Suppl. Group 2			Misc. Groups		
	Lach	Barq	Shech	Amm	Qau	Most	Matm	Meg	Mirg	Sedm
6A	1	1	-	-	1	-	-	-	-	-
6B	2	2	2	1	-	-	2	2	-	1
6C	4	-	1	2	3	-	1	-	1	-
7A	4	-	2	-	-	1	-	3	-	1
7B	4	-	1	1	-	2	-	1	-	1
7C	-	1	-	1	1	-	-	-	-	-
8	-	-	-	-	1	1	-	-	1	-
9A	2	-	-	2	-	-	-	1	-	-
9B	-	-	2	1	1	-	-	-	1	-
9C	1	1	1	1	-	1	1	-	4	1
9D	1	-	-	-	-	-	-	-	1	-
9E	1	1	1	1	-	4	-	-	-	-
9F	-	-	-	-	3	-	-	-	1	-
9G	-	-	-	-	-	-	-	-	1	-
9H	-	-	-	-	-	-	-	-	-	-
10A	4	1	2	3	6	1	-	1	-	1
10B	1	-	-	-	-	-	1	1	1	-
10C	1	-	-	2	-	-	-	-	1	1
10D	1	-	-	-	1	-	-	-	2	1
10E	-	-	-	-	-	-	-	-	-	-
10F	-	-	-	-	-	-	-	-	-	-
11A	-	1	-	1	-	-	-	-	2	-
11B	-	-	-	-	2	-	-	-	4	1
11C	-	-	-	-	-	-	-	-	-	-
11D	-	-	-	-	-	-	-	-	-	-
No. Scar.	72	14	20	30	47	35	13	28	31	45

Table E. Summary Percent of Use: Periods IV-V, Suppl. Groups 1 and 2.

	Period IV	Suppl. Group 2	Period V	Suppl. Group 1
Heads				
X	1	5	1	2
A	17	17	19	11
B	50	25	36	20
C	2	7	1	1
D	29	45	45	66
Backs				
LN	9	4	4	6
LS	6	19	4	9
PN	33	14	28	20
PS	52	56	64	65
Sides				
a	-		-	-
b	-	not	-	-
c	-		-	-
d	48	known	44	41
e	52		56	59
Designs				
1	5	3	6	4
2	7	8	9	6
3 ear	-	-	-	-
3A	14	27	6	21
3B	16	14	15	24
3C	10	14	8	13
3D	4	-	3	3
3E	4	2	4	6
4	7	7	4	3
5	2	-	2	4
6	9	7	10	11
7	18	4	11	9
8	9	2	7	-
9	10	10	14	12
10	11	9	16	11

E. Test Groups: Typological Classification

"No." refers to the number given in the original publications.

Lachish: Tufnell 1958, pls. 30-32

No.	Size	Classification	Design
23	17	D6 PS e10	3C 7A2
24	18	D6 PS e9	3B3b 6C3
25	22	D6 PS e9	10C1a
26	18	D6 PS d d6	3C 3E1
27	14	B3 PS -	2B1
28	20	D7 PS -	2A
30	18	D6 PS e9	10A1a
31	25	D5 PS -	6C1
32	13	D9 PS d e11a	6C2
33	19	D7 PS d5	3A3
34	22	A4 PN d5	3C 3E4
60	17	- PS e9	3B1b 3C
61	17	D5 PS e11a	6B2b
62	13	B3 PS e6	2B1
67	17	A6 PN d5	3A3 7B1
68	15	D9 PS d5	2A
69	11	D1 PS e11a	4E
70	18	D5 PS e9	3A3 3E1
71	24	D5 PS d6	9E
72	13	B2 PS e11	10B1f
73	16	B3 PS d5	9C1
74	17	D6 PS d e9	1E3 3A3b
75	14	D1 LS d e10	3A4
76	16	D7 PS d5	9A
77	11	D3 PS e6	3A3c 3B2
78	20	A4 PN e6	3B3b 3B6
79	14	B2 PS d15	3B2 3B6
80	11	D4 PN d5	3B2
81	18	- PS -	1B
82	24	D5 PN d5	6B2b
83	26	B2 PS -	3A3
85	11	A3 PN d5	3B5
86	11	B2 PN d5	3A3
87	10	D7 PS e11a	3C
88	11	D1 PS e2	3C
89	11	B2 PS e11a	3C
90	21	B7 PN e6	3C 7A2
91	14	A6 PN e6	3A3 7B3
92	15	B6 LS d e10	3B4 3B5
93	19	D5 PN d5	2A 3A3
94	16	A7 PN d5	2A 3B6
95	18	D2 PS d6	2A
96	24	D6 PS e9	9D
97	15	D5 PS e11a	10A1e
98	13	D5 PS d5	10A1b

Lachish (cont.)

No.	Size	Classification	Design
99	17	B7 PN d5	10D1
100	14	D9 PS d7	1B
101	16	B7 PN d5	3B6 7B1
102	18	D6 PN e10	3B5 6A
103	16	B7 PN d5	3C
104	22	D6 PS d e10	3C 3D4
105	21	D6 PS e10	3C 3D3 4D2
106	17	D3 PS e10	7B2
107	21	B7 LN d d6	2B2
108	19	A3 LN d d6	4B2
109	15	B4 PN d5	3A3 3B5 7A2
110	18	A6 PN d6	7A1
111	20	D6 PS e10	5
112	14	B2 PS e10	5
113	14	B2 PS e11a	6C1
114	17	D1 PS d5	10A1a
115	17	B2 PS e10	3A4
116	17	D3 LS d e10	3A3
117	17	D3 LS e10	9A
118	15	D6 LS e10	3A3
119	14	D3 LS e10	3A3
120	14	D6 LS e9	3A3
121	15	- - e10	3A1 3B3b
122	18	D8 LS e10	3B1a 3B3b
123	17	B7 PS e6	3B5 3B6
124	16	D1 LS e10	1E3 3A3
125	14	D6 PS e10	3A3

Barqai: Gophna and Sussman 1969, fig. 10

No.	Size	Classification	Design
1	21	A6 PN d6	7C2 11A
2	18	D1 PS e6	3C 3E2
3	16	D9 PS e11a	9C3
4	21	D1 PS e9	3B6
5	21	A1 PN d5	3B6
6	23	D6 PS d5	3B1b 3C 3D1 5
7	14	D1 PN e10	5
8	19	D6 PS e10	6B2b
9	18	A1 LS v e10	6B3
10	17	C7 PN d5	3B5 6A
11	19	D1 LN d5	3C 10A1d
12	19	D9 LN v d5	9E
13	20	B3 PN d5	4E2
14	14	D7 PS o	plain

Shechem: Horn 1962; 1966; 1973

No.	Size	Classification			Design
22	17	X1	PS	-	3A3 7B2
23	22	A5	LN	-	10A1c
24	17	B2	PS	-	2A 3E4
25	21	D1	PS	-	6B2
26	18	B2	PS	-	3A3
27	21	B2	PS	-	3E1
30	14	D9	PS	-	1E3 3A3
46	12	impression			3A4
48	15	D5	LS	-	4A2
50	17	impression			6B1 7A2
51	13	D8	PS	-	9B
57	19	A5	LN	e8	4B3
59	22	D6	PS	e8	3E1
60	17	D9	PN	e11a	9B
61	20	D6	PS	d5	6C1
62	23	D8	PS	e10	10A1b
66	16	D9	LS	e11a	9C3
72	11	impression			3B6
73	18?	impression			9E
74	17?	impression			7A2

Amman: Ward 1966

No.	Size	Classification			Design
6224	21	D6	PS	e11a	10A2
6225	21	D6	PS	e10	3B3b 3B4
6226	18	B3	PS	e6	3B4 3D4
6227	22	C3	PS	d6	3A3 3B1a
6228	15	-	PS	e11	7B1
6230	19	D8	PS	e11a	9A1
6232	16	D6	PS	d5	9B
6233	12	D5	PN	d6	3B2
6234	19	X2	PS	e5	1E 9A2
9373	23	D5	PN	d5	10A1d
9374	20	D6	PS	e10	3B1b
9375	21	D2	PS	e10	9E
9376	19	D6	PS	d5	10C1c
9377	21	B2	PN	d5	6B2
9378	18	D6	PS	d5	9C2
9379	19	D3	PS	e10	5
9380	17	D6	PS	d5	10C1a
9381	15	D7	PS	e11a	3A3 3B5
9382	22	A1	LN	d6	3C 3E5
9383	17	D6	PS	e10	3B1d 3C
9384	18	D6	LN d	e10	10A1f
9385	18	D2	PS	e11a	3A3
9386	23	D7	PS	d5	7C2 11A
9387	16	D5	PS	d5	3A3
9388	16	D6	PS	d5	3B5

Amman (cont.)

No.	Size	Classification			Design
9389	14	D8	PS	e11a	6C2
9393	19	D6	PS	e10	3A2
9390	17	D6	PS	e5	3C
9391	14	D8	PS	e11a	6C2
9395	13	D6	PS	d6	5

Qau: Brunton 1930, pl. 19

No.	Size	Classification			Design
19	25	B2	PN	-	11B
21	23	D5	PN	-	3A3 3B2
23	13	B1	PS	-	2B1 3E4
35	19	B2	PN	-	3A1 3B3b 3C
37	16	D8	PS	-	9F
38	17	D1	PS	-	9F
40	18	D9	PN	-	10A1c
41	20	D6	PS	-	10A2c
42	16	B2	PN	-	10A2c
51	10	B2	LS	-	3A3 3B5
52	17	D2	PN	-	3A3 3B5
53	21	B2	LS	-	3B1e 3B3e
54	15	D5	LN	-	3A3
55	13	A6	LN	-	3A3
56	13	C1	LS	-	3A3
60	13	D1	PS	-	2A1 3A2
61	16	C2	PS	-	6C2
62	13	A5	LS	-	3A3
63	9	A1	PS	-	3C
64	5	A1	LS	-	3C
66	15	B2	PS	-	3A2
73	15	D8	PS	-	4E2
74	11	D8	PS	-	4E2
76	8	B2	PS	-	4E2
77	11	A1	PS	e5	12B
20	18	-	-	-	11B
22	26	-	-	-	7C2a
24	10	-	-	-	2A
26	25	-	-	-	2A 8BB
27	18	-	-	-	3E4 6C3
28	17	-	-	-	6C3
29	9	-	-	-	3A3
31	18	-	-	-	3B3b
32	22	-	-	-	3A3
33	27	-	-	-	2A 3A3
34	18	-	-	-	6A
36	17	-	-	-	9B
39	18	-	-	-	9F
43	15	-	-	-	10A2b
45	25	-	-	-	10A1e

Qau (cont.)

No.	Size	Classification			Design
46	22	-	-	-	10A1b
47	22	-	-	-	10D2
50	17	-	-	-	3B4 3B5
70	12	X1	MSc	-	3C
71	8	-	MSc	-	3C
72	8	-	MSc	-	3C
75	9	-	-	-	4E

Mostagedda: Brunton 1937, pl. 69

No.	Size	Classification			Design
13	12	D5	LS	e11a	2A
14	23	C2	LN	d12	3A3 7A1
15	18	B8	PN	d6	3A3 7B2a
16	13	A4	PS	-	3A3 7B3a
17	14	B2	LS v	d11	3A3 3B5
18	14	D5	PS d	-	3B1c
19	14	D7	PS	d5	3A3 3B5
20	9	D5	LS	e4	1E3
21	14	D1	PS	e9	3A3
22	12	A3	LS	e5	3A3
23	11	D8	LS	e11a	3A3
24	12	D8	PS	-	3A3
25	14	B2	PS	d5	3A3
26	14	D8	PS	e11a	1E2
27	14	D8	PS	e11a	1E2
28	19	D6	PS	d5	12A
30	12	B2	PS	o	12A
32	19	B2	PS	e11a	10A2c
33	15	D1	PS	d5	9E
34	16	C7	PS	e11a	9E
35	20	D8	PS	d5	9E
36	19	D9	PS	e11a	9E
37	15	D8	PS	e11a	9C3
38	11	B1	LS	e5	3C
39	17	D5	PS	d5	3C
40	10	D5	PS	e9	3C 8B
41	12	C2	PS	e5	3C
42	6	B1	PS	e5	3C
43	6	A3	PS	e5	3C
44	11	D8	PS	e11a	4E2
45	11	D8	PS	e11a	4E2
46	27	X2	LS	e11	12B
47	30	B1	LS	e11	12B
51	8	-	MSc	o	3C
52	8	X2	MSc	o	plain

Matmar: Brunton 1948, pl. 43

No.	Size	Classification			Design
25	19	A1	LS	-	9C2 10B2f
26	17	A1	LS	-	2B1
27	16	D8	PS	-	3A3
28	11	B1	PS	-	3A3
29	15	D3	PN	-	2B2
30	16	B2	PS	-	6B2a
31	16	D6	PS	-	6B2b
32	13	D9	PN	e11a	6C1
33	14	D3	PS	-	3A3
34	16	B2	PS	-	3A3
35	12	A2	PS	-	3C
36	16	B2	PS	-	3B5
37	17	D8	PN	-	3B1c

Megiddo Tomb 24: Guy 1938, pls. 105-06

No.	Size	Classification			Design
pl. 105					
1	17	A4	PN	d6	6B2a
2	15	D2	PS	e9	3A3 7A2a
3	14	B2	PS	e9	5
4	15	B2	PN	d5	4B3
5	21	A5	LN	d6	6B2b
6	16	D2	PS	e10	5
7	12	A4	PS	d5	2A
8	18	A4	PN	e6	3A1
9	17	D2	PS	d5	3A3 7A1a
10	25	D8	LN	d6	3A3 7A2a
11	16	D6	LN	e10	3A3 7B2a
12	22	D4	LS	e11	12A
13	16	A4	PN	e6	3B1c 3B4
14	16	B2	LN	e9	9A1
pl. 106					
1	16	D6	xx	e9	3A3 3C 3D4
2	13	A4	PS	e6	3A3 3B5
3	15	D6	PS	e9	3B1a 3B6
4	17	D6	PS	e9	3C 3E5
5	19	A4	PN	e6	3A3 3B1d 3D1
6	19	B2	xx	e9	3A3 3C
7	16	D5	PS	e9	3B3e 3B6
8	18	A5	LN	e9	3B3b 10B1b
9	18	D6	PS	e9	3C 10A1b
10	13	A6	PN	d6	3A3
11	19	B2	LS	e11	12A
12	18	D8	PS	e7	3B5
13	19	D6	LN	e6	3A1
14	18	B2	PN	d5	3B3b 3B4 3B5 3B6

Mirgissa: Vercoutter 1970; 1976

No.	Size	Classification	Design
1970, pl. 26			
1	22	C5 LN -	11B
2	25	B4 PN d6	10B2b 11A
3	24	B8 PN d -	4D 11B
4	17	- - -	5
5	18	A1 PS -	9C5
6	20	X1 PS -	9C5
7	17	D8 PN -	3B5 3B6
8	12	A6 LN -	10D2
1976, fig. 19			
2	11	B2 LS -	2A
4	15	D5 PS -	3B3e 3C
5	9	D8 PS -	4E
1976, fig. 21			
1	18	D7 PS -	9C4 10C2b
4	14	B1 PS -	3A3
7	14	D6 PN -	9G
8	15	B2 PS -	12A
1976, fig. 23			
1	12	A6 PN -	3A1
1976, fig. 24			
1	10	D8 LS -	9C1
1976, fig. 26			
72.1	11	D8 PS -	4E
72.2	20	B3 PS -	3B6
72.3	16	D6 PS -	11B
80.1	13	D8 PS -	10D2
1976, fig. 27			
2	15	D8 PS -	9B
1976, fig. 36			
24	15	D8 PN -	2A
1976, fig. 55			
10	24	D9 PS -	3A3 8C
11	15	D8 LS -	plain
12	21	D8 PS -	3C
27	18	D9 PS -	3E2 11A
1976, fig. 63			
5	20	D7 PS -	9D
40	9	D8 PS -	3C
1976, fig. 71			
1	26	D6 LN d -	2A 3C
1976, fig. 82			
1	32	D8 LS -	11B

Sedment: Petrie and Brunton 1924, pl. 43

No.	Size	Classification	Design
1	19	D1 PN e9	3B5 3B6 7A2a
2	12	D9 MSc -	4E
3	17	D8 PS -	6B1
4	9	X2 PS -	12B
8	15	- PS -	12B
9	20	D9 PS -	10A2c
10	20	A4 PN -	3A1
11	21	D8 PS -	3A3 3B5
12	16	D8 PS -	3C
13	16	D5 PS -	10C2c
14	18	X4 PS -	3A3
15	19	B6 PN -	3C
16	11	- PS -	12B
18	15	D8 PS -	1E
20	11	B2 PS -	4E
21	10	D8 PS -	4E
22	22	impression	7B3a 11B
23	19	D8 PS -	3B1c 9C3
24	17	X1 PS -	12A
25	12	B2 PS -	3A3 3C
26	9	B2 PS -	4E
27	8	D9 PS -	4E
28	8	B2 PS -	4E
5	15	- LS -	3A3
7	11	A3 LS -	3C
29	8	D8 PS -	4E
30	9	B2 PS -	4E
31	15	D8 PS -	3A3
32	12	B2 PS -	4E
33	10	B2 PS -	4E
36	7	Face xx -	3C
37	10	B2 PS -	4E
38	9	D8 PS -	4E
39	9	X2 PS -	4E
40	26	X3 LS e7	12B
42	16	X4 LS e7	12B
44	13	B3 PN -	2B2
46	12	X2 PS -	3A3
47	10	D5 PS -	3A3
48	12	Face LN d11	10D2
49	18	B7 PN d -	3B5 3B6
64	14	A4 PS -	5
65	15	B2 PS -	12A
66	13	D8 PS -	3A4
67	8	D8 PS -	3A3

NOTES

[1]Ward 1978, nos. 5, 11, 25, 126 (Mesheikh); nos. 3, 12, 18, 45, 152 (Abydos). The Mesheikh cemeteries are now being prepared for publication by WAW. The associated archaeological material leaves no doubt about the date.

[2]Tufnell 1984, nos. 3112, 3113, 3117, 3125, 3126, 3127, None are illustrated, though the original publications show similarities in engraving style; typologically, they are all the same. Differences in the engraving of the hieroglyphs, however, lead one to assume that more than one artist was involved in producing the designs. It is not out of character in the production of Egyptian artistic works involving texts that one workman would produce the scarab itself, accounting for the uniform typology of these pieces, and others would engrave the designs on the base.

[3]Cf. Ward 1993. Others working on Canaanite scarabs also see local manufacture. Richards 1992: 42, suggests a local workshop at Pella, Jordan, "with several unique design concepts and a style of seal engraving that is noticeably different to its contemporaries," though one wishes she had defined this a bit more clearly. Two Israeli experts are now examining this question as well, and their research may well produce more evidence of local manufacture.

[4]The full range of back decoration, of course, is larger than that represented in the present work; other designs are shown in Martin 1971, pls. 53-54, Rowe 1936, pls. 33-34, etc. While a full investigation would be necessary to prove the point, the general impression is that decorated backs are more frequent percentage-wise before the NK. There are datable NK and later examples with such decoration (e.g., Jaeger 1982, §460; Hornung and Staehelin 1976, nos. 256, 446, 500, 714; etc.), but decorated backs seem more at home in the pre-NK repertoire.

[5]Only four examples are found in the design scarab sample, one in the royal name sample. Others come from Megiddo Tomb 24 and Sedment Cemetery K (Table B). In general, criss-cross backs with scarab heads are unusual in all collections: four examples in Rowe 1936, three in Hornung and Staehelin 1976, none in Petrie 1917 or Martin 1971. Scaraboids with true hedgehog backs portraying the actual animal appear in the 15th Dynasty, but are much more common in later times; Droste zu Hülshoff 1980: 37-38, and Chap. 4. The criss-cross back with a human head -- known from the NK and later -- represents a wig; cf. Hornung and Staehelin 1976: 190-93.

[6]On the latter, see Ward 1978: 23-24. The difference between 3 Early and the class 3 designs -- Egyptian signs and symbols -- from the 12th Dynasty on is a matter of both subject matter and technique.

[7]As long recognized, the humeral callosity was not used prior to the end of the period of the 15th Dynasty. The earliest example in the royal name series is on a scarab naming King Apophis (Tufnell 1984, no. 3460). Examples on design scarabs are extremely rare before the 18th Dynasty, and then only in late 15th Dynasty or late MB III contexts: Brunton 1937, pl. 69:17; Gophna and Sussman 1969, fig. 10: 9, 12, from the latest MB III phase of a burial at Barqai. All three of these examples have the V-marks in unnatural positions, indicating the first attempts at portraying this feature of the live beetle.

[8] While the present work is not concerned with possible historical implications of royal name scarabs, the fact that most of this class were amulets and not official seals has a significant bearing on their interpretation when found in foreign contexts. It has been frequently proposed that royal name scarabs offer some clue as to an Egyptian presence or influence in Canaan and elsewhere. That is, the geographical spread of royal name scarabs in a foreign region somehow equates to Egyptian control over that region or the extent of Egyptian rule. This is not a valid hypothesis once one realizes that the production of scarabs with royal names was merely one facet of the production of scarabs in general and that royal names were considered protective or good luck symbols much the same as the *Neferzeichen* class.

Much has been made of the fact, for example, that numerous royal name scarabs of the Hyksos Age have been found at Canaanite sites. While such objects have value in establishing a relative chronology, they have no other historical meaning once their amuletic character is understood. Scarabs naming the rulers of this period would be included as a matter of course in any shipment of scarabs going abroad. It is quite incorrect to assume that because one or more scarabs naming, say, Mayibre Sheshi were discovered at a given site that this indicates an official Egyptian interest in that site. Such objects were of no more intrinsic value than any others, except for their use in relative chronology. One can even seriously question whether their basically amuletic character had any significance in a foreign culture which may simply have viewed all scarabs as decorative jewelry. Scarabs with royal names should certainly not be endowed with a historical or political value they did not represent.

[9] The most successful attempt to distinguish contemporary royal name scarabs from later re-issues is that of Jaeger 1982. Using the evidence of stylistic details, engraving techniques, and the like, Jaeger has produced a corpus of contemporary scarabs naming Thutmosis III and established a set of principles by which scarabs naming that king can be dated into Saite times. Following Jaeger's lead, Wiese 1990 has now applied these principles in his own study of royal name scarabs picturing rulers of the whole New Kingdom and later.

It is possible to apply this methodology only to a limited degree to royal name scarabs of the Middle Kingdom since they are far less numerous than those of the New Kingdom. This approach, however, has been employed wherever possible and a substantial number of Middle Kingdom royal name scarabs has been omitted from the Tufnell 1984 corpus as a result.

[10] No one would seriously argue today that royal name scarabs were manufactured prior to the beginning of the 12th Dynasty. The same can be said for private name scarabs, though here perhaps the evidence is not quite as conclusive; cf. Ward 1978: 61. On the scarabs of Wah, formerly assigned to the 11th Dynasty, see Chap. 1, n. 4.

[11] The same is true for private name scarabs, though the border designs are more or less restricted to scroll and rope borders; Martin 1971, passim. Borders of paired signs were not used except for rare examples (*Ibid.*, pl. 40, types 6a, 6b) and borders of concentric circles were not used at all. This simply emphasizes again that the three main classes of scarabs -- royal name, private name, design -- have somewhat different typologies which must be taken into consideration in any history of scarab style.

[12] While the tradition of spiralform decoration is widely attested on scarabs of the FIP (Ward, 1971: 109-18), spiral borders of any kind are exceedingly rare; Ward 1978: 58.

---

13 Based primarily on the extensive scarab evidence of the period; the full argument is in Ward 1984: 162-72. The tentative sequence in fig. 7:5 makes no attempt to isolate the six rulers of the 15th Dynasty, though the Kamose Stela and Turin King List establish Apophis and Khamudy as the last two. The other four are probably included in the "Main Sequence" of fig. 7:5, though it is not now possible to identify them except for Seuserenre Khayaranu (Khyan) by virtue of his contemporary monuments. The sequence in fig. 7:5 differs markedly from that obtained from Manetho and his copyists, but this tradition is so garbled that it has little value with respect to individual names of this period and is best ignored. This sequence based on scarabs is accepted by O'Connor (1987: 41) but rejected by Redford (1992: 110, n. 66). Kempinski (1985:132), working along other lines, produces the same sequence as Redford: Mayibre Sheshi, Meruserre Yakubhar, Seuserenre Khayaranu, Aauserre Apophis, Khamudi.

The "King's Eldest Son *Ynss-idn* ," mentioned on a stela fragment of Seuserenre Khayaranu (Khyan) from Tell el-Dab^{c}a (Bietak and Görg 1981) has been included here. Unfortunately, this object was not found *in situ* , but was reused in a later building as a door-post. Bietak and Görg suggest this may be the Iannas of Manetho, while Redford (1992: 110) identifies this prince as Manetho's Assis; both names appear only in Josephus (von Beckerath 1964: 15). The full name as it now appears is read *Ynss-idn* = *Yanassi-adôn* , "The Lord exalts" (Bietak and Görg 1981: 72; Kempinski 1985: 135, n. 6), the first element being a semitic *Yaqattil* form from *ns'*. In Egyptian, however, semitic doubled consonants were never represented, as would be the case here, two of the signs making up the first element were engraved in a fashion different from the others suggesting a re-working of the text, and the reading of the second element is possible but not certain. But at present this reading of the name seems the most plausible. Assuming this prince did succeed his father, he is placed as the fourth ruler of the 15th Dynasty by Bietak, Redford and Kempinski, as the second ruler in fig. 7:5.

14 The associated pottery supports this as there are "certain large groups ... containing forms clearly allied to well known types of both the M.K. [i.e., the 12th Dynasty] and N.K...."; Brunton 1930: 10.

CHAPTER 8

DATING SCARABS

A. INTRODUCTION

The preceding chapters have shown that the practical matter of dating scarabs is by no means simple and that there are limits beyond which the factual evidence will not allow us to go. It has also been emphasized that the dating criteria developed in the early decades of the present century in large part do not reflect the reality of scarab history. It is not possible, for example, to create a workable scheme of typological chronology based only on back types and/or design classes. The most naturalistic and the most schematic backs appear side by side at any given time and many designs tend to have a long period of use, often several centuries. While the present project has developed an essentially new typology which accounts for the whole scarab and is more detailed than its predecessors, it must be stated clearly that even this admittedly complex systematization of typological features has limits.

Chief among these is the inability of this or any other typological system to provide unequivocal dates for many individual scarabs. The Tufnell typology works best with groups of scarabs where a sufficient range of typological details is available to fit a given group into the overall pattern of scarab history. And there are many individual scarabs which can be dated on the basis of distinctive or diagnostic details. But there are scarabs with a combination of such common or rare features that, with no supporting evidence, the date of their manufacture remains impossible to define.

A good example is a scarab from the ᶜAjjûl Courtyard Cemetery (fig. 5:1, no. 4, Chap. 5). Without its archaeological context, this scarab could not be assigned an unquestioned date. Head D5 was used throughout Periods IIA-VI (Table 5); back PS was very common during the same long time range (Table 6); side e9 is the most common side type in IIA and III, but was used in IV-V (Table 7); design 1E is found from Periods I-VI to varying degrees: design 3A1 is rare, but slightly more used in IIA-III (Table 8) though it is found from the 12th Dynasty into the New Kingdom (Ward 1978: 72-74). In short, while the percent of use of side e9 and design 3A1 point to Periods IIA-III, the combination of all features could occur from IIA-V. The MB I context, of course, assures the earlier date,[1] but lacking this context this particular scarab could only tentatively be placed in the 12th Dynasty.

On the other hand, there are individual scarabs having no archaeological or other context which can be fairly accurately dated:

Fig. 8:1, no. 1, is a surface find from Tell Jerishe, Israel, hence has no archaeological context. It is now in the collection of the Institute of Archaeology, Tel Aviv University, and is published in Giveon's posthumous work (1988, no. 67) on material from recent Israeli excavations. The date assigned to this object is "Dyn. XV or a later imitation of that style." Two features of this scarab point to the second alternative. Head A3 was very common at the outset of scarab history, was little used throughout the 12th to 15th Dynasties, and is one of those features which suddenly reappear as characteristic at the beginning of the 18th Dynasty (Table 5). Back LS is quite rare in the 15th Dynasty but is another early feature used extensively in the New Kingdom (Table 6). The e11a side is characteristic only of the 15th Dynasty but does continue rarely into the New Kingdom (e.g., Hornung and Staehelin 1976, nos. 238,

365). On the evidence of the head and back, this scarab is better placed in the early New Kingdom than the 15th Dynasty.

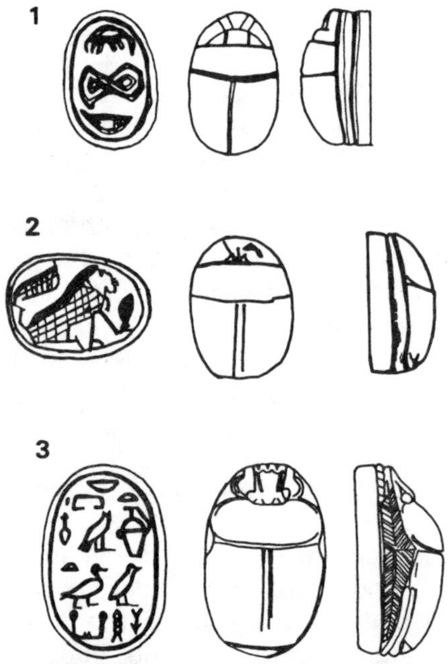

Fig. 8: 1. Datable Scarabs.

Fig. 8:1, no. 2, is from the former von Bissing Collection (Hornung and Staehelin 1976, no. 781) and, while the editors give no specific date, this piece can be placed in the 15th Dynasty. As just noted, side e11a becomes characteristic at this time though it continues into the New Kingdom. However, head D9 which does not continue into the New Kingdom is a diagnostic feature of the 15th Dynasty. The design is of little help since the lion with two cobras[2] begins before the 15th Dynasty and was used into the New Kingdom. This factor is not generally considered in the literature and this particular design is usually automatically labelled "Hyksos Period." In this instance, it is the head and side types which determine the date.[3]

Fig. 8:1, no. 3, is a private name scarab dated by Giveon to the "Late Period" presumably because of the personal names: "Khnum-neferu, daughter of Sen-Heqa" (Giveon 1985: 134, no. 4). However, this scarab shows good Middle Kingdom style (head B4, back PN, side e6) and the name Khnum-neferu (var. Neferu-Khnum) does appear in Middle Kingdom texts (Ranke 1935: 199, 15; Franke 1984, Dossier 472). The father may rather be "the Physician (*swnw*) Heqa" which can also be Middle Kingdom. All told, there is no reason to date this piece to the post-New Kingdom and substantial evidence in favor of a Middle Kingdom date.

B. Test Group from Harageh

To illustrate the procedure in using the Tufnell typology, it seems best to apply it to scarabs from an excavation where the general context provides a known chronological range. An ideal group of scarabs for this purpose is the small group of 17 from eleven burials at Harageh collected in Kemp and Merrillees 1980, figs. 18-19. This is part of a lengthy analysis of much of the Harageh material with an eye to fixing a general chronological range for both the settlement and the numerous contemporary cemeteries (Kemp and Merrillees 1980: 23-57). This study of Engelbach's excavation is extremely useful and its main conclusions are assumed to be correct in the present context. These are: cemeteries C and D date to the FIP and early Middle Kingdom, perhaps down to the reign of Sesostris II; cemeteries A, B, E and F belong essentially to the Middle Kingdom; the Harageh Middle Kingdom period extends from the reign of Sesostris II to just before the Hyksos age (Kemp and Merrillees 1980: 17, 54, 56). The scarabs in question come from the cemeteries and are given a range in date "from within the Twelfth Dynasty until well into the Thirteenth, perhaps approaching very closely to the beginning of the Hyksos Period."[4] Within this chronological framework, we can apply the Tufnell typology to this group of scarabs.

The procedure itself is obvious. Each scarab must first be typed according to head, back, side, and design(s), preferably from good photographs or the actual objects; drawings are suspect unless done by someone with some experience. In general, the typing is fairly simple, though there are examples where personal judgement may be involved. A case in point is the scarab noted above from Tell Jerishe, Israel (fig. 8:1, no. 1). In the publication, the head is classified as a D5 trapezoidal head. In reality this is a much enlarged lunate A3 head, a form which frequently appears on scarabs carved with little attention to detail. Since it is the A3 head which is a good indicator of date, it is important that the initial classification be done carefully. Once a satisfactory classification has been made, this can be compared first with Summary Table One which shows the percent of use of the major typological categories. This Summary Table will not often indicate a particular date, but will point to a general time range. One should then consult the Dating Charts that accompany Tables 5-8; the Dating Charts are simplified versions of the Tables in that they record ranges in frequency of use. In those cases where the Dating Charts do not offer a clear-cut date, reference to the actual frequencies of use in the Tables will usually do so. Most scarabs can be assigned a date within one or two periods on this basis. For example, the scarab from Harageh tomb D 660 -- classification A1 LS d1 3(early) -- is typical of Periods I-II; side d1 and design 3(early) are found only then, head A1 and back LS were far more common at that time than in the 12th to 15th Dynasties. Collectively, these factors are more common in Period I, hence this scarab is so dated.

A comparison of individual design scarabs with the royal name series is of somewhat limited use; such comparisons produce satisfactory results only when a group of design scarabs is involved. As is shown in Summary Table Two and Tables 9-12, the typology of royal name scarabs is different at points from that of design scarabs. For example, design 3E panels is rarely found on design scarabs but is characteristic of royal name scarabs of the 15th Dynasty; design 7A is characteristic of early 12th Dynasty royal name scarabs, but does not become relatively common on design scarabs until Periods IV-V. And there is the major problem that royal name scarabs of the 13th Dynasty are atypical on most counts, hence cannot be compared at all.

We may now turn to the Harageh scarab group. The sequence in the following discussion is that of the original publication. Since a few burials contained more than one scarab, it is best to take these as groups. In order to illustrate the use of each feature clearly, the percent of use is given for each scarab in figs. 8:2 to 8:5, extracted from Tables 5 to 8.

It must be emphasized that a date should not be assigned simply on the basis of the highest frequency of use. Other factors must be taken into account such as when a given head or side is first attested. Also, in any typology with few clear-cut chronological divisions and showing a continuous development and change over an extended range of time, *it is the collective frequency of use in a given chronological period which is important.* Most individual features are attested over long periods of time so that the main dating indicator is when most features represented on a scarab or group of scarabs are most likely to occur together.

In the following discussion of the Harageh scarabs, KM = Kemp and Merrillees 1980.

Tomb A 70. Periods IIA-III. Fig. 8:2

The highest concentration of use of the features on these scarabs is in Periods II to III; head B1 is too rare to indicate a specific date.[5] Period II is ruled out since side d5 does not appear until Period IIA. This combination of backs and sides is thus most likely to occur in IIA-III. Note that all the highest frequencies occur before and after this time range, emphasizing that this is not the decisive chronological factor in every case.

Tomb A 40. Period III. Fig. 8:2.

A date for this group is not immediately apparent since all 13 features represented are found in Periods III to V, all but two in Period IIA. Head D3 and design 3B2 begin in Period III which suggests that Period IIA should be omitted here, and the

Tomb A 70. Periods IIA-III.
KM, fig. 18:1. Classification: B1-LS-d5-2A
KM, fig. 18:2: Classification: B1-LN-e6-plain

		I	II	IIA	III	IV	V
Head	B1	1	4	2	2	1	-
Backs	LN	56	41	28	17	9	4
	LS	43	50	12	13	6	4
Sides	d5	-	-	12	15	32	28
	e6	-	21	17	10	7	11
Design	2A	7	21	2	-	1	4

Tomb A 40. Period III
KM, fig. 18:3. Classification: D3-LN-d5-5
KM, fig. 18:4. Classification: A1-LS-e5-3C
KM, fig. 18:5. Classification: B2-PN-d5-3B2
KM, fig. 18:6. Classification: A6-LS-d5-3A3

		I	II	IIA	III	IV	V
Heads	A1	29	31	5	8	4	1
	A6	-	-	7	10	7	5
	B2	1	12	25	25	25	10
	D3	-	-	-	9	6	9
Backs	LN	56	41	28	17	9	14
	LS	43	50	12	13	6	4
	PN	-	6	25	28	33	28
Sides	d5	-	-	12	15	32	28
	e5	-	26	3	4	2	1
Designs	3A3	-	-	11	13	8	4
	3B2	-	-	-	4	1	1
	3C	-	-	8	12	11	7
	5	1	7	8	7	2	2

Fig. 8:2. Harageh Scarabs: Tombs A 70, A 40.

cemetery does not extend into Period V. The choice is thus between Periods III and IV. With the exception of head D3 and design 3B2, Period III is remarkably similar to IIA, less so to IV. This group should therefore date to Period III.

Tomb A 116. Periods IIA-III
KM, fig. 18:7. Classification: D8-PS-d6-1C
KM, fig. 18:8. Classification: B2-PS-e2-3A3
KM, fig. 18:9. Classification: B2-LS-e9-1E

		I	II	IIA	III	IV	V
Heads	B2	1	12	25	25	25	10
	D8	-	3	3	3	8	4
Backs	LS	43	50	12	13	6	4
	PS	1	3	34	42	52	64
Sides	d6	-	-	8	7	12	12
	e2	1	6	2	-	-	-
	e9	-	-	30	38	16	10
Designs	1C	10	1	-	-	-	-
	1E	21	9	6	4	4	4
	3A3	-	-	11	13	8	4

Tomb A 91. Period IIA.
KM, fig. 18:10. Classification: ?-LN-d6-2B

		I	II	IIA	III	IV	V
Back	LN	56	41	28	17	9	4
Side	d6	-	-	8	7	12	12
Design	2B	2	7	16	3	6	5

Tomb B 287. Period IV
KM, fig. 18:11. Classification: B3-PS-d5-1B

		I	II	IIA	III	IV	V
Head	B3	-	-	5	5	5	9
Back	PS	1	3	34	42	52	64
Side	d5	-	-	12	15	32	28
Design	1B	22	6	2	-	1	1

Fig. 8:3. Harageh Scarabs: Tombs A 116, A 91, B 287

Tomb A 116. Periods IIA-III. Fig. 8:3.

In this group, the use of design 3A3 and sides d6 and e9 (thus including all three scarabs) indicates a date no earlier than IIA; Period V is excluded by the chronological range assigned to Harageh Cemetery A. The most probable date for this group is IIA-III where the largest concentration of the features represented occurs.

This group illustrates a rather common phenomenon: individual typological features which have an early date range often appear sporadically later on, in this case, side e2 and design 1C. Side e2 was used only in Periods I-II in the design scarab series used in the present survey; it does not occur at all in the royal name series. But rare examples do occur after Period II, notably the present example and one from a MB III deposit at Lachish (Tufnell 1958, pl, 41:35). The 1C design of fig. 18: 7 is difficult to classify: a *ẖrd* -sign with flanking plants. This "child + plant" combination is probably shown on several scarabs of Period I[6] and another scarab of this age seems to express the wish "may many children (*ẖrdw)* live." This date, of course, is much too early for the Harageh piece. In later periods, the *ẖrd*- sign alone is quite rare (Hornung and Staehelin 1976, no. 764; Petrie 1925, no. 968) though it does appear with the *nfr*-sign in what may be intended to express a wish "may the child be good," or the like.[7] At any rate, the use of the child-symbol (not to be confused with the Harpocrates sign) is too rare to be of value here.

Tomb A 91. Period IIA. Fig. 8:3.

The head of this scarab, provided the drawing is accurate, is unique; its vertical oval shape does not equate with any variety in the present or in any other typology. It comes closest to D1 though only an examination of the original can determine what was intended. This head has therefore been omitted from the discussion. The other features of this scarab indicate a probable date in Period IIA.

Tomb B 287. Period IV. Fig. 8:3.

The combination of features on this scarab is most likely to date to Periods III-V, though the latter is outside the general chronological limits of this cemetery. Period IV thus remains the most likely date. The use of design 1B, characteristic only of Period I, is another good example of an early feature appearing sporadically later on.

Tomb B 255. Periods IIA-III. Fig. 8:4.

Side d9 rules out Periods I-II, though it is too rare to suggest a date. Periods IIA-III seem the most likely. The single pot from this burial supports such a date (see below).

Tomb D 660. Period I. Fig. 8:4.

This classification is typical of Period I. The two ovoids also from this burial (KM, fig. 18: 13-14) are consistent with this date as is the early date of Cemetery D in general.

Tomb S 549. Periods IIA-III. Fig. 8:4.

While both these scarabs are assigned to tomb S 549 by Kemp and Merrillees, only the first is listed in the tomb register (Engelbach 1923, pl. 62) and one assumes that museum or other records validate the ascription of the second scarab. Both are datable only in general terms to Periods IIA-V, though back PS is much more common from Period III on and uninscribed scarabs are more likely to appear at that time. Periods IIA-III seem the most likely date, with Period IV a possibility. The use of D6, e5, e10, and 1E together, however, tend toward an earlier date.

Tomb W1 527. Period ?, Fig. 8:5.

The drawing may be inaccurate; the head could be D8 and the side fits into the general style of e8-10 though these do not have notched front legs only. A date is not possible though if this is indeed an A1 head, this and the design point to an earlier rather than later date.

Tomb B 255. Periods IIA-III.
KM, fig. 18:12. Classification: D4-LS-d9-2B

		I	II	IIA	III	IV	V
Head	D4	1	1	3	1	2	1
Back	LS	43	50	12	13	6	4
Side	d9	-	-	2	1	-	1
Design	2B	2	7	16	3	6	5

Tomb D 660. Period I.
KM, fig. 18:15. Classification: A1-LS-d1-3 Early

		I	II	IIA	III	IV	V
Head	A1	29	31	5	8	4	1
Back	LS	43	50	12	13	6	4
Side	d1	10	3	-	-	-	-
Design	3 Early	23	15	-	-	-	-

Tomb S 549. Periods IIA-III.
KM, fig. 18:16. Classification: D6-PS-e10-1E
KM, fig. 19:20. Classification: D4-PS-e5-plain

		I	II	IIA	III	IV	V
Heads	D4	1	1	3	1	2	1
	D6	-	-	7	3	4	5
Back	PS	1	3	34	42	52	64
Sides	e5	-	26	3	4	2	1
	e10	-	-	15	8	10	11
Design	1E	21	9	6	4	4	4

Fig. 8:4. Harageh Scarabs: Tombs B 255, D 660, S 549.

Tomb W1 527. Period ?
KM, fig. 18:18. Classification: A1-PS-e?-3 Early

		I	II	IIA	III	IV	V
Head	A1	29	31	5	8	4	1
Back	PS	1	3	34	42	52	64
Design	3 Early	23	15	-	-	-	-

Tomb B 354. Period IV.
KM, fig. 14: Ash. 1914.649.
Classification: B2-PN-d13-2B

		I	II	IIA	III	IV	V
Head	B2	1	12	25	25	25	10
Back	PN	-	6	25	28	33	28
Side	d13	-	-	-	-	1	-
Design	2B	2	7	16	3	6	5

Tomb D 586. Periods I-II.
KM, fig. 19:19. Classification: A1-LS-?-2B

		I	II	IIA	III	IV	V
Head	A1	29	31	5	8	4	1
Back	LS	43	50	12	13	6	4
Design	2B	2	7	16	3	6	5

Fig. 8:5. Harageh Scarabs: Tombs W1 527, B 354, D 586.

Tomb B 354. Period IV. Fig. 8:5.

This scarab has been classified with a PN back in spite of the fact that "careful examination of the worn back disclosed a faint marking in the surviving glaze down the middle of the back which may derive from a wing-case division"(Kemp and Merrillees 1980: 34) Such a line would be in the stone itself no matter how much the glaze had been worn off. Some scarabs do show wear, but not usually enough to erase all back markings in the stone. The d13 side is not an indicator of date, even if grouped with the similar d12 and d14; they are distinguished only by which legs are fringed or notched (fig. 9:3). Collectively, these side varieties are quite rare, appearing only in isolated examples throughout the 12th to 15th Dynasties on both design and royal name scarabs. While this scarab could be dated anywhere in that period -- its features are either very common or very rare -- its archaeological context places it in Period IV (see below, n. 10).

Tomb D 586. Periods I-II. Fig. 8:5.

The side is not illustrated in the publication. The other features, however, point to an early date, Periods I-II being the most likely. It could be somewhat later, depending on the side type which could be the decisive factor.

Period	Scarab Analysis	Pottery Seriation, etc.
I	D 586 D 660	D 586 D 660
IIA	A 91	A 91
IIA-III	A 70 A 116 B 255 S 549	A 70 A 116
III	A 40	
IV	B 287 B 354	B 287 B 354

Fig. 8:6. Order of Harageh burials containing scarabs by scarab analysis and pottery seriation.

The preceding analysis and dating of this scarab group can now be compared with the pottery seriations and other information given in the detailed examination of the Harageh cemeteries by Kemp and Merrillees. Of the eleven burials represented by the scarabs in question, nine have been dated here on the scarab evidence, seven by Kemp and Merrillees on the basis of pottery and other archaeological evidence.[8] Even if one allows for the fact that neither the analysis of the individual scarabs nor the seriations of the pottery can give a precise sequence of burials, the resulting comparison still shows remarkably similar results (fig. 8:6). Both analyses place tombs D 586 and D 660 in Period I,[9] tomb B 354 in Period IV; tomb B 287 can also be placed at the end of the pottery series due to the single jar from this burial.[10] The single jar from tomb B 255 indicates the middle segment of the pottery series.[11] The two approaches are thus complimentary as they arrive at the same conclusions using two different categories of archaeological material.

The Harageh group illustrates once again that it is somewhat easier to date groups of scarabs than individual pieces since several scarabs found together yield more typological features to consider. It also shows that one must emphasize the percent of use of each feature individually and determine at which time the collective features are most likely to occur together. That such a procedure is not precise and that unequivocal dates are often difficult to ascertain is a drawback that can probably never be overcome. The material is too complex so that uncertainty here and there is an aspect that must be accepted as inevitable.

C. Scarabs from Hazor Cistern 9024.[12]

In Tufnell 1984 the ten scarabs from Hazor Cistern 9024 Str. 5-4 (Yadin 1958, pl. 118) were dated to about the time of Ruweisé tomb 66. This, however, is incorrect as this is a mixed deposit of the MB II period; see Chap. 3F.1

No.	Length	Head	Back	Side	Designs		Date
24	20mm	C5	PN	e6	2B1	7A1	III-IV
25	21	A6	LN	d6	3B1	3B3	IIA-III
26	19	A6	LN	d5	5		III-IV
27	17	D5	PS	e9	3A3		IIA-III
28	20	A6	PN	d5	3B1	3B4	III-IV
29	18	D3	PS	e9	3E1	3C	III-IV
30	17	A6	LN	e9	3A3		IIA-III
31	16	B2	xxx	e9	3A3		IIA-III
32	14	D6	PS	e9	3A4		IIA-III
33	14	D8	PS	e11	2B1		IV

Fig. 8:7. Scarabs from Hazor Cistern 9024; classification and date.

Since Hazor Cistern 9024 is a mixed deposit, one cannot insist that the scarabs are a homogeneous group. Indeed, as fig. 8:7 indicates, when examined individually, there is some difference in date. As Tufnell pointed out (1984: 56), the emphasis on design classes 2 and 3 tends to indicate an earlier date for the group as a whole. One can likewise observe that the extensive use of side e9 also points in that direction, while the absence of such features as side e11a, designs 9 and 10, head D9, as well as the mixture of head and back types, suggests that Period V (MB III) does not come into the question here. Periods I and II, of course, need not even be considered. It seems evident that this group fits into the general range of Periods III-IV (note, for example, the distinction on all counts between nos. 25 and 33) though it leans more toward the former.

D. Choosing the Evidence for Statistical Analysis

Certainly the most significant problem in the process of defining a typological history of scarabs is their diversity. Unless made of composition in molds, scarabs are almost always unique. The range of typological variation available to an artist was such that a very large number of combinations was possible; even when two or more scarabs have the same general classification, there is always some detail -- in the design, for example -- that individualizes each piece. One can almost say that every scarab is in some way different from every other scarab. This can be put in more concrete terms. In theory, by Period V the varieties of heads (38), backs (4), and sides (33) which had been actually used at one time or another allow 5,016 possible combinations of these three features alone. Adding the wide range of design variations, the possible combinations rise to half a million! In practise, of course, by Period V many typological varieties were no longer in use and relatively few new ones had been added. Still, the heads, backs, sides, and designs recorded for Period V in the main sample used in the present work permit over 61,000 combinations.

It is for this reason that in Ward 1978 and Tufnell 1984 the stylistic analysis considered separately the general categories (head, side, etc.) and their sub-types rather than combinations of sub-types from different general categories, e.g., head A6 + side e9. For the present volume, an analysis of typological combinations was attempted to see if new information could be added that might help in determining chronological development. To this end, all the scarabs used in the project were entered in a data processing program which has allowed a much more precise examination of the total evidence. The results were disappointing, though not unexpected. The reason is that even the small number of typological features which actually occur in this material (relative to the total which *could* appear)offer thousands of possible combinations in each chronological period. Therefore, no matter what combination of features is examined, a large percent of such combinations are represented only by single scarabs.

A thorough analysis of all the head+side combinations represented in this volume provided nothing of real chronological value. With regard to back types, the four back types now used in this project are not nearly as helpful except as a very general guide for dating groups. A group of scarabs dominated by lined backs will come early in the series; one dominated by plain backs, especially PS, will come late in the series. Lined backs again dominate in the New Kingdom, but groups of scarabs of this date will show features such as the humeral callosity and divine figures and names which immediately place them after Period V. These facts, of course, have long been known and the present survey simply confirms them to be true. Contrary to what has been frequently stated, decorated backs are not a 13th Dynasty phenomenon, at least in the present sample. They are fairly evenly distributed throughout Periods IIA-V, but tend to be more common in Periods IIA-III, the classical Middle Kingdom style (Table 6). Decoration is found equally on lined and plain backs. As they are used with other features, decorated backs tend to go with sides e9-e10 in Periods IIA-III, sides d5-d6 in Periods IV -V. The design repertoire of scarabs with decorated backs is practically limited to classes 3 to 5 in IIA-III; these continue in IV-V with the addition of classes 6 to 10.

The tabulation of design classes as they are used with other typological features does not produce usable results. As has been shown throughout the course of the present project, design is the least likely feature to determine date simply because designs tended to be used over long periods of time. Certain designs, of course, do offer helpful, though limited, information. For example, classes 3A4 (Horus hawk with *nṯr*), 3B3 (pairs of red crowns), and 5 (cross patterns) tend to be of the 12th Dynasty rather than later; such general observations are easily seen in Table 8. The conclusion of importance in the present context is the obvious one: in any given period, designs appear with the scarab heads and sides used at that time. In other words, there is no relation between design, heads, and sides beyond the connections evident in Tables 1-8.

It is evident, after a detailed examination of the possible chronological relationships between different typological categories, that very little can be achieved along these lines. The possible combinations are so numerous, even those that are actually represented, that no consistent pattern emerges. Therefore, dating groups of scarabs or individual pieces is best done by the method suggested for the sample test group from Harageh, the admittedly complicated procedure of examining each typological feature separately.

There remains the question as to how detailed the statistical presentation ought to be. This is not a concern with head, back, and side types since the number of varieties is not such that the statistics have little or no value. Design classes and their numerous varieties are a different matter. Tufnell (1984: 29-30) lists a total of 157 designs while the present work examines only 62. The substantial difference is due to a single factor: a large number of the design variations listed by Tufnell do not appear often enough, some not at all, in both the main sample and the supplementary test groups to be statistically significant.

Tufnell's aim in developing her complicated design typology was primarily to create a system that allowed for expansion when more dated material becomes available. Tufnell herself (1984: 45-51) omitted all design variations and limited her statistical tables to the main design classes only, taking the further step of combining even some of these. Classes 7 and 8 were taken together, for example, as were classes 9 and 10. While this reduced the statistical tables in size, hence in complexity, the resulting picture of the use of design is somewhat inaccurate.

	IIA	III	IV	V	Sup.	VI		IIA	III	IV	V	Sup.	VI
10A1a	-	-	3	2	2	-	10B2a	-	-	1	1	-	-
10A1b	1	-	2	10	4	1	10B2b	-	-	-	-	1	-
10A1c	-	-	3	7	1	-	10B2c	-	-	-	-	-	-
10A1d	-	-	1	4	1	-	10B2d	-	-	-	-	-	-
10A1e	-	-	-	-	2	-	10B2e	-	-	-	-	-	-
10A1f	-	-	1	14	1	-	10B2f	-	-	-	1	1	-
10A2a	-	-	-	1	-	-	10C1a	2	1	3	-	-	-
10A2b	-	-	1	3	1	-	10C1b	1	-	2	3	-	1
10A2c	-	-	1	2	4	-	10C1c	-	-	-	1	1	-
10A2d	-	-	-	-	-	-	10C1d	-	-	-	-	-	-
10A2e	-	-	-	-	-	-	10C1e	-	-	-	-	-	-
10A2f	-	-	1	4	-	-	10C1f	-	-	-	1	-	1
10B1a	-	-	-	-	-	-	10C2a	-	-	-	1	-	-
10B1b	-	1	1	2	1	-	10C2b	-	-	-	1	1	-
10B1c	-	-	-	-	-	-	10C2c	-	-	2	3	1	-
10B1d	-	-	-	-	-	-	10C2d	-	-	-	-	-	-
10B1e	-	-	-	1	-	-	10C2e	-	-	-	-	-	-
10B1f	-	1	2	3	1	-	10C2f	-	-	1	2	-	-

Fig. 8:8. Design Class 10: all varieties, actual numbers. "Sup." column gives examples from the Supplementary Test Groups of Chap. 7D.

The present work expands the design statistics to include all the main classes and their more important sub-types, but does not go beyond this. The reasons are evident in fig. 8:8 which lists the actual numbers of all 36 varieties of designs 10A-10C, human and mythical figures. Statistically, these numbers are uninformative. The largest number for a single design is 14 examples of 10A1f in Period V which represents only 3% of the scarabs in that group. 11 of these designs are represented by only one to three examples, 12 by none at all. Therefore, with the amount of material collected in the present volume, statistically significant results can only be obtained by tabulating design class 10 just to the first main sub-type --10A, 10B, 10C, etc. -- as in Table 8. As more dated examples become available in the future, it is possible that the now empty spaces in fig. 8:8 can be filled in and eventually one can show a much more detailed statistical analysis of design class 10 as a whole. The same problems are evident with other design classes having numerous varieties such as 3B, 4, 7, and 9.

NOTES

[1]Cf. Chap 3F.13. It is of interest that the current back typologies would place this scarab in the 15th Dynasty: Martin 1971, pl. 54, type 10; O'Connor 1987, figs. 2 and 4, type 10 schematic. This date is out of the question due to the archaeological context.

[2]The editors identify the shape before the lion as a *nb*-sign; it is really the body of a degenerated cobra in the lion with cobras fore and aft motif; similar examples in Tufnell 1984, pl. 40: 2605, 2631.

[3]According to O'Connor 1987, figs. 2 and 4 (type 8), this scarab would be placed incorrectly in the 13th or 18th Dynasties.

[4]Kemp and Merrillees 1980: 50. The evidence for the lower limit is a "Hyksos plaque" from tomb 613 of Cemetery S (= Engelbach 1923, pl. 20: 86) and three scarabs from various cemeteries at the site. The plaque is certainly of the deeply cut, hollowed out style which characterizes the Hyksos Period and the grave in question comes at the end of the pottery seriation for Cemetery S; Kemp and Merrillees 1980, fig. 20. This date can therefore be accepted, probably the closing years of the 13th Dynasty.

[5]The head of KM, fig. 18:1 is difficult to classify since the drawing shows the triangular clypeus of D8, but the circular eyes within the outline of the head reminiscent of B1. Because of the latter detail, it is here considered a B1 head though only an examination of the original would settle the matter.

[6]Ward 1978, nos. 140-42, though in none of these does the upraised hand actually touch the mouth as in the hieroglyph. Another scarab of this age seems to express the wish "may many children (*ẖrdw*) live; *ibid.,* 51, no. 152. The same grouping of signs *ꜥnẖ, ꜥš3, ẖrd* occurs on a contemporary ivory plaque from Nag' ed-Dêr and an unpublished design amulet in the Ashmolean Museum.

[7]Cairo: Newberry 1907, no. 27169; Uronarti: Dunham 1967, nos. 161, 355-57. The Uronarti sealings may instead record the word *nfr(w),* "elite trooper," coming as they do from an administrative and military center. The Cairo piece also includes a plant.

[8]Kemp and Merrillees 1980: 25-34, with figs. 9, 11, 13, 20. Burials without pottery or only a single example could not be used in this analysis so that the seriation tables include only part of the cemetery material.

[9]Kemp and Merrillees 1980: 51, 54; cemeteries C and D are FIP and into the early 12th Dynasty. The scarabs from these burials are classic FIP types.

[10]Tomb B 354: Kemp-Merrillees, 34-36, figs. 9 and 14. While B 287 does not figure in the pottery seriation, the one jar from this burial is Kemp-Merrillees type 25 (also found in B 354) which is one of the latest in the pottery series; *ibid.,* fig. 9.

[11]Kemp-Merrillees fig. 9, pot type 20. B 255 is not included in the pottery seriation since it contained only this single pot.

---

[12]A few changes in classification have been made from that given by Tufnell 1984, fig. 17. The head type of no. 33 has been changed to D8, four designs have been added, and the new back types are used. The dates were arrived at by the same procedure as that outlined above for the test group from Harageh.

CHAPTER 9

SCARAB TYPOLOGY AND STATISTICAL ANALYSIS

A. NOTES ON FIGS. 9:1 TO 9:5: DRAWINGS OF TYPES

Fig. 9:1. Heads. One new head type (B9) has been added as this appears in Period VI (earlier 18th Dynasty).

Fig. 9:2. Backs. Tufnell's original typology of backs (1984:34-35) has been replaced by a modified version of O'Connor's back types -- with only the elytra and pronotum considered -- in four modes based on lined or plain backs done in naturalistic or stylistic modes. Decorated and criss-cross backs are also listed, although they are in general statistically insignificant. "Decorated" includes curls, lotuses, branches, and other motifs.

Fig. 9:3. Sides. Side d3 was never used and is therefore omitted. Side e3 has been omitted; the three examples thus classified are better taken as e2. Tufnell's division of side e6 into three varieties has not been followed since her e6a and e6b are more or less the same and her e6c is almost nonexistent in the sample studied here. Side type e11a, characteristic of Period V, has been added. Hopefully, the side type drawings given in the present work clarify a few obscurities in those of Tufnell 1984.

Figs. 9:4 and 9:5. Designs. The type-drawings are highly selective in that almost every one has numerous varieties. This is especially true of design classes 1, 2, 3 Early, 3A3, 9, and 10. The full range in each class is fairly well represented in the plates in Ward 1978 and Tufnell 1984, though even the vast design repertoire illustrated there is certainly not exhaustive. Variations in design are limited only by the surface available for engraving and the creativity of the engraver. Class 9A is new as this appears in the 18th Dynasty (Period VI).

B. Description of Typological Classes and Varieties

Fig. 9:1. Typology of Scarab HEADS

X Head not represented or shown only in elementary fashion
- X1 no markings, straight base
- X2 clypeus only, shown by notches or lines
- X3 V-shaped base with arc or lines for head
- X4 straight or slightly curved line for head
- X5 diamond-shaped head in cut-out area

A Lunate head
- A1 plain (rarely with vertical strokes)
- A2 base line incomplete or omitted
- A3 eyes shown by single lines
- A4 plain (sometimes rounded) with horn
- A5 eyes shown by double lines
- A6 depressed head (sausage-shape) with and without eyes and horn
- A7 as A6 but rounded or squared
- A8 head as semi-circle, sometimes with horn

B Open head, mostly "hour-glass" outline, combining head and clypeus
- B1 eyes shown
- B2 eyes not shown, sometimes with horn
- B3 eyes outlined at base
- B4 eyes marked off, sometimes depressed base line
- B5 eyes not shown, depressed base
- B6 eyes not shown, depressed base, with horn
- B7 eyes not shown, depressed base, with trapezoid and horn
- B8 eyes shown by single line, depressed base, sometimes with horn
- B9 open curved outline, no eyes or horn

C Square head
- C1 plain square, eyes sometimes marked
- C2 plain square, horn marked, sometimes with B outline
- C3 gabled with horn, with B outlines
- C4 double square, eyes and horn on exterior outline
- C5 double side lines, horn and eyes marked on exterior outline
- C6 double square with eyes outlined at base, with horn
- C7 squared oblong shape, eyes marked by single line, sometimes with horn

D Trapezoidal heads
- D1 plain, eyes sometimes marked in various ways
- D2 plain, with horn, eyes sometimes marked
- D3 plain with B outlines, sometimes with horn
- D4 plain, no eyes or horn indicated (rarely with vertical strokes)
- D5 double side lines, sometimes with horn
- D6 double side lines, eyes marked, sometimes with horn
- D7 triangle within trapezoid or B outline, eyes shown, sometimes with horn
- D8 triangle with or without horns, no eyes shown, sometimes in B outline or with pointed clypeus merging with D4
- D9 triangle with or without horns, pointed clypeus merging with D5 or D6

Fig. 9:1. Typology of Scarab Heads

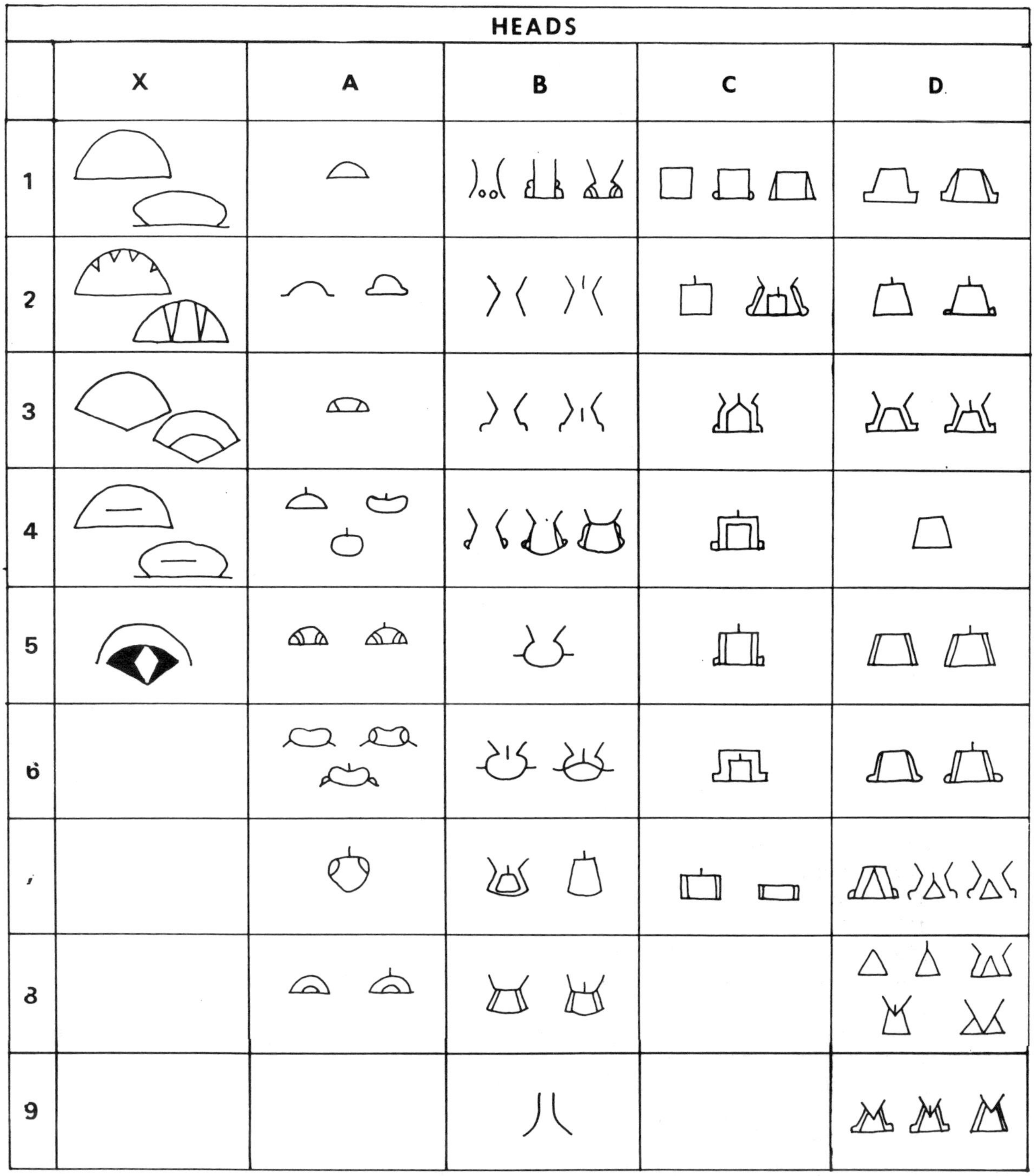

Fig. 9:2. Typology of Scarab BACKS
(replaces classification in Ward 1978 and Tufnell 1984)

LN	Lined naturalistic: rounded pronotum, wing-cases divided by line(s), side indentation between pronotom and wing-cases clearly deliniated
LS	Lined stylistic: straight outline for pronotum and wing-cases, latter divided by line(s)
PN	Plain naturalistic: rounded pronotum, side indentation between pronotum and wing-cases clearly marked, no lines marking off pronotum or wing-cases
PS	Plain stylistic: straight outline for pronotum and wing-cases, indention between pronotum and wing-cases reduced to incised mark
Dec.	Lined or plain back with curls, lotus, branches, etc.
XX	Criss-cross pattern ("hedgehog" back)

Fig. 9:3. Typology of Scarab SIDES

a	Single deep groove, legs not shown	
	a1	head undefined or only slightly defined
	a2	head sharply defined
b	Chip carved, legs plain or notched, head and tail separated from base	
	b1	legs plain
	b2	legs notched
	b3	legs meet where pronotum and elytra join
c	Chip carved, pierced (hollowed), legs plain or notched	
	c1	legs plain
	c2	legs notched
	c3	legs meet where pronotum and elytra join
d	Chip carved, squared profile, legs shown	
	d1	legs plain and shown summarily
	d2	legs plain or notched; very rare early forms of d5 and d6
	d4	hind leg notched
	d5	legs plain, squared base
	d6	fore, mid, and hind legs notched
	d7	fore and mid legs notched
	d8	fore and hind legs notched
	d9	fore leg notched
	d10	mid leg notched
	d11	legs natural
	d12	fore and mid legs fringed
	d13	fore leg notched, mid leg fringed
	d14	fore and hind legs notched, mid leg fringed
	d15	head defined, hind leg notched
e	scored, squared profile, plinth grooved, legs shown by grooving, notching or fringing	
	e1	groove incomplete
	e2	groove incomplete, hind leg marked
	e4	groove incomplete, with cross strikes
	e5	groove incomplete, hind leg diagonal
	e6	fore and hind leg notched, mid leg fringed (varieties in Tufnell 1984: 36)
	e7	scored as for e6, but surface plain
	e8	hind leg diagonal, all legs notched
	e9	hind leg diagonal, fore and/or hind leg notched
	e10	complete groove, straight notches on fore and hind legs
	e11	complete goove, no legs marked
	e11a	wide and deeply cut groove, no legs marked

Fig. 9:2. Typology of Scarab Backs

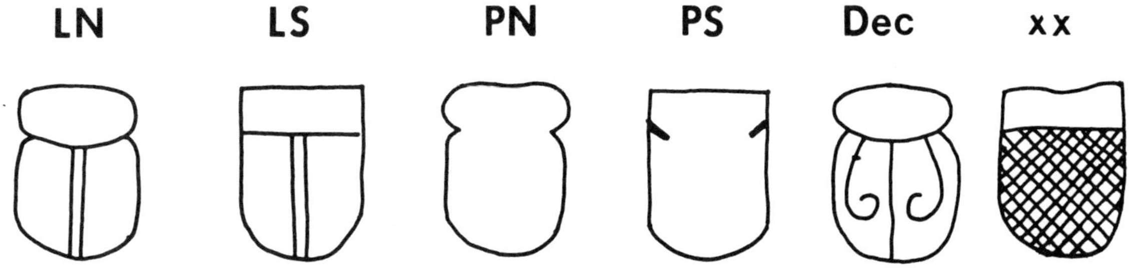

Fig. 9:3. Typology of Scarab Sides

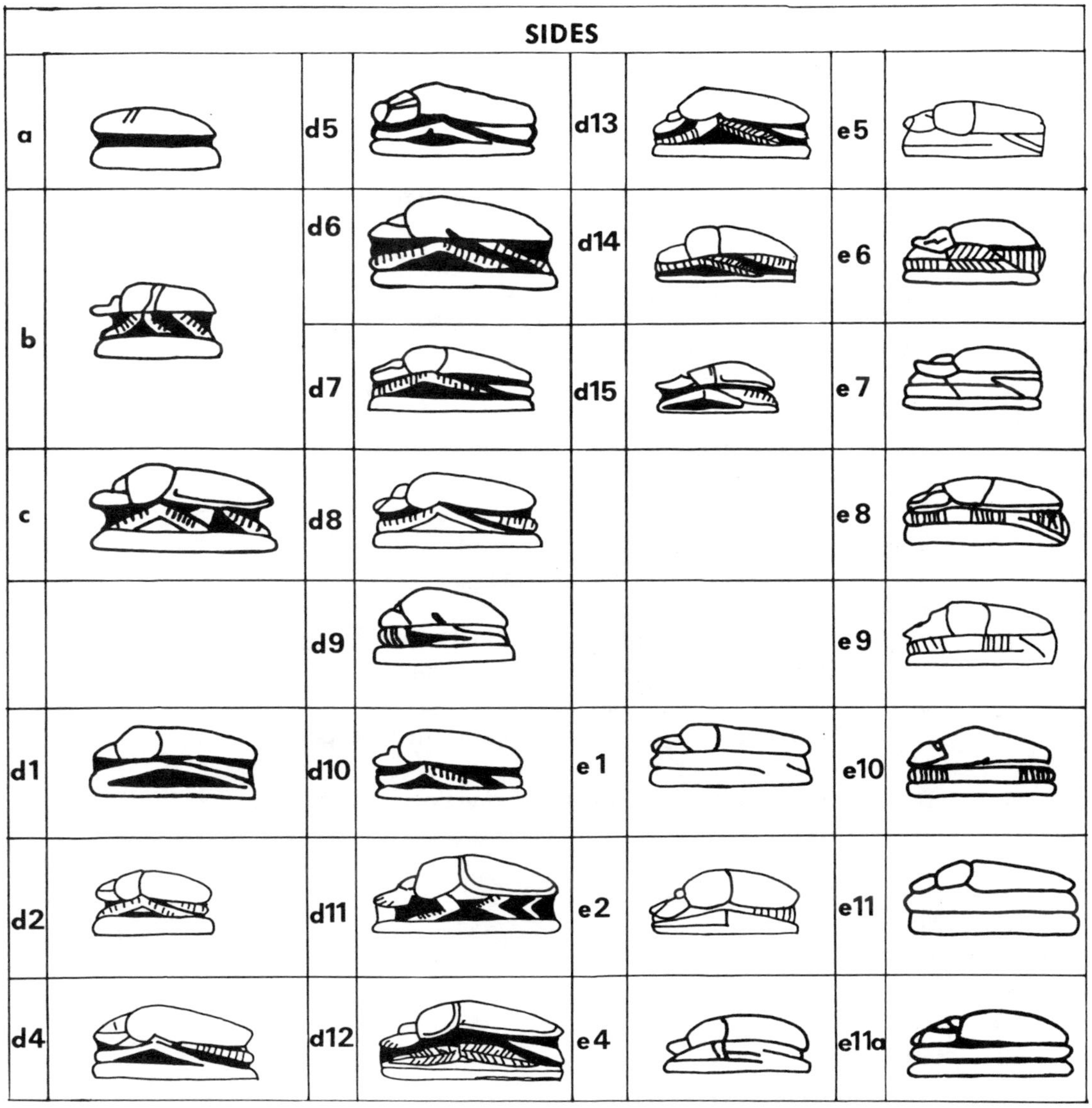

Fig. 9:4. Typology of Scarab DESIGNS, Classes 1 to 5
(*= varieties omitted; cf. Tufnell 1984: 29-30)

1 Linear patterns
- 1A maze
- 1B geometric
- 1C human figures
- 1D animals and insects
- 1E* floral motifs

2 Scrolls and spirals
- 2A Z-, S-, and C-scrolls
- 2B* round, interlocking spirals

3 Egyptian signs and symbols
- 3 Early (cf. Ward 1978: 55-56)
- 3A Monograms and varia
  - 3A1 Sign of union, *sm3*
  - 3A2 *nb.ty* with plants
  - 3A3 varia
  - 3A4 Horus hawk with *nṯr* and other signs
- 3B Symmetric patterns
  - 3B1* paired cobras
  - 3B2 King of Upper and Lower Egypt, *nsw bit*
  - 3B3* paired red crowns
  - 3B4 paired Horus eyes,*wḏ3 t*
  - 3B5 paired sedge plant, *swt*
  - 3B6 Gold-sign, *nbw,* in longitudinal setting
  - 3B7 paired forepart of lion, *fi 3 t*
- 3C Formulae
- 3D Cartouches
  - 3D1 simple oblong
  - 3D2 oblong with single base-line
  - 3D3 base-line joined by lines
  - 3D4 triangular base
  - 3D5 neck between oblong and base
  - 3D6 varia
- 3E Panels marked off longitudinally from border to border
  - 3E1 three or more signs in side panels
  - 3E2 two signs in side panels
  - 3E3 double *nṯr* signs, one reversed, in side panels
  - 3E4 cross-bars in side panels
  - 3E5 squared "shrine" -- panel divisions touch only one border
  - 3E6 varia

4 Concentric circles
- 4A* with lines
- 4B* linked
- 4C* small
- 4D* border
- 4E* varia

5 Cross patterns

Fig. 9:4. Typology of Scarab Design Classes 1 to 5.

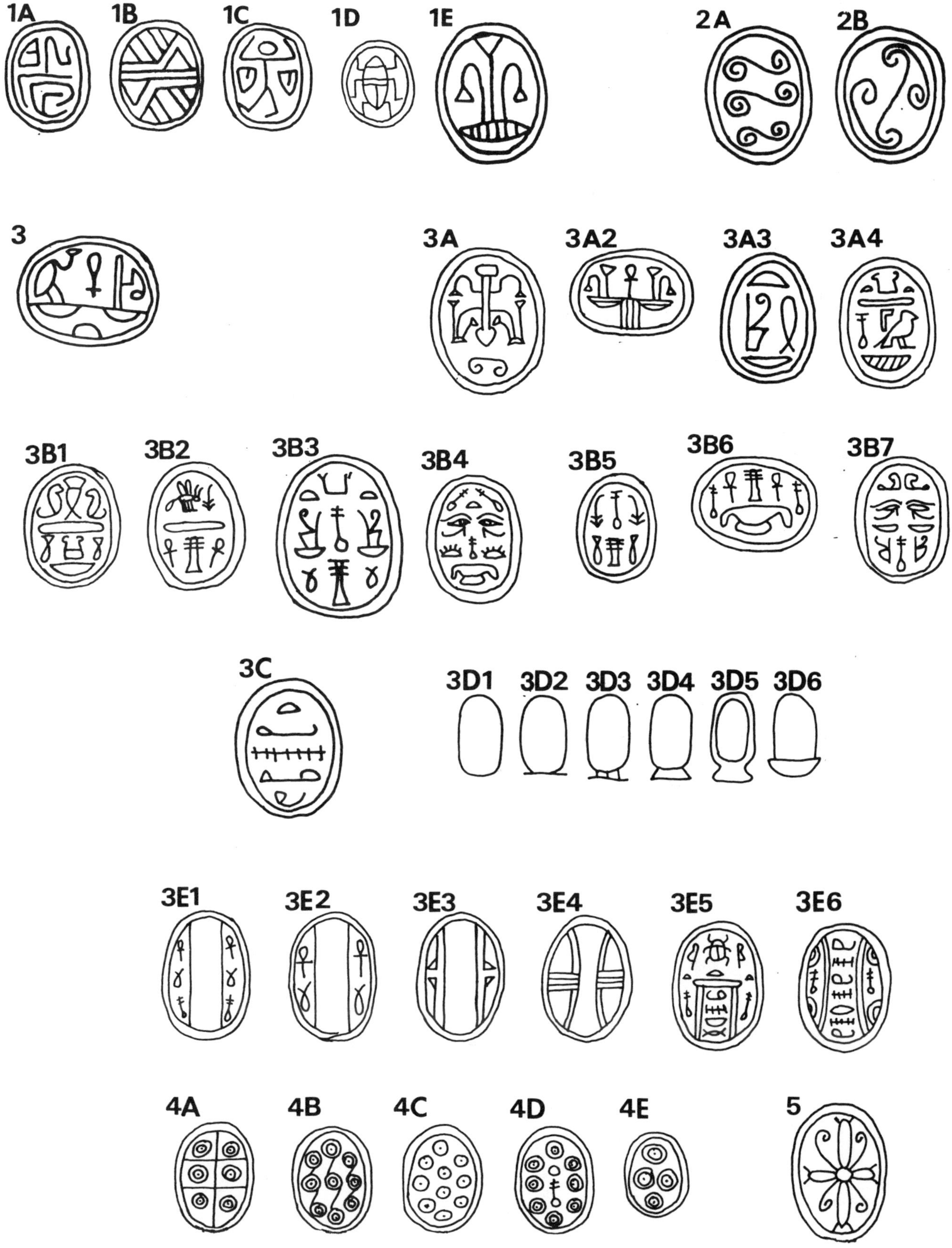

Fig. 9:5. Typology of Scarab DESIGNS, Classes 6 to 11

6 Coiled and "woven" patterns
- 6A single-line thread
- 6B* convoluted
- 6C* encompassed

7 Scroll borders
- 7A* continuous
- 7B* paired scrolls, top loop
- 7C* paired scrolls, open at top and/or base

8 * Rope borders

9 Animals and heraldic beasts
- 9A single or multiple cobras
- 9B antelopes
- 9C* cobras confronted
- 9D crocodiles
- 9E lions
- 9F heraldic beasts
- 9G equids

10 Human and mythical figures
- 10A* standing
- 10B* two or more figures standing and/or kneeling
- 10C* kneeling
- 10D* goddess
- 10E deities
- 10F kings

11 Names and titles
- 11A royal names
- 11B private names and titles
- 11C royal and private names, doubtful readings
- 11D names of deities

Fig. 9:5. Typology of Scarab Design Classes 6 to 11.

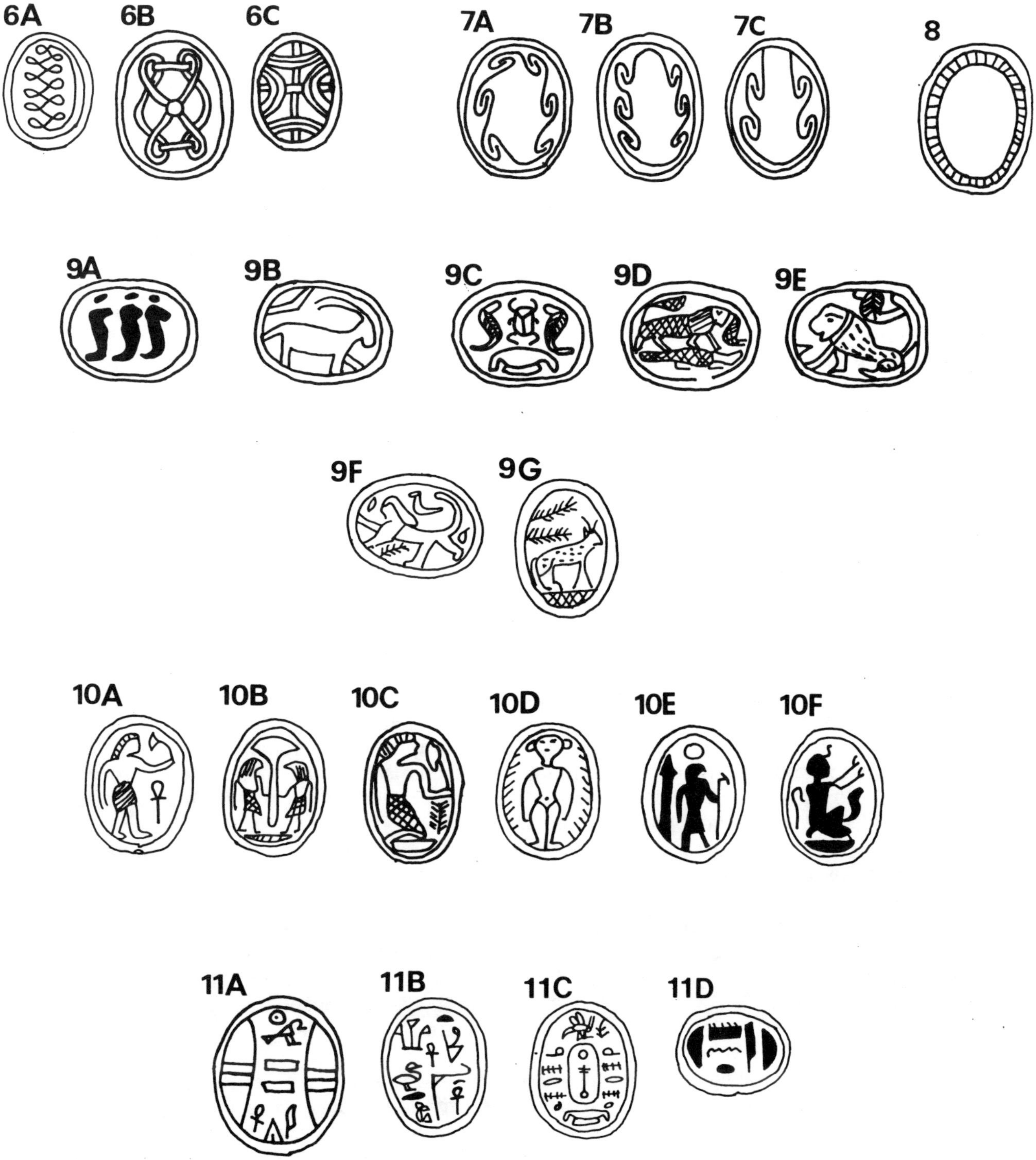

C. NOTES ON STATISTICAL TABLES 1 TO 13.

The Tables which follow are organized into five groups.

1. Summary Tables One and Two for the design and royal name scarabs used in the main sample series. These offer an overall picture of the main typological categories which are useful in determining the mix of heads, backs, etc., in a given Period. The Summary Tables are of help where groups of scarabs are involved, but do not apply in dating single scarabs.

2. Tables 1 to 4 give the actual number of design scarabs showing each typological feature.The total number of scarabs involved is noted at the bottom of each Table. These totals may vary since a few features here and there cannot be classified due to damage to the original object or insufficient publication. These four Tables thus catalogue all the design scarabs used as the basic test sample in the present work. Equivalent tables for the royal name series have been published in Ward 1984: 185-87 (there called Distribution Lists). The Distribution List for back types in that volume, as in Ward 1978, follows the original back classification, not that adopted in Ward 1987 and the present work. In spite of this, it seemed unnecessary to duplicate all the pertinent statistics here. Those for heads, sides, and designs remain the same. The actual number of backs under the new classification (LN, LS, PN, PS) can easily be tabulated by reference to Tufnell 1984, pls. 51-62.

3. Tables 5 to 8 give the percent of use by Period for all typological features for the design scarab series.

4. Tables 9 to 12 do the same for the royal name series.

5. Table 13 gives the basic statistics for scarab length.

The use of extensive tables of this kind was adopted in Ward 1978 and Tufnell 1984 after long discussion by the authors of those works and many trials at representing this complex material by graphs or other pictorial methods. Tufnell at one time preferred graphs (e.g. 1973: 80), but such graphs must sometimes be reduced because of space and become difficult to read. Block charts such as those used here with Tables 5-12 do have some value when the material so illustrated is sufficient to show trends graphically. Further precision is obtained by reference to the Tables they accompany. In the end, percentage tables were considered the best method of representing all the material as it actually is and that practice is continued in the present volume. The nature of the material -- a long, steady change with few chronological milestones -- requires such an approach. The only times in earlier scarab history when a large number of new typological features were introduced are the second phase of Period I (Tables 1-4), the 12th Dynasty (Periods IIA and III) and the 18th Dynasty (Period VI). While these represent clearly delineated phases in the development of scarab style, they are hardly sufficient if closer dating is desired.

Such closer dating is only possible by examining each typological variety represented by a scarab or a group of scarabs. But many features were in use over long periods time: heads A1 and B2, for example, occur in all periods covered by the present survey. The only way to establish when these heads were most likely to have been used is by statistical analysis to determine when they formed a characteristic part of the head repertoire; a use of 10% or more seems reasonable to define a "characteristic" feature. Head A1 can thus be shown to have been overwhelmingly most used in Periods I and II, very little used from Periods IIA to V, and again very common in Period VI (Table 5).

Head B2, used extensively from Periods II to VI, is most common in the range IIA to IV. For each head, then, the percent of use within each period can establish when it was used most often. As indicated elsewhere, very few typological features can be found in only one Period. The most probable date for a scarab or group of scarabs is thus the highest percent of use of the majority of features they evidence; this is the approach used in Chap. 8B to date the Harageh scarabs.

It should be emphasized again that while the statistics of Tables 1to12 are based on a relatively small sample, ten test groups with datable contexts measured against this sample show the same typological profile (Chap. 7D). Therefore, the statistics set forth in the Tables can be assumed to be accurate within reason. Due to the very wide range of features in the stylistic repertoire as a whole, new scarab groups will always show some differences from the typological history presented here. These are usually minor, however, and the system can easily be adapted to accommodate them.

Following are some general remarks on the statistical tables.

1. All percentages have been rounded off to the nearest whole number. "1" = less, or slightly more than 1%. Reference to Tables 1-4 will show how many scarabs are actually involved which may be as few as 1 out of 307 (Period III).

2. The ^{c}Ajjûl material published in Tufnell 1984 on which the present statistics for ^{c}Ajjûl Lower and ^{c}Ajjûl Upper are based, was classified by Tufnell according to her original typology. Since then, a new back classification has been introduced and an important distinction made between sides e11 and e11a. While it has not been possible to re-examine this group for the present volume, this has been partially compensated for as follows:

<u>a.</u> Table 2, BACKS: ^{c}Ajjûl Lower has been omitted. The figures for ^{c}Ajjûl Upper are based on the 100 scarabs from this site published in Giveon 1985: 60-100. The Giveon material is used only in Table 2. Elsewhere, back types from ^{c}Ajjûl are not included in the statistics.

<u>b.</u> Table 3, SIDES: for ^{c}Ajjûl Upper, there are 12 e11 sides classified in Tufnell 1984. Half of these have been arbitrarily assigned to e11a which is a minimum number for Period V. It is of interest that the Giveon material just noted shows ella sides at 24%. No such accommodation was made for e11a sides in the ^{c}Ajjûl Lower column since this side is extremely rare prior to Period V.

3. In the Tables on designs, since a single scarab often has more than one design: the total numbers of scarabs (Table 4) may be less than the total designs; the percent of use (Tables 8, 12) may be more than the number of scarabs

Summary Table One. Design Scarab Main Series. Percent of use, major typological categories.

	I	II	IIA	III	IV	V	VI
Heads							
X	15	6	-	2	1	1	2
A	74	58	25	27	17	19	66
B	3	16	35	42	50	36	18
C	4	6	8	3	2	1	3
D	2	9	32	25	29	45	15
Backs							
LN	56	41	28	17	9	4	26
LS	43	50	12	13	6	4	43
PN	-	6	25	28	33	28	6
PS	1	3	34	42	52	64	25
Sides							
a	19	-	-	-	-	-	-
b	35	6	-	-	-	-	14
c	33	8	-	-	-	-	17
d	11	3	27	31	48	44	35
e	2	81	63	69	52	56	30
Design							
1	81	19	10	5	5	6	7
2	10	28	18	3	7	9	6
	25	15	-	-	-	-	-
3ear							
3A	-	-	30	25	14	6	20
3B	-	-	30	42	16	15	10
3C	-	-	8	12	10	8	3
3D	-	-	4	4	4	3	4
3E	-	-	1	6	4	4	1
4	1	34	8	9	7	4	1
5	1	9	8	7	2	2	4
6	1	6	4	7	9	10	2
7	1	-	2	16	18	11	3
8	-	-	-	8	9	7	-
9	-	-	-	1	10	14	8
10	-	-	6	3	11	16	14

Summary Table Two. Royal Name Series.
Percent of use, major typological categories.

	E XII	L XII	E XIII	L XIII	E XV	L XV
Heads						
X	-	-	-	-	-	-
A	29	42	3	13	9	4
B	43	38	13	4	19	14
C	4	8	49	38	1	1
D	24	12	35	45	71	81
Backs						
LN	10	19	66	60	3	5
LS	10	7	21	30	3	5
PN	31	30	9	-	34	9
PS	49	44	3	10	60	81
Sides						
a	-	-	-	-	-	-
b	5	-	-	-	-	-
c	5	6	1	-	-	-
d	36	47	7	60	19	48
e	50	47	92	40	81	52
Design						
1	-	2	-	8	-	1
2	-	2	-	2	-	1
	-	-	-	-	-	-
3ear						
3A	-	2	-	-	-	-
3B	52	50	3	2	11	8
3C	-	-	-	-	-	-
3D	26	30	100	96	42	16
3E	-	2	-	-	55	78
4	4	8	-	-	1	-
5	-	-	-	-	-	-
6	-	-	-	-	-	-
7	40	20	-	6	37	5
8	4	18	-	-	1	-
9	-	-	-	-	-	-
10	-	-	-	-	-	-

Table 1. HEADS. Design Scarab Series; actual number by Period and site

	I			II	IIA	III		IV				V				VI
	1	2	3			Jer II	Meg A-D	Jer III	Jer IV	Meg E-F	Ajj Low	Jer V	Meg G	Fara	Ajj Up	
X1	2	5	1	4	-	3	-	1	-	-	-	1	-	-	-	1
X2	6	4	-	-	-	-	-	-	-	-	-	1	-	-	-	1
X3	9	3	1	-	-	-	-	-	-	-	-	-	-	-	-	-
X4	5	2	-	-	-	-	-	-	-	-	-	-	-	-	-	-
X5	7	2	-	-	-	-	-	-	-	-	-	-	-	-	-	-
A1	17	50	18	21	3	10	-	5	2	-	2	1	-	1	-	34
A2	-	2	5	7	-	-	-	-	-	-	-	3	-	-	1	-
A3	2	56	58	11	-	-	-	-	-	-	-	1	-	-	2	27
A4	-	1	-	1	5	2	2	2	4	2	-	1	3	1	4	4
A5	-	1	4	-	3	4	3	3	2	-	-	2	3	4	6	12
A6	-	-	-	-	4	13	-	8	8	1	-	14	-	-	2	1
A7	-	-	-	-	-	-	-	1	-	-	-	-	-	-	1	1
A8	-	-	-	-	-	-	-	-	-	-	-	-	-	-	-	1
B1	-	1	1	3	1	2	-	1	1	-	-	-	-	-	1	2
B2	-	1	2	8	15	23	8	36	22	2	-	22	1	2	3	7
B3	-	-	-	-	3	1	5	5	5	1	1	6	-	13	6	-
B4	-	1	-	-	-	3	-	4	9	-	1	2	-	6	3	3
B5	-	-	-	-	1	6	2	12	2	1	-	9	-	-	1	1
B6	-	-	-	-	1	2	1	3	6	1	1	1	1	6	3	1
B7	-	-	-	-	-	2	-	1	3	-	-	1	-	5	3	-
B8	-	-	-	-	-	-	-	-	-	-	-	-	-	4	2	-
B9	-	-	-	-	-	-	-	-	-	-	-	-	-	-	-	6
C1	-	6	13	3	1	-	-	-	1	-	-	1	-	-	-	2
C2	-	-	1	1	-	-	1	-	-	-	2	-	-	-	-	-
C3	-	-	-	-	-	-	-	-	-	-	-	-	-	-	-	-
C4	-	-	-	-	2	-	-	-	-	-	-	-	-	-	-	-
C5	-	-	-	1	1	1	-	-	-	1	1	-	1	-	1	-
C6	-	-	-	-	1	-	1	-	-	-	-	-	-	-	1	-
C7	-	-	-	-	-	-	-	-	-	-	-	-	-	-	-	1
D1	-	1	1	3	1	6	-	1	2	-	-	1	-	-	-	3
D2	-	-	-	1	-	1	-	-	-	-	-	-	-	-	1	1
D3	-	-	-	-	4	6	5	3	6	1	5	2	4	9	12	3
D4	-	-	1	1	2	1	-	1	4	-	-	3	-	-	-	5
D5	-	-	-	-	5	2	-	5	5	1	1	7	1	7	2	2
D6	-	-	-	-	4	3	1	5	2	1	2	3	-	8	4	1
D7	-	-	-	-	1	1	-	-	-	-	-	5	-	4	5	-
D8	-	-	-	2	2	2	2	9	12	-	2	6	-	2	3	1
D9	-	-	-	-	-	-	-	1	1	-	2	2	4	24	12	-
No. Sca	48	136	106	67	60	94	31	108	97	12	20	97	18	96	80	120

Table 2. BACKS. Design Scarab Series; actual number by Period and site.

	I			II	IIA	III		IV				V				VI
	1	2	3			Jer II	Meg A-D	Jer III	Jer IV	Meg E-F	Ajj Low	Jer V	Meg G	Fara	Ajj Up	
LN	5	81	86	28	18	16	6	16	5	1		3	3	3		33
LS	47	60	24	34	8	12	6	8	2	3		7	1	-		54
PN	-	-	-	4	16	31	6	40	36	-		26	4	28		7
PS	-	3	1	2	22	35	19	50	57	13		62	13	57		31
Dec.	-	-	-	-	8	6	5	7	5	1	1	1	3	6	1	1
xx	-	-	-	-	1	1	-	1	-	-	-	-	-	-	-	1
No. Sca	52	144	111	68	65	94	37	114	100	17		98	21	88		125

Table 3. SIDES. Design Scarab Series; actual number by Period and site.

	I			II	IIA	III		IV				V				VI
	1	2	3			Jer II	Meg A-D	Jer III	Jer IV	Meg E-F	Ajj Low	Jer V	Meg G	Fara	Ajj Up	
a1	24	5	-	-	-	-	-	-	-	-	-	-	-	-	-	-
a2	12	9	-	-	-	-	-	-	-	-	-	-	-	-	-	-
b1	10	32	6	2	-	-	-	-	-	-	-	-	-	-	-	2
b2	2	31	3	-	-	-	-	-	-	-	-	-	-	-	-	-
b3	-	8	6	2	-	-	-	-	-	-	-	-	-	-	-	2
c1	1	11	1	-	-	-	-	-	-	-	-	-	-	-	-	1
c2	-	16	22	2	-	-	-	-	-	-	-	-	-	-	-	-
c3	-	1	39	3	-	-	-	-	-	-	-	-	-	-	-	4
d1	-	14	14	2	-	-	-	-	-	-	-	-	-	-	-	-
d2	-	-	3	-	-	-	-	-	-	-	-	-	-	-	-	-
d5	-	-	-	-	7	13	4	23	24	7	4	12	6	31	19	6
d6	-	-	-	-	5	5	3	11	8	1	2	11	2	6	9	3
d7	-	-	-	-	1	1	-	1	1	-	-	-	-	-	-	1
d8	-	-	-	-	1	3	1	1	-	-	1	-	1	1	2	-
d9	-	-	-	-	1	1	-	-	-	-	-	2	-	-	-	-
d10	-	-	-	-	-	-	-	-	-	-	-	-	-	2	-	-
d11	-	-	-	-	-	-	1	-	-	-	-	-	-	-	-	-
d12	-	-	-	-	-	-	-	-	-	-	-	-	-	-	-	-
d13	-	-	-	-	-	-	-	-	-	-	1	-	-	-	-	-
d14	-	-	-	-	-	-	2	-	-	1	-	-	-	-	1	-
d15	-	-	-	-	1	1	-	1	1	-	-	-	-	-	1	-
e1	-	-	-	3	-	-	-	-	-	-	-	-	-	-	-	-
e2	-	-	3	6	1	-	-	-	-	-	-	-	-	-	-	1
e4	-	-	-	10	1	1	-	-	1	-	-	-	-	2	-	-
e5	-	-	-	17	2	5	-	4	-	-	-	2	-	-	-	1
e6	-	-	1	14	10	11	1	5	6	-	2	3	-	14	9	5
e7	-	-	-	-	-	3	-	3	-	1	-	1	-	-	-	-
e8	-	-	-	1	1	1	-	-	-	-	-	-	-	-	-	-
e9	-	-	-	-	18	26	18	14	11	3	1	2	4	6	11	-
e10	-	-	-	-	9	5	4	6	9	3	1	5	2	9	11	-
e11	1	1	-	3	1	5	2	9	7	-	7	6	1	6	13	3
e11a	-	-	-	-	-	-	-	-	1	-	2	-	4	18	6	-
No. Sca.	50	128	98	65	59	81	36	78	69	16	21	44	20	95	82	29

Table 4. DESIGNS. Design Scarab Series; actual number by Period and site.

	I			II	IIA	III		IV				V				VI
	1	2	3			Jer II	Meg A-D	Jer III	Jer IV	Meg E-F	Ajj Low	Jer V	Meg G	Fara	Ajj Up	
1A	36	22	-	-	-	-	-	-	-	-	-	-	-	-	-	-
1B	6	51	8	4	2	-	-	-	-	-	1	2	-	4	-	1
1C	7	23	1	1	-	-	-	-	-	-	-	-	-	-	-	-
1D	2	19	15	1	1	2	-	1	1	-	1	1	-	1	2	2
1E	1	26	41	7	5	4	1	3	7	-	-	2	2	8	8	6
2A	-	5	18	14	2	-	-	1	1	-	1	2	1	4	12	4
2B	-	-	8	5	13	4	-	5	9	2	-	4	2	10	5	4
3 Ear	2	18	59	10	-	-	-	-	-	-	-	-	-	-	-	-
3A1	-	-	-	-	3	4	-	1	1	-	1	1	-	2	1	1
3A2	-	-	-	-	1	-	-	1	-	-	1	-	-	1	-	3
3A3	-	-	-	-	9	12	5	12	6	1	2	8	1	5	4	22
3A4	-	-	-	-	7	7	5	8	4	-	1	2	-	-	3	1
3B1	-	-	-	-	4	12	7	3	3	-	1	3	1	6	5	4
3B2	-	-	-	-	-	5	-	-	1	-	1	-	-	4	2	-
3B3	-	-	-	-	10	11	5	7	4	-	1	4	1	1	3	4
3B4	-	-	-	-	3	5	1	2	2	1	-	2	1	2	3	1
3B5	-	-	-	-	2	1	1	2	2	1	-	5	-	4	7	2
3B6	-	-	-	-	1	5	1	3	6	-	2	4	1	3	4	2
3B7	-	-	-	-	4	1	1	1	-	-	-	-	-	-	-	-
3C	-	-	-	-	6	12	4	8	13	1	6	8	2	15	11	4
3D	-	-	-	-	3	5	1	4	3	-	3	1	-	6	8	5
3E1	-	-	-	-	1	1	2	1	-	-	2	-	1	3	4	-
3E2	-	-	-	-	-	-	-	-	-	-	-	-	-	1	1	-
3E3	-	-	-	-	-	-	-	-	-	-	-	-	-	-	-	-
3E4	-	-	-	-	-	-	-	-	1	-	1	-	-	2	2	1
3E5	-	-	-	-	-	3	1	2	2	1	-	-	-	-	1	-
3E6	-	-	-	-	-	1	-	1	-	-	-	-	-	-	1	-
3E7	-	-	-	-	-	-	-	-	-	-	-	-	-	-	-	-
4A	-	-	-	13	1	-	-	-	-	-	-	-	-	-	1	-
4B	-	-	1	6	5	5	2	4	3	-	-	3	2	1	3	-
4C	-	-	-	5	-	1	-	-	-	-	-	-	-	4	1	1
4D	-	-	-	-	1	-	3	3	-	1	-	3	-	1	-	-
4E	-	-	-	-	-	1	-	-	2	1	-	-	-	-	-	-
5	-	-	2	6	6	8	2	4	-	1	1	2	1	5	1	5

Table 4. DESIGNS. Design Scarab Series (cont.)

	I			II	IIA	III		IV				V				VI
	1	2	3			Jer II	Meg A-D	Jer III	Jer IV	Meg E-F	Ajj Low	Jer V	Meg G	Fara	Ajj Up	
6A	-	-	2	2	1	3	-	-	1	-	-	2	-	1	1	1
6B	-	-	1	2	2	5	-	4	3	2	7	3	1	5	7	-
6C	-	-	-	-	1	1	1	-	6	2	2	2	1	12	12	2
7A	-	1	-	-	-	3	1	8	3	-	2	7	2	8	5	3
7B	-	-	1	-	2	12	4	14	15	2	1	18	-	6	9	1
7C	-	-	-	-	-	1	-	-	2	-	1	1	-	-	2	-
8	-	-	-	-	-	9	2	14	9	1	1	17	1	8	7	-
9A	-	-	-	-	-	-	-	-	-	-	-	-	-	-	-	3
9B	-	-	-	-	-	-	-	3	2	1	1	3	-	7	9	-
9C	-	-	-	-	-	-	-	3	4	1	4	6	2	4	4	-
9D	-	-	-	-	-	-	-	-	1	-	1	1	1	1	4	-
9E	-	-	-	-	-	-	-	2	2	-	1	2	-	8	5	3
9F	-	-	-	-	-	-	1	2	1	-	-	2	3	-	3	1
9G	-	-	-	-	-	-	-	-	-	-	-	-	-	-	-	1
9H	-	-	-	-	-	-	-	-	-	-	-	-	-	-	-	3
10A	-	-	-	-	1	-	-	5	6	-	2	7	-	16	19	1
10B	-	-	-	-	-	1	1	-	1	1	1	-	1	4	5	-
10C	-	-	-	-	3	-	2	4	2	-	1	1	-	6	4	2
10D	-	-	-	-	1	-	-	2	3	-	-	1	-	3	3	1
10E	-	-	-	-	-	-	-	-	-	-	-	-	-	-	-	6
10F	-	-	-	-	-	-	-	-	-	-	-	-	-	-	-	9
11A	-	-	-	-	3	-	-	1	1	-	1	1	-	1	7	19
11B	-	-	-	-	1	1	1	1	-	-	2	1	-	2	2	3
11C	-	-	-	-	-	2	-	2	1	-	2	-	-	2	1	-
11D	-	-	-	-	-	-	-	-	-	-	-	-	-	-	-	20
No. Sca	53	152	114	68	79	96	38	110	100	17	42	99	21	139	196	134

Table 5. HEADS. Design Scarab Series: percent of use by Periods.

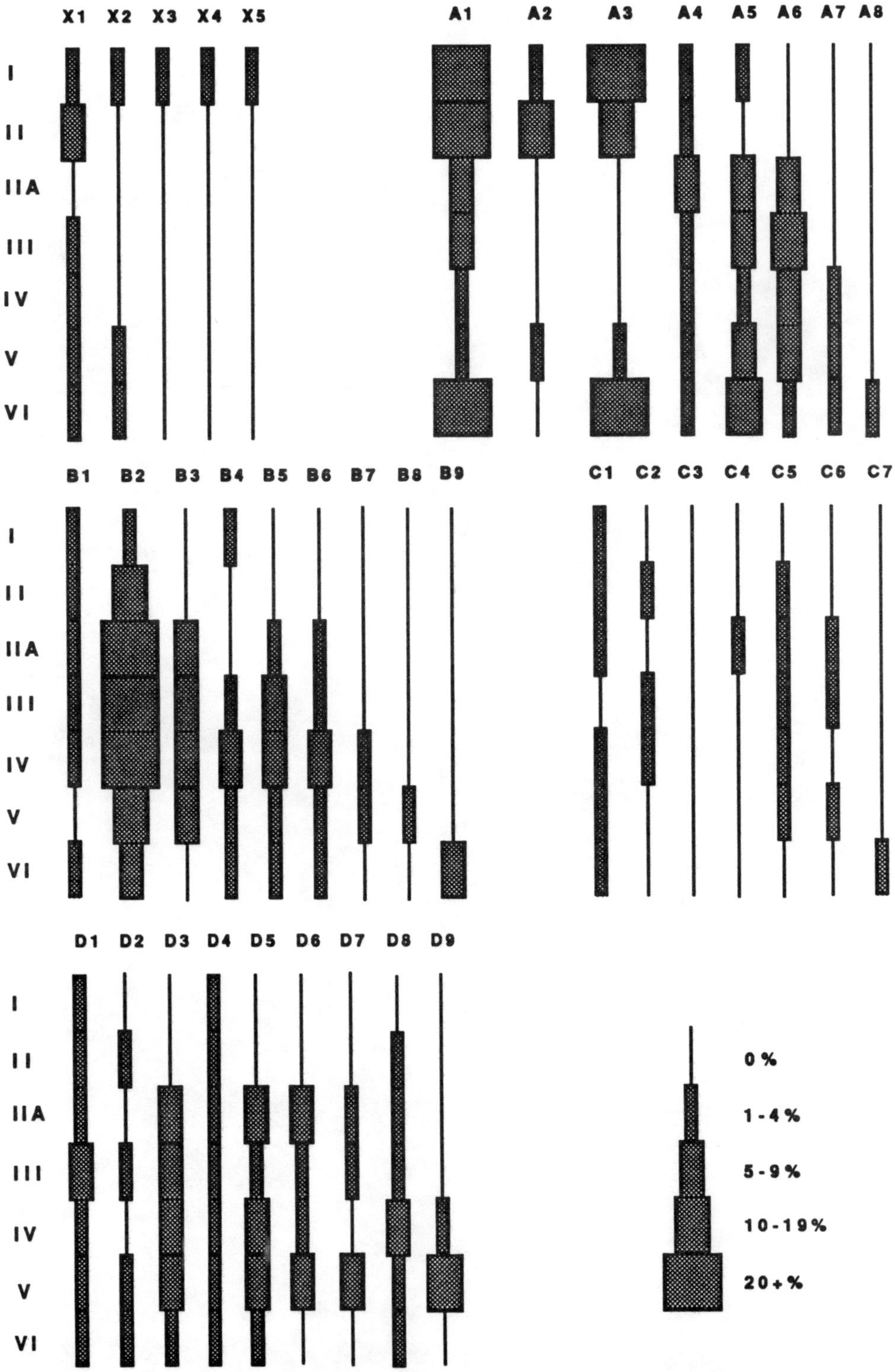

Table 5. HEADS. Design Scarab Series; percent of use by Periods.

	I	II	IIA	III	IV	V	VI
X1	3	6	-	2	1	1	1
X2	3	-	-	-	-	1	1
X3	4	-	-	-	-	-	-
X4	2	-	-	-	-	-	-
X5	3	-	-	-	-	-	-
A1	29	31	5	8	4	1	28
A2	2	10	-	-	-	1	-
A3	40	16	-	-	-	1	22
A4	1	1	8	3	3	3	3
A5	2	-	5	6	2	5	10
A6	-	-	7	10	7	5	1
A7	-	-	-	-	1	1	1
A8	-	-	-	-	-	-	1
B1	1	4	2	2	1	-	2
B2	1	12	25	25	25	10	6
B3	-	-	5	5	5	9	-
B4	1	-	-	2	6	4	3
B5	-	-	2	6	6	4	1
B6	-	-	2	2	5	4	1
B7	-	-	-	-	2	3	-
B8	-	-	-	-	-	2	-
B9	-	-	-	-	-	-	5
C1	4	4	2	-	1	1	2
C2	-	1	-	1	1	-	-
C3	-	-	-	-	-	-	-
C4	-	-	3	-	-	-	-
C5	-	1	2	1	1	1	-
C6	-	-	2	1	-	1	-
C7	-	-	-	-	-	-	1
D1	1	4	2	5	1	1	3
D2	-	1	-	1	-	1	1
D3	-	-	7	9	6	9	3
D4	1	1	3	1	2	1	4
D5	-	-	8	2	5	6	2
D6	-	-	7	3	4	5	1
D7	-	-	2	1	-	5	-
D8	-	3	3	3	8	4	1
D9	-	-	-	-	2	14	-

Table 6. BACKS. Design Scarab Series. Percent of use by Periods

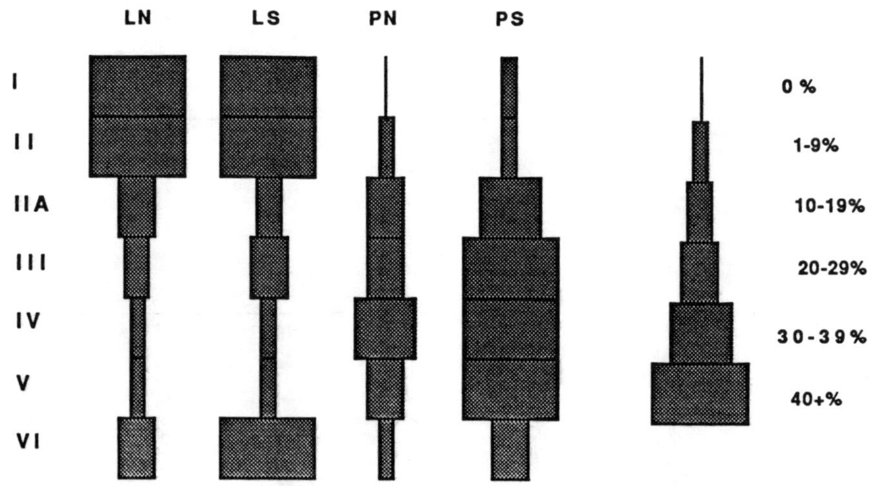

Table 6. BACKS. Design Scarab Series; percent of use by Periods.

	I	II	IIA	III	IV	V	VI
LN	56	41	28	17	9	4	26
LS	43	50	12	13	6	4	43
PN	-	6	25	28	33	28	6
PS	1	3	34	42	52	64	25
Dec.	-	-	12	8	6	5	1
XX	-	-	1	1	1	-	1

Table 7. SIDES. Design Scarab Series. Percent of Use by Period

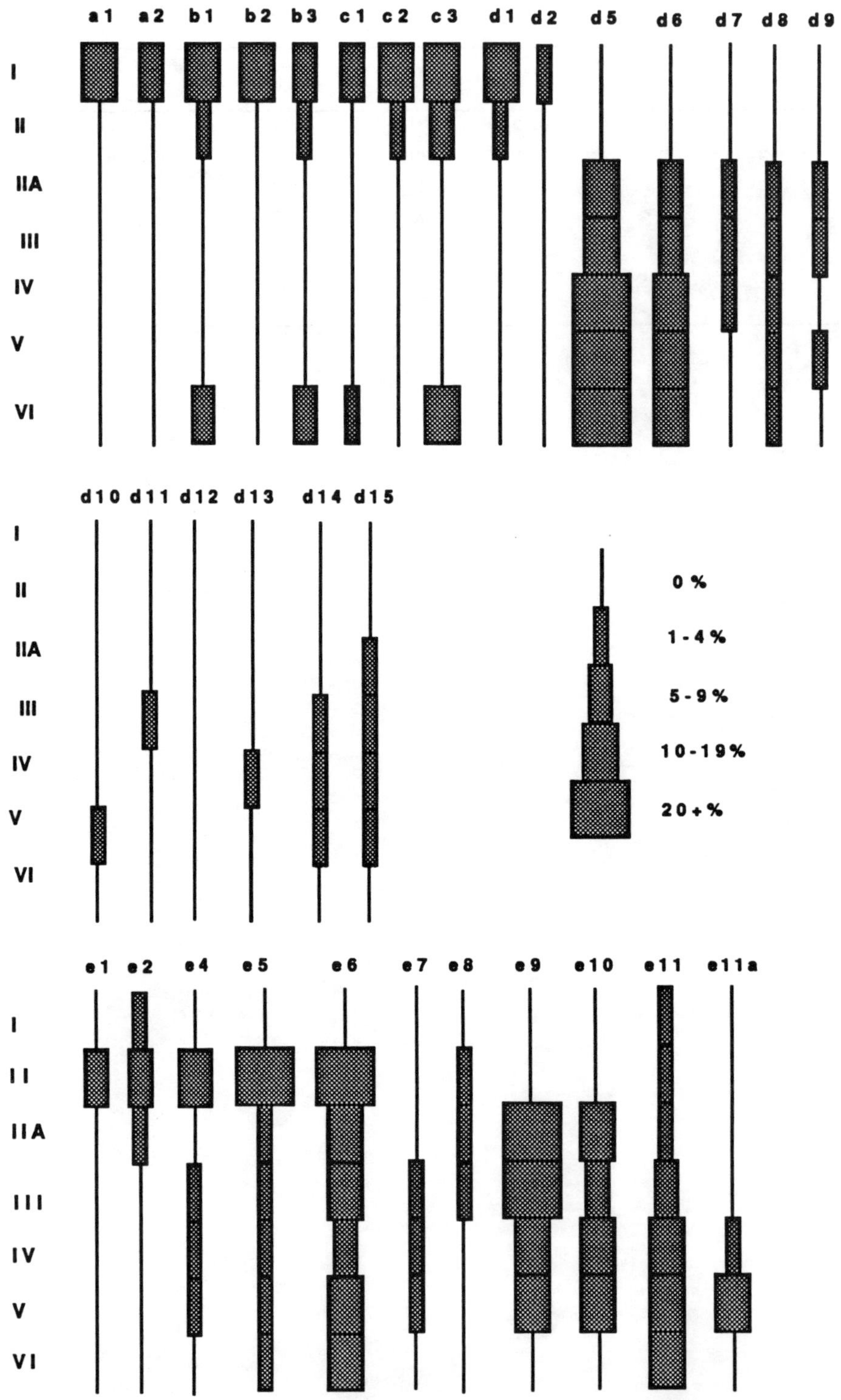

Table 7. SIDES. Design Scarab Series; percent of use by Periods.

	I	II	IIA	III	IV	V	VI
a1	11	-	-	-	-	-	-
a2	8	-	-	-	-	-	-
b1	17	3	-	-	-	-	7
b2	13	-	-	-	-	-	-
b3	5	3	-	-	-	-	7
c1	5	-	-	-	-	-	3
c2	14	3	-	-	-	-	-
c3	14	5	-	-	-	-	14
d1	10	3	-	-	-	-	-
d2	1	-	-	-	-	-	-
d5	-	-	12	15	32	28	21
d6	-	-	8	7	12	12	11
d7	-	-	2	1	1	-	-
d8	-	-	2	3	1	2	3
d9	-	-	2	1	-	1	-
d10	-	-	-	-	-	1	-
d11	-	-	-	1	-	-	-
d12	-	-	-	-	-	-	-
d13	-	-	-	-	1	-	-
d14	-	-	-	2	1	1	-
d15	-	-	2	1	1	1	-
e1	-	5	-	-	-	-	-
e2	1	9	2	-	-	-	-
e4	-	15	2	1	1	1	-
e5	-	26	3	4	2	1	3
e6	-	21	17	10	7	11	17
e7	-	-	-	3	2	1	-
e8	-	1	2	1	-	-	-
e9	-	-	30	38	16	10	-
e10	-	-	15	8	10	11	-
e11	1	4	2	6	12	11	10
e11a	-	-	-	-	1	12	-

Table 8. DESIGNS. Design Scarab Series. Percent of use by Period.

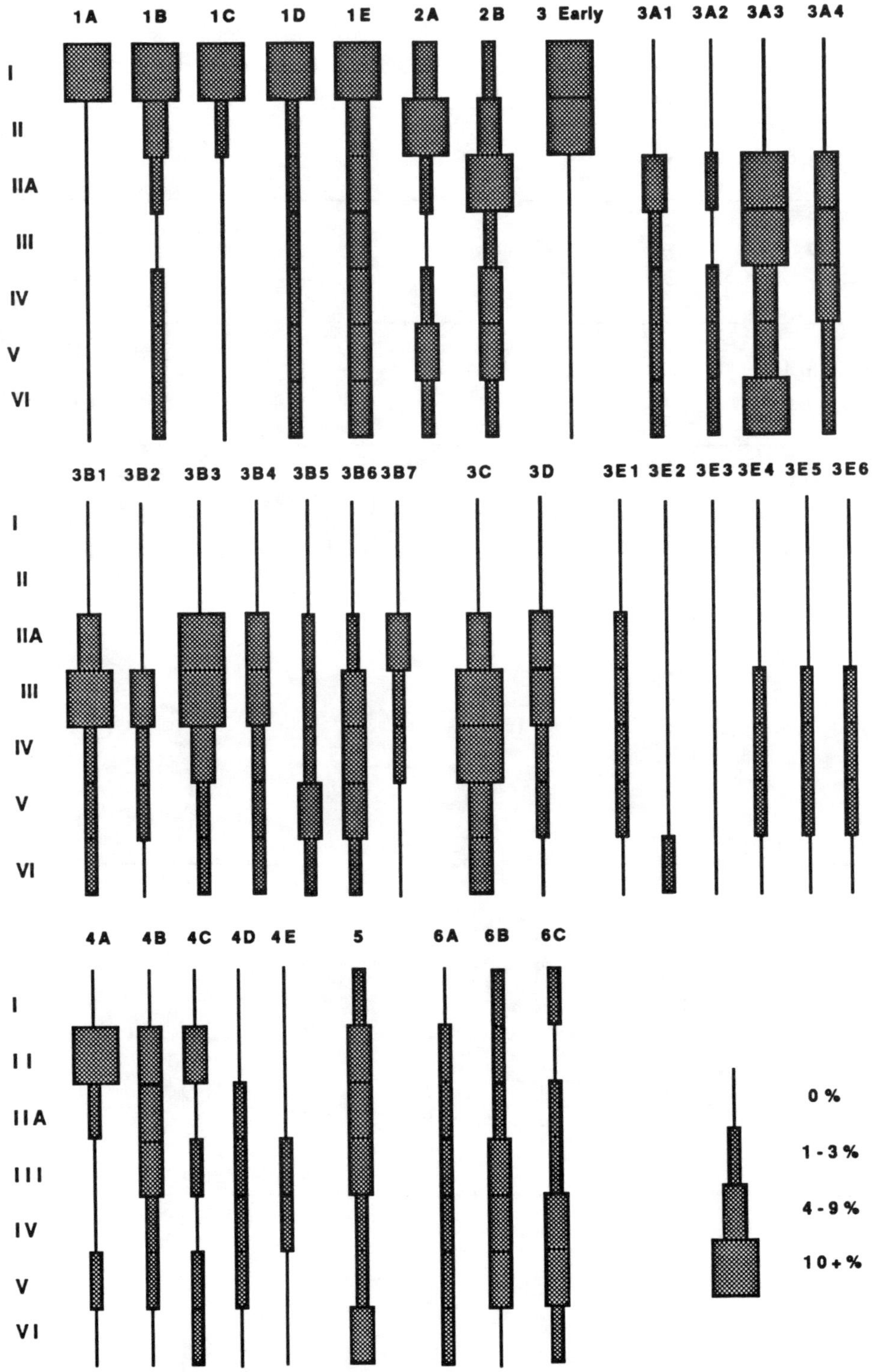

Table 8. DESIGNS. Design Scarab Series; percent of use by Periods.

	I	II	IIA	III	IV	V	VI
1A	18	-	-	-	-	-	-
1B	20	6	2	-	1	1	1
1C	10	1	-	-	-	-	-
1D	11	1	1	1	1	1	1
1E	21	9	6	4	4	4	4
2A	7	21	2	-	1	4	3
2B	2	7	16	3	6	5	3
3 Early	23	15	-	-	-	-	-
3A1	-	-	4	3	1	1	1
3A2	-	-	1	-	1	1	2
3A3	-	-	11	13	8	4	16
3A4	-	-	9	9	5	1	1
3B1	-	-	5	14	2	3	3
3B2	-	-	-	4	1	1	-
3B3	-	-	13	12	5	2	3
3B4	-	-	4	4	2	2	1
3B5	-	-	2	1	2	4	1
3B6	-	-	1	4	4	3	1
3B7	-	-	5	1	1	-	-
3C	-	-	8	12	11	7	4
3D	-	-	4	4	3	3	-
3E1	-	-	1	2	1	2	-
3E2	-	-	-	-	-	1	-
3E3	-	-	-	-	-	-	-
3E4	-	-	-	-	1	1	1
3E5	-	-	-	3	2	1	-
3E6	-	-	-	1	1	1	-
4A	-	19	1	-	-	1	-
4B	1	9	6	5	3	2	-
4C	-	7	-	1	-	1	1
4D	-	-	1	2	2	1	-
4E	-	-	-	1	1	-	-
5	1	7	8	7	2	2	4
6A	-	3	1	2	1	1	1
6B	1	3	2	4	5	4	-
6C	1	-	1	1	4	6	1

Table 8. DESIGNS (cont.)

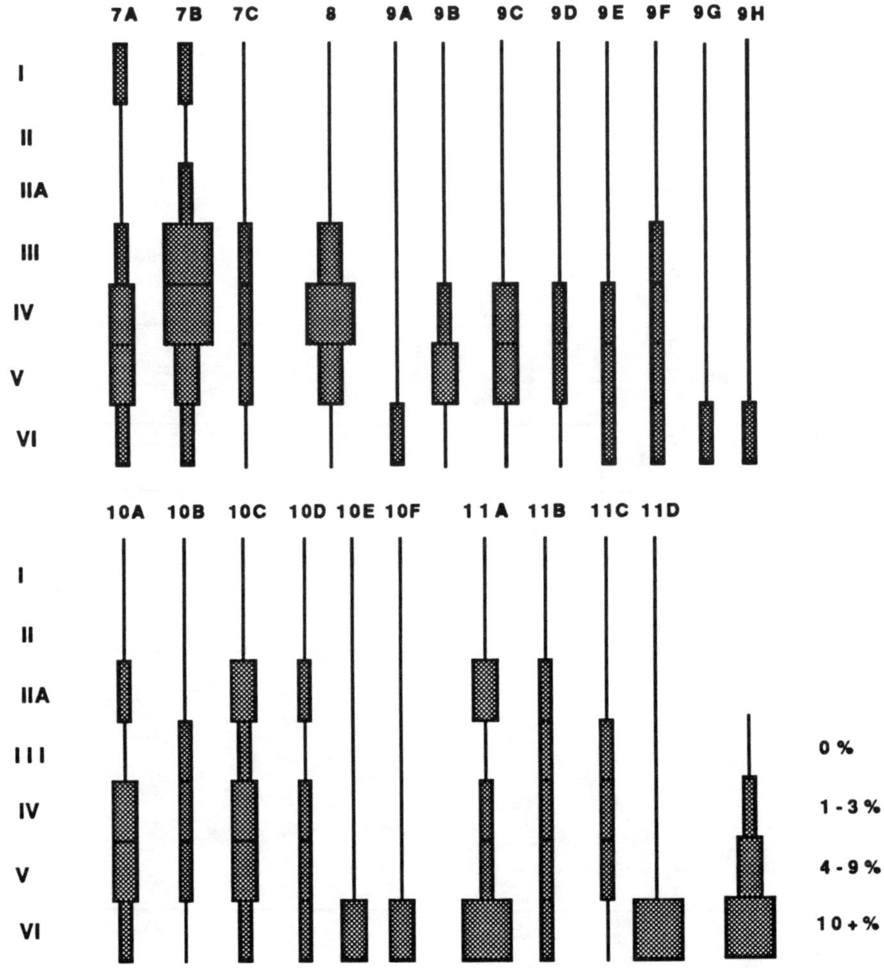

Table 8. DESIGNS. Design Scarab Series (cont)

	I	II	IIA	III	IV	V	VI
7A	1	-	-	3	5	5	2
7B	1	-	2	12	12	6	1
7C	-	-	-	1	1	1	-
8	-	-	-	8	10	7	-
9A	-	-	-	-	-	-	2
9B	-	-	-	-	3	4	-
9C	-	-	-	-	5	4	-
9D	-	-	-	-	1	2	-
9E	-	-	-	-	2	3	2
9F	-	-	-	1	1	2	1
9G	-	-	-	-	-	-	1
9H	-	-	-	-	-	-	2
10A	-	-	1	-	5	9	1
10B	-	-	-	1	1	2	-
10C	-	-	4	1	3	3	1
10D	-	-	1	-	2	2	1
10E	-	-	-	-	-	-	4
10F	-	-	-	-	-	-	7
11A	-	-	4	-	1	2	14
11B	-	-	1	1	1	1	3
11C	-	-	-	1	2	1	-
11D	-	-	-	-	-	-	15

Table 9. HEADS. Royal Name Series. Percent of use by Period.

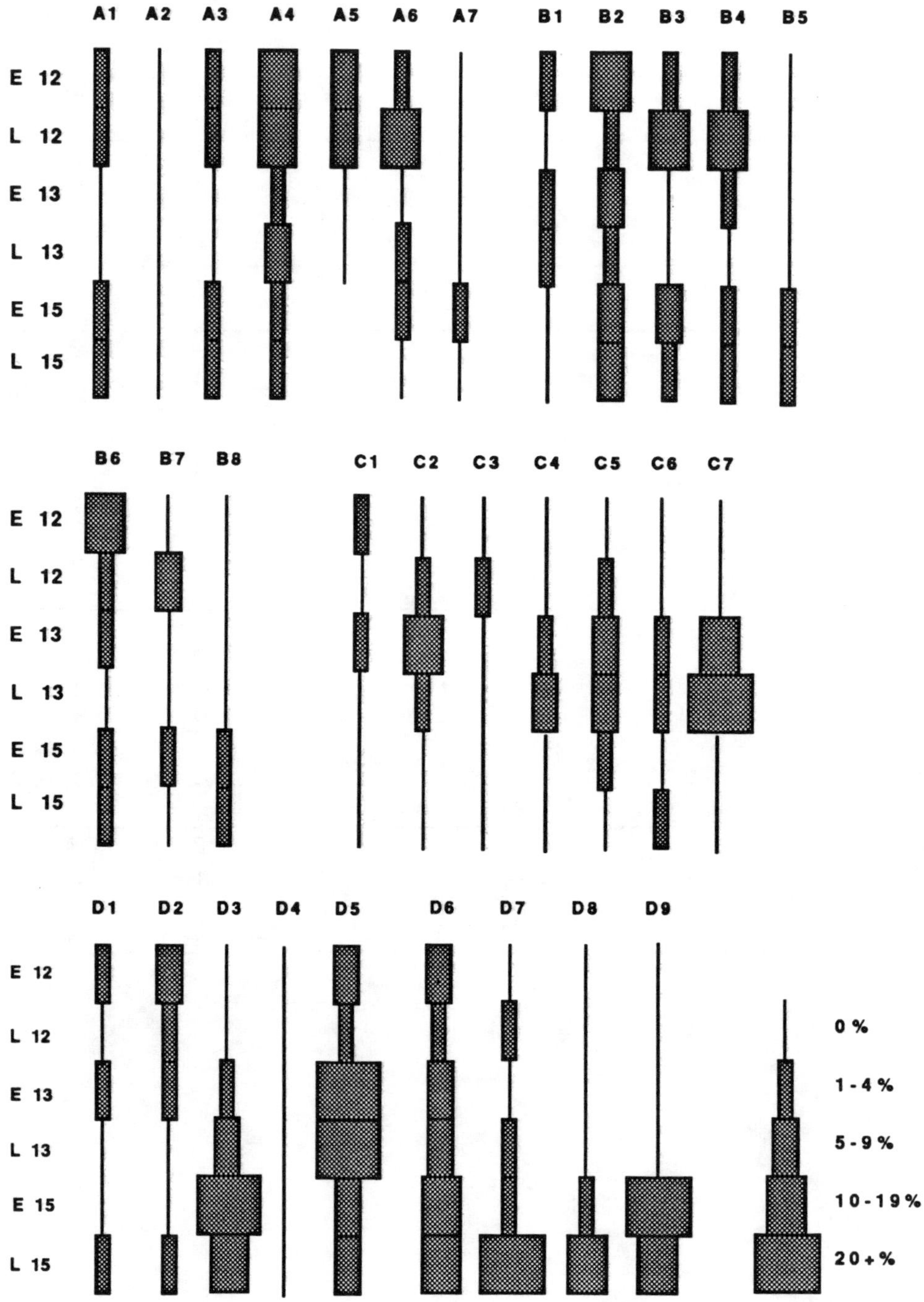

Table 9. HEADS. Royal Name Series; percent of use by Periods

	E 12	L 12	E 13	L 13	E 15	L 15
A1	2	2	-	-	1	1
A2	-	-	-	-	-	-
A3	2	4	-	-	1	1
A4	11	17	3	9	1	3
A5	9	6	-	-	2	1
A6	4	10	-	2	3	-
A7	-	-	-	-	1	-
B1	2	-	1	2	-	-
B2	17	2	9	2	5	8
B3	2	15	-	-	5	3
B4	4	10	1	-	2	1
B5	-	-	-	-	2	1
B6	17	4	1	-	1	1
B7	-	6	-	-	3	-
B8	-	-	-	-	1	1
C1	4	-	3	-	-	-
C2	-	4	12	2	-	-
C3	-	2	-	-	-	-
C4	-	-	4	5	-	-
C5	-	2	7	5	1	-
C6	-	-	3	2	-	1
C7	-	-	16	21	-	-
D1	2	-	4	-	-	1
D2	9	2	1	-	-	1
D3	-	-	1	5	25	12
D4	-	-	-	-	-	-
D5	6	2	21	28	7	6
D6	6	4	7	9	10	10
D7	-	4	-	2	4	22
D8	-	-	-	-	4	15
D9	-	-	-	-	20	13

Table 10. BACKS. Royal Name Series. Percent of use by Periods.

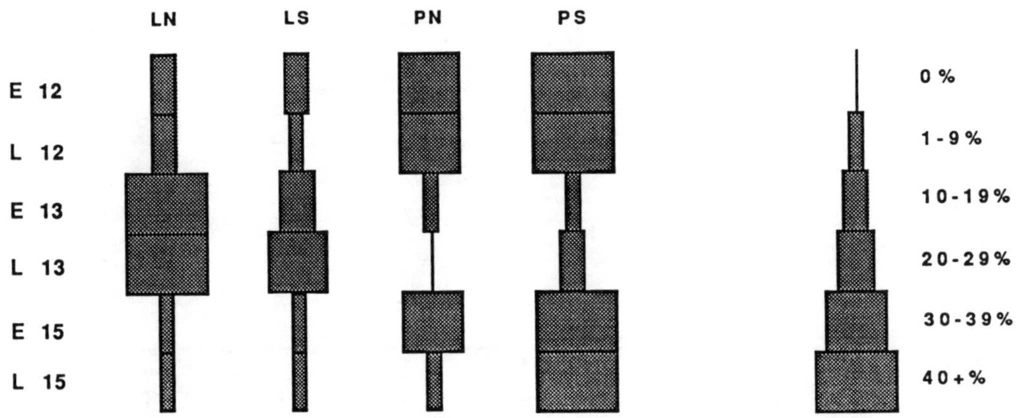

Table 10. BACKS. Royal Name Series; percent of use by Periods.

	E 12	L 12	E 13	L 13	E 15	L 15
LN	10	19	66	60	3	5
LS	10	7	21	30	3	5
PN	31	30	9	-	34	9
PS	49	44	3	10	60	81
Dec.	1	1	1	-	10	4
XX	1	-	-	-	-	-

Table 11. SIDES. Royal Name Series. Percent of use by Periods.

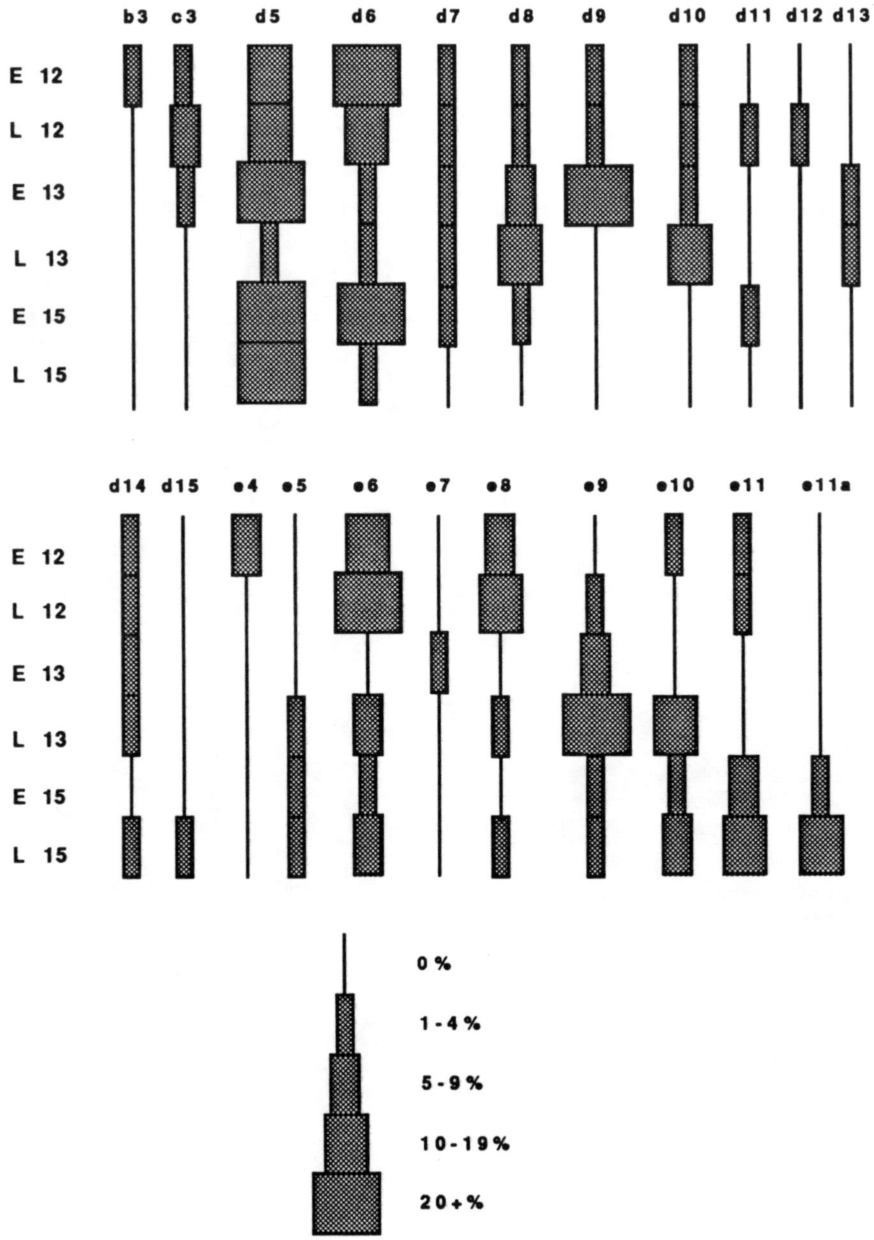

Table 11. SIDES. Royal Name Series; percent of use by Periods

	E 12	L 12	E 13	L 13	E 15	L 15
b	4	-	-	-	-	-
c	4	6	1	-	-	-
d5	13	17	27	4	49	49
d6	24	13	1	4	28	1
d7	2	2	3	2	1	-
d8	2	2	8	11	1	-
d9	2	4	46	-	-	-
d10	2	2	3	13	-	-
d11	-	2	-	-	2	-
d12	-	2	-	-	-	-
d13	-	-	1	2	-	-
d14	4	2	1	2	-	1
d15	-	-	-	-	-	1
e4	7	-	-	-	-	-
e5	-	-	-	2	1	4
e6	18	30	-	7	2	5
e7	-	-	1	-	-	-
e8	7	13	-	4	-	1
e9	-	2	5	33	2	3
e10	2	-	-	13	4	5
e11	2	2	-	-	6	15
e11a	-	-	-	-	3	14

Table 12. DESIGNS. Royal Name Series. Percent of use by Periods.

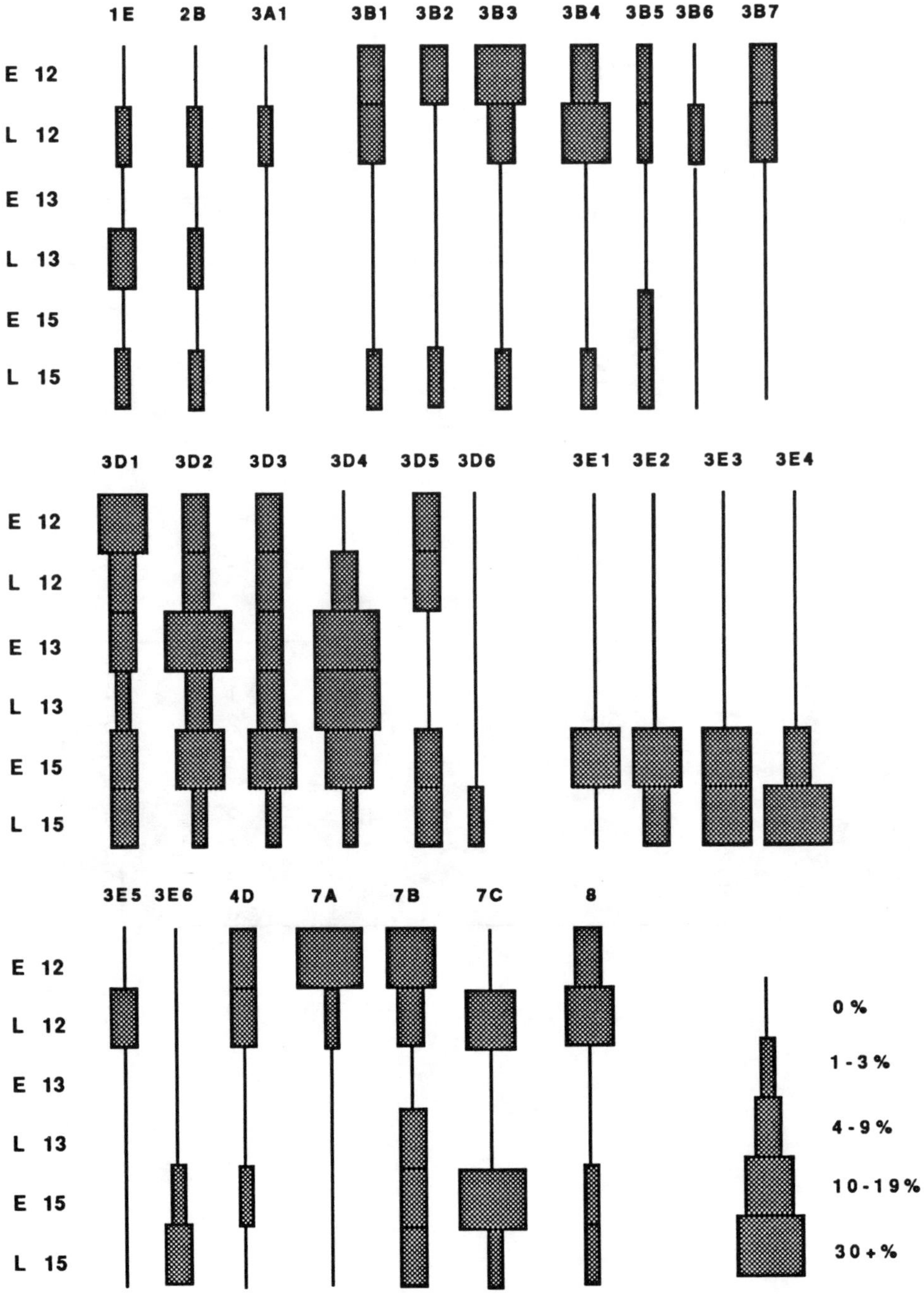

Table 12. DESIGNS. Royal Name Series; percent of use by Periods.

	E 12	L 12	E 13	L 13	E 15	L 15
1E	-	2	-	8	-	1
2B	-	2	-	2	-	1
3A1	-	2	-	-	-	-
3B1	6	4	-	-	-	1
3B2	6	-	-	-	-	1
3B3	12	8	-	-	-	-
3B4	4	16	-	-	-	1
3B5	2	2	-	-	2	1
3B6	-	2	-	-	-	-
3B7	6	4	-	-	-	-
3D1	12	6	6	2	9	9
3D2	4	6	36	8	11	2
3D3	4	6	5	4	17	1
3D4	-	6	51	84	10	1
3D5	2	2	-	-	1	1
3D6	-	-	-	-	-	1
3E1	-	-	-	-	13	-
3E2	-	-	-	-	18	8
3E3	-	-	-	-	14	12
3E4	-	-	-	-	7	50
3E5	-	4	-	-	-	-
3E6	-	-	-	-	2	8
4D	10	2	-	-	1	-
7A	30	2	-	-	-	-
7B	10	8	-	6	5	4
7C	-	10	-	-	32	1
8	4	18	-	-	1	1

Table 13. Summary of Scarab Length (in mm). Design scarab series (upper) and royal name series (lower). Bar shows mid 50% length span, dot shows average length.

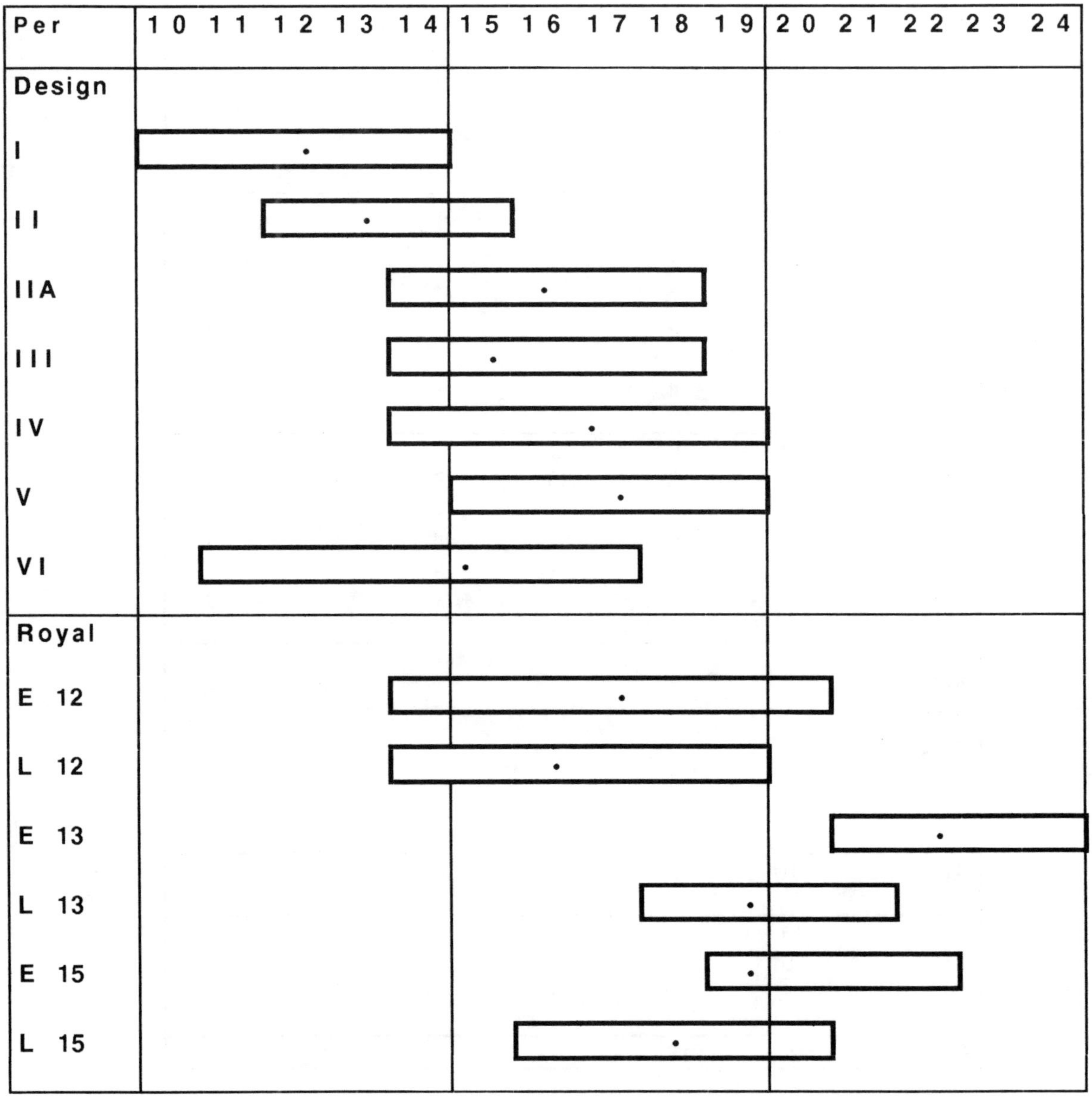

Abbreviations

ÄA	Ägyptologische Abhandlungen
ADAJ	*Annual of the Department of Antiquities of Jordan*
ÄF	Ägyptologische Forschungen
AJA	*American Journal of Archaeology*
AJSL	*American Journal of Semitic Languages and Literature*
ASOR	American Schools of Oriental Research
BA	*Biblical Archaeologist*
BAR	British Archaeological Reports
BASOR	*Bulletin of the American Schools of Oriental Research*
Berytus	*Berytus Archaeological Studies*
BibOr	*Bibliotheca Orientalis*
BMB	*Bulletin du Musée de Beyrouth*
CAH[3]	*Cambridge Ancient History.* Third edition.
CdÉ	*Chronique d'Égypte*
EAEHL	*Encyclopedia of Archaeological Excavations in the Holy Land*
HÄB	Hildesheimer Ägyptologische Beiträge
IEJ	*Israel Exploration Journal*
IFAO	Institut Français d'Archéologie Orientale
JAOS	*Journal of the American Oriental Society*
JEA	*Journal of Egyptian Archaeology*
JJS	*Journal of Jewish Studies*
JNES	*Journal of Near Eastern Studies*
JSSEA	*Journal of the Society for the Study of Egyptian Antiquities*
Levant	*Levant. Journal of the British School of Archaeology in Jerusalem*
LIA Bull.	*Bulletin of the Institute of Archaeology, London*
MÄS	Münchner Ägyptologische Studien
MDAIK	*Mitteilungen der Deutsches Archäologisches Institut. Abteilung Kairo*
MMJ	*Metropolitan Museum Journal*
MonAeg	Monumenta Aegyptiaca. Brussels
NAWG	Nachrichten von der Akademie der Wissenschaften zu Göttingen
ÖAW	Österreichischen Akademie der Wissenschaften
OBO	Orbis Biblicus et Orientalis
OIP	Oriental Institute Publications
ÖJh Beiblatt	*Jahreshefte des Österreichischen Instituts in Wien. Beiblatte*
OMRO	*Oudheidkundige Mededeelingen uit het Rijksmuseum van Oudheiden te Leiden*
PEQ	*Palestine Exploration Quarterly*
QDAP	*Quarterly of the Department of Antiquities of Palestine*
RDAC	*Report of the Department of Antiquities in Cyprus*
RevEg	*Revue d'Égyptologie*
SAK	*Studien zur altägyptischen Kultur*
SMA	Studies in Mediterranean Archaeology
SMAL	Studies in Mediterranean Archaeology and Literature
Syria	*Syria. Revue d'art oriental et d'archéologie*
UF	*Ugarit-Forschungen*
ZÄS	*Zeitschrift für Ägyptische Sprache und Altertumskunde*
ZDPV	*Zeitschrift des Deutschen Palästinavereins*

BIBLIOGRAPHY

Aḥituv, S.
1978 Economic Factors in the Egyptian Conquest of Canaan. *IEJ* 28: 93-105.

Albright, W. F.
1932 The Excavation of Tell Beit Mirsim. IA.The Bronze Age Pottery of the Fourth Campaign. *Annual ASOR* 13: 55ff. New Haven: Yale University Press.
1938 The Chronology of a South Palestinian City, Tell el-^{c}Ajjul. *AJSL* 55: 337-59.
1954 *The Archaeology of Palestine.* Baltimore: Penguin.
1966 Remarks on the Chronology of Early Bronze IV - Middle Bronze IIA in Phoenicia and Syria-Palestine. *BASOR* 184: 26-35.

Amiron, R.
1969 *Ancient Pottery of the Holy Land.* Rutgers: Rutgers University Press.

Arnold, D.
1977 Zur Keramik aus dem Taltemplebereich der Pyramide Amenemhets III in Dahschur. *MDAIK* 33: 21-26.
1982 Keramik Bearbeitung in Dahschur 1976-1981. *MDAIK* 38: 25-65.
1991 Amenemhat I and the Early Twelfth Dynasty at Thebes. *MMJ* 26: 5-48.

Arnold, D., and Stadelmann, R.
1977 Dahschur, Zweiter Grabungsbericht. *MDAIK* 33: 15-20.

Artzy, M.
1993 Nami: A Second Millennium B.C. International Maritime Trade Center in the Eastern Mediterranean. Forthcoming in *Recent Excavations in Israel: A View to the West,* ed. S. Gitin. Boston: Archaeological Institute of America.

Beck, P.
1975 The Pottery of the Middle Bronze Age IIA at Tel Aphek. *Tel Aviv* 2: 45-85.
1985 The Middle Bronze Age IIA Pottery from Aphek, 1972-1984: First Summary. *Tel Aviv* 12: 181-203.

Beckerath, J. von
1964 *Untersuchungen zur politischen Geschichte der Zweiten Zwischenzeit in Ägypten.* ÄF 23. Glückstadt: J. J. Augustin.

Ben-Dor, I.
1950 A Bronze-Age Temple at Nahariyah. *QDAP* 14: 1-41.

Ben-Tor, A.
1982 The Relations Between Egypt and the Land of Canaan during the Third Millennium B.C. *JJS* 33: 3-18.

Ben-Tor, A., Portugali, Y., and Avissar, M.
1981 The First Two Seasons of Excavations of Tel Qashish, 1978-1979: Preliminary Report. *IEJ* 31: 137-64.

Beste, I.
1979 *Skarabäen.* Part 3. Corpus Antiquitatum Aegypticarum, Kestner-Museum, Hanover. Mainz am Rhine: von Zabern.

Bienkowski, P.
1989 The Division of Middle Bronze IIB-C in Palestine. *Levant* 21: 169-79.

Bietak, M.
1968 Vorläufiger Bericht über die erste und zweite Kampagne der österreichischen Ausgrabung auf Tell ed-Dab^{c}a im Ostdelta Ägyptens (1966, 1967). *MDAIK* 23: 79-114.
1970 Vorläufiger Bericht über die dritte Kampagne der österreichischen Ausgrabungen auf Tell ed-Dab^{c}a im Ostdelta

Ägyptens (1968). *MDAIK* 26:15-42.
1979 *Avaris and Piramesse: Archae-ological Exploration in the Eastern Nile Delta.* London: British Academy.
1984 Problems of Middle Bronze Age Chronology: New Evidence from Egypt. *AJA* 88: 471-85.
1984a Tell el-Dab[c]a. *ÖJh Beiblatt* 55: 1-9.
1989 The Middle Bronze Age of the Levant -- A New Approch to Relative and Absolute Chronology. Pp. 78-123 in *High, Middle or Low? Acts of an International Colloquium on Absolute Chronology held at the University of Gothenburg 20th-22nd August 1987.* Part 3, ed. P. Åström. SMAL Pocket Book 80. Gothenburg: Åströms Förlag.
1991 Egypt and Canaan During the Middle Bronze Age. *BASOR* 281: 21-72.
1991a *Tell El-Dab[c]a V. Ein Friedhofs-bezirk der Mittleren Bronzezeitkultur mit Totentempel und Siedlungsschichten.* Vienna: Österreichischen Akademie der Wissenschaften.

Bietak, M. and Görg, M.
1981 Eine Stela des ältesten Königssohnes des Hyksos Chajan. *MDAIK* 17: 63-73.

Bishara, S. I.
1978 Biology and Identification of Scarab Beetles. Appendix D in Ward 1978.

Blackman, A. M.
1915 *The Rock Tombs of Meir III.* London: Egypt Exploration Fund.

Bonimovitz, S.
1992 The Middle Bronze Fortifications in Palestine as a Social Phenomenon. *Tel Aviv* 19: 221-34.

Broshi, M., and Gophna, R.
1986 Middle Bronze Age II Palestine. Its Settlement and Population. *BASOR* 261: 73-90.

Brunton, G.
1930 *Qau and Badari III.* London: British School of Archaeology in Egypt.
1937 *Mostagedda and the Tasian Culture.* London: Quaritch.
1948 *Matmar.* London: Quaritch.

Brunton, G. and Engelbach, R.
1927 *Gurob.* London: British School of Archaeology in Egypt.

Chéhab, M.
1939 Tombe phénicienne de Sin el Fil. Pp. 803-10 in *Mélanges syriens offerts à René Dussaud II.* Paris: Geuthner.

Cole, D. P.
1984 *Shechem I. The Middle Bronze IIB Pottery.* Winona Lake, IN: Eisenbraun's.

Coote, R. B., and Whitelam, K. W.
1987 *The Emergence of Early Israel in Historical Perspective.* Sheffield: Almond.

Courtois, J. Cl.
1974 Ugarit Grid, Strata, and Find Localizations. A Reassessment. *ZDPV* 90: 97-114.

Daton, G.
1969 Theoretical Issues in Economic Anthropology. *Current Anthropology* 10: 63-102.

Dalton, G. ed.
1967 *Tribal and Peasant Economies: Readings in Economic Anthropology.* Garden City, NY: Natural History Press.

D'Auria, S., Lacovara, P., and Roehrig, C.
1988 *Mummies and Magic. The Funerary Arts of Ancient Egypt.* Boston: Museum of Fine Arts.

Dever, W. G.

1973 The EB IV-MB I Horizon in Transjordan and Southern Palestine. *BASOR* 210: 37-63.

1974 The MB IIC Stratification in the Northwest Gate Area at Shechem. *BASOR* 216: 31-52.

1975 MB IIA Cemeteries at ᶜAin es-Sâmiyeh and Sinjil. *BASOR* 217: 23-36.

1976 The Beginning of the Middle Bronze Age in Syria-Palestine. Pp. 3-38 in *Magnalia Dei: The Mighty Acts of God. Essays on the Bible and Archaeology in Memory of G. Ernest Wright.* eds. F. M. Cross, W. E. Lemke, and P. D. Miller. Garden City, NY: Doubleday.

1980 New Vistas on the "EB IV-MB I" Horizon in Syria-Palestine. *BASOR* 237: 31-59.

1985 Relations Between Syria-Palestine and Egypt in the "Hyksos" Period. Pp. 69-87 in *Palestine in the Bronze and Iron Ages: Papers in Honour of Olga Tufnell.* ed. J. N. Tubb. Institute of Archaeology, Occasional Publication 11. London: Institute of Archaeology.

1987a The Collapse of the Urban Early Bronze Age in Palestine -- Toward a Systemic Analysis. Pp. 225-46 in *L'urbanisation de la Palestine á l'âge du bronze ancien,* ed. P. de Miroschedji. Oxford: BAR International Studies.

1987b The Middle Bronze Age: The Zenith of the Urban Canaanite Era. *BA* 50:148-77.

1990 "Hyksos," Egyptian Destructions, and the End of the Palestinian Middle Bronze Age. *Levant* 22: 75-81.

1991 Tell el-Dabᶜa and Levantine Middle Bronze Age Chronology: A Reply to Manfred Bietak. *BASOR* 281: 73-79

1992 The Chronology of Syria-Palestine in the Second Millennium B.C.E.: Current Issues. *BASOR* 288: 1-25.

1993a Pastoral Nomadism and the End of the Urban Early Bronze Age in Palestine. Forthcoming in *Pastoral Nomadism in the Levant: Archaeological Materials in Anthropological Perspective,* eds. O. Bar-Yosef and A. Khasanov.

1993b Social Structure in the Early Bronze IV Period in Palestine. Forthcoming in *The Archaeology of Society in the Holy Land,* ed. T. E. Levy. Leicester: Leicester University.

1993c The Rise of Complexity in Palestine in the Early Second Millennium B.C. Forthcoming in *Proceedings of the Second International Congress on Biblical Archaeology. Jerusalem, 1990.*

1993d Settlement Patterns and Chronology of Palestine in the Middle Bronze Age. Forthcoming in *Cultural Connections in the Eastern Mediterranean: The Hyksos and the Middle Bronze Age,* ed. E. D. Oren. Philadelphia: University Museum.

1993e From Tribe to Nation: State Formation Processes in Ancient Israel. Forthcoming in *Nuove fondazioni nel Vicino Oriente antico: realitá ed ideologia,* ed. S. Mazzoni. Pisa: University of Pisa.

Dever, W. G., Lance, H. D., and Wright, G. E.

1970 *Gezer I: Preliminary Report of the 1964-66 Seasons.* Jerusalem: Hebrew Union College.

Dever, W. G., *et al.*

1974 *Gezer II. Report of the 1966-70 Seasons in Fields I and II.*

Jerusalem: Hebrew Union College.
1984 *Gezer IV. The 1969-71 Seasons in Field VI, the "Acropolis."* Jerusalem: Hebrew Union College.

Dewachter, M.
1976 Le roi Sahathor et la famille de Neferhotep I. *RevEg* 28:66-73.

Dothan, M.

1956 The Excavations at Nahariyeh. *IEJ* 6: 14-25.

Drenkhahn, R.
1976 Bemerkungen zu dem Titel *ḫkr.t nswt*. *SAK* 4: 57-67.

Droste zu Hülshoff, V. von.
1980 *Der Igel im alten Ägypten.* HÄB 11. Hildesheim: Gerstenberg.

Druks,
1982 Early Tombs on Tel ᶜAmr. *ᶜAtiqot* 8: 1-6 (Hebrew Series).

Dunayevsky, I., and Kempinski, A.

1973 The Megiddo Temples. *ZDPV* 89: 161-87.

Dunand, M.
1939 *Fouilles de Byblos 1926-1932* . Vol. I. *Texte.* Paris: Geuthner.
1954-58 *Fouilles de Byblos 1933-1938.* Vol. II. *Texte.* Paris: Geuthner.

Dunham, D.
1967 *Second Cataract Forts II. Uronarti, Shalfak, Mirgissa.* Boston: Museum of Fine Arts.

Earle, T. K.
1985 Prehistoric Economies and the Evolution of Social Complexity. Pp. 106-11 in *Prehistoric Production and Exchange: The Aegean and Eastern Mediterranean,* eds. A. B. Knapp and T. Stech. Los Angeles: University of California at Los Angeles.

Earle, T. K., and Christianson, A., eds.
1980 *Modeling Change in Prehistoric Subsistence Economics.* New York: Academic Press.

Earle, T. K., and Ericson, J. E.
1977 *Exchange Systems in Prehistory.* New York: Academic Press.

Engelbach, R.
1923 *Harageh.* London: British School of Archaeology in Egypt.

Epron, L., *et al.*
1939 *Le tombeau de Ti.* Fasc. I. Cairo: IFAO.

Epstein, C.
1965 An Interpretation of the Megiddo Sacred Area During Middle Bronze II. *IEJ* 15: 204-21.
1974 Middle Bronze Age Tombs at Kfar Szold and Ginosar. *ᶜAtiqot* 7: 13-39. (Hebrew Series).

Ericson, J. E., and Earle, T. K.
1982 *Contexts for Prehistoric Exchange.* New York: Academic Press.

Falconer, S. E.
1987 *Heartland of Villages: Reconsidering Early Urbanism in the Southern Levant.* Unpublished doctoral dissertation, University of Arizona.

Falconer, S. E., and Magness-Gardiner, B.
1984 Preliminary Report of the First Season of the Tell el-Hayyat Project. *BASOR* 255: 49-74.
1989 Bronze Age Village Life in the Jordan Valley: Archaeological Investigations at Tell el-Hayyat and Tell Abu En-Niaj.

National Geographic Research 5: 335-47.

Finkelstein, I.
1988-89. The Land of Ephraim Survey 1980-1987. Preliminary Report. *Tel Aviv* 15-16: 117-83.

Furshpan (Walker), A. M.
1975 Une sepulture collective du Bronze Moyen II AB á Kh. Minfia (Munfiata), Israel. The Pottery. Pp. 89-111 in *Report on Work at Suwwanet eth-Thaniya, Tananir, and Khirbet Minfia (Munfiata),* ed. G. M. Landes. Missoula, MT: Scholars Press.

Fischer, H.
1961 Three Old Kingdom Palimpsests in the Louvre. *ZAS* 86: 21-31.

Franke, D.
1984 *Personendata aus dem Mittleren Reich. Dossiers 1-796.* ÄA 41. Wiesbaden: Harrasowitz.

Gal, Z.
1991 A Note on the Settlement Pattern of the MB II Jezreel and Beth Shan Valleys. *BASOR* 284: 29-31.

Gale, N. H.
1991 *Bronze Age Trade in the Mediterranean.* SMA 90. Jonesred: Åström.

Gardiner, A. H.
1946 Davies's Copy of the Great Speos Artemidos Inscription. *JEA* 32: 43-56.

Garelli, P.
1963 *Les Assyriens en Cappadoce.* Paris: Adrien Maisonneuve.

Garfinkle, Y., and Bonfil, R.
1990 Graves and Burial Customs of the MB IIA Period in Gesher. *Eretz-Israel* 21: 132-47 (the Ruth Amiran volume; in Hebrew).

Gerstenblith, P.
1980 A Reassessment of the Beginning of the Middle Bronze Age in Syria-Palestine. *BASOR* 237: 65-84
1983 *The Levant at the Beginning of the Middle Bronze Age.* ASOR Dissertation Series 5. Winona Lake, IN: ASOR.

Gittlen, B. M.
1981 The Cultural and Chronological Implications of the Cypro-Palestinian Trade During the Late Bronze Age. *BASOR* 241: 49-59

Giveon, R.
1967 Royal Seals of the XIIth Dynasty from Western Asia. *RevEg* 19: 29-37
1973 Review of Ward 1971. *CdÉ* 95: 88-92.
1985 *Egyptian Scarabs from Western Asia from the Collections of the British Museum.* OBO, Ser. Arch. 3. Freiburg: Universitätsverlag.
1988 *Scarabs from Recent Excavations in Israel.* OBO 83. Ed. D. Warburton and C. Uehlinger. Freiburg: Universitätsverlag.

Gophna, R.
1986 The Settlement Landscape of Palestine in the Early Bronze Age II-III and Middle Bronze Age II. *IEJ* 34: 20-31.

Gophna, R., and Portugali, Y.
1988 Settlement and Demographic Processes in Israel's Coastal Plain from the Chalcolithic to the Middle Bronze Age. *BASOR* 269: 11-38.

Gophna, R., and Sussman, V.
1969 A Middle Bronze Age Tomb at Barqai. *ᶜAtiqot* (Hebr. Ser.) 5: 1-13.

Graefe, E.

1971 Das sog. Mundöffnungsgerät "*pss-kf*". *JEA* 57: 203.

Grant, E., ed.

1986 *Central Places, Archaeology and History.* Sheffield: University of Sheffield.

Gregori, B.

1986 "Three-Entrance" City-gates of the Middle Bronze Age in Syria and Palestine. *Levant* 18: 83-102.

Guigues, P. O.

1937 Lébé[c]a, Kafer-Garra, Qrayé: Nécropoles de la région sidonienne. *BMB* 1: 37-56.

1938 Lébé[c]a, Kafer-Garra, Qrayé: Nécropoles de la région sidonienne. *BMB* 2: 27-72.

Guy. P. L. O.

1938 *Megiddo Tombs.* OIP 33. Chicago: University of Chicago Press.

Habachi, L.

1951 Notes on the Altar of Sekhemre[c]-Sewadjtowe Sebkhotpe from Sehel. *JEA* 37: 17-19.

1981 New Light on the Neferhotep Family, as Revealed by Their Inscriptions in the Cataract Area. Pp. 77-81 in *Studies in Ancient Egypt, the Aegean and the Sudan. Essays in Honor of Dows Dunham,* eds. W. K. Simpson and W. M. Davis. Boston: Museum of Fine Arts.

Hall, H. R.

1913 *Catalogue of Egyptian Scarabs, etc., in the British Museum.* Vol. 1. *Royal Scarabs.* London: The British Museum.

Hawkins, J. D., ed.

1977 *Trade in the Ancient Near East.* London: British School of Archaeology in Iran.

Helck, W.

1967 Einige Bemerkungen zum Mundöffnungsritual. *MDAIK* 22: 26-41.

1971 *Die Beziehungen Ägyptens zu Vorderasien im 3. und 2. Jahrtausend v, Chr.* 2d ed. ÄA 5. Wiesbaden: Harrassowitz.

1975 *Historisch-biographische Texte der 2. Zwischenzeit und neue Texte der 18. Dynastie.* Kleine Ägyptische Texte. Wiesbaden: Harrassowitz.

1989 (Remarks in discussion). Pp. 40-45 in *High, Middle or Low. Acts of an International Colloquium on Absolute Chronology held at the University of Gothenburg 20th-22nd August 1987,* ed. P. Åström. SMAL Pocket Book 80. Gothenburg: Åströms Fölag.

Heltzer, M

1971 *Goods, Prices and the Organization of Trade in Ugarit. Marketing and Transportation in the Eastern Mediterraenan in the Second Half of the II Millennium B.C.* Wiesbaden: Harrassowitz.

Hodder, I.

1974 Regression Analysis of Some Trade and Marketing Practices. *World Archaeology* 6: 172-89.

Hodder, I., ed.

1978 *The Spatial Organization of Culture.* Cambridge: Cambridge University.

Hoffmeier, J. K.

1989 Reconsidering Egypt's Part in the Termination of the Middle Bronze Age in Palestine. *Levant* 21: 181-93.

1991 Some Thoughts on William G. Dever's "Hyksos," Egyptian Destructions, and the End of the Palestinian Middle Bronze Age. *Levant* 22: 83-89.

Holladay, J. S.
1982 *Cities of the Delta. Part III: Tell el-Maskhuta. Preliminary Report of the Wadi Tumilat Project 1978-1979.* Malibu, CA: Undena.

Horn, S.
1962 Scarabs from Shechem. *JNES* 21:1-14.
1966 Scarabs and Scarab Impressions from Shechem - II. *JNES* 25:48-56.
1973 Scarabs and Scarab Impressions from Shechem - III. *JNES* 32: 281-89.

Hornung, E. and Staehelin, E.
1976 *Skarabäen und andere Siegel-amulette aus Basler Sammlungen.* Mainz: Philipp von Zabern.

Ilan, D.
1991 "Stepped-Rim" Juglets from Tel Dan and the "MB I-II (MB IIA-B) Transitional Period." *IEJ* 41: 229-38.
1993 The Dawn of Internationalism -- The Middle Bronze Age. Forthcoming in *The Archaeology of Society in the Holy Land,* ed. T. E. Levy. Leicester: Leicester University.

Iliffe, J. H.
1936 Pottery from Râs el [c]Ain. *QDAP* 5: 113-26.

Jaeger, B.
1982 *Essai de classification et datation des scarabées Menkhéperrê.* OBO Ser. Arch. 2. Freiburg: Universitätsverlag.

Joffe, A. H.
1991 Early Bronze I and the Evolution of Social Complexity in the Southern Levant. *Journal of Mediterranean Archaeology* 4/1: 3-58.

Johnson, P.
1982 The Middle Cypriote Pottery Found in Palestine. *Opuscula Atheniensa* 14: 49-72.

Kantor, H. J.
1947 *The Aegean and the Orient in the Second Millennium B.C.* Bloomington, IN: Principia Press.

Kaplan, J.
1955 A Cemetery of the Bronze Age Discovered Near Tel Aviv Harbour. [c]Atiqot I; 1-12 (English series).

Kaplan, M. F.
1980 *The Origin and Distribution of Tell el Yehudiyeh Pottery.* SMA 62. Göteborg: Åström.

Kaplony, P.
1981 *Die Rollsiegel des Alten Reichs II. Katalog der Rollsiegel.* MonAeg 3. Brussels: Fondation Égyptologique Reine Élisabeth.

Keel, O., and Schroer, S.
1985 *Studien zu den Stempelsiegeln aus Palästina/Israel I.* OBO 67. Freiburg: Universitätsverlag.

Keel, O., *et al.*
1989 *Studien zu den Stempelsiegeln aus Palästina/Israel II.* OBO 88. Freiburg: Universitätsverlag.

Kemp, B. J. and Merrillees, R. S.
1980 *Minoan Pottery in Second Millennium Egypt.* Mainz: von Zabern.

Kempinski, A.
1983 *Syrien und Palästina (Kanaan) in der letzten Phase der Mittelbronze IIB Zeit (1650-1570 v. Chr.).* Wiesbaden: Harrassowitz.
1985 Some Observations on the Hyksos (XVth) Dynasty and its Canaanite Origins. Pp. 129-37 in *Pharaonic Egypt, the*

Bible and Christianity, ed. S. Israelit-Groll. Jerusalem: Magnus Press.

1992 a Urbanization and Town Plans in the Middle Bronze Age II. Pp. 121-26 in *The Architecture of Ancient Israel,* eds. A. Kempinski and R. Reich. Jerusalem: Israel Exploration Society.

1992 b The Middle Bronze Age. Pp. 159-210 in *The Archaeology of Ancient Israel,* ed. A. Ben-Tor. New Haven: Yale University.

Kenyon, K. M.

1957 *Digging Up Jericho.* London: Ernst Benn.

1958 Some Notes on the Early and Middle Bronze Age Strata of Megiddo. *Eretz-Israel* 5: 51*-69* (the Mazar volume).

1965 *Excavations at Jericho II. The Tombs Excavated in 1955-58.* London: British School of Archaeology in Jerusalem.

1966 *Amorites and Canaanites.* London: Oxford University Press.

1971 Syria and Palestine c. 2160-1780 B.C. The Archaeological Sites. *CAH* 3 Vol. 1, Part 2: 567-94.

1973 Palestine in the Middle Bronze Age. *CAH* 3, Vol. II, Part 1: 525-56.

Kirkbride, D.

1965 Scarabs. Appendix E in Kenyon 1965.

Kitchen, K. A.

1967 Byblos, Egypt and Mari in the Early Second Millennium B.C. *Orientalia* 36: 39-54.

1987 The Basics of Egyptian Chronology in Relation to the Bronze Age. Pp. 37-55 in *High, Middle of Low? Acts of an International Colloquium on Absolute Chronology held at the University of Gothenburg 20th-22nd August 1987.* Part 1, ed. P. Äström. SMAL Pocket Book 56. Gothenburg: Äströms Förlag.

1989 Supplementary Notes on 'The Basics of Egyptian Chronology'. Pp. 152-59 in *High, Middle or Low? Acts of an International Colloquium on Absolute Chronology held at the University of Gothenburg 20th-22nd August 1987.* Part 3, ed. P. Åström. SMAL Pocket Book 80. Gothenburg: Åströms Förlag.

Knapp, A. B.

1992 *Archaeology, Annales, and Ethnohistory.* Cambridge: Cambridge University.

Knapp, A. B., and Stech, T., eds.

1985 *Prehistoric Production and Exchange: The Aegean and Eastern Mediterranean.* Los Angeles: University of California at Los Angeles.

Kochavi, M.

1975 The First Two Seasons of Excavations at Aphek-Antipatris. *Tel Aviv* 2: 17-42.

Kotter, W.

1987 *Spatial Aspects of Urban Development of Palestine During the Middle Bronze Age.* Unpublished doctoral dissertation, University of Arizona.

Krauss, R.

1985 *Sothis und Monddaten. Studien zur astronomischen und technischen Chronologie altägyptens.* HÄB 20. Hildesheim: Gerstenberg.

LaBianca, Ø. S.

1990 *Hesban I. Sedentarization and Nomadization: Food System Cycles at Hesban and Vicinity in Transjordan.* Berrien Springs, MI: Andrews University.

Lacau, P. and Chevrier, H.
1977 *Une sanctuaire d'Hatshepsout à Karnak.* Cairo: IFAO.

Lapp, P. W.
1961 Review of K. M. Kenyon, *Excavations at Jericho*, Vol. I. *AJA* 65: 69, 70.

Larsen, M. T.
1976 *The Old Assyrian City-State and its Colonies, Mesopotamia.* Copenhagen: Akademisk Forlag.

Leibovitch,
1955 Description of the Scarabs Found in a Cemetery Near Tel Aviv. *ᶜAtiqot* 1: 13-18.(English Series).

Leitz, Ch.
1989 *Studien zur ägyptischen Astronomie.* ÄA 49. Wiesbaden: Harrassowitz.

Lilyquist, C.
1979 *Ancient Egyptian Mirrors from the Earliest Times through the Middle Kingdom.* MÄS 27. Berlin: Deutsche Kunstverlag.
1993 Granulation and Glass: Chronological and Stylistic Investigations at Selected Sites, ca. 2500-1400 B.C.E. *BASOR* 290-291: 27-92.

Loud, G.
1948 *Megiddo II: Seasons of 1935-39.* OIP 62. Chicago: University of Chicago.

Luft, U.
1992 *Die chronologische Fixierung des ägyptischen Mittleren Reiches nach dem Tempelarchiv von Illahun.* ÖAW phil-hist. Kl., Sitz., Band 598. Vienna: Verlag der Österreichischen Akademie der Wissenschaften.

Mabry, J.
1986 The Canaanite Countryside. Unpublished manuscript, University of Arizona.

Macadam, M. F. Laming
1951 A Royal Family of the Thirteenth Dynasty. *JEA* 37: 20-28.

Macalister, R. A. S.
1912 *The Excavation of Gezer, 1902-1905 and 1907-1909.* 3 vols. London: Murray.

Malamat, A.
1989 Hazor and Mari. *Eretz-Israel* 20: 68-71 (Hebrew; the Yadin Volume).

Mallet, J.
1973 *Tell el-Farᶜah (Region Naplouse): L'installation du Moyen Bronze antérieur au rampart.* Paris: J. Gabalda.

Martin, G. T.
1971 *Egyptian Administrative and Private-name Seals Principally of the Middle Kingdom and Second Intermediate Period.* Oxford: Griffith Institute.

Marfoe, L.
1979 The Integrative Transformation: Patterns of Socio-Political Organization in Southern Syria. *BASOR* 243: 1-42.

Matthiae, P.
1979 Scavi a Tell Mardikh-Ebla, 1978: rapporto summario. *Studi Eblaiti* I/9-12: 129-84.
1980 Two Princely Tombs at Tell Mardikh-Ebla. *Archaeology* 33: 8-17.
1984 New Discoveries at Ebla: The Excavation of the Western Palace and the Royal Necropolis of the Amorite Period. *BA* 47: 18-32.

Maxwell-Hyslop, K. R.
1971 *Western Asiatic Jewellery c. 3000-612 B.C.* London: Methuen.

Mazar, B.
1968 The Middle Bronze Age in Palestine. *IEJ* 8: 65-97.

du Mesnil du Buisson, R.
1948 *Baghouz, l'ancienne Corsôte: le tell archaique et la nécropole de l'âge du bronze.* Leiden: Brill.

Montet, P.
1928 *Byblos et l'Égypte. Quatre campagnes de fouilles à Gebeil.* Paris: Geuthner.

Muhly, J. M.
1982 The Nature of Trade in the Late Bronze Age Eastern Mediterranean: The Organization of the Metals' Trade and the Role of Cyprus. Pp. 251-66 in *Acta of the International Archaeological Symposium: Early Metallurgy in Cyprus, 4000-500 B.C.,* eds. J. D. Muhly, R. Maddin, and V. Karageorghis. Nicosia: Perides Foundation.
1986 The Role of Cyprus in the Economy of the Eastern Mediterranean During the Second Millennium B.C. Pp. 45-62 in *Acts of the International Archaeological Symposium "Cyprus Between the Orient and the Occident" Nicosia 1986,* ed. V. Karageorghis. Nicosia: Department of Antiquities of Cyprus.

Murray, M.
1949 Some Canaanite Scarabs. *PEQ* 81: 92-99.

Na'aman, N.
1981 Economic Aspects of the Egyptian Occupation of Canaan. *IEJ* 31: 172-85.

Naumann, R.
1971 *Architektur Kleinasiens.* Second edition. Tübingen: E. Wasmuth.

Naveh, J.
1982 *Early History of the Alphabet. An Introduction to West Semitic Epigraphy and Paleography.* Jerusalem: Magness.

Negbi, O. and Moskowitz, S.
1966 The "Foundation Deposits" or "Offering Deposits" of Byblos. *BASOR* 184: 21-26.

Newberry, P. E.
1906 *Scarabs. An Introduction to the Study of Egyptian Seals and Signet Rings.* London: Constable.
1907 *Scarab-shaped Seals.* Catalogue Général des Antiquités Égyptiennes du Musée du Caire, nos. 36001-37521. London: Constable.

Niccacci, A.
1980 *Hyksos Scarabs.* Jerusalem: Museum of the Studium Biblicum Franciscanum.

Niemeier, W.
1993 Tel Kabri: Cretan Frescoes in a Canaanite Palace. Forthcoming in *Recent Excavations in Israel: A View to the West,* ed. S. Gitin. Boston: Archaeological Institute of America.

North, R.
1973 Ugarit Grid, Strata, and Find Localizations. *ZDPV* 89: 113-60.

O'Connor, D.
1969 Nubian Archaeological Material of the First to Second Intermediate Periods. Unpublished doctoral dissertation, Cambridge University.
1974 Political Systems and Archaeological Data in Egypt: 2600-1780 B.C. *World Archaeology* 6: 15-38.
1983 Review of Ward 1978. *CdE* 115-116: 163-72.

1987 The Chronology of Scarabs of the Middle Kingdom and the Second Intermediate Period. *JSSEA* 15: 1-41 (for 1985).

Oren, E.
1971 A Middle Bronze Age I Warrior Tomb at Beth-Shan. *ZDPV* 87: 109-39.

Ortiz, S., ed.
1983 *Economic Anthropology.* Lanham, MD: University Press of America.

Ory, J.
1936 Excavations at Ras el-^{c}Ain. *QDAP* 5: 111-12.
1937 Excavations at Ras el-^{c}Ain. *QDAP* 6: 99-120.
1948 A Bronze-Age Cemetery at Dhahrat el Humraiya. *QDAP* 13: 75-89.

Palumbo, G.
1991 *The Early Bronze Age IV in the Southern Levant. Settlement Patterns, Economy, and Material Culture of a "Dark Age."* Rome: University of Rome.

Paynter, R. W.
1983 Expanding the Scope of Settlement Analysis. Pp. 233-75 in *Archaeological Hammers and Theories,* eds. J. A. Moore and A. S. Keene. New York: Academic.

Petrie, W. M. F.
1889 *Historical Scarabs: a series of drawings from the principal collections.* London:
1901 *Diospolis Parva. The Cemeteries of Abadiyeh and Hu.* London: Egyptian Exploration Fund.
1917 *Scarabs and Cylinders with Names. Illustrated by the Egyptian Collection in University College London.* London: British School of Archaeology in Egypt.
1925 *Buttons and Design Scarabs: Illustrated by the Egyptian Collection in University College London.* London: British School of Archaeology in Egypt.
1932 *Ancient Gaza II: Tell el-Ajjûl.* London: British School of Archaeology in Egypt.

Petrie, W. M. F. and Brunton, G.
1924 *Sedment II.* London: British School of Archaeology in Egypt.

Piccirillo, M.
1978 Una tomba del bronzo medio ad Amman? *Liber Annuus* 28: 73-86.

Philip, G.
1989 *Metal Weapons of the Early and Middle Bronze Ages in Syria-Palestine.* BAR International Series 526. Oxford: British Archaeological Reports.

Pieper, M.
1927 Skarabäen. Cols. 447-59 in Reihe III.1 of *Real-Encyclopädie der klassischen Altertumswissenschaft,* ed. A. Pauly, G. Wissowa, and W. Kroll. Stuttgart: Metzlersche Verlagsbuchhandlung.

Polanyi, K., Arensberg, C. M., and Pearson, H. W., eds.
1957 *Trade and Market in the Early Empires.* Glencoe, IL: Free Press.

Porter, B., and Moss, R. L. B.
1972 *Topographical Bibliography of Ancient Egyptian Hieroglyphic Texts, Reliefs and Paintings. II. Theban Temples.* Oxford: Clarendon Press.

Price Williams, D.
1977 *The Tombs of the Middle Bronze II Period from the "500" Cemetery at Tell Fara (South).* Occasional Papers 1. London: Institute of Archaeology.

Ranke, H.
1935 *Die Ägyptischen Personennamen I.* Glückstadt: Augustin.
1952 *Die Ägyptischen Personennamen II.* Glückstadt: Augustin.

Redford, D. B.
1986 *Pharaonic King-lists, Annals and Day-books.* Mississauga: Benben Publications.
1992 *Egypt, Canaan, and Israel in Ancient Times.* Princeton: Princeton University Press.

Reisner, G. A., and Smith W. S.
1955 *A History of the Giza Necropolis II. The Tomb of Hetep-heres The Mother of Cheops.* Cambridge, MA: Harvard University Press.

Renfrew, A. C.
1969 Trade and Culture Process in European Prehistory. *Current Anthropology* 10: 151-69.
1977 Alternate Models for Exchange and Spatial Distribution. Pp. 71-90 in *Exchange Systems in Prehistory,* eds. T. K. Earle and J. E. Ericson. New York: Academic.
1984 *Approaches to Social Archaeology.* Cambridge: Harvard University.

Richards, F. V.
1992 *Scarab Seals from a Middle to Late Bronze Age Tomb at Pella in Jordan.* OBO 117. Freiburg: Universitätsverlag.

Rowe, A.
1936 *Catalogue of Egyptian Scarabs, Scaraboids, Seals and Amulets in the Palestine Archaeological Museum.* Cairo: IFAO.

Runnels, C., and Van Andel, T. H.
1988 Trade and the Origins of Agriculture in the Eastern Mediterranean. *Journal of Mediterranean Archaeology* I/1: 83-109.

Saghieh, M.
1983 *Byblos in the Third Millennium B.C.* Warminster: Aris and Phillips.

Sahlins, M. D.
1972 *Stone Age Economics.* Chicago: Aldine.

Salz, D. L.
1977 The Chronology of the Middle Cypriote Period. *RDAC* 1977: 51-70.

Sass, B.
1988 *The Genesis of the Alphabet and its Development in the Second Millennium B.C.* Wiesbaden: Harrassowitz.

Säve-Söderbergh, T.
1951 The Hyksos Rule in Egypt. *JEA* 37: 53-71.

Scandone Matthiae, G.
1979 Un oggetto faraonico della XIII dinastia dalla "Tomba del Signore dei capride." *Studi Eblaiti* 1: 119-28.

Schaeffer, Cl.
1939 *Ugaritica II.* Mission de Ras Shamra V. Paris: Geuthner.

Schneider, H. K.
1974 *Economic Man: The Anthropology of Economics.* New York: Free Press.

Schott, S.
1955 *Zum Krönungstag der Königen Hatschepsût.* NAWG 1955, 6. Göttingen: Vandenhoeck & Ruprecht.

Sheridan, A., and Bailey, G., eds.
1981 *Economic Archaeology: Towards an Integration of Ecological and Sociological Approaches.* BAR International Series 96. Oxford: BAR.

Smith, H. S., and Smith A.
1976 A Reconsideration of the Kamose Texts. *ZÄS* 103: 48-76.

Smith, R.H.
1962 *Excavations in the Cemetery at Khirbet Kufin, Palestine.* London.

Stock, H.
1955 *Studien zur Geschichte und Archäologie der 13. bis 17. Dynastie Ägyptens.* ÄF 12. Glückstadt: J. J. Augustin.

Tubb, J
1983 The MB IIA Period in Palestine: Its Relationship with Syria and its Origin. *Levant* 15: 49-62.

Tufnell, O.
1958 *Lachish IV (Tell ed-Duweir). The Bronze Age.* London: Oxford University Press.
1962 The Courtyard Cemetery at Tell el-cAjjul. *LIA Bull.* 3: 1-37.
1969 The Pottery from Royal Tombs I-III at Byblos. *Berytus* 18: 5-33.
1970 Some Scarabs with Decorated Backs. *Levant* 2: 95-99
1973 The Middle Bronze Age Scarab-seals from Burials on the Mound at Megiddo. *Levant* 5: 69-82.
1975 Seal Impressions from Kahûn Town and Uronarti Fort. *JEA* 61: 67-102.
1975-76 Tomb 66 at Ruweisé, Near Sidon. *Berytus* 24: 5-25.
1980 A Review of the Contents of Cave 303 at Tell el-cAjjûl. *cAtiqot* 14: 37-48 (English Series).
1984 *Scarab Seals and Their Contribution to History in the Early Second Millennium B.C.* Studies on Scarab Seals II. Warminster: Aris and Phillips.

Tufnell, O. and Ward, W. A.
1966 Relations Between Byblos, Egypt and Mesopotamia at the end of the Third Millennium B.C. A Study of the Montet Jar. *Syria* 32: 165-241.

Van den Brink, E. C. M.
1982 *Tombs and Burial Customs at Tell el-Dabca and their Cultural Relationshiop to Syria-Palestine during the Second Intermediate Period.* Vienna: AFRO-PUB.

Vandersleyen, C.
1971 *Les guerres d'Amosis Fondateur de la XVIIIe Dynastie.* Monographies Reine Élisabeth 1. Brussels: Fondation Égyptologique Reine Élisabeth.

Van Walsem, R.
1978-79 The *psš-kf.* An Investigation of an Ancient Egyptian Funerary Instrument. *OMRO* 59-60: 193-249.

Vercoutter, J.
1956 *L'Égypte et le monde égéen préhellénique. Étude critique des sources égyptiennes.* IFAO Bib. d'Étude 22. Cairo: IFAO.
1970 *Mirgissa I.* Paris: Geuthner.
1976 *Mirgissa III. Les nécropoles II.* Paris: Geuthner.

Ward, W. A.
1966 Scarabs, Seals and Cylinders from Two Tombs at Amman. *ADAJ* 11: 5-18.
1971 *Egypt and the East Mediterranean World 2200-1900 B.C. Studies in Egyptian Foreign Relations During the First Intermediate Period.* Beirut: American University of Beirut.
1976 Some Personal Names of the Hyksos Period Rulers and Notes on the Epigraphy of Their Scarabs. *UF* 8: 353-69.

1977 Scarabs of "Nubkheperra": A Note on the Interpretation of Design. *Berytus* 25: 163-72.
1978 *Pre-12th Dynasty Scarab Seals.* Studies on Scarab Seals I. Warminster: Aris and Phillips.
1978 a Scarabs from the Montet Jar. *Berytus* 26: 37-53.
1984 Royal-name Scarabs. Chapter 6 in Tufnell 1984.
1986 *Essays on Feminine Titles of the Middle Kingdom and Related Subjects.* Beirut: American University of Beirut.
1987 Scarab Typology and Archaeological Context. *AJA* 91: 507-32.
1991 Early Contacts Between Egypt, Canaan, and Sinai: Remarks on the Paper by Amnon Ben-Tor. *BASOR* 281: 11-26.
1992 The Present Status of Egyptian Chronology. *BASOR* 288: 53-66.
1993 Review of Keel, *et al.* 1989. *BibOr* 49: 733-39.
1994 Egypt and the East Mediterranean World: Defining Cultural Interchange. Forthcoming in *BA*.

Webb, M.
1974 Exchange Networks and Prehistory. *Annual Review of Anthropology* 3: 357-83.

Weill, R.
1953 *XIIe dynastie royauté de Haute Égypte et domination hyksos dans le nord.* Cairo: IFAO.

Weinstein, J.
1975 Egyptian Relations with Palestine in the Middle Kingdom. *BASOR* 217: 1-16.
1981 The Egyptian Empire in Palestine: A Reassessment. *BASOR* 241: 1-28.
1991 Egypt and the Middle Bronze IIC/Late Bronze IA Transition in Palestine. *Levant* 23: 105-15.
1992 The Chronology of Palestine in the Early Second Millennium B.C.E. *BASOR* 288: 27-46.

Weise, A.
1990 *Zum Bild des Königs auf ägyptischen Siegelamuletten.* OBO 96. Freiburg: Universitätsverlag.

Wright, G. E.
1965 *Shechem: The Biography of a Biblical City.* New York: McGraw-Hill.
1971 The Archaeology of Palestine from the Neolithic through the Middle Bronze Age. *JAOS* 91: 276-93.

Yadin, Y
1972 *Hazor, the Head of all Those Kingdoms.* London: Oxford.

Yadin, Y., *et al.*
1958 *Hazor I.* Jerusalem: Magness Press.
1960 *Hazor II.* Jerusalem: Magness Press.

Yoffee, N.
1977 *The Economic Role of the Crown in the Old Babylonian Period.* Malibu: Undena.

Yoffee, N., and Cowgill, G. L.
1988 *The Collapse of Ancient States and Civilizations.* Tucson: University of Arizona.

Yogev, O.
1985 A Middle Bronze Age Cemetery South of Tel Rehov. *ᶜAtiqot* 17: 90-113 (English Series).

Zevulun, V.
1990 Tell el-Yahudiyah Juglets from a Potters' Refuse Pit at Afula. *Eretz-Israel* 21: 174-90 (the Ruth Amiran volume; Hebrew).

INDEX